A PRIMER
FOR
POLICY
ANALYSIS

A PRIMER FOR POLICY ANALYSIS

Edith Stokey and **Richard Zeckhauser**
Kennedy School of Government, Harvard University

W · W · NORTON & COMPANY

New York · London

We dedicate this PRIMER *to our families.*

W. W. Norton & Company, Inc., 500 Fifth Avenue, New York, N.Y. 10110
W. W. Norton & Company Ltd., 10 Coptic Street, London WC1A 1PU

ISBN 0-393-09098-1

890

Contents

Preface

Policy makers in the public sector face difficult problems in deciding how public resources are to be allocated. If these resources—land, manpower, energy, and the like—were unlimited, or if the dollars to buy them could be obtained without sacrifice, no choices would be necessary. But in our finite world it is usually possible to promote one worthy objective only at the expense of another. If the Delaware River is dammed at Tocks Island to protect against floods and provide a lake for recreation, a natural wilderness will be lost. If university funds are devoted to a Shakespeare festival, they will have to be diverted from such other uses as student scholarships or (heaven forbid) faculty salaries. If the federal government orders a power plant to convert to coal, oil will be conserved and generating costs reduced, but air quality may deteriorate sharply and more miners will be injured. In all these cases no sensible policy choice can be made without careful analysis of the advantages and disadvantages of each course of action. How to conduct such an analysis is the subject of this book.

In recent years we have heard more and more about policy analysis. This burgeoning interest has led to new course offerings, at both the undergraduate and graduate levels, in a variety of applied areas. Indeed, new programs and schools in public policy designed to train individuals for careers in the public sector are being established all over the country. Many of the new courses are still in the experimental stage; those who teach them are all too aware of the dearth of expository materials in this field. Specific examples of public policy analysis abound, and so do systematic treatments of decisions in the private sector. This volume is an attempt to bridge that gap. Our aim is to set forth a comprehensive overview of the principles of policy analysis in the public sector, and to introduce you to the important tools of the trade and to the structure common to all policy problems that ties these tools together.

This is a do-it-yourself book: the more effort you put into it, the more understanding you will get out of it. Some of you will merely want to read through it quickly to grasp the general principles, and will then use it as a reference work. We hope that most of you will work through the examples, one by one, to gain a fuller grasp of the tools, and that you will then go a step further and practice applying the tools to some of your own problems. Deciding if you should install storm windows to save energy and make a building more comfortable requires the same kind of analysis whether the building is City Hall or your own home. And it is a question that can be addressed only with the aid of some of the tools presented here. On other matters your role may be that of the private citizen who wishes to clarify his own thinking about some of the fundamental issues of the day. How, for example, should we trade off the increased health risks accompanying certain methods for generating electricity against the higher resource costs of alternative technologies? The concepts you will wrestle with in this volume should prove useful in illuminating such questions.

If you have glanced ahead and seen a landscape littered with diagrams, numbers, and symbols, don't let it alarm you. The level of mathematics required is high school algebra. (Honestly!) We use these devices because much of what we have to say is most easily conveyed with the aid of such shorthand, and also because we think you too will find it useful, once you become accustomed to it.

In this book you will find no (she), no him/her, no spokespersons, for we believe that insisting on such affronts to the language is a poor way to advance the status of women. As one female and one male author, we are quite comfortable in treating "he" as a genderless pronoun.

A Primer for Policy Analysis has been a completely joint venture; our names are listed alphabetically. We have both worked on every bit of it, word by painful word. The materials presented have been developed and refined over several years of Harvard teaching, both at the Kennedy School of Government and at the Law School; the contributions of our colleagues and students are beyond measure. Many readers provided helpful comments; Aanund Hylland, Nancy Jackson, and Earl Steinberg merit particular mention. Special thanks go to our good friends Holly Grano and Linda Jacobson for their superb typing and remarkable restraint in the face of endless revisions.

Cambridge, Massachusetts
September 1977

Part **I**

Cornerstones

1 Thinking About Policy Choices

Should the federal government require oil-burning power plants to switch to coal? Given the declining birthrate, should Memorial Hospital convert some of its maternity rooms to a cardiac unit? Should the state university develop a master's program in public policy? Should the Transport Authority extend the subway system to the outer suburbs? Should the United States stockpile grains to diminish extreme price fluctuations? To address these questions one must understand the principles of policy analysis; introducing you to those principles is the goal of this book.

Our Approach to Policy Analysis

The approach to policy analysis throughout this *Primer* is that of the rational decision maker who lays out goals and uses logical processes to explore the best way to reach those goals. He may perform the analysis himself or he may commission others to do parts or all of it for him. The decision maker may be an individual or a group that acts essentially as a unit. We will not consider explicitly the situations in which several decision makers with conflicting objectives participate in a decision. Nonetheless, our approach should prove helpful to an individual who takes part in such a process of shared decision making, whether as a legislator deciding how to vote or as a bureaucrat trying to line up support for a proposal.

In any case, the emphasis in this book is on how decisions ought to be analyzed and made, rather than on the details of the information that should serve as inputs to the decisions. In establishing this framework we rely heavily on the analytic techniques developed in economics, mathematics, operations research, and systems analysis. In actual practice, to be sure, policy analysis is much more broadly eclectic, drawing on a great variety of disciplines, including law, sociology, and political and organizational analysis. We will have little to say about these important complementary disciplines, although you should recognize their relevance for the working analyst. If he is designing a program for welfare reform, he must take account of the capabilities of the state bureaucracies that will implement the program. If he is drawing up safety regulations, he must understand the administrative and judicial processes through which the regulations will ultimately be enforced. Nor will we discuss the natural sciences here, even though understanding how pollutants spewing from tailpipes mix with pollutants escaping up chimneys may be critical for drawing up a set of environmental regulations. In short, understanding and predicting how the world will actually behave is essential for any process of policy formulation. Our concern here, however, is with how the decision maker should structure his thinking about a policy choice and with the analytic models that will aid understanding and prediction, not with all the disciplines that could conceivably provide helpful information.

Most of the materials in this book are equally applicable to a socialist, capitalist, or mixed-enterprise society, to a democracy or a dictatorship, indeed wherever hard policy choices must be made. In deciding whether a vaccine should be used to halt the spread of a threatened epidemic we need not worry about the political or economic ideology of those innoculated. Nor will the optimal scheduling for refuse trucks depend on whether it is capitalist or socialist trash that is being collected.

Questions of values are, nevertheless, a critical and inevitable part of policy analysis. Nothing can be written on the subject without making value judgments, at least implicitly. No specific policies are recommended here; policy issues are used merely for illustration. Still, the very nature of the tools and concepts we expound reflects a philosophical bias and a particular set of ethical concerns. For one thing, the subject itself, policy analysis, is a discipline for working within a political and economic system, not for changing it. For another, we follow in the predominant Western intellectual tradition of recent centuries, which regards the well-being of individuals as the ultimate objective of public policy. We turn in the last few chapters to a further exploration of these points. No doubt those who search for it will find a backward trickle from these later chapters to the more tool-oriented chapters that are the main body of the book.

The Plan of Attack

A Primer for Policy Analysis consists of three major sections. In the first, "Cornerstones," we establish a framework for thinking about policy problems and making choices. The second and much the longest section, "Nuts and Bolts," focuses on the use of models to represent real-world phenomena, and the more general use of analytic methods to assist in the entire process of making decisions. We will work through a toolbox of techniques, starting with fairly simple situations and gradually adding such important complexities as outcomes that are uncertain or that have consequences over future time periods. We deal initially with techniques that help us see clearly what the decision maker's choices are, and then with techniques that assist in identifying and formulating his preferences.

Each technique is to be understood as part of a total structure for thinking about policy choice, as a means of determining some of the pieces of that total structure, and not as an end in itself.

The third section, "Ends and Means," is broader in scope and less technical. To provide a background against which policy analysis can be viewed, it considers critical ethical questions: who should make what policy choices, and on what basis? It lays out the basic criteria for policy choice, identifies the circumstances in which the government should play a role in allocating the resources of society, and reviews briefly the alternative forms that government intervention might take. We might have begun the book with this more philosophical discussion. We did not because this *Primer* is meant to be an essentially practical work emphasizing the structural aspects of policy analysis. Moreover, we want to get you thinking right away in terms of analytic methods, especially if this is a mode of thought you find a bit unfamiliar.

A Framework for Analysis

What do you do when a complicated policy issue lands on your desk? Suppose it's your first day on the job as a policy analyst in a New York State agency; you are directed to investigate and evaluate alternative pollution control measures for the Hudson River. The problem has so many ramifications you wonder how you will ever sort them out—and even where to begin. You can always muddle along, hoping eventually to develop a feel for the situation, but such a hit-or-miss approach rather goes against the grain. You would prefer to have a standard procedure that will at least help you make a start on digging into a complex policy issue.

Many policy analysts have experimented with a variety of ways to structure complex problems like this one. We suggest the following five-part framework as a starting point. As you gain experience in thinking analytically about policy choices, you will perhaps wish to revise it to suit your own operational style; so much the better.

1. *Establishing the Context.* What is the underlying problem that must be dealt with? What specific objectives are to be pursued in confronting this problem?
2. *Laying Out the Alternatives.* What are the alternative courses of action? What are the possibilities for gathering further information?
3. *Predicting the Consequences.* What are the consequences of each of the alternative actions? What techniques are relevant for predicting these consequences? If outcomes are uncertain, what is the estimated likelihood of each?
4. *Valuing the Outcomes.* By what criteria should we measure success in pursuing each objective? Recognizing that inevitably some alternatives will be superior with respect to certain objectives and inferior with respect to others, how should different combinations of valued objectives be compared with one another?

5. *Making a Choice*. Drawing all aspects of the analysis together, what is the preferred course of action?

We do not mean to imply that an analyst will always proceed in an orderly fashion from one stage of the analysis to the next. Real people— even those who are models of administrative efficiency—can rarely operate so neatly, nor should they try to. But we do insist that each of these five critical areas must be dealt with. The conduct of an analysis will usually turn out in practice to be an iterative process, with the analyst working back and forth among the tasks of identifying problems, defining objectives, enumerating possible alternatives, predicting outcomes, establishing criteria, and valuing tradeoffs, to refine the analysis. This is an entirely sensible approach. We claim only that it is easier to keep track of where you are in this iterative process, and to avoid going around in circles (a disease with which even the best analysts are occasionally afflicted), if you keep in mind a basic framework to which every aspect of the analysis must be related. Furthermore, the consumers of your analysis will thank you, for strict adherence to a clearly visible structure makes for far easier reading and comprehension, and opens up the analysis for evaluation and debate.

We believe you will also find the outline useful as a background for the rest of this book, to help tie together the wide array of methods and concepts that are considered. The techniques described in the following chapters are all aimed at enabling us to provide better answers to one or another of the questions in the outline. At every point as you work your way through the following chapters, ask yourself, "How does this method fit into the overall picture?"

To be sure, not all the questions we bring together here will be addressed in every piece of policy analysis. The analyst will frequently be asked merely to predict outcomes, or will enter the decision process at an intermediate stage, after the range of possible actions has already been delineated. He may be asked to set forth the nature of the tradeoffs that must be made among objectives without making a final choice. This is particularly likely to be the case when a decision revolves around what are sometimes labeled "fragile values," such as risks to health or to the ecosystem. Perhaps the decision maker will be pressed for time, so that waiting for further information (an option that is frequently understressed) is out of the question. And often an analyst will be asked to "suboptimize," to find a best choice for a lower level problem without worrying about the overall problem. Almost all budget decisions are made in this way; the local library trustees are expected to make their expenditure decisions within a given total sum without reference to how the highway department will be spending its funds.

Some Practical Advice

Many of the policy decisions you will encounter will not fit neatly and automatically into the models presented here, for the real world is rich and complex. Policy analysis is not an assembly line process, where a single-purpose tool can be applied repeatedly to whatever problem comes along. These are a craftsman's tools; you must learn to wield them with skill. Reading about policy analysis is only a beginning. An academic mastery of the tools will hardly prove sufficient; judgment and sophistication in applying them should be your ultimate goal. Therefore our perennial advice to students is *"Practice!"* Practice on all kinds of situations, large and small, public and private. Look regularly at the front page of the newspaper and think hard about one of the policy problems featured. Perhaps a proposed plan for energy conservation is under discussion; see if you can define the immediate objectives of the plan and their relationship to the underlying problem. What procedures would you use to predict the practical outcome of the plan? How would you treat uncertainty? What further information would you want? Should the plan be implemented sequentially? By what criteria would you evaluate the success of a proposed policy? On what basis should the decision be made?

Practice thinking informally in terms of objectives in your day-to-day work. When you are taking part in a budgeting process, say for a committee or a voluntary organization, consider what the organization's objectives might be and what various expenditures would accomplish. For example, suppose you are serving on a committee to allocate limited student aid funds. What are the committee's objectives? How should they be traded off against one another? How do various types and amounts of aid satisfy these objectives?

Practice on your own problems and decisions, using models to get your thinking straight or to illuminate commonplace events. For example, when you find yourself waiting in line, ask yourself what could be accomplished with additional service capacity, and what the benefits of such a move would be. When the local school committee advocates an inexpensive building with high maintenance costs, think about the tradeoff between present and future spending that is implied.

Above all, practice presenting your conclusions systematically; you don't need to become a gifted and sophisticated analyst before you can upgrade your output. Make up your mind that at least once every day you will deliberately apply the outline set forth above to a problem you face. You'll be amazed at what it will do for your reputation for perceptiveness and good judgment.

2 Models:
A General Discussion

Of all the terms that policy analysts like to toss about, *model* is perhaps the most confusing to the layman, for models are many things to many people. A model is a simplified representation of some aspect of the real world, sometimes of an object, sometimes of a situation or a process. It may be an actual physical representation—a globe, for instance—or a diagram, a concept, or even a set of equations. It is a purposeful reduction of a mass of information to a manageable size and shape, and hence is a principal tool in the analyst's workbox. Indeed, we will be employing models throughout this book.

Models are of particular importance for public policy analysts, who are frequently forced to make policy recommendations in the face of a bewildering conglomeration of facts and estimates. The analyst must strip away the nonessentials that cloud a problem to expose the structural relationships among the important variables, so that the consequences of a particular policy choice may be predicted. The statement "No one can predict what will happen," while perhaps correct in a very narrow sense, is extraordinarily dangerous. It may allow the status quo to persist unquestioned, or it may lead more or less inevitably to the selection of the alternative that is most popular at the moment. We prefer the risks of decisions based on predictions, including predictions that admit to uncertainties, to decisions made by default.

We all rely on models in the conduct of our daily lives. A parent marks the heights of his growing children on the wall; you draw a map so that your friends may find their way to your house; we frequently use an average value for some sequence of events in the past (the weather, for example) in planning for the future. The models of policy analysts are merely extensions—albeit sometimes highly sophisticated—of such simple models as these. In justifying the use of any model, whether we use it to describe Mrs. Smith's behavior in the fruit market or to inform the federal government's deliberations about the appropriate policies for energy re-

search and development, we must always come back to the same fundamental question: Do the gains in insight and manageability outweigh the
sacrifice in realism that we incur by stripping away descriptive details?

Types of Models

It is customary to start off a discussion of models with a taxonomic listing.
We will not attempt to draw up such a formal tabulation, for there is an
infinite number of dimensions in which models may differ. Rather, we will
list some of the kinds of models in common use, more or less in order of
increasing difficulty or abstractness.

A model may be a model in the sense that we have used the term since
childhood: a physical model that is a more or less accurate physical
representation or image of some real-life phenomenon. Sometimes the
scale is very much reduced, as with a model airplane. On the other hand, a
model of the human eye might be many times enlarged. Urban planners
frequently use models of proposed projects to show how things will look
and facilitate public discussion. A still more abstract model of classroom
space is used by the registrars of many schools in assigning rooms.
Typically, a large wall chart will have slots for each classroom and each
hour of the week; availability of space is seen by a glance at the open slots.

A step removed from these models are the diagrammatic models; a
road map is a familiar example. The traditional map tries to capture the
essential features of a road network to assist us in getting from one place to
another. It regards as nonessential such details as which route has the best
restaurants, although that might be given high priority in a guide for the
traveling gourmet. It enables us only to guess at which route is the least
congested, although it distinguishes superhighways from country roads.
Yet it is usually adequate for the purpose at hand. Blueprints of a house,
another example of this type of model, tell the builder what he needs to
know. The painter would find them less helpful.

Flow charts are a particularly valuable sort of diagrammatic model,
especially in situations where some commodity or some portion of the
population passes at a regular rate of flow from one condition to another.
In recent years we have often seen flow charts indicating the processes by
which crude oil becomes gasoline or some other petroleum product. A flow
diagram may be useful in describing how an individual apprehended for a
crime passes through the stages of a criminal justice system. Figure 2–1
illustrates a flow chart designed to model the dynamics of heroin use. The
population is divided into three major categories: nonusers of heroin,
unsupervised users, and those in supervised programs. Each of these
categories is in turn subdivided. In addition, the model includes the
possibility of death. The arrows indicate the movement of people from one
category to another. The government's objective may then be thought of as
influencing favorably the rates at which these movements occur.

Drawing boxes and showing the connections between them is a good

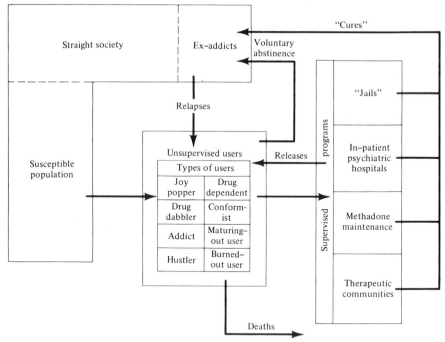

Fig. 2–1. *A Dynamic Model of the Heroin-Using Population*
Source: Mark H. Moore, "Anatomy of the Heroin Problem: An Exercise in
Problem Definition," *Policy Analysis* 2, no. 4 (Fall 1976): 656.

way to begin to attack numerous problems. Many skeptics, once into the
process, have discovered how tough and challenging it is and how much is
learned in trying to do it. If you find it difficult to draw up such a model,
you probably do not understand all aspects of the system you are trying to
model.

Decision trees are first cousins to the flow chart; both identify distinct
stages in a complex process. Figure 2–2 shows the simple decision tree
(which is read from left to right) for a power authority that must decide
whether to install conventional generators or a new, untested type in its
projected power plant. If it takes action B and installs the new type, it must
then await the outcome of a chance event (designated by the circle): either
the new type of generator works or it doesn't. Decision trees move beyond
flow charts, however, in pointing us toward the best choice. They have
been developed primarily to aid decisions that must allow for chance

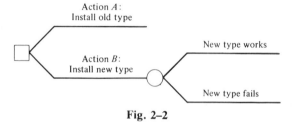

Fig. 2–2

events in the outside world. Chapter 12 is devoted to models of this type, which fall under the general heading of decision analysis.

Graphs and charts are another type of diagrammatic model. We will see in the next chapter that the economist uses an indifference map as a graphical model of preferences, and a possibility frontier to trace out the combinations of available outputs.

The term *model* is also used for what are essentially conceptual models. In a simple way, the person slicing a pie has the model of a circle in the back of his mind. He knows that the easiest way to divide a circle evenly is to cut it into wedge-shaped pieces. Rarely do we see anyone try to cut a round pie into concentric circles.

Long division sometimes serves as a conceptual model. It is easily applied and almost always helpful. Most of us instinctively employ it when we want to find out how much we are getting for a given level and type of expenditure. Large numbers are sometimes confusing; we can't think as intelligently as we would like when we are confronted by all those zeros in front of the decimal point. But we can try to convert them to terms we can come to grips with. The original estimate of the cost to the federal government of the swine flu immunization program was $130 million. Most of us have had little acquaintance with that kind of money or that type of program. But most of us also instinctively performed a little long division. If half the people in the country are immunized, $130 million comes to a bit more than $1 per person. A $2 million housing project that provides homes for 40 families comes out to $50,000 per family dwelling unit, a number we can understand and readily compare with alternatives.

On a more complex level, such terms as *feedback* or *contagion* are often used as conceptual models of processes that are widely understood. A thermostat is a familiar example of a feedback mechanism. Many suburban fire departments have an analogous mutual aid mechanism to reassign engines routinely from one town to another when one department is overburdened. The heroin study from which Figure 2-1 was reprinted includes a contagion model to show how heroin use spreads among a susceptible population. Such concepts can serve as appropriate metaphors in a variety of situations that differ drastically on the surface.

One of the most famous conceptual models of recent years is Garrett Hardin's model of the commons, the common grazing ground of the medieval English village.[1] Cattle owners holding the rights to pasture their animals on the commons, like car owners who have the right to use a common expressway, ignore the cost that their own use imposes on others. The inevitable result is overgrazing or overcongestion that is costly to all. And as Hardin observed, the problem of the commons arises in countless contexts that have nothing to do with cows or cars.

Conceptual models are often used to make nonquantified predictions about the behavior of individuals or institutions. Many of the theoretical

[1] "The Tragedy of the Commons," *Science* 162, no. 3059 (December 13, 1968): 1243-48.

constructs of sociology and political science are designed to help us understand such behavior.

A Simple Model: Compound Interest

Our definition of model seems to be getting broader and broader, so perhaps it is time to turn to a more restricted type that is in fact what many analysts mean when they speak of models. These are the formal mathematical models that describe explicitly the quantitative changes in a particular variable or system in response to various stimuli. For example, suppose we wish to investigate what happens to a sum of money that is left in a savings bank for a number of years. (We deliberately choose this simple situation because it is one with which all our readers will be thoroughly familiar.) What facts do we need? We need to know the initial sum of money (call it S_0), the rate of interest paid on the sum on deposit (call it r), and how long the money is to be left in the bank (let n be the number of years). These are the parameters of the problem. The term *parameter* is used to suggest that the particular variable in question is fixed, at least for the duration of the present exercise. The decision maker is to take it as given; he cannot change it. It implies, however, that the model is formulated in such a way that it can handle a parameter change should one occur.

Following this notation, S_n will be the sum at the end of n years. We can illustrate the progression from the original deposit to the sum after n years with the following diagram:

$$\begin{array}{cc} r & n \\ \downarrow & \downarrow \end{array}$$

$$S_0 \rightarrow \boxed{\text{model}} \rightarrow S_n$$

What does this model actually look like? Suppose $r = .05$. At the end of the first year we have a sum S_1, which is related to the original sum by the formula:

$$S_1 = (1.05)S_0$$

That is, $1 will yield just $1.05. (The rather backward bank of this example compounds interest annually, though its real-world competitors have been driven to daily compounding.) At the end of the second year we have

$$S_2 = (1.05)S_1 = (1.05)(1.05)S_0 = (1.05)^2 S_0$$

And at the end of n years we have an amount

$$S_n = (1.05)^n S_0$$

This, then, is the analytical model for compound interest at 5 percent. The general model for any rate r is

$$S_n = (1 + r)^n S_0$$

The mathematical models in the chapters that follow are more complex, but we will continue to make use of the simple compound interest model for purposes of definition and exposition. One class of mathematical models, those involving statistical inference, are not discussed in this book, since they are well covered in many elementary texts.[2]

Frequently the study of a complex problem will make use of several subsidiary mathematical models to predict the changes in important variables, or the consequences of different policy choices or of different assumptions about the true state of the world. Many people find that the use of physical or conceptual models comes naturally to them, although they may have to remind themselves, say, to try a flow chart in a particular situation. It is the mathematical models and their quantitative implications that seem more difficult, and for this reason disproportionate attention is devoted to them in the subsequent discussion.

Before moving on, we should mention one further use of the term *model* that has proven confusing to some students of policy analysis. Some people in the field have come to use the term broadly to refer to several separate models addressed to a common issue. As an example, suppose Alice Smith has analyzed the problem of public transportation in the city of Brownbury, using a number of subsidiary models to predict population growth, changing land-use patterns, or what have you. Even though she may not provide a comprehensive model of the complete transportation system, her entire product will often be referred to as "the Smith model." This is not a strictly accurate use of the term, but most of us have learned to live with it.

Formal models are used increasingly in the analysis of public systems. Hence, merely for purposes of speaking the language, a familiarity with them is of growing importance for people in associated fields. In acquiring this familiarity, the student must necessarily start with narrow and specific applications of various models. He thus runs the risk that he will overemphasize the solution aspect of modeling, which is really its least significant feature. Much more important is learning how to use models to formulate problems better, especially those broad, fuzzy problems where it is hard to know how to begin, and to get others to discuss what they feel to be their essential elements. As a further payoff, you will find that as you use models more and more, you begin to develop analytic insights in other situations where you do not consciously engage in a modeling process.

What we have presented here is by no means an exhaustive list of all the kinds of models you may encounter or use. To reiterate, however, all models have one basic feature in common—they aim at reducing the complexity of the problem at hand by eliminating nonessential features so that we may concentrate on the features that describe the primary behavior of the significant variables.

Descriptive vs. Prescriptive Models

Improved decision making is the goal of model building. The ultimate justification for models must thus rest on their usefulness in aiding decisions. Some models illuminate choices by showing us more clearly

[2] See, for example, Ralph E. Beals, *Statistics for Economists* (Chicago: Rand McNally, 1970).

what those choices entail, what outcomes will result from what actions. These models are called *descriptive*; they describe the way the world operates. Others go further and provide rules for making the optimal choice. They are categorized as *prescriptive*; they help prescribe courses of action. The distinction is worth pinning down, so let's try to be more precise.

A descriptive model is just what you would expect: it attempts to describe or explain something, or to predict how some variables will respond to changes in other parts of a system. The "something" may be an entire system or only a piece of it. We mentioned earlier that the relation between action and consequence may be complex indeed. It is this relationship that the descriptive model focuses on, perhaps on its entirety, perhaps on only a part of it. For example, an environmentalist may model the flow of pollutants through a particular body of water; an econometrician may construct a model of the entire economy in an attempt to predict the effects of alternative tax proposals.

A prescriptive or normative or optimizing model—take your pick— consists of two parts. The first part is a descriptive model that encompasses all the choices open to the decision maker and predicts the outcome of each. (If he has no choice as to the actions he may take, or if all actions lead to the same outcome, then he has no problem and there is no need for a prescriptive model.) The second part of a prescriptive model is a set of procedures for choosing among alternative actions, given the decision maker's preferences among the outcomes. Prescriptive modeling includes procedures to help the decision maker sort out those preferences.

We may illustrate these definitions with the descriptive model of accumulating compound interest that we discussed earlier. Generalizing the model so that it holds for any interest rate r, we find that

$$S_n = (1 + r)^n S_0$$

where S_0 is the initial sum of money and S_n the amount to which S_0 accumulates after n years. As it stands, this is a simple descriptive model; it predicts the amount to which a given sum of money will accumulate if it is left in the bank for a given number of years at a given annual interest rate. It is not a prescriptive model because (1) as it is constructed, no indication is given that the decision maker has any choice as to the values of r or n or S_0. In other words, the model is not formulated in terms of alternatives. The choices may be there, but if they are we have not been told what they are. And (2) even if we were to redraft the model so that it relates the outcome S_n to some sort of a choice of r or n or S_0, we have no criteria for evaluating different S_ns.

Let's construct an artificial situation in which we can convert this into a prescriptive model. Suppose, first, that our decision maker has a fixed sum, $10,000, which he has already decided will be left in a savings bank for 2 years. He can deposit the money in any of five banks, which are essentially identical in every respect that is important to the decision maker except one—they do not all pay the same rate of interest. The first bank pays r_1 percent, the second r_2, and so on. Now our compound interest model becomes

$$S_{2i} = (1 + r_i)^2(10,000), \qquad i = 1, \ldots, 5$$

where S_{2i} is the accumulation at the end of two years if $10,000 is deposited in the ith bank, and r_i is the rate paid by the ith bank. Now the decision maker has a choice among actions (i.e., among banks) and these actions lead to different outcomes. This takes care of the first part of the prescriptive model discussed above.

To satisfy the second part of a prescriptive model, we need a rule for choosing among actions that reflects the decision maker's preferences as to the outcomes or S_{2i}s. Let us assume that our decision maker is a straightforward person who prefers more to less. The decision rule in this case is obvious: to maximize S_{2i}, choose the bank with the largest r. The model is now prescriptive, albeit trivial.

How might this model become more complicated? Well, for one thing, different banks may have different kinds of service charges associated with their accounts, or may offer different borrowing privileges to depositors. Some may reward a new depositor with an electric blanket; others offer him tickets to the World Series or a collapsible dinghy. The interest rates may be guaranteed for different periods of time, or the notice of withdrawal requirements may differ. Most important, different types and degrees of risk may be involved, especially if one is choosing not just among savings banks but among different types of investment instruments. Such complications would require a more elaborate descriptive model, as well as a far more complex decision rule to deal with the decision maker's preferences for income, convenience, risk, and the like.

If all this sounds easy, don't be misled; it isn't. Constructing a descriptive model may be extremely difficult, especially when the relation between action and outcome is complex or remote. Determining objectives and finding ways to evaluate outcomes in terms of those objectives is likely to be even harder. If complications can conveniently be introduced one by one, however, we may learn to deal with increasingly complex situations.

Deterministic vs. Probabilistic Models

We have defined models as simplified representations of reality, and it is natural to think of reality as consisting of hard facts and sure things. Many models deal with situations where each action has a certain outcome. You flick the switch and the light goes on; you take an automobile plant and add prescribed quantities of materials and labor, and a given number of cars come off the assembly line. This does not mean that nothing ever goes wrong. Now and then something obviously does. What it does mean is that the outcome of an action is so close to being a sure thing that the model may take it as certain.

In other situations the true state of affairs is not at all certain; nevertheless, you are satisfied to treat it as certain. Perhaps some element in your model behaves randomly, but you know that using an average value will provide a sufficiently good approximation. Per pupil expenditures, for example, are frequently used in models of school systems. Or perhaps you would like to test the implications of various alternative assumptions. In population forecasts, for example, a model of how population changes over time may make use of several alternative sets of assumptions about birth and death rates, without any commitment as to which set is the most likely. If you assess the likelihood that each of these sets of assumptions is correct, then you may be able to predict the likelihood that each corresponding outcome will be observed. Note, however, that for each set of assumptions the outcome is taken as certain.

Models such as these, in which the outcome is assumed to be certain, are called *deterministic*. Given the relationships, the initial conditions, and the actions (which may be simply the passage of time, as in a population model), the outcome is uniquely determined.

You might think that this is as far as we can go with models, but it isn't. In some situations the outcome of a particular action is not unique. Instead there is a range or a number of possible outcomes, for which the probabilities may be estimated. Many models relating to health policies are of this sort. We might wish to model, for example, the progress of an epidemic. Suppose that, on average, 30 percent of the people coming in contact with the victim of a certain disease will themselves catch it. If 10 people are exposed, on average 3 will get sick. But sometimes 2 or 4 will catch the disease, and there is a small chance that all 10 will. A model that considers the various possible outcomes can help health planners estimate the probabilities of experiences of various sizes.

In such cases it is frequently possible to construct a model that will help us to trace the consequences of various actions that have probabilistic outcomes. Such a probabilistic model will illuminate the kinds of choices we are facing far better than a model that relies simply on an average value.[3] Since some of the inputs or some of the processes are probabilistic in nature, we will necessarily end up with a probability distribution of possible outcomes.

Let us milk one more illustration out of the compound interest model. Suppose you have decided to deposit $10,000 in the local bank and let it sit there for 2 years. At present the bank pays 5 percent per year, compounded annually, but realistically you know that next year's interest rate is subject to change. You estimate that the probability that it will remain at 5 percent is .6; that it will increase to 5¼ percent, .3; and that it will drop to 4¾ percent, .1.

---

[3] The distinction between a deterministic and a probabilistic model isn't very important in itself. But you should know that there are more ways to cope with variables that behave randomly than just taking an average and letting it go at that. Looked at from the proper angle, a deterministic model is simply a probabilistic model in which the probabilities of various outcomes happen to be either 0 or 100 percent. For example, a thrown ball has a 100 percent chance of coming down, a 0 percent chance of continuing upward indefinitely.

In tabular form,

$$p(.05) = .6$$

$$p(.0525) = .3$$

$$p(.0475) = .1$$

where $p(.05)$ means "the probability that the interest rate in the second year is .05."

The model that predicts how we'll make out with our money is

$$S_2 = (\$10,000)(1.05)(1 + r_2)$$

where S_2 is the sum on deposit at the end of 2 years and r_2 is the interest rate in the second year.

We might simply find the average of the possible values that S_2 could achieve. But in fact we can do better than that. Given our probability estimates for each interest rate, we can predict that

$$p(S_2 = \$11,025) = .6$$

$$p(S_2 = \$11,051.25) = .3$$

$$p(S_2 = \$10,998.75) = .1$$

Thus in this primitive probabilistic model, the probability distribution for S_2 coming out of the model happens to be the same as that for r_2 going in.

As an example of a more complex probabilistic model, consider the IRS office where people queue up to wait for assistance in preparing their income tax returns. They arrive irregularly, according to some probability distribution; the time it takes to serve each taxpayer is also irregular, and follows another probability distribution. If we model the queuing process, we will be able to predict the waiting times, or the length of the queues, in the form of still more probability distributions that will hardly be identical to or as simple as those with which we started. This distribution will be valuable in helping the director of the office to balance personnel costs against waiting times for the customers.

These probabilistic models are descriptive; without additional inputs they tell us nothing about how to make choices among chancy outcomes. Later in this book we will consider an important prescriptive model for decision making under uncertainty; it is generally known as decision analysis.

Choosing the "Right" Model

Our choice among models depends on the type of situation we confront, what we want to know, the level of detail we need, and the variables that we can control. The model will be judged by how well it works, or by how accurately it predicts, whether it is a complex set of equations fed into a computer or merely a few pencil scratches on the back of an envelope. This means that the assumptions that drive a good model must be accurate. We must take great care with assumptions that play an important role in determining the model's predictions. Some of these assumptions—the more obvious ones—will be quantitative; cost estimates are a familiar example. Other critical and more subtle assumptions take the form of deciding what we can safely leave out of the model; in other words, the design of the model itself reflects our assumptions. Therein lies a major part of the art of model building. Many situations can be modeled in more than one way. A regional road map may be fine for getting us from Jacksonville to Atlanta, but something more specialized is required to get us to the corner of Peachtree and Ponce de Leon. Makers of road maps recognize this and frequently tuck more detailed maps of larger cities away in a corner. And even then we are occasionally inconvenienced by the failure to indicate the No Left Turn sign inevitably found at a crucial intersection.

Consider models for projecting the future population of a city. If a new school site is our concern, the model should concentrate on younger children and potential parents, and how they are distributed among neighborhoods. If the major decision relates to modernizing the city hospital, local geography would be of less interest. Instead we would want a breakdown of the types of illness and the utilization of medical facilities. Or suppose that as a part of a suburban planning project we need to predict population 10 years hence. Someone suggests a simple model based on the birth rate b, the death rate d, and present population P_0:

$$P_{10} = P_0 (1 + b - d)^{10}$$

It probably occurs to you immediately that, however closely we estimate birth and death rates, the model will mislead us if we omit other factors, such as net immigration. On the other hand, for some closed populations— such as microbes in a test tube—we would be completely justified in ignoring immigration. Note, incidentally, that population models need not be confined to human beings. They work for microbes, rabbits, or, for that matter, business enterprises.

Every day most of us enjoy (or suffer) the outputs of weather prediction models. For the cranberry grower trying to decide whether to flood his bogs or to conserve his limited water supply for more urgently needed flooding later on, longer term projections are desirable. If we were attempting to control the weather itself, perhaps through cloud seeding, we would need to secure much more detailed information about atmospheric conditions.

The point to recognize is that all models of a system or process, whether of the population of a nation, crime patterns in a city, or the immunological system of the human body, are not and should not be the same. To be manageable, all models must simplify and streamline. Which elements are omitted and which highlighted in any particular model will depend on the variables that are important for policy purposes. These variables may be critical because they are themselves valued outputs or because they interact significantly with variables that are subject to choice. Other factors being equal, the more important the decisions that are to be made, the greater the resources we should be willing to spend to refine the model and enhance its accuracy. If we must decide whether to carry an umbrella, a glance at the sky usually provides a sufficient weather forecast. For harvesting many acres of a delicate crop like raisin grapes, however, a more sophisticated and expensive forecast would almost certainly be warranted.

How do we know which type of model to use in a particular situation? Sometimes the choice is easy. If customers must line up for service, clearly a queuing model is called for. If the benefits and costs of a proposed project will be felt over many years, we must think about benefit–cost analysis and how impacts felt in future years should be valued or discounted. If uncertainty is a crucial element, decision analysis is indicated. The array of models set forth in the following chapters is sufficiently rich that most situations are addressed by one or more of them. Some cases require more judgment than others, but selecting the right model or models on which to base your analysis is not an esoteric art—it's a matter of experience and plain everyday common sense. It is our aim in these pages to give you a start on gaining that experience. The common sense you will have to provide for yourself.

The Advantages and Limitations of Models

What should you get out of this discussion? You should first of all understand the advantages of using models. One major advantage is that the discipline of constructing a model helps us get our thinking straight; it makes us get down to fundamental principles. Models provide an economical description of the essential features of a complex situation. Formal analytical models, in particular, enable us to use more variables than we can comfortably carry in our heads. By temporarily setting aside unimportant variables, they serve as powerful tools for the study of interrelationships among the important variables.

Models provide a bookkeeping mechanism of a sort. An input cannot get lost—it has to go somewhere. And you are less likely to overlook an output. For example, one of the purported virtues of public transport is that it lures some drivers away from the highways. If it reduces congestion, it will provide a positive benefit to those who continue to use highways and to others who breathe the nearby air. And yet, although the driver who has been lured to the bus is no longer available to jam the roads, the diminished traffic may in turn attract other drivers. If you never bothered to model the transport situation, you might miss some of these factors. The model will help you keep track of people and the transportation modes they use. Moreover, in a complex situation it is sometimes impossible to tell what all your choices are without a model, or to think systematically about what these choices may be. Modeling forces you to identify the levers that will influence outcomes, which are in actuality the true policy alternatives. In any case, unless you can describe alternatives with sufficient accuracy, you cannot sensibly choose among them.

Construction of a model may tell us a lot about what kinds of information are desirable before a decision can be made, and about the value of different types of information. It may focus our attention on how little we know about a situation. If more information may be available in the near future, the desirability of postponing all or part of a decision in order to maintain flexibility becomes obvious. It may even be advisable to spend time and money to get more information before making a decision.

A further advantage is the possibility of experimenting with the model rather than with the system itself. This is likely to be particularly valuable in planning a new public facility, such as a hospital. Planners need to know the implications for design of assumptions about a host of variables such as intensive care load, emergency arrival rate, and the like. In such a case it may be impossible to experiment with the hospital itself, and it certainly would be prohibitively expensive in terms of time, money, morale, and health. The model highlights the critical tradeoffs, such as longer stays for chronic-care patients versus an extra day for maternity cases.

In other situations, experiments with a model may suggest potential beneficial changes in a system that warrant cautious moves in a particular direction. In 1965 a famous case of this sort resulted in a dramatic improvement in the service provided by the Northeast Frontier Railway in India. On this single-line railway, trains moving in opposite directions could cross only at crossing stations, which necessarily involved halting at least one of the trains. Delays were monumental. Analysts experimented with a simplified mathematical model and found that the number of such crossing delays rises sharply with the number of trains using the line. In fact, the number of delays increases more rapidly than the square of the number of trains. Thus an increase from 10 to 11 trains per day would bring about not just a 10 percent increase in the number of crossing delays, but rather an increase of $(11^2 - 10^2)/10^2$, or 21 percent. This finding suggested that the railroad should try running 2 of its 15 trains coupled. When the experiment resulted in a better than 20 percent improvement in the average number of kilometers each diesel engine covered in a day, the scheme was extended.[4]

Constructing a model frequently facilitates communication among those concerned with a policy issue. It makes specific the definition of the problem (or at least of a piece of it); it sets out on paper what might otherwise remain buried in the analyst's mind. (This seems to be the one point on which harmony prevails among admirers and critics of that famous volume modeling world economic behavior, *The Limits to Growth*.)[5] Moreover, when we refer to frequently employed classical models—linear programming, for instance—we employ a common language that permits shortcuts in communication. To be sure, this degree of precision makes it harder to smudge over some factors, and in some situations (especially those political in nature) this may be a disadvantage as well as an advantage.

Perhaps most important of all, experience with modeling helps us

---

[4] For a description of the model, see Jagjit Singh, *Great Ideas of Operations Research* (New York: Dover Publications, Inc., 1968), p. 165.

[5] Donella H. Meadows, Dennis L. Meadows, Jørgen Randers, and William W. Behrens III (New York: Universe Books, 1972).

develop general insights that can be applied even to unfamiliar situations. For example, we soon learn that systems involving queues often behave in an almost counterintuitive fashion: even a very small increase in service capacity offered may radically reduce waiting time at a facility.

How much should the individual who desires a broad, rather than deep, comprehension of policy analysis know about actual models? We suggest the following five goals, in no particular order of priority:

1. You should become aware of a few conceptual models that are widely useful because they provide a shorthand description of situations or processes that pervade our society. Earlier we cited feedback and contagion as widely used conceptual models, and mentioned Hardin's famous model of the commons. You should become knowledgeable about the existence of the formal models most commonly used in statistics, in project evaluation, and in operations research. Some of these, such as benefit–cost analysis, linear programming, and decision analysis, are discussed in some detail later in this volume.

2. You should acquire the habit of asking yourself, when faced with a complex problem, if constructing a model would shed any light on the problem or subject you to the discipline of testing your own understanding. You should develop both an ability to construct simple models of your own and the habit of relying on an expert to refine the model and develop empirical data as a problem becomes more technical.

3. You should learn to use some of the more basic formal models in thinking about the structure of a problem even when you do not carry your thinking to the point of quantification. The insights gained through this nonrigorous use of modeling concepts may well be the most valuable outcome of a study of modeling.

4. To accompany your enhanced technical proficiency, you should develop a healthy and informed skepticism about models, and become aware of their limitations. A good way to start is by making sure that you understand all the assumptions about the relationships that the model implies and the data that it uses. Test the model's plausibility by seeing how it performs under simple conditions. Ask some probing questions: What are the critical features of the model that is being presented to you? Where may it diverge from reality in a manner that might lead our reasoning astray? What about causality—are you dealing with a situation where it is essential to understand why the variables in a system behave the way they do, or is simply modeling the observed relationship sufficient for your purposes? What parameter values are significant, in the sense that changing them would drastically change the predictions made or choices suggested by the model? Indeed, you should be careful to develop your own models in such a way that you can answer these questions.

5. You should keep the real world of policy making in mind as you build or use a model. A model so vast and so complex that no one can understand how it works will benefit neither the modeler nor the client of the analysis.

In the next chapter we will begin to discuss types of mathematical models in greater detail. We will then introduce a variety of widely used modeling techniques that have proven particularly useful in practice.

3 The Model
of Choice

An economist approaches a decision by asking "What do we want and what can we get?"[1] Ordinarily we want more than we can get, and because our capabilities are limited and the resources available to us scarce, choices must be made among our competing desires. The Port Authority would like to expand airport operations and at the same time reduce noise levels. It cannot do both; as headlines testify, the choice is difficult. How choices should be made—the whole problem of allocating scarce resources among competing ends—is the stuff of economics and the subject of this book. We focus on choices in the public sector, on how decisions should be made by governments at all levels and by nonprofit institutions. As we are by now all well aware, the government is not a business, and in many respects it cannot be run like a business. Its goals are different and it operates under different constraints. Yet the basic elements of good decisions are the same in all arenas, and the methods for making them set forth here are applicable for all decision makers, public and private.

Our starting point is a fundamental model of choice, a model that those who have studied economics will doubtless find familiar. We have seen that a model is a simplified representation of some aspect of the real world, a deliberate distillation of reality to extract the essential features of a situation. The fundamental choice model is particularly valuable because it offers a universal yet succinct way of looking at problems in terms of the two primary elements of any act of choice:

1. The alternatives available to the decision maker; and
2. His preferences among these alternatives.

Moreover—and this is not to be taken lightly—the model forces the decision maker to express the alternatives he faces and his preferences

---

[1] Some of the examples in this chapter were drawn from Richard Zeckhauser and Elmer Schaefer, "Public Policy and Normative Economic Theory," in Raymond Bauer, ed., *The Study of Policy Formation* (New York: The Free Press, 1968).

among them in comparable units. You will see from our examples that the alternatives may sometimes be described in tangible terms, actual outputs that can be seen and counted, such as electricity and water, or allergy tests and electrocardiograms. At other times the outputs of the alternative choices will be described in terms of intangible attributes such as intelligence and beauty, or taste and nutrition, or safety and speed. Some of these intangibles can be measured more or less objectively; others cannot. The model is flexible; it easily handles all types of attributes, whether described by hard numbers or paragraphs of prose, so long as the decision maker's preferences are expressed in the same terms as the alternatives.

In this chapter we set forth the model of choice and deduce from it the characteristics of best decisions. We begin by looking at the model in drastically simplified situations, deliberately limited to two variables—two outputs or attributes—so that we can plot the results on a graph. Tradeoffs—painful tradeoffs—are the essence of difficult decisions, and there is no clearer way to visualize the nature of these tradeoffs than with a graph. In general, of course, many more than two variables will be considered by a policy maker; the concepts are readily extended to many variables, and the geometric representation to many dimensions.

Our perspective is that of the unitary decision maker, whether an individual or a corporate body, who faces no significant uncertainties. The model applies equally well to a person making a choice about his own consumption or career, or a firm making a production or research or marketing choice, or a public official facing a decision about a government project.

The Alternatives Available to the Decision Maker

The first element of the basic model describes the alternatives available to the decision maker. If this were a standard economics text, we would introduce you to apples and oranges and ask you to consider the plight of the grocery shopper who must allocate his fruit budget between those two goods. But this is a book about public decisions, so we ask you instead to play the part of a public official who must choose among several alternative dam projects. These projects are identical in every respect—costs, environmental consequences, and so on—except two: they produce different amounts of electric power and water for irrigation. In other words, the decision maker faces a certain number of alternative quantities of power and water. Suppose there are five possibilities with the outputs shown in Table 3–1. We plot these five alternatives on a graph, as shown in Figure 3–1. In this diagram, point A represents an electric output of 22 thousand kilowatt-hours per day and a water output of 20 million gallons of water per day.

Increases in both outputs would clearly be desired by the decision maker. (Remember that we have assumed that the projects are the same with respect to all other factors, including cost.) This means that any point

Table 3-1

Dam	Electric output in thousands of kilowatt-hrs/day	Water output in millions of gallons/day
A	22	20
B	10	35
C	20	32
D	12	21
E	6	25

(such as C) lying both north and east of another point (such as D) is superior to it. In technical language, C *dominates* D; it is better in every respect. The decision maker would never choose D in preference to C regardless of his relative preferences for electricity and water. A combination of outputs or attributes is said to be *efficient* if, given the available alternatives, it is impossible to increase one output without giving up some of at least one other. In Figure 3-1, points A, B, and C are efficient; D is not because we can have more of both water and electricity, at the same cost, by choosing C. Similarly, E is not efficient because we can have more of both water and electricity by choosing either B or C. Obviously, dominated points can never be efficient; thus all points are either dominated or efficient.[2]

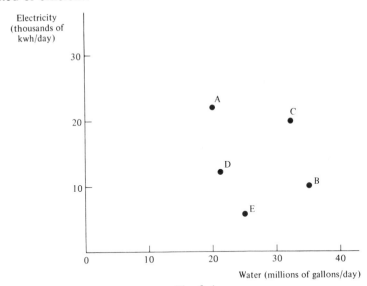

Fig. 3-1

It need not be the case that the decision maker has only a small number of discrete alternatives open to him. He might well be able to vary the output combinations in small steps so that he could always get a little more hydroelectric power by giving up a little more water for irrigation. If it is possible to make these continuous tradeoffs we are not limited to five

---

[2] You may come across the expression "X weakly dominates Y." This means that X is equally as good as Y in some respects, better in at least one, and worse in none.

or eight or even twenty-five separate points; we can draw a whole curve that delineates the location of efficient points. This curve (shown in Figure 3–2 as *EW*) tells us the maximum achievable output of water for every possible output of electricity. For example, point *F* indicates that with an electrical output of 8 thousand kilowatt-hours, the maximum water output is 32 million gallons, and conversely. We call this collection of efficient points the *possibility frontier*.[3]

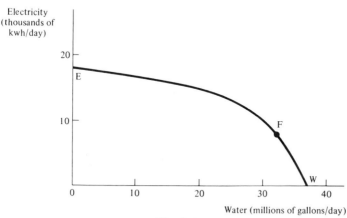

Fig. 3–2

The possibility frontier may be applied in numerous contexts. It may describe tangible goods or intangibles. It may refer to a public project, as here, or to a private firm or individual. It may be used to describe the combinations of goods available to a consumer or the tradeoff of intangible attributes for a proposed public building, for example flexibility of space and privacy of offices. The frontier may be straight or curved, continuous or discrete, or it may consist merely of a few isolated points. Whatever shape it takes, it is the set of efficient alternatives, the contenders for the best available choice.

The following examples illustrate the wide applicability of the possibility frontier:

1. A transit authority has a $10 million budget for new rolling stock. Buses cost $65,000 each and subway cars $465,000. The efficient choices for that budget are indicated by its possibility frontier, line *CB* in Figure 3–3. The authority would never spend $10 million for interior combinations even though they are feasible.[4]

A similar straight-line possibility frontier is appropriate for a municipal highway department that can readily transfer its men and equipment from

---

[3] Some readers will recognize that this particular curve is in fact the *production possibility frontier* talked about so frequently by economists. We deliberately drop the word *production* because we use the term *possibility frontier* in a somewhat broader sense.

[4] This possibility frontier is simply the straight line represented by the equation $65,000B + 465,000S = \$10,000,000$, where B is the number of buses purchased and S is the number of subway cars. You may wonder about the smooth line and the problem of fractional buses and subway cars. Under most circumstances, when outputs are indivisible, the best choice indicated by the model will be only approximate; the basic principles still hold.

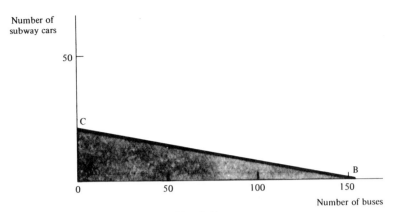

Fig. 3–3

street repairs to snowplowing as the need arises.

In a more familiar vein, a straight line sets forth the maximum combinations of apples and oranges that the consumer can buy, at going prices, for a given sum of money. A frontier of this type is frequently termed a budget line.

2. An urban renewal project includes a high-rise building. The lower floors will be rented as commercial space; the upper floors will be used for apartments. It is undecided where the line should be drawn, although certainly no more than five floors will be rented commercially. The tradeoff between the value of the commercial rentals and the amount of housing space available is shown by the curve CR in Figure 3–4. The curvature reflects the fact that because of the escalator and elevator configuration, commercial space is less valuable as you go higher in the building.

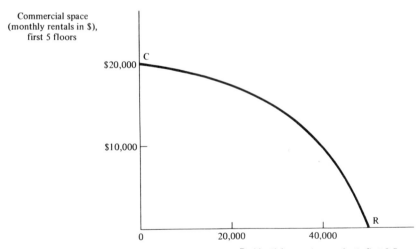

Fig. 3–4

If the municipal highway department's maintenance and plowing equipment were less than fully flexible, a tradeoff curve similar in shape to this one would result. If all equipment is being used for maintenance when a snowstorm strikes, the trucks diverted first to plowing should be those that will produce the most miles plowed relative to the maintenance capability sacrificed. If the storm is a really bad one, trucks that are less satisfactory will have to be pressed into service, at a greater maintenance sacrifice.

3. A legal aid office provides two kinds of services to its clients, "domestic relations" and "landlord–tenant." The maximum combinations of cases are indicated by the curve DL in Figure 3–5. This sort of curvature would arise if the average time required to handle a type of case shrinks as the legal staff handles more and more cases of that type.

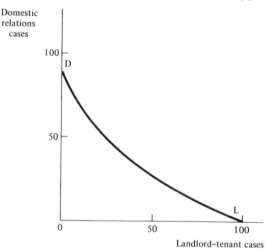

Fig. 3–5

4. Three sites (1, 2, and 3) are available for a new health clinic. Each is rated A, B, C, or D with respect to the two characteristics deemed relevant, accessibility to the community and quiet. The possibility frontier, which is shown in Figure 3–6, consists of three points. (This figure,

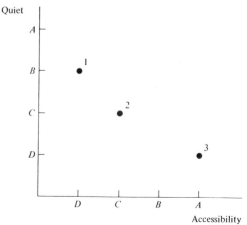

Fig. 3–6

incidentally, shows us a common way of constructing a diagram when only letter grades or ordinal rankings—such as first, second, and so on—are available. The letters or numbers run "backward" from the origin because we are accustomed to seeing things get better as we move north and east.)

In short, the set of feasible alternatives may be specified in many different ways. The efficient choices are those from which it is not possible to make an improvement in one respect without accepting a sacrifice in some other respect.

The Decision Maker's Preferences

The second element of the fundamental choice model describes the decision maker's preferences. We assume throughout the technical part of this book that these preferences are given, though occasionally we point out where a particular technique is helpful in defining preferences. In Part III of this volume we turn to a discussion of the source of these preferences.

We have seen that frequently the available alternatives combine many outputs or attributes, all of which are valued by the decision maker. The problem of choice is not difficult if one alternative is superior to all others with respect to all attributes—in other words, if one alternative is dominant. Of the five dam projects considered above, C dominates D, and B dominates E, but no single alternative is dominant over all the others. We can eliminate D and E, but there is still more than one efficient alternative.

Unfortunately we are rarely presented with a dominant choice. Consider the case of three applicants for a job, Anderson, Barker, and Corcoran, who are equally qualified in all attributes but two, technical capability and ability to get things done. Their rankings with respect to these two attributes are summarized in Table 3–2. Here there is no dominant choice, for the applicant who is the best technician of the three is not best in ability to get things done. An employer might even prefer Barker, who is neither the best technician nor the most able, to either Anderson or Corcoran.

Table 3–2

Applicants for a position	Attribute	
	Technical capability	Ability to get things done
Anderson	1st	3rd
Barker	2nd	2nd
Corcoran	3rd	1st

Such conflicts in attribute rankings lie at the core of many difficult decisions that must be made in the public sector. These conflicts may arise because the decisions affect many people; although policy A is better for one group in the society, policy B is better for another; a battle over an airport location is an example. How would you weight the attributes "better for group 1" and "better for group 2"? Or if time is a crucial element we may find, for example, that policy *A* (screening for bladder cancer) is more immediately beneficial, but that policy *B* (cancer research) will be better for a long period starting 20 years from now. How would you weight the attributes "better now" and "better later"? In a third context, policy *A* will be superior if some uncertain events turn out favorably, but policy *B*—flood plain zoning, for instance—is a better hedge against misfortune. Again, how would you weight the attributes "better if no flood" and "better if flood"? Conceptually, these conflicts among attributes are no different from the conflict between the attribute rankings of Anderson, Barker, and Corcoran. What is needed in all these cases is a method for determining and displaying the decision maker's preferences among different combinations of attributes. If we develop a perfectly general formulation that applies to all combinations, we can then apply it to some of the more complex problems we will encounter later on.

As in the last section, we will restrict our discussion to situations in which there are only two relevant attributes, because this permits graphing. The ideas may be extended readily to many dimensions.

Let's get back to our dam planner, whom we left contemplating the five projects and wondering what to do. Forget, for the moment, about the particular dams in question and think only about his unrestricted preferences for electricity and water. Suppose we consider just one combination of outputs, say 11 thousand kilowatt-hours of electricity per day and 25 million gallons of water per day. This combination is shown at point *P* in Figure 3–7. The model presumes that as far as the decision maker is concerned there are other combinations of electricity and water that are just as good—and no better. Say he is neutral between points *P* and *Q*, where *Q* represents 7 thousand kilowatt hours per day and 36 million gallons of water per day. And he regards *P* and *Q* as exactly as satisfactory as *R* (19 thousand kilowatt hours and 17 million gallons), and *S* (24 and 14).

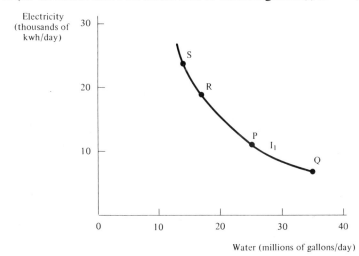

Fig. 3–7

We draw a curve, I_1 in Figure 3–7, through these four points and all others that he regards as equally desirable; we call it an *indifference curve*. Note that we say nothing about the amount of satisfaction depicted by this curve. We state only that all points on it are equally good from the decision maker's point of view; that is why we have drawn it as we have. This causal relationship is crucial; it is not because they lie on the same curve that the points on an indifference curve are equally satisfactory—rather, they lie on the same indifference curve *because* they are equally satisfactory. Note further that when we draw a smooth curve such as I_1, we in effect assume that the decision maker's preferences are continuous.

Similarly, we could draw other indifference curves I_0, I_2, and I_3, depicting lower and higher levels of satisfaction, respectively, as shown in Figure 3–8.

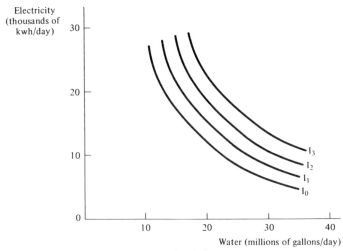

Fig. 3–8

Again, we do not assign specific values to these levels of satisfaction; we merely state that I_1 is better than I_0, I_2 than I_1, and I_3 than I_2. In particular, there is no implication that movements of equal distance across the graph are equally valuable. We could draw more and more indifference curves, until there is one (and only one) through every point in electricity–water "space." As in the diagrams of available alternatives, things get better as we move north and east. The decision maker's preferences for possible combinations of electricity and water are thus completely described. Such a family of curves is called an *indifference map*. In other contexts, as we shall shortly see, the preferences may take the form of equal profit or cost lines. Conceptually, all of these curves are identical to the isobars that show all points of equal temperature on a meteorological map, or the contour lines that indicate equal altitudes on a topographical map. We will use the general term *preference function* to describe whatever formal information we have about the decision maker's preferences. (A function is, strictly speaking, a mathematical relationship between two sets of variables. Used more loosely, as here, it means simply that we can write down what the decision maker's preferences depend on.) Like the possibility frontier, the preference function may refer to tangibles or intangibles, and it may be represented with varying degrees of completeness. On some occasions it will be the whole map, on others a piece of a map, while on still others only a few isolated points may be known. The following are examples of preference functions:

1. A firm that produces thermometers and barometers makes a profit of $1 per thermometer and $3 per barometer. If it is seeking to maximize profits, its preference function will consist of parallel lines (P_{1000}, P_{2000}, P_{3000}) as shown in Figure 3–9. Along each preference contour profits are equal. Any point on P_{2000} is preferred to any on P_{1000}, and so on.

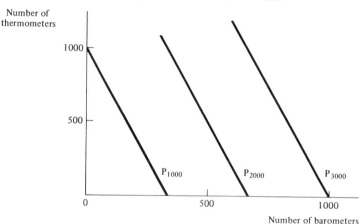

Fig. 3–9

2. A municipal government wishes to maximize the use of a projected recreation facility, which will consist of tennis courts and softball diamonds. The criterion is the number of people who can use the facility simultaneously. The line N_{100} in Figure 3–10 joins combinations of courts and diamonds that are equally satisfactory; any of these combinations will permit 100 people to play at one time. Any N_{200} point is preferred to any

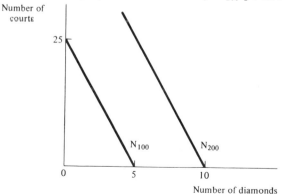

Fig. 3–10

N_{100} point, and so on. (Incidentally, we should remind ourselves that we wouldn't build fractional courts or diamonds, just as the transit authority mentioned on page 00 wouldn't buy fractional buses or subway cars. Each contour really consists of a succession of discrete points.)

3. An individual is a swimming and theater enthusiast; he likes to spend some time doing each. The more he swims, the less theater time he will give up for still another hour of swimming. His preferences are diagrammed in Figure 3–11. I_2 is preferred to I_1, and so on.

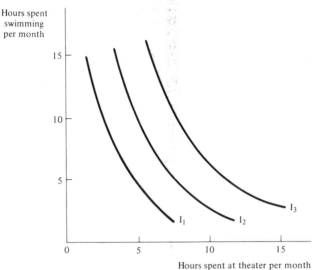

Fig. 3–11

4. A hospital outpatient clinic provides two types of medical services, allergy tests and electrocardiograms. The directors of the clinic originally considered three possible allocations of space and staff, which would permit the combinations of services shown in Table 3–3. The directors concluded that of these B was the most desirable and A the least desirable. They are now given the opportunity to consider additional mixes of services. What can we say about their preference function, on the basis of the rankings already provided? Strictly speaking, we know only that point B is preferred to C, which in turn is preferred to A. This suggests that the indifference map bears some resemblance to that shown in Figure 3–12, but we can be sure only of the ordering indicated.

In sum, there is a wide range of situations in which we can model the decision maker's preferences. In the next section we consider how preferences and alternatives can be put together to define the best choice.

Table 3–3

Alternative	EKGs/day	Allergy tests/day
A	80	20
B	65	30
C	40	65

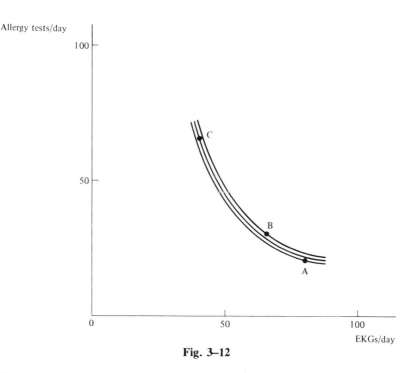

Fig. 3–12

The Best Choice

We have now represented on a geometric diagram the two elements in the act of choice, the set of alternatives from which the choice is to be made and the set of preferences according to which the chooser ranks these alternatives. What use can we make of these representations of options and preferences? Because both are measured in the same units, which in the dam example were kilowatt-hours of electricity per day and gallons of water per day, we can plot both on the same graph. (This is a very important point; we'll get back to it in a minute.) The nature of the best choice is then indicated. If the alternatives are limited to the five specific dams originally considered, our diagram will look like Figure 3–13, which combines Figures 3–1 and 3–8. The policy planner should choose alternative C, for it is the project preferred according to his own ranking; it is the project that places him on the highest indifference curve.

On the other hand, Figure 3–14 shows that a different indifference map might well produce a different ranking of the alternatives. (We use J's to label this set of indifference curves.) Now B is preferred to C. Of course no map would ever show D or E as the best choice; we might as well have stopped plotting them on the graph several pages back. Figure 3–14, incidentally, shows a decision maker who really likes his water; it takes a lot of electricity to persuade him to give up a little water.

Figures 3–13 and 3–14 demonstrate the preferred choice when the decision maker confronts discrete alternatives. What happens when continuous tradeoffs between electricity and water are possible, as in Figure 3–2?

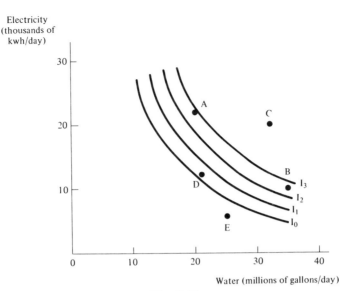

Fig. 3–13

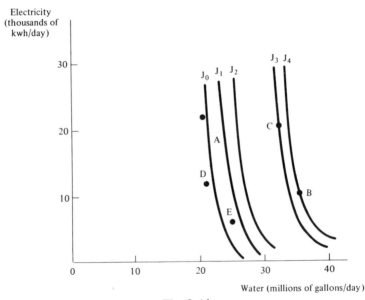

Fig. 3–14

Figure 3–15 combines the continuous possibility frontier of Figure 3–2 and the indifference map of Figure 3–8. Examining this composite diagram, we see that the best choice for the dam planner is the combination of electricity and water represented by point T, because only at that point can he reach the highest possible indifference curve. A rational decision maker would never choose a point inside the frontier—an inefficient point—because larger outputs of both attributes would be attainable at points on the frontier at no additional cost. And he would not choose a different

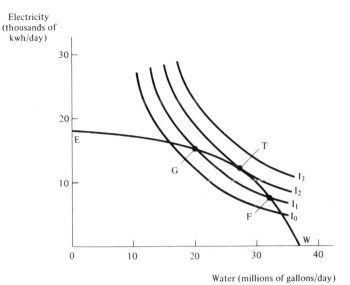

Fig. 3–15

point on the frontier (*F*, for example) because, as his indifference map tells us, all the points along the *FG* segment of the frontier are better for him than *F*. He would like to choose a point on I_3, but he can't—he can't move beyond the possibility frontier. Note very carefully the relationship between the possibility frontier and the indifference map: they are bulging toward each other, and at point *T* they just touch. That is, at that point the possibility frontier is tangent to an indifference curve; their slopes are equal.[5]

---

[5] The slope of a curve at any point *P* is equal to the slope of the straight line that is tangent to the curve at *P*, for at the point where they touch they are both going in identical directions. And what is the slope of a straight line? It is the ratio of the vertical increase between any two points on the line to the horizontal increase between the same two points. (It doesn't matter which points you choose for this purpose, thanks to the happy properties of the right triangle.) Thus the slope of the straight line *AB* is length *BC* divided by the length *AC*, 2/4 in this case; this is also the slope of the curve *DE* at point *P*. Note that the slope of a straight line is a constant, whereas the slope of a curve changes as you move along the curve. A line that slopes up to the right has a positive slope; the implication is that the variables measured on the two axes move in the same direction. A line that slopes down to the right has a negative slope; the two variables move in opposite directions. A vertical line has an infinite slope, a horizontal line a zero slope.

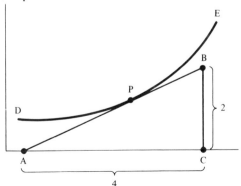

Before reading on, you should convince yourself that the point of tangency is indeed the best choice in this diagram, and that it will always be the best choice if the curves have the general shape shown in the diagram.[6]

We noted that at point T the possibility frontier is tangent to the planner's indifference curve, and the slopes of these two curves are equal. This is a geometric representation of an important characteristic of the optimum choice. Before discussing the significance of this equality for the model of choice, we must interpret the meaning of these slopes.

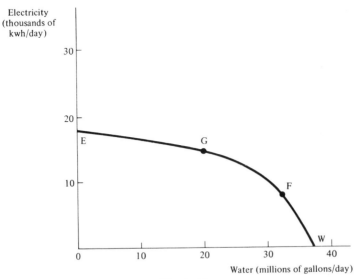

Fig. 3–16

Look again at the possibility frontier EW; it is reproduced in Figure 3–16. As we move down along this curve from E toward W, we are in effect reducing the output of electricity in return for an increased production of water. The rate at which this tradeoff is taking place is called, quite reasonably, the *rate of transformation*, and the possibility frontier is sometimes called the *transformation curve*. For the possibility frontier we have assumed, points G and F have the numerical values shown in Table 3–4.

Table 3–4

Point	Electricity in thousands of kilowatt-hours/day	Water in millions of gallons/day
G	15	20
F	8	32
Change	7	12

[6] It may occur to you that we require certain assumptions about the shape of the curves if this statement is to hold. You are quite right. Fortunately the assumptions are ordinarily plausible; they are discussed in the next section.

Over the range from G to F, we say that the rate of transformation of electricity for water is 7000 kilowatt-hours for 12 million gallons or 1 kilowatt-hour for 1714 gallons.[7] We are dealing, however, with transformation possibilities that change continuously as we move along the curve. Although we can average only 1714 units of increased water production for every kilowatt-hour of electricity sacrificed over the entire GF range, we would have to sacrifice less than 1 kilowatt-hour of electricity to get the first 1714 additional gallons of water at point G. (Analogously, while a man may drive from Chicago to Denver at an average speed of 50 miles an hour, part of the time he is going faster than 50—say, 60—and part of the time he is going more slowly.) At any point on the curve, the rate at which one output can be transformed into another is given by the slope at that point on the possibility frontier. The steeper slope at point F indicates that the rate of transformation at which electricity can be traded for water is greater there than it is at point G. We refer to the rate at which one output can be transformed into the other at a particular point as the *marginal rate of transformation,* or MRT. The use of the word marginal suggests that we are considering only a very small region, and that we should be alert to the possibility that the MRT will change if we move a significant distance along the curve. For the individual consumer who has no influence over the prices of the things he buys, regardless of how much he buys the MRT is constant. Hence his budget line is a straight line.

The slope of an indifference curve may be interpreted in similar fashion. It represents the way in which the decision maker is willing to trade electricity for water while still remaining at the same level of satisfaction, in other words, on the same indifference curve. The steepness of the indifference curve indicates the rate at which he is willing to trade off between the two outputs; the steeper the curve, the greater the amount of electricity output he is willing to trade for a unit of water production. Thus in Figure 3–17 he would give up more electricity at point M in return for an extra unit of water than he would at point N. We refer to this tradeoff rate as the individual's *rate of substitution* between the two goods; the tradeoff rate at a particular point is called the *marginal rate of substitution* or MRS. It is a logical complement to the marginal rate of transformation or MRT.

The relationship between the marginal rate of transformation and the marginal rate of substitution is an important one to grasp. The MRT is the rate at which one is *able* to exchange one good for another at a particular point; the MRS is the rate at which the decision maker is *willing* to exchange one good for another. The former is defined by the typical constraints of the production process, the latter by the subjective preferences of the decision maker. The preferences of the public decision maker,

[7] To be strictly accurate, the rate of transformation is a negative number, for the changes in the two variables are of opposite sign as we move along the curve. Since the essential idea of this model is tradeoffs, tradeoffs that involve less of one thing in return for more of something else, all these rates would have minus signs if we insisted on rigor. In other words, all the curves slope down to the right. Because the slopes are all negative, it is customary to drop the minus sign in verbal discussions such as this.

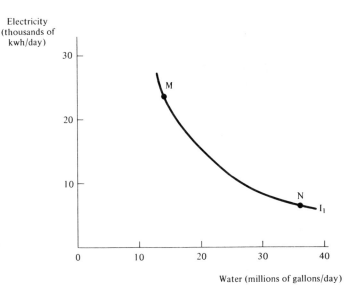

Fig. 3–17

to be sure, should not be his own, for he is not the consumer. Rather they should reflect his view of the preferences of the society he represents. The way social preferences should be determined is no easy matter; it is discussed at length in Chapter 13.

We saw that for the optimal choice the slopes of the possibility frontier and the indifference curve are equal, because the two curves are tangent at that point. Thus at the best point the marginal rate of transformation between two goods must equal the decision maker's marginal rate of substitution between them. The objective rate at which the planner is capable of carrying out the tradeoff between electricity and water power is exactly equal to the subjective rate at which he is willing to substitute between these two outputs. Why must this be the case? Consider point G in Figure 3–18, at which the rate of transformation between electricity and water (the rate at which electricity output can be traded for water output) is less than the decision maker's rate of substitution. He will find it to his advantage to pursue options that yield more water and less electricity. At G, he is able to get 2200 gallons of water output by giving up 1 kilowatt-hour of electricity, whereas he would be willing to sacrifice 1 kilowatt-hour for as little as 1050 additional gallons of water. Clearly, then, it is in his interest to trade off electricity for water at the advantageous rate available at point G. In this manner, the decision maker will continue to move along the possibility frontier until he reaches point T, where the willingness rate and the possibility rate are equal. If he strays beyond T, this same type of marginal analysis will lead him back to the point of tangency.

We have seen in our example that the model of choice may be interpreted in various ways. The chooser may be an individual, a group operating as a unit, or a government. The alternatives may be simple combinations of goods or outputs like those we've considered here, or they

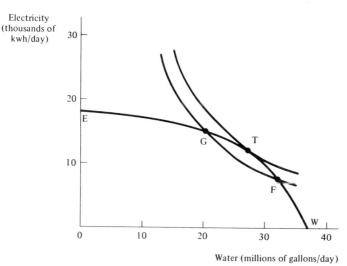

Fig. 3-18

may be far more complex. Uncertain prospects such as alternative lottery tickets, or the choice among elaborate plans for an individual's entire life, or decisions about sweeping programs of social reform are all encompassed by the model. The principle of rational choice is unchanged. The decision maker should attempt to select the available alternative that he values most highly in terms of his own preferences.

Marginal Analysis

This discussion of marginal rates of transformation and substitution is only one example of the type of analysis that forms the core of traditional microeconomic theory. In a nutshell, in order to achieve an optimal result, the allocation of scarce resources among competing uses must satisfy certain marginal equalities. For example, the consumer should allocate his budget so that he gets the same satisfaction from the last dollar he spends on orange juice and the last dollar he spends on going to the ballet. And a rational consumer will do just that, even though he will rarely do so consciously. A farmer or the manager of a pencil factory should expand production just to the point where his last dollar of sales costs him exactly $1. Producing more diminishes his profit, producing less means that he forgoes some of the profit he might have reaped. Similarly, a public decision maker—a mayor, say—should allocate spending on park mainte-nance and on fire protection so that the last dollar spent on each is equally satisfying to the society he represents.

Marginal analysis is conventionally expounded in terms of the private sector. Because scores of texts in microeconomic theory cover the subject admirably, we will not delve into its details here.[8] We will, however, return

---

[8] See, for example, Edwin Mansfield, *Microeconomics* (New York: W. W. Norton, 1975).

briefly to the subject in Chapter 9, where marginal benefit and marginal cost concepts are discussed.

Pathological Cases

We have followed the conventional practice in constructing the shape of our indifference and possibility curves. That is, the possibility frontier has been drawn so that it is concave to (bowed away from) the origin and the indifference curves are convex to (bowed toward) the origin. It has been found that most decision makers do indeed behave as though their indifference curves could be drawn in this way. In other words, the amount of output II that they will give up for more of output I decreases as they acquire more of output I. Furthermore, experience has shown that possibility curves are usually either concave to the origin or straight lines. Often the curvature results simply from the technological facts of life; that is, as we continue to increase our production of output I, we must continually give up more and more units of output II for each additional unit of output produced. In other situations, the outputs may be traded off at a constant rate, so that the possibility frontier is a straight line. We noted above that this is the case for the individual consumer. When indifference curves and the possibility frontier are thus appropriately shaped, equality between MRT and MRS indicates the best choice.

But occasionally we come across pathological cases in which MRT and MRS are not equal at the optimum. If for any particular decision problem the possibility or indifference curves are not conventionally shaped, the point of tangency may be a worst rather than a best point, a pessimum rather than an optimum. In Figure 3–19 we show a pathological possibility frontier *PP* (convex to the origin) and indifference curves

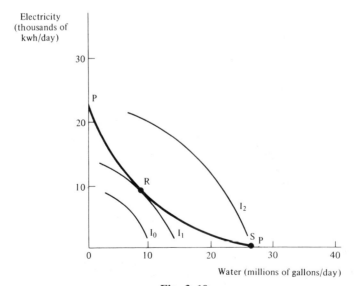

Fig. 3–19

(concave to the origin). (*PP* has been drawn as a heavier line to make the graph easier to read.) MRT equals MRS at the point of tangency *R*, but *R* is a dreadful point, the worst of all those on the possibility frontier. We can see that the highest possible indifference curve is reached at point *S*. The optimal solution involves the production of water only; point *S* is a *corner solution*, because the best choice lies in a corner of the feasible set of points. Any feasible choice that includes both water and electricity is inferior.

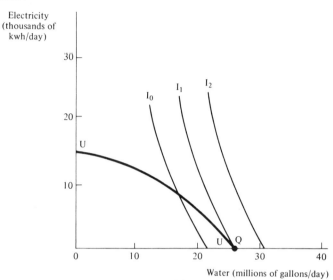

Fig. 3–20

It is possible that the best choice is represented by a corner solution even when the curves are conventionally shaped. Figure 3–20 shows such a situation in which there is no point of tangency, no point at which MRT and MRS are equal. The best choice is at point *Q*.

Indivisibilities

A much more common problem is that encountered when it is impossible to make continuous tradeoffs between the outputs. If, for example, the outputs are aircraft carriers and bombers, or sheep and goats, it is not possible to swap one for the other continuously until a point of tangency is reached and the best choice thereby determined. One cannot fly two-thirds of a bomber nor raise half a sheep. When the outputs are indivisible, they should (strictly speaking) be represented by a series of points rather than a continuous possibility frontier. Even though incremental optimization procedures are then ruled out, the decision maker can move stepwise from point to point and thus reach the best choice, provided the efficient points can be connected by a curve that is concave to the origin. Such a curve is drawn through points *W*, *X*, *Y*, and *Z* in Figure 3–21. The point *P* at which

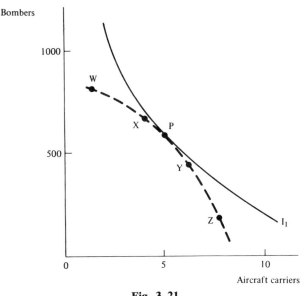

Fig. 3–21

the indifference curve I_1 is tangent to this broken curve is an approximate solution; the best choice will be one of the two neighboring alternatives, X or Y.

More on Dimensions

The model of choice requires that preferences be expressed in the same units as the outcomes of the various alternatives proposed. Thus, if the decision maker is offered a choice among assorted combinations of apples and oranges, his preferences must be expressed also in terms of apples and oranges. Conversely, if he is to choose a mix of strange fruit whose attributes are a mystery to him, although he knows his preferences for, say, vitamins and juiciness, the outcomes of the various possible choices must be expressed not as bundles of fruit but as combinations of these attributes. In other words, he must be able to measure these fruits in terms of the characteristics he understands, cares about, and can work with.

For most of us, apples and oranges are familiar goods; if we select a given bundle, we know what we are getting and we can think directly in terms of our preferences for its contents. In contrast, the outcomes of policy choices are rarely obvious and frequently subtle. In considering a proposal made for a new national park on Boston's harbor islands, the knowledge that the choice is between developing the islands and leaving them as they are tells us little about the ultimate outcomes of these two courses, for the bare choice between developing and not developing is almost meaningless. It is the impact of that choice on recreation, the environment, the local economy, and so on, that we care about. In the case of the dam proposals, the planner's preferences for electricity and water presumably depend on the uses to which these outputs will be put. That is to say, his true preferences relate to such considerations as the number of homes served by the electricity and the number of acres irrigated by the water. But unless he can translate these preferences into kilowatt-hours of electricity and gallons of water, he can't determine which dam is the best choice. Alternatively, of course, he could have expressed the output of each dam in terms of homes served and acres irrigated.

This matter of dimensions may seem embarrassingly obvious, but it is not trivial. We are all familiar with controversies about ongoing public programs—public housing, for instance—in which the proponents point with pride to admirable intangible goals while the opponents add up the broken windows and the muggings in the elevators. In short, being forced into a model of choice is useful, for it compels us to get the ground rules straight on what we value and how the alternatives before us measure up in these respects.

What Practical Use for the Model of Choice?

Of what use is the model of choice to the decision maker? Is not the ability to make difficult choices among competing ends the very asset that has placed him in his policy making position? The economist would answer that systematic analyses and formal statements of procedure can be valuable. He might invoke an analogy to sailing and the theories that underlie it: even the experienced yachtsman benefits from a knowledge of aerodynamics.

For expository purposes, we ordinarily describe the fundamental model in terms of simple choices, so simple that they can easily be made without recourse to analytic methods. (After all, we need neither a theory nor a model to choose among ice cream cones of different flavors, although we would argue that implicit models do in fact govern such choices.) Moreover, the model of choice assumes an individual decision maker who is confronted with a fixed menu of alternatives in a world he can't change. He faces no significant uncertainties, and he has complete command over his preferences. These are stringent conditions; they are unlikely to be fulfilled precisely in most real-world situations. Nevertheless, it is important to understand the framework that produces the best decision in a well-behaved situation. This model can serve as the foundation on which to build choice procedures for more complex situations, many of which are considered in the remainder of this volume.

What new complications arise in public policy choices? At the outset, the mere process of constructing the possibility frontier and the preference function is vastly more difficult. The choice between allocating $100 million to job training programs and using it for bolstering Title I grants for the education of disadvantaged children may not only plumb to the roots of our value system, it will involve us in difficult problems of predicting the costs and benefits that each will generate for quite different groups of people. Even in the evaluation of individual projects we may encounter exceptional difficulties. How can we weigh the losses of those families displaced by our hypothetical urban renewal project against the gains of those who will enjoy improved living conditions in the completed housing? How can we relate the basic model to decision making in the real world, to issues such as how to allocate funds for biomedical research or how to regulate automobile safety equipment?

Our approach is to extend the fundamental model by employing it as a prescriptive model for analyzing and making such complex decisions. Note carefully that this is the converse of the descriptive use of the model in economic theory. The economist would construct the possibility frontier and the decision maker's preference map by observing the choices that can be made and that actually are made, and would then argue that the decision maker behaves *as if* he were following such a model. The economic model is thus interpreted as a descriptive theory of behavior, a theory that can be tested by seeing whether actual choices correspond to those predicted by the model. We ask our decision maker to invert this process. We expect him to think about and determine, consciously and explicitly, what the alternatives and their outcomes are and what his preferences among these outcomes are, and to make his choice accordingly. In the public sphere this task is frequently extraordinarily hard. The rest of this book is aimed at helping the analyst and decision maker to make these determinations.

Part II

Nuts and Bolts

4 Difference Equations

Highway engineers forecasting traffic density, biologists observing the rate at which cells multiply, economists tracking GNP growth rates, businessmen evaluating investment opportunities—all rely on difference equations. Difference equations are a tool for exploring the way things change over time; they are concerned with dynamic processes rather than static situations. They offer powerful insights and at the same time are easy to understand and use. Moreover, difference equations have significant pedagogical advantages. They are a convenient vehicle for introducing a variety of concepts, including the general subject of mathematical notation, and provide good practice in the technique of translating verbal statements into equations. Consequently, we devote our first "Nuts and Bolts" chapter to difference equations, a particularly valuable type of mathematical model, and one that has proven useful for modeling dynamic processes in a wide variety of fields.

A General Description and Some Easy Illustrations

There are two ways we can represent dynamic processes. We can view things as changing continuously over time, which is in fact generally the case, or we can break in on a process or system at specified time intervals and see where things are. Parents, for example, are likely to measure a child's height each year on his birthday, although they recognize that he grows throughout the year.

Difference equations take the period-by-period or discrete approach: they relate the value of a variable in a given time period to its values in periods past. They are an essential feature of the financial world; indeed, the compound interest model that we used in Chapter 2 is a simple difference equation:

$$S_1 = (1 + r)S_0$$

Here S_1, the sum of money in a savings bank account at the end of a year, is related to the initial sum S_0; r is the rate of interest. We use letters rather than precise numbers in order to make our statements more generally applicable. For example, this equation is valid whether r is 5 percent, 7 percent, or 100 percent. Note the use of subscripts, numbers or letters written to the right of and a little below the symbol for the variable, to indicate the specific time at which a variable is being valued. They are typical of difference equations: using the subscripted variables S_0 and S_1 rather than completely different symbols such as A and B for the variables serves to remind us that we are talking about a particular chunk of money, even though the exact sum in question is different at different times.

Another simple model describes the number of miles of bicycle paths, M, in a town that builds 2 additional miles of path per year:

$$M_1 = M_0 + 2$$

By now you have probably noticed that we use mnemonic or memory-assisting notation whenever possible. This is simply a matter of convenience; it is easier to remember M for miles, or S for sum and r for rate, than the more familiar x, y, and z. Note also a small scrap of terminology: the sum of money in the savings bank grows at a constant *rate*, whereas the number of miles of bike paths increases by a constant *amount*.

Listed below are a few illustrations of the many sorts of situations in which difference equation models are useful:

1. A couple wishes to set aside money to supplement Social Security when they retire in twenty years. They want to know what their savings will be when they retire if they invest $2000 per year at 7 percent interest, and how long those savings will last if after retirement they withdraw $5000 per year, continuing to earn 7 percent on the balance left in their account.
2. A school district has overcrowded classrooms. There is pressure to relieve this overcrowding, either by building a new school or by renting temporary facilities. In order to decide between these two alternatives, the school board needs projections of the school-age population in the district over the next two decades.
3. The president of a university is concerned about its ability to fund ongoing programs. He needs projections of income and expenses over the next 10 years to help him decide what policies to follow with respect to tuition, scholarship aid, and faculty hiring.
4. A state department of public health is considering a new program to detect and treat hypertensives. It has guesstimates of how many new hypertensives would be discovered every month, what propor-

tion would then enter treatment, and what the attrition rate from the program would be. In order to put together a budget, the department needs estimates of the number of people in treatment during the first two years of the program.

5. The 1970 Clean Air Act mandates stepped reduction in the permissible level of pollutants emitted by new cars. The possibility of requiring the owners of older cars to add pollution control devices has been discussed. Given the rates at which older cars go out of service, how much difference would such a policy make in the total amount of auto emissions?

6. A mosquito control district is considering several alternative spraying programs, all of which have the same dollar cost. It needs a model of mosquito reproduction and of the effects of different spraying programs in order to determine the most effective plan.

The choice of the appropriate time interval—the amount of time that elapses between time 0 and time 1—to use in a difference equation depends on the particular problem at hand. If we were examining the growth of a flu epidemic, for instance, days or weeks might be appropriate, whereas for the growth of world population we would be more likely to look at years or decades.

Nonmathematicians sometimes find it difficult to translate verbal statements into mathematical equations. Difference equations provide good practice in this; before going further you should try to express the following statements as difference equations, relating the value in period 1 to that in period 0 (answers will be found at the end of the book).

1. A totalitarian country that prohibits migration has a birth rate b and a death rate d. How does population change from one year to the next?

2. There are no births in a Shaker community, only R recruits per year. The death rate is d. What is the difference equation that describes this situation?

3. The Eastville School Committee agrees to an annual $200 per year salary increase for each Eastville teacher. Express this as a difference equation.

4. The Westtown School Committee is more generous. It agrees to a 5.5 percent cost-of-living increase per year, plus a one-time only $200 "adjustment" for past sins of omission. Express this as a difference equation.

5. A well-incubated staphylococcus population doubles in about 1 hour. How does the population change from one period to the next?

Before proceeding, you should try to think of dynamic situations in your own field of interest that can be illuminated by a model that uses difference equations.

A Few Words About Notation

Cumbersome notation is an impediment to the use of difference equations. It may alarm the nomathematician; many laymen turn and run at the sight of a subscript, and accelerate if it's a double subscript. If they would only stick it out, they would learn that their difficulties are more apparent than real; subscripts become tame on even short acquaintance. Here are some hints.

The time period of a variable is usually denoted by subscripts: S_0, S_1, S_n, and S_{t+1} are examples. Any respectable discussion of a model will tell you what all the variables are and what all the subscripts stand for. (If it doesn't, you are entitled to label it "bad" writing.) When you build your own models, you should follow the tradition of telling the readers what your notation stands for, rather than making them guess. Our simplest compound interest model used S_0 to denote an initial sum of money and S_1 the amount a year later. The use of a "0" subscript usually implies an initial or starting condition. If you're reading it aloud, you say "S zero" or "S sub zero" to tell your listeners exactly where the zero can be found, or "S nought" to give it a British flair. Some people start up their models at time 1, not time 0. That too is fine—just so long as they tell us.

Frequently a single subscript isn't enough. If you will refer back to the choose-the-bank version of the compound interest model that we discussed in Chapter 2, you will recall that the sum of money after n years depended both on how long it was left in the bank and on the bank in which it was deposited. Therefore we wrote S_{ni} for the amount accumulated after n years in the ith ("eyeth") bank. Note that if we had assigned actual numbers to n and i, say 2 years in the third bank, and if we then wrote S_{23}, it might look as though there were a single subscript "twenty-three." To prevent this confusion we could write "$S_{2,3}$" or "$S_{2\ 3}$." Whether or not the comma or space is inserted depends on the individual circumstances; frequently no confusion is possible so it's left out.

Another way to handle the multiple subscript problem is to write $S_i(n)$, where i, the subscript, indicates which bank we mean and n, the value in the parentheses, is the time period. In the case of our compound interest problem, be sure that you understand the meaning of expressions such as $S_2(5)$ or $S_4(3)$.

Still another method of handling the subscript problem is to use superscripts. Sometimes a superscript is placed in parentheses so that it won't be confused with an exponent, but don't rely on that: S_{ni} could also be written $S_n^{(i)}$ or S_n^i.

One of the most common uses of double subscripts is to describe a location in a rectangular table (or matrix, as they say in the trade) of numbers. Ordinarily "a_{ij}" means the number in the ith row and the jth column. If the table were three-dimensional, you would need a third subscript and the general term would be "a_{ijk}."

The important thing about subscripts is not to let them intimidate you. As with the characters you meet in a Russian novel, it often pays to make notes as to how they're defined as you go along. You can then readily refer to your notes as you work your way througy an analysis.

One further comment: Computers can't write subscripts as such; everything has to go on the same line; they use parentheses instead. S_0, for example, becomes $S(0)$; S_{ij} becomes $S(i,j)$. Once again it's a matter of convention, and again you must make sure the convention is explained, this time to a machine.

The General Form of a Difference Equation

Thus far our difference equations have modeled changes for specific periods of time, an initial period (0) and one period later (1). Usually we are more interested in a general statement that relates the value of the variable in any time period to its value in the preceding period. In the compound interest model, it would be useful to have an expression for S_n, the sum at the nth period, in terms of what S was in period $(n - 1)$. This of course offers greater flexibility in applying the formula. In this case it is clear what that formula must be; we simply write:

$$S_n = (1 + r)S_{n-1}, \qquad \text{for all } n \geq 1^1$$

where S_{n-1} is the sum on deposit at the end of the $(n - 1)$th period. This equation is called the *general form* of the difference equation, because it holds in general and not just for specific values of n. It is a *first-order* difference equation because the variable S_n can be determined from its value in the one preceding period only. We don't need to know its history before that. Before reading on, you should try writing the five exercises on page 49 as general difference equations for the nth period, including any restrictions on the values n may take (answers will be found at the end of the book).

Difference Equations of Higher Order

Consider the following statement:

> The Bonex Company prefers, earnings permitting, to pay dividends according to the following rule: The dividend on a share of common stock should be equal to 90 percent of last year's dividend plus one and one-half times the previous year's change in dividend.

This exercise is designed to illustrate a situation slightly more complicated than those previously encountered. Here we are concerned with a dividend, D, that depends on its value not only in the last period but also in the period before last. The general difference equation is:

$$D_n = .90D_{n-1} + 1.5(D_{n-1} - D_{n-2}) = 2.4D_{n-1} - 1.5D_{n-2}, \quad n \geq 2$$

---

[1] The symbol $>$ means "greater than"; $<$ means "less than." Similarly, $\geq$ is translated as "greater than or equal to," $\leq$ as "less than or equal to."

The earliest period for which this equation is valid is period 2, for both D_1 and D_0 are needed in order to determine D_2. We call D_1 and D_0 the initial conditions; we must know what each equals if we are to calculate a numerical value for D_2. Suppose, for example, that the Bonex dividend was $2.10 per share last year and $1.50 two years ago; what does the company policy indicate it should be this year?[2] This is a second-order difference equation, so called because the difference between the highest and lowest subscript in the equation is 2; we must go back two periods to predict this period's values. It follows from the above discussion that a difference equation may be valid only for n sufficiently large; this one is valid for $n \geq 2$, whereas those we encountered earlier were valid for $n \geq 1$. The higher the order, the more initial conditions that must be known, and the larger n must be in order for the general equation to be valid.

At times we may find that one general equation is valid for certain values of n, say n odd, and another or others for different values of n. We'll meet up with such cases later on in this chapter. Here are some other examples of general difference equations:

$$w_{n+1} = w_n - .1w_{n-1} + 5 \tag{4-1}$$

$$x_{n+1} = 1.05x_n + n \tag{4-2}$$

$$y_n = y_{n-1} + y_{n-2} - y_{n-4} \tag{4-3}$$

$$z_n = 1.2z_{n-1} - .000002(z_{n-1})^2 - 1500 \tag{4-4}$$

The four variables, w, x, y, and z are unspecified; w might be sales of a new automobile accessory, x the sum of money accumulated as the result of an annual birthday present that follows a pleasant path of its own, and y the population of a certain short-lived animal species. Equation (4-4) is a nonlinear equation; i.e., one of the variables is raised to a power other than 1. Equations of the general form of (4-4) are commonly used to describe the growth patterns of many biological species—whales, for example—when unchecked by human activity.

"Solving" Difference Equations

Ordinarily we use difference equations for more than just the period-to-period applications we have discussed thus far. We are usually more interested in exploring the implications of a situation for some time in the future, perhaps the far distant future. Of course we could calculate that future value, period by period, starting from the initial period. For example, suppose in the compound interest model

$$S_n = (1 + r)S_{n-1}$$

---

[2] The answer is $2.79 per share.

we set S_0 equal to \$10,000 and r equal to .05. We ask to what sum the initial deposit will accumulate in 20 years; in other words, what S_{20} will be. If we grind out the answer period by period we find that:

$$S_1 = (1.05)(10,000) = 10,500$$

$$S_2 = (1.05)(10,500) = 11,025$$

$$S_3 = (1.05)(11,025) = 11,576.25$$

$$\vdots \qquad \vdots$$

$$S_{20} = (1.05)(25,269.49) = 26,532.96.^3$$

This is tiresome; it would be handy to have a formula that relates S_{20} directly to S_0 so that we don't have to drudge through all the intervening steps. To put it more generally, we need a formula that relates S_n to the initial conditions. In this case the desired equation is obvious from inspection:

$$S_1 = 1.05 S_0$$

$$S_2 = 1.05 S_1 = 1.05^2 S_0$$

$$\vdots \qquad \vdots$$

$$S_n = 1.05^n S_0, \quad \text{for all } n \geq 1$$

This expression for S_n is known as the *general solution* of the difference equation; it is valid for all values of n for which the difference equation itself is valid. For practice, try to find the general solutions for the five exercises on page 49 (the answers are given at the end of the book).

Is there any special technique for finding the general solution to a difference equation? In certain areas, like the one we just saw, a solution may be evident upon inspection. In others, solutions may be difficult or impossible to find. Our recommendation is to try hammer and tongs: write out the equations for a few periods and see if a clear pattern emerges. One useful simplifying trick for computing the sum of a geometric series is demonstrated below.

Frequently, the general solution of a difference equation will not be readily apparent, or it will be so messy that it is easier to generate the values period by period. If the general solution is elusive, the best course is simply to find the equation for the nth period in terms of the immediately preceding period or periods and then run the equation on a computer, starting at period 0. (Better yet, find someone to run it for you.) The three difference equations (4–1), (4–2), and (4–3) on page 52 are examples of linear difference equations that are not easily solved. Even when the solutions can be found, they are too cumbersome to be of any use. Nonlinear equations are even less promising, for it is far less likely that an

---

³ Three dots, either vertical or horizontal, are used to indicate that (1) something has been left out, and (2) whatever it is fits into a logical progression that you should be able to figure out for yourself.

analytic solution can be found. And when you need to calculate the value of several interacting variables over time, as you might if dealing with the age distribution of a population, you'll probably want to resort to a computer anyway. We will have more to say on this in our discussion of simulation.

Solving difference equations was a more rewarding occupation 25 years ago than it is today. When all computations had to be ground out laboriously on an old-fashioned desk calculator, even an arduous search for a streamlined way of doing things was worthwhile. Nowadays it is rarely worth the trouble for the occasional user to struggle to find a general solution; a computer will carry out period-by-period iterations in a second or two, and will offer far fewer opportunities for human error. A solution may still be an elegant exercise, but it has lost much of its advantage in computational speed. In this age of microseconds, the primary reason for searching for a solution, or at least for attempting to ferret out its form, is to gather insights that might not be available if we merely cranked out the numbers. Bundles of numbers may make it difficult to discern certain patterns or regularities. For example, we may not be sure from looking at the numbers whether a dwindling animal species is inexorably threatened with extinction, or whether it is merely adjusting to a changed environment and can be expected to stabilize permanently at a lower level, or possibly at a higher level.

For many problems, the properties of the solution will not be of great interest; we will just want to know the numerical values. For example, we may want to determine the budgetary cost of a pending state pension scheme in each of the next 50 years. A calculation of this sort should routinely inform labor negotiations with public employees, in which retirement benefits are often a major bone of contention. In the heat and press of negotiations, it may be impossible to run to a computer. A hand calculator can prove quite satisfactory in yielding quick approximations. A number of computational shortcuts might be employed; the ones that follow have many uses.

A Mathematical Digression: The Sum of a Geometric Series

Rabbit populations and money in the bank grow at regular rates. So too, until recent years, did electricity use. In a great variety of contexts it may be important to sum up the year-by-year quantities of a regularly growing commodity. What will be the primary school population of Ruritania 10 years from now if the number of babies born each year is growing at a 3 percent rate? How much natural gas will we consume in the next decade if consumption grows at 8 percent per year? Indeed, predictions of the future demand for energy are among the most crucially important uses of difference equations. We saw above that one way to calculate the value of a variable at a time in the future is to go at it year by year. This is sometimes described as "iterating it out," a laborious pastime that is fine for computers but not recommended for people. If we have to do the work ourselves, we would like to find an easier way to do it, a general solution that relates S_n directly to the initial conditions without working through all the steps. Frequently this is impossible, but now and then we can use the following helpful trick.

A geometric series is an expression of the form

$$a^n + a^{n-1} + \ldots + a^2 + a + 1$$

Fortunately, sums of this sort may be expressed as a simple fraction:

$$a^n + \ldots + a + 1 = \frac{a^{n+1} - 1}{a - 1} \tag{4-5}$$

Naturally it's a lot easier to calculate the right-hand side of (4–5) than the left.[4]

How would you use this formula? Let's go back to our compound interest example and complicate the situation a bit. Suppose our saver starts with an initial amount S_0, but he also deposits an additional S_0 dollars

---

[4] One of the authors rarely forgets a phone number, a formula, or a bridge hand. The other has a mind like a sieve and has to rederive the formula every time. In case you identify with the latter, here is the trick:

Consider the sum

$$A = a^n + a^{n-1} + \ldots + a^2 + a + 1$$

If we multiply both sides of this equation by a, we have

$$Aa = (a^n + a^{n-1} + \ldots + a^2 + a + 1)a$$

Performing the multiplication on the right-hand side, we get

$$Aa = a^{n+1} + a^n + \ldots + a^2 + a$$

If we now subtract $A = a^n + a^{n-1} + \ldots + a + 1$ from Aa, we have

$$Aa - A = a^{n+1} + a^n + \ldots + a^2 + a$$
$$- a^n - \ldots - a^2 - a - 1$$
$$= a^{n+1} - 1$$

Thus

$$Aa - A = a^{n+1} - 1$$

Dividing through by $(a - 1)$ gives:

$$A = \frac{a^{n+1} - 1}{a - 1}$$

This formula works for any value of a, positive or negative, except $a = 1$. What happens then? The formula yields $A = 0/0$, which has no meaning. But if we go back to the original definition of A, we see that

$$A = a^n + a^{n-1} + \ldots + a^2 + a + 1$$
$$= 1 + 1 + \ldots + 1 + 1 + 1$$

to a total of $(n + 1)$ terms. So if $a = 1$, this expression must simply give $A = n + 1$.

Note finally that if a is a fraction that is less than 1 (i.e., $0 < a < 1$) and if n becomes very large, then the term a^{n+1} becomes very small so that A, the sum of the geometric series, approaches $1/(1 - a)$. We then write $A \approx 1/(1 - a)$. The approximation holds also for $-1 < a < 0$.

each year. This gives:

$$S_1 = (1 + r)S_0 + S_0$$

$$S_2 = (1 + r)S_1 + S_0 = (1 + r)^2 S_0 + (1 + r)S_0 + S_0$$

$$S_3 = (1 + r)S_2 + S_0 = (1 + r)^3 S_0 + (1 + r)^2 S_0 + (1 + r)S_0 + S_0$$

$$\vdots \qquad \vdots$$

and in general

$$S_n = [(1 + r)^n + (1 + r)^{n-1} + (1 + r)^{n-2}$$
$$+ \ldots + (1 + r)^2 + (1 + r) + 1]S_0$$

This simplification may look as though it hasn't accomplished much—there is still an enormous amount of computation to do. But the expression in the brackets is the sum of a geometric series, i.e., it is of the form

$$a_n + a^{n-1} + \ldots + a^2 + a + 1$$

where the a terms have been replaced by terms in $(1 + r)$. If we set $(1 + r)$ equal to a and substitute in (4–5) we get:

$$(1 + r)^n + (1 + r)^{n-1} + \ldots + (1 + r) + 1$$
$$= \frac{(1 + r)^{n+1} - 1}{(1 + r) - 1} = \frac{(1 + r)^{n+1} - 1}{r}$$

Thus we can write:

$$S_n = \frac{(1 + r)^{n+1} - 1}{r} S_0$$

an expression within easy reach of any hand calculator.

A Useful Rule of Thumb: Doubling Time and the Rule of 72

In working with difference equations, it's often helpful to have a quick estimate of how long it will take to double a sum of money or a population.

Table 4–1
Time Required to Double a Population

Rate of growth per year	Actual years required (to nearest tenth)	Years predicted by Rule of 72
.01	69.7	72
.02	35.0	36
.03	23.4	24
.04	17.7	18
.05	14.2	14.4
.10	7.3	7.2
.20	3.8	3.6
.40	2.1	1.8

Naturally it all depends on the rate at which it grows. Those analysts and businessmen who have come across it rely on the "Rule of 72," which says that money invested to yield x percent per year will double in roughly $72/x$ years, provided that x is not too large. (The interest rates we ordinarily encounter in the real world are "not too large.") Thus the rule predicts that money left in a bank where it grows at 5 percent per year will double in about $72/5 = 14.4$ years. Table 4–1 shows how closely the rule approximates the actual numbers.

More on Difference Equations in General

One point to note about difference equations is that you have to be very careful about specifying when within a time period an event occurs. In the compound interest example, we implied by the way we wrote the difference equation that a deposit is made at the end of a period; it doesn't start earning interest until the beginning of the next period. There are no mathematical rules for this; you simply have to apply your common sense, asking questions when necessary, to figure out how a system works and then get it down on paper. Sunday, for example, might give us some trouble unless we are precise. Do we view it as the first day of next week, which tradition suggests it should be, or the last day of this week, which it is for most of us in practice? For the sake of those who will use your model, it's desirable to state explicitly the assumptions you have made about when things happen. In many situations, of course, the context of the problem will dictate which assumptions are appropriate. The Westtown School Committee exercise on page 00 illustrates an ambiguous situation. The new teachers' contract calls for a 5.5 percent per year cost of living increase, plus a $200 lump sum payment. It is not clear on the stated facts whether the 5.5 percent applies before or after the $200 payment is made. If you find it necessary to use a model developed by someone who has failed to describe his variables fully, you simply have to take one view or another, stating explicitly the assumptions you have made.

Incidentally, the shorter the time period, the less crucial is the assumption as to when within it events occur. This is because, as the period becomes shorter, the model more closely resembles a continuous model.[5] As a practical matter, the length of the time period to be used in a

---

[5] As banks and other savings institutions often explain, the more frequently interest is compounded, the better it is for the depositor. If a bank advertises 6 percent interest compounded semiannually, it means that the bank pays 3 percent at the end of each 6-month period, which turns out to be 6.09 percent, since $1.03^2 = 1.0609$ annually. If 6 percent is compounded quarterly, it is equivalent to an annual rate of 6.135 percent. The general formula for n years at a rate r, compounded t times during the year, is

$$S_n = \left(1 + \frac{r}{t}\right)^{tn} S_0$$

You may wonder what happens if interest is compounded at shorter and shorter intervals. Does the effective annual rate increase indefinitely? No, there is a limit to this process, namely e^r, where $e = 2.718 \ldots$, a number as indispensable to mathematicians as π (as is

difference equation may be determined by the data available. In predicting economic events we might find it helpful to have monthly data; frequently only quarterly or even annual statistics can be obtained.

Equilibrium and Stability

We have seen that models using difference equations are valuable for tracking a variable over time. Sometimes in examining the long-run behavior of a variable we find that it more and more closely approaches some limiting value, which we call the *equilibrium* value.

Equilibrium is a most important concept. A system that has reached an equilibrium stays there—i.e., the values of its variables remain the same—unless it is disturbed by some outside force. If the equilibrium is *stable,* the system will return to equilibrium (although not necessarily very quickly) once the disturbance ceases. (Think of a child's swing: it always comes to rest in the same place once it is no longer pushed or pumped.) If the equilibrium is *unstable,* the system will stay put as long as nothing disturbs it. But once it is nudged or jiggled, there will be no tendency for the system to return to this equilibrium. (Imagine, if you can, an orange balanced on the edge of a knife. Tip it, and it is gone from the knife edge forever.) Some systems have equilibria that are stable if the outside disturbance is small and unstable if it is large. (A television tower sways in the wind and eventually returns to its original position—unless the wind is so strong that it topples the tower.)

The term *equilibrium* carries no favorable connotation whatsoever, a point that is too often forgotten. An equilibrium may be a good or bad or neutral state of affairs. If our only goal is prediction, of course, being at an equilibrium will substantially ease our task.

Frequently our main interest in a system that can be modeled using difference equations is in whether or not the system will approach an equilibrium. For example, consider a reservoir that currently holds 1200 million gallons of water. Springs, streams, rainfall, and pumping from deep wells provide an inflow of 200 million gallons a month; consumption is 150 million gallons a month. Loss from seepage and evaporation is 5 percent per month. Water Department officials observe that the water level in the reservoir is dropping noticeably; they are worried about what will happen to this reservoir over the long run.

A difference equation model sheds some light on this situation. Letting

---

evidenced by its appearance in the more expensive pocket calculators). When r is .06, continuous compounding leads to

$$S_t = (e^{.06})^n S_0 = (1.06184)^n S_0$$

A bank that compounds continuously at 6 percent interest will give you 6.184 percent per year. This discussion, by the way, suggests why difference equations are so named: the time that elapses between one period and the next is a finite measurable quantity, a difference. If the difference becomes infinitesimally small, it merges into the continuous case. You probably have heard a good deal about exponential growth in recent years. This is it; it's nothing more than the continuous version of geometric growth.

W_m equal the millions of gallons of water in the reservoir at month m, we may write

$$W_0 = 1200$$

$$W_1 = .95W_0 + 50$$

$$W_2 = .95W_1 + 50 = .95^2 W_0 + .95(50) + 50$$

$$\vdots \qquad \vdots$$

$$W_m = .95^m W_0 + 50\left(\frac{.95^m - 1}{.95 - 1}\right) = .95^m W_0 - 1000(.95^m - 1)$$

$$= .95^m(W_0 - 1000) + 1000$$

Now as many, many months pass and m becomes very large, $.95^m$ will get smaller and smaller, until eventually the term $.95^m(W_0 - 1000)$ becomes insignificant compared to the other term, 1000.[6] Thus in the long run the amount of water in the reservoir comes closer and closer to 1 billion gallons. Note that in computing the equilibrium we never had to make use of the fact that $W_0 = 1200$; it turned out to be irrelevant. However, this is due to our concern with the very long run only. It is evident that the closer the current level of the reservoir, W_0, is to its ultimate equilibrium, the more quickly the reservoir will approach that level. Moreover, in a different system (as we'll see shortly) the starting point might play a role in determining the equilibrium that is eventually reached.

Can we determine directly whether the level of this reservoir—or any variable—reaches such an equilibrium value, and whether that equilibrium is stable or unstable? The logic required to address these questions is straightforward. At the equilibrium, the variable will by definition have the same value in period after period. In other words, an equilibrium value of the variable will produce that same value in the following period.

In the case of the reservoir, the general difference equation is:

$$W_m = .95W_{m-1} + 50$$

If this system reaches an equilibrium level, which we will denote by W_e, it must be that in every month thereafter there will also be W_e gallons of water in the reservoir. This follows from the definition of an equilibrium. In other words, it must be that

$$W_e = .95W_e + 50$$

Solving this equation, we find that $W_e = 1$ billion gallons.

An equilibrium is stable if the variable tends toward the equilibrium value over the long run, even if it is occasionally disturbed as in the case of the child's swing. In mathematical notation, we express this condition as

$$\lim_{n \to \infty} P_n = P_e$$

---

[6] For example, $.95^{10} \approx .599$, and $.95^{100} \approx .006$.

where P is whatever population we are investigating. (This is read aloud as, "The limit of P_n, as n approaches infinity, equals P_e.") "Population" has no human or even animal connotation here; it could just as well be water, as in the reservoir above, or dollars, as in the compound interest example.

We can improve our understanding of this whole matter of stable and unstable equilibria, and at the same time demonstrate the insights that a simple model may offer (provided we administer it with a little common sense) by looking at the whole family of simple difference equations having the form

$$P_n = aP_{n-1} + b$$

where P is the population under study and a and b are parameters that describe the behavior of this particular population. The equilibrium value is given by

$$P_e = aP_e + b \quad \text{or} \quad P_e = \frac{b}{1-a}$$

The easiest way to visualize this situation is with a diagram. In Figure 4–1, we plot P_n along the horizontal axis and P_{n+1} along the vertical axis.

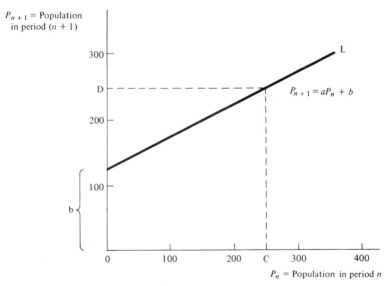

Fig. 4–1

The curve on the diagram, in this instance the straight line L, tells us what value P_{n+1} will take, given the value of P_n. For example, if P_n is C, P_{n+1} will be D.

The difference equation

$$P_{n+1} = aP_n + b$$

is the equation of the straight line with slope a that intercepts the P_{n+1} axis at b. (To verify this, set P_n equal to 0 in the above equations; P_{n+1} will then equal b.) To be sure, we can't actually draw this line accurately unless we know what a and b are. The line L in Figure 4-2 shows the case where $a = \frac{1}{2}$ and $b = 125$.

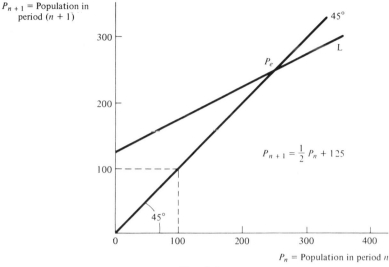

Fig. 4-2

We have seen that the equilibrium condition is simply

$$P_{n+1} = P_n$$

This equation may be represented by a 45° line through the origin, for at every point along that line $P_{n+1} = P_n$. Thus it is a neat device for transferring us from a given value (100, say) on one axis to the same value on the other axis, as is shown by the dotted lines in Figure 4-2. It also means that the intersection of the two lines in the figure is the equilibrium point, for only at this point will the value taken by P in the nth period be the same in the $(n + 1)$th period. For this particular situation, $P_e = 250.$[7]

We can use Figure 4-3 to investigate the stability of the equilibrium. Let's suppose we have as the initial condition $P_0 = 300$. We start by locating P_0 on the P_n axis. We then read the corresponding value of P_1 by following the arrows up to line L and over to the vertical axis; we find that $P_1 = 275$, which we could of course have found algebraically. Now we repeat the process, starting from $P_1 = 275$ on the P_n axis and moving to P_2

---

[7] Recall that the intersection of two straight lines may be found by solving the pair of simultaneous equations represented by the lines. In this case these equations are

$$\begin{cases} P_{n+1} = \frac{1}{2}P_n + 125, & \text{and} \\ P_{n+1} = P_n \end{cases}$$

This immediately reduces, by substitution, to $P_n = \frac{1}{2}P_n + 125$ or $P_e = 250$, the equilibrium value.

More generally, solving the pair of equations

$$\begin{cases} P_{n+1} = aP_n + b \\ P_{n+1} = P_n \end{cases}$$

yields the equilibrium value $P_e = b/(1 - a)$.

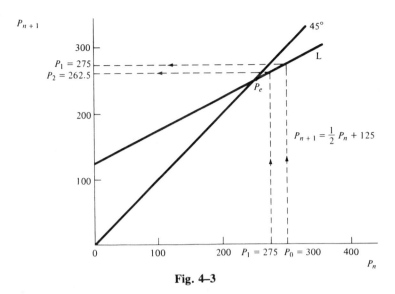

Fig. 4-3

= 262.5 on the vertical axis. We could keep this up indefinitely, and it is evident that if we try it will move down L, getting closer and closer to P_e, but never quite getting there.

Better yet, we can make use of the 45° line to shortcut this process. In Figure 4-4, the solid line and arrows indicate the net route the iterative process takes, in the sense that this is the route if we eliminate the parts where we retrace our steps.

Although we have dealt here with specific values of a and b, the lessons to be drawn are more general. Whewnever $0 < a < 1$ and $b > 0$, the diagram will essentially look like this one, and the system will move toward its equilibrium value. If $b < 0$, the equilibrium value will be

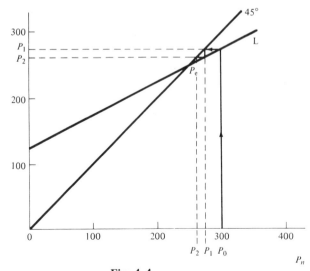

Fig. 4-4

negative. Sometimes this makes sense and sometimes it doesn't. If P refers to rabbits, negative numbers have no meaning: the population can't fall below zero; zero is a stable equilibrium. However, if P is a sum of money, negative numbers might well be possible, as many an overdrawn bank customer has discovered.

Will P_n always converge toward its equilibrium value in this way? By no means. Consider the case $a > 1$, $b < 0$; Figure 4–5 shows the unstable situation where $a = 2$, $b = -200$. There is still an equilibrium at $P_e = b/(1 - a)$, the intersection of line L and the 45° line, but it is unstable. If P_0 is greater than $b/(1 - a)$, P_n gets larger without limit as n increases, as the arrows indicate. If P_0 is less than $b/(1 - a)$, the population decreases and eventually is wiped out.[8] Thereafter it remains at 0, so 0 is in fact a stable equilibrium. If P_0 equals $b/(1 - a)$, the population remains at $b/(1 - a)$ only as long as nothing happens to upset it. The equilibrium is unstable, and the starting point is crucial for determining what eventually happens.

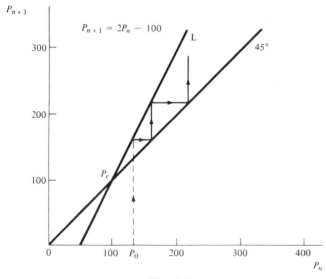

Fig. 4–5

Thus by examining what happens under various assumptions about a and b—and you may want to experiment on your own with some other assumptions—we gain valuable insights into systems that behave in this general fashion.

Let's return briefly to the Water Department and its reservoir. How might a difference equation model be used for further policy decisions? Suppose that planners project a 20 percent increase in water consumption over the next decade. The Water Department, concerned that the reservoir be maintained at all times at a minimum volume of 250 million gallons, is

---

[8] Occasionally it is possible for P to take negative values, as when P refers to a sum of money and debts may be incurred. Then, once the system falls below its unstable equilibrium, the debt will increase without limit, or at least will do so as long as lenders can be found.

requesting funds for more wells and pumping equipment. Is the request reasonable? A 20 percent increase in water consumption means a total monthly use of 180 million gallons and a net inflow of 20 million gallons. The future equilibrium, with no additional water sources, is therefore

$$W_e = .95W_e + 20$$

or a quite comfortable 400 million gallons. It appears that the Water Department's request is premature.

An Equilibrium Exercise: The Endowment Fund

An independent secondary school is concerned about its financial future. The overall rate of return (dividends, interest, and capital gains) on the school's investment portfolio is 10 percent per year. In order to meet expenses, $300,000 must be withdrawn from endowment income (and if necessary, from the principal) each year. Contributions to endowment are $200,000 per year. Will the endowment reach an equilibrium?

The general equation is

$$E_{n+1} = 1.10E_n - 300,000 + 200,000$$

where E is the endowment. Consequently the equilibrium (if it exists) is found by solving the equation

$$E_e = 1.10E_e - 100,000$$

$$E_e = 1,000,000$$

Figure 4–6 shows the diagram for this problem.

Is the equilibrium stable? In this equation $a = 1.10$; since it is greater than 1, the equilibrium is unstable. If initial endowment is greater than $1 million, it will grow without limit. If it is less, the endowment will shrink to $0 and remain there.

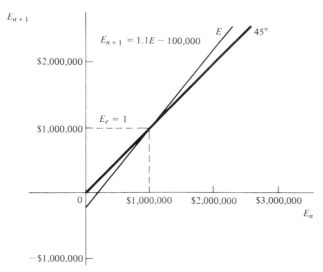

Fig. 4–6

As any fund raiser for an institution knows, the endowment problem is more complex than is implied here. Contributors are likely to be sensitive to both the size of the endowment and changes in it. If it is growing very quickly, the alumni may feel that their help is less crucial and may cut back their gifts accordingly. On the other hand, if the endowment is being heavily tapped, they may decide that further contributions are money down the drain. Attitudes such as these are depicted by the curve *EE* in Figure 4–7.

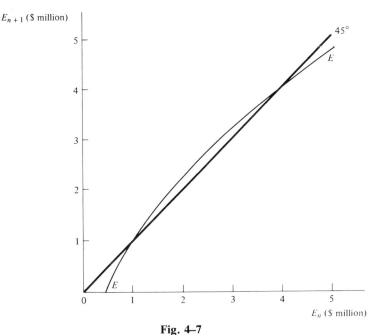

Fig. 4–7

As before, $1 million is a critical level. But now if endowment is greater than this amount, it will eventually reach a stable equilibrium at $4,000,000.[9]

The lower, unstable equilibrium is a typical "critical mass" or "over the hump" phenomenon, the sort of behavior that is encountered frequently in the real world. (The critical mass concept, incidentally, is another example of a conceptual model.) An automobile manufacturer trying to maintain a viable share of the market, the presidential primary candidate trying to qualify for matching funds, the Patuxent biologists trying to save the whooping crane from extinction—all are concerned with preventing their relevant populations from dwindling to extinction. They must achieve a certain critical level.

Thus far we have seen that a population whose growth pattern may be modeled with a first-order difference equation may increase without limit, dwindle to nothing or even less than nothing, reach a stable equilibrium, or

---

[9] One difference equation that will produce this result is $E_{n+1} = (3\sqrt{E_n}) - 2$, where E is endowment in millions of dollars.

(though unlikely) remain at an unstable equilibrium. When a more complex equation is required to describe the workings of the system, the model may imply the existence of multiple equilibria, some stable, others unstable. There is a further possibility: the population may oscillate indefinitely. For example, suppose we have a population whose behavior may be described by the following model:

$$P_{n+2} = P_n$$

This difference equation requires two initial conditions, P_0 and P_1. Assume that $P_0 = 100$ and $P_1 = 200$. Then our general equation becomes:

$P_n = 100$, n even;
$P_n = 200$, n odd.

And this will oscillate indefinitely between 100 and 200.

If this strikes you as an implausible model, consider a junior college with a fixed enrollment of 300 students and a board of trustees who thought it a good idea to start with an entering class of only 100 students when the college first opened. There are no failures, no dropouts, no transfers . . . and eventually a sadder but wiser board of trustees.

Any training program that must absorb a lot of spring graduates runs into this kind of problem. A baby boom that later subsides will produce oscillations. But because the effects in succeeding generations are spread out over longer and longer periods of time, the oscillations will be damped. We can expect to see the recurring effects of the post-World War II baby boom for several generations, but as time passes they will be more difficult to discern. Even when a population will eventually reach a stable equilibrium, the effects of an unusually large cohort (all those in a particular age bracket) are likely to be felt for a surprisingly long time; the ripple effect is dissipated only gradually.

Practice in Finding Equilibria

Here are two exercises to test your understanding of equilibrium and stability in first-order difference equations:

1. Every year 10 percent of the public housing units in a particular city deteriorate to the point where they are uninhabitable and must be demolished. Current plans and budget constraints call for the construction of 800 new units per year. Is there an equilibrium number of public housing units, and if so, is it stable?
2. A well-incubated staph population doubles in one hour, but now we introduce white blood cells, each of which can destroy 100 staph germs per hour. Is there an equilibrium, and if so, is it stable?

(Answers will be found at the end of the book.)

Difference Equations with More Than One Variable

Thus far our discussion has focused on the use of difference equations to predict the change over time in a single variable. This restriction has been helpful for expository purposes, but most of the more interesting cases involve more than one variable. These are called multivariable problems. Among them probably the most common and most important are the investigations of the changing structure of a population. The analysis is applicable to any situation where individuals progress in some systematic fashion from one state to another.

As a simple example of plausible growth patterns that lead to unexpected results, consider a population where there are 100 children (those aged 0 through 19) and 100 workers (those aged 20 through 39). In each period, 70 percent of the children survive to become workers in the following period; a period is 20 years in length. The workers reproduce at a rate of 1.3 children per worker per period, and expire when they reach age 40. What can we say about the ratio of children to workers in the long run? If we let C_n equal the child population at the nth period and W_n the worker population at the same period, we have the figures shown in Table 4–2.

Table 4–2

Period	C_n	W_n	Total population	Ratio of children to workers
0	100	100	200	$1:1$
1	130	70	200	$1.857:1$
2	91	91	182	$1:1$
3	118.3	63.7	182	$1.857:1$
4	82.81	82.81	166	$1:1$

The general equations are:

$$n \text{ odd:} \begin{cases} C_n = (.7)^{(n-1)/2}(1.3)^{(n+1)/2} W_0 \\ W_n = (.7)^{(n+1)/2}(1.3)^{(n-1)/2} C_0 \\ C_n/W_n = 1.3W_0/.7C_0 \end{cases}$$

$$n \text{ even:} \begin{cases} C_n = (.7)^{n/2}(1.3)^{n/2} C_0 \\ W_n = (.7)^{n/2}(1.3)^{n/2} W_0 \\ C_n/W_n = C_0/W_0 \end{cases}$$

Check these out and make sure you believe them.[10] This particular example is intended to show that without a model it's hard to predict the long-run structure of a population. With the model, we can make a very good guess as to what the population in, say, period 10 will look like. If we refined this

---

[10] The general equations were derived by the hammer-and-tongs method, in other words, by writing the equations down period by period until a clear pattern emerged.

Period 1: $C_1 = 1.3W_0$
$W_1 = .7C_0$

Period 2: $C_2 = 1.3W_1 = (.7)(1.3)C_0$

$W_2 = .7C_1 = (.7)(1.3)W_0$

Period 3: $C_3 = 1.3W_2 = (.7)(1.3)^2 W_0$

$W_3 = .7C_2 = (.7)^2(1.3)C_0$

(Footnote continues page 68.)

model and added a third category, retired workers, it could readily be adapted for studying the Social Security trust fund problems that are now so troubling to our nation.

Policy Issues Involving Stock and Flows

A number of the policy situations you may encounter are fruitfully analyzed with models employing stocks and flows. The stock is the total existing supply of a commodity; the flow is the additions or subtractions from that supply in each period. Stocks are thus a quantity measured in units such as dollars or gallons or people. Flows are quantities per time period and are measured in units such as dollars per year, or gallons per minute, or people per day. Stock-flow problems arise in many types of activity. One might encounter them, for example, with patients on kidney dialysis machines, numbers of practicing physicians, students in college, subway cars that are operative, water in a reservoir, soldiers in the army, or dollars in the Social Security trust fund.

Stock and flow models can readily be developed with the aid of difference equations. The fundamental relationship between the stock and the flows can be expressed mathematically as

$$S_{t+1} = S_t + I_t - O_t$$

where S is the stock, I the inflow, and O the outflow. Typical examples of inflows and outflows to the stocks just listed are shown in Table 4–3.

Table 4–3

Stock	Inflow	Outflow
Patients on dialysis	New patients	Transplants, deaths
Practicing physi- cians	New medical school gradu- ates	Retirements, deaths
Students in college	Freshmen, reenrollments	Graduates, dropouts
Operative subway cars	Purchases, rehabilitations	Breakdowns, removals from service
Water in reservoir	Rain, springs, streams	Spillway, use, evaporation
Soldiers in army	Recruits, reenlistments	Retirements, deaths
Social Security trust fund	Employee and employer contributions, possibly general revenues	Benefits paid

---

[10]   Period 4: $C_4 = 1.3W_3 = (.7)^2(1.3)^2C_0$

$W_4 = .7C_3 = (.7)^2(1.3)^2W_0$

Period 5: $C_5 = 1.3W_4 = (.7)^2(1.3)^3W_0$

$W_5 = .7C_4 = (.7)^3(1.3)^2C_0$

Period 6: $C_6 = 1.3W_5 = (.7)^3(1.3)^3C_0$

$W_6 = .7C_5 = (.7)^3(1.3)^3W_0$

By now the pattern is clear. Looking at these equations, you should be able to convince yourself that this particular population is doomed to extinction.

If the stock is large relative to the flow, which is likely when inflows survive for a long time in the stock, dramatic changes in inflows or outflows will not significantly affect stock size. Attention to this simple insight might have tempered the federal government's effort to expand people's access to medical services by increasing the size of entering medical school classes. With a physician population of 300,000, raising the number of new medical school freshmen from 13,000 to 18,000 per year will not significantly increase the number of doctors in the near future.

Army Manpower

In a great number of policy contexts, we will have control only over the flow variable, though the stock variable will be the primary target of our policy concern. U.S. Army staff who are responsible for manpower, for example, try to maintain the service as a whole and particular specialties and ranks within it at a desired size by manipulating enlistment, reenlistment, and retirement inducements. Even when the size of the army may be controlled directly, as was the case when the draft was in effect, thorny analytic problems may arise. In the early 1960s, for example, the construction of the Berlin wall led to a rapid buildup in the size of the U.S. Army; many men were enrolled within a short period of time. At the times when the regular tours of duty for these buildup draftees came to a close, many new trainees were required as replacements. At these times training camps were jammed. During intervening periods the camps were substantially underutilized. In an earlier section we raised the possibility that a system might oscillate indefinitely. Oscillations of this sort are frequently observed in stock-flow situations. The utilization of the training camps provides a graphic illustration of this phenomenon. The policy question for the army was how to phase in trainees so as to balance two objectives: (1) maintaining an army stable in size, and (2) reducing the alternate overcrowding and underutilization of training camps. Difference equations are most helpful in analyzing this type of problem, as the following simplified example makes evident.

A tour of duty for a member of the army lasts for four periods; each period may be thought of as being 6 months long. Fifty percent of the personnel reenlist for another tour when their enlistment runs out. At time zero, the structure of the army is as follows:

$$S_1(0) = 500,000$$
$$S_2(0) = 100,000$$
$$S_3(0) = 100,000$$
$$S_4(0) = 100,000$$

where $S_1(0)$ is the number of men starting their first period, $S_2(0)$ those starting their second period, and so on. The total initial size of the army is thus 800,000 men. Three of the transition relationships are straightforward:

$$S_2(t + 1) = S_1(t)$$
$$S_3(t + 1) = S_2(t)$$
$$S_4(t + 1) = S_3(t)$$

In other words, once someone has enlisted in the army, he has to stick with it through four periods; he can't drop out part-way through. For the first period the situation is slightly more complicated, for in that period the number will include both the new soldiers recruited during the previous period and those who have reenlisted after having just completed a tour of duty. [For convenience, we'll assume that those recruited during period t actually begin their training at the start of period $(t + 1)$.] Then we have

$$S_1(t + 1) = .5S_4(t) + R(t)$$

where $R(t)$ are the men recruited during period t, who must then be trained during period $(t + 1)$. Training lasts for one period.

We are now in a position to determine the size of the army as a function of the size of the training program. Let's assume that it has been decided to train 150,000 recruits per period. The army would then evolve as shown in Table 4–4. Note that the original uneven distribution among the four periods gradually smoothes out. The equilibrium configuration will have an army of 1,200,000 men, with 300,000 in each cohort.[11]

Table 4–4
Size of Army (thousands of men)

(1) Period (t)	(2) Trainees	(3) Reen- listments	(4) $S_1(t) =$ (2) + (3)	(5) $S_2(t)$	(6) $S_3(t)$	(7) $S_4(t)$	(8) $T(t) =$ total
0	—	—	500	100	100	100	800
1	150	50	200	500	100	100	900
2	150	50	200	200	500	100	1,000
3	150	50	200	200	200	500	1,100
4	150	250	400	200	200	200	1,000
5	150	100	250	400	200	200	1,050
6	150	100	250	250	400	200	1,100

It is highly unlikely that the optimal strategy would be to train the same number of men in each period. If the sole objective were to maintain the size of the army at a constant 800,000 men, then a quite different approach would be called for. It would be necessary to train 50,000 men in each of periods 1, 2, and 3, and then 250,000 in the fourth period. This four-year cyclical pattern would continue as long as the army was maintained at that size.

---

[11] At the equilibrium, the total army size $T(t)$ will be the same year after year. This may be calculated directly by solving the equation

$$T(t + 1) = T(t)$$

or

$$S_1(t + 1) + S_2(t + 1) + S_3(t + 1) + S_4(t + 1) = S_1(t) + S_2(t) + S_3(t) + S_4(t)$$

Substitution gives

$$.5S_4(t) + 150,000 + S_1(t) + S_2(t) + S_3(t) = S_1(t) + S_2(t) + S_3(t) + S_4(t)$$

or $S_4 = 300,000$. The other values follow directly.

The stable training level strategy leads to significant variations in the size of the army; the stable army strategy leads to wide oscillations in the number of trainees. The preferred strategy would presumably be some compromise between these pure cases.

A difference equation model could be and indeed was employed in 1962 to test the implications of alternative training and recruitment strategies. The army became sensitive to this problem only when impending size fluctuations and training camp congestion were visible on the horizon. Systematic use of a difference equation model would have led to an earlier recognition of the problem, and most likely would have changed early decisions about training programs. Even with the army's belated recognition, a difference equation model was of significant assistance in formulating policy.[12]

A situation similar to the army recruiting problem has arisen in recent years. In the glow of the postwar baby boom, it seemed to many decision makers, both in the public sector and in private nonprofit institutions, that teacher shortages were to be a permanent feature of the landscape. Training programs were expanded and additional teachers were turned out by the hundreds of thousands. Many more teachers were trained than ultimately could be absorbed by school systems; many of them are without jobs or have been forced to find other work. The teacher glut probably could not have been entirely foreseen, for the problem has indeed been exacerbated by falling fertility rates and the return of women (including former teachers) to the work force in unexpected numbers. But a relatively simple stock-flow model would have exposed the possibility of future difficulties as early as 1950. In particular, it would have indicated that even if fertility rates had continued high, the smaller cohort born during the thirties would result in fewer parents to produce the schoolchildren of the late sixties and seventies.

Two lessons should be drawn from these experiences with training programs. First, difference equations can be helpful in enabling a policy maker to make informed predictions about the future, and also in enabling him to recognize the possible existence of future problems. Second, stock-flow analyses frequently lead to surprising results, particularly if a system is far from an equilibrium. These results can readily be analyzed with the aid of difference equations.

Oil Reserves

Difference equations are invaluable for investigating the troubling question "When will the oil run out?" In 1977 the world demand for oil was roughly 15 billion barrels a year; proven world reserves were estimated at 600

---

[12] One of the authors was involved in this analysis when he was a summer intern at the Pentagon, working closely with a senior army officer. The officer lamented that although he was a terrific field operations man, he had had no experience with this form of higher mathematics. With a little effort, however, he soon mastered the principles of elementary difference equations.

billion barrels.[13] Simple arithmetic tells us that the proven reserves would be exhausted by the year 2017 if world demand held constant. We know, however, that demand will not remain constant; it is currently growing at about 5 percent a year. Even with a worldwide conservation effort, the demand for oil will continue to grow with world population and with the increased industrialization of the developing countries. What are the implications of a continued rate of growth of 5 percent in the demand for oil?

The difference equations that describe the situation are

$$D_n = 1.05 \, D_{n-1} \tag{4-6}$$

where D_n is the world demand for oil (in billions of barrels) in year n, with $D_0 = 15$, and

$$C_n = D_0 + D_1 + \ldots + D_n \tag{4-7}$$

where C_n is cumulative world consumption of oil (also in billions of barrels) from now through year n. The proven reserves will run out when

$$C_n = 600 \tag{4-8}$$

Substituting (4–6) and (4–7) in (4–8) gives

$$D_0(1 + 1.05 + 1.05^2 + \ldots + 1.05^n) = 600 \tag{4-9}$$

And we found above that the expression in parentheses is equal to

$$\frac{1.05^{n+1} - 1}{1.05 - 1}$$

Simplifying, and recalling that $D_0 = 15$, we have

$$15\left(\frac{1.05^{n+1} - 1}{.05}\right) = 600$$

$$1.05^{n+1} = 3, \quad \text{or}$$

$$n \approx 22$$

In short, if world demand for oil grows at 5 percent per year, proven reserves will run out about 1999.

It has been proposed in many circles that stern conservation measures be undertaken. What would be the effect of policy measures (including perhaps a higher price for oil) that restrict the growth of demand to 3 percent a year? Solving the same equations for a growth rate of 3 percent gives $n \approx 26$ years, implying exhaustion of proven reserves about 2003. If

[13] These figures are for the non-Communist world only; no reliable figures are available for Communist countries. The numbers given here are a consensus of estimates, and no more than that. (See *Newsweek*, May, 23, 1977, pp. 48 and 53, and June 27, 1977, pp. 71–73.) It is evident, however, that the exact numbers are not crucial; the conclusions are essentially the same for rather substantial variations in the estimates.

draconian conservation measures succeeded in reducing the rate of growth of demand to 2 percent, exhaustion would be delayed until 2006.

All the calculations are of course based on proven reserves only; they do not allow for the possibility of new discoveries. Estimates of total world resources, in the sense of potentially recoverable oil, are necessarily soft. The current consensus, however, puts the total at somewhere around 1600 billion barrels. If we use the same difference equations to investigate the implications of resources of this magnitude, we find that with a demand growth rate of 5 percent, world supplies of oil will be exhausted in 2014; with 3 percent, in 2025; and with 2 percent, 2034. The 2034 estimate is perhaps encouraging, but we should record a cautionary note: it will be much more difficult to institute conservation measures if estimates of reserves continue to be revised upward. The 3 percent/1600 barrels scenario is highly optimstic, and the 2 percent version more so.

The Use of Difference Equations in Modeling

Ordinarily we expect to see difference equations used as submodels, to predict parts of a system rather than the system as a whole. This is not to downgrade the importance of difference equations. Indeed, few people would view predictions about the future availability of oil as unimportant. As noted above, more sophisticated versions of the children–workers model set forth on page 67 are used in projecting the future path of the U.S. Social Security system. Many people fear that the changing age structure of the U.S. population will at some future time seriously threaten the system, because a relatively small working population will be asked to carry too heavy a Social Security tax burden for a bloated elderly population. In constructing their models, policy analysts rely on the existing age structure and predictions as to the future behavior of variables such as age-specific birth rates, death rates, migration rates, percent of the population gainfully employed, retirement rates, wage rates, and the like, with difference equations playing a central role.

On the local level, failure to develop accurate models of structural changes in population has cost many suburban towns dearly. Naive projections of population growth now manifest themselves in empty classrooms, in large part because citizens' committees did not ask the right questions.

A third area where the use of difference equations lends insights is in the development of guidelines for affirmative action. If the federal government requires an organization to undertake compensatory hiring of women or minorities, what are the implications for future patterns of employment and promotion? Alternatively, to achieve such patterns in specified periods of time, what must be the composition of present hirings and layoffs?

In this chapter we have used difference equations primarily as a vehicle for introducing a variety of concepts and techniques. We must keep in mind that our main goal in developing these models is better predictions of the outcomes of policy alternatives.

5 Queues

Agencies that are in the business of delivering services to individuals must often decide how much delivery capacity they should have. Licensing bureaus, health clinics, and courts, to name but a few, all dislike making people wait for service. Yet installing additional service capacity is expensive. Choices of this type are always difficult for they involve competing objectives, but they can be made less blindly if we model the service delivery process to see what sort of tradeoffs are available.

Queuing problems arise whenever a service facility is too limited to provide instantaneous service to all of its customers on all occasions. When the customers arrive more swiftly than they can be serviced, lines or queues will develop. Bottlenecks are familiar to all of us—we seem to be perennially waiting in line, and much of the time the waiting is for some kind of public service. The situation may be as mundane as the wait for a traffic light to turn green, or as fundamental as the diminution of a constitutional right when a judicial backlog blocks the way to a speedy trial. Sometimes those who wait are physically present in a line, say a health clinic. In other circumstances the wait is a delay in securing service; many a senior citizen has had to wait months or even years to gain admission to subsidized housing for the elderly.

Waiting is costly; frequently we would pay to avoid it. At best, it is a mere annoyance, as at the traffic light. Sometimes the costs are more significant; we all remember the gasoline lines during the OAPEC oil cutbacks. And at times those who must wait are flirting with disaster, perhaps in a crowded hospital emergency room, perhaps because a fire breaks out while the engines are out on another alarm.

It is, of course, impossible to eliminate waiting altogether; the costs would be prohibitive. A fire engine for every house in a rural area would protect against the one in a trillion possibility that all the engines will be needed at the same time, but it would obviously be undesirable. This is a straightforward matter of tradeoffs: the shorter we wish waiting time to be, the more facilities we must have available. Consequently we should try to strike a careful balance between holding down waiting time and limiting our investment in service capability. How shall we make this tradeoff? A queuing model won't define our preferences for us—but it will set forth the nature of the tradeoffs very clearly, rather than leaving the whole matter to guesswork. To be more specific, the model can tell us how the waiting time for service will respond to the level of facilities that is made available. How much, for example, can the local Social Security office shorten clients' waiting times by opening another window? Occasionally it is also possible to change the time required for service; what would be the result of improving procedures so as to cut service time by two minutes?

Studying the way queues behave is important for public policy because the relationship between waiting times and service capacity is far from obvious, while the cost of providing extra capacity is likely to be large. Even simple models can help us grasp the essence of a great variety of real-world situations, and the results are often surprising.

A Simple Deterministic Model of a Toll Bridge

Suppose a single-lane, one-way toll bridge is the only convenient westward exit from a city. A toll booth can serve one car every 10 seconds. Every day, 7200 cars cross the bridge. This averages out to one car every 12 seconds, and hence is less traffic than the bridge can handle on a 24-hour basis. The trouble is that half the traffic, 3600 cars, crosses between 4:00 and 6:00 P.M. when the city empties. The other 3600 cars are spread uniformly over the remaining 22 hours, for an average load of 3600/22 ≈ 164 cars per hour. What will happen if the city is so foolish as to operate

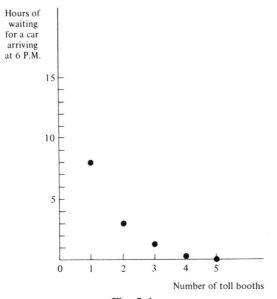

Fig. 5–1

only one toll booth? Assuming, as is likely, that no cars are waiting when the 4 o'clock rush begins, when will the mess straighten itself out so that cars can again cross the bridge without waiting? Not until after 8 o'clock the next morning! (We won't spoil the fun of those who want to work it out to the precise minute.)

What will happen to the traffic jam if more toll booths are added? We can calculate this directly. For example, two booths can handle 720 cars an hour. Therefore at 6 P.M. there will be 3600 − (2 × 720) = 2160 cars in line. Given the subsequent flow of 164 cars per hour, the backlog will be eaten into at the rate of roughly 720 − 164 = 556 cars per hour. Figure 5–1 shows how long you would have to wait, with various numbers of booths, if you were so unfortunate as to arrive at the bridge at 6 P.M. Even with four booths, you would have more than a half-hour wait; a fifth booth would eliminate waiting altogether. A little additional arithmetic produces the interesting result that with only one booth, you would have a longer wait if you arrived well after the rush hour—say at 9 P.M.—than if you got in line at 5 P.M., the peak of the rush hour.

Probabilistic Queuing Models

When customers arrive for service at a regular and predictable rate, as we assumed they did at the toll bridge, long lines may develop as a result of sheer numbers; expected arrivals may exceed the service capacity. A deterministic model that pays no attention to uncertainties (such as the one we used above) can then predict directly the effects of adding or subtracting stations. Most queuing problems are not so tractable; customers usually arrive at irregular rates. Take the case of a facility that can serve up to 12 people per hour if they arrive at regular intervals. One day 3 people may arrive during the first hour and 18 during the next hour. As a result, people must queue up even when there is, on average, enough service capacity. In other words, a facility may be able on paper to serve a given number of customers per day provided they arrive regularly. But if they arrive irregularly, as a practical matter the facility will serve far fewer than its theoretical capacity. As the average number demanding service each day rises, waiting times will become intolerable. The following example shows how waiting times respond to the number of people who want service.

Irregular Arrivals: The Registry of Motor Vehicles

The Registry of Motor Vehicles tests the eyesight of individuals who wish to renew their driver's licenses. Three test machines are used; the test takes 10 minutes. The facility opens at 9 A.M. and closes at 5 P.M., but no new applicants are accepted after 3 P.M. Thus its maximum capacity is 144 people per day (3 machines × 8 hours per day × 6 persons per machine per hour). Some days lots of people come in to be tested, arriving randomly

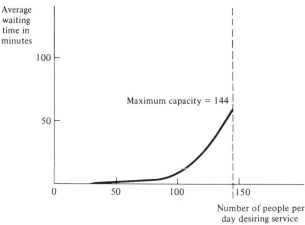

Fig. 5–2

throughout the day; on other days business is poor.[1] As a result of the random arrivals, one or more machines at times stand idle, and the time then lost can never be made up. Hence in practice the effective capacity of the test facility is less than 144. As the number of people demanding service nears 144, waiting lines become longer and longer. Experiments with a queuing model indicate that the average waiting time for those who eventually are served rises sharply as the number demanding service increases, as shown in Figure 5–2. Moreover, when more than about 125 people demand service, usually some of them will still be waiting when testing stops at 5 o'clock.[2]

Constructing a Probabilistic Queuing Model: The Hypertension Clinic

We have just seen that when rates of arrival are irregular, average rates provide less information than we need. In fact, relying on averages can lead to disaster. A fire department in an isolated community that averages 100 fires a year (less than one-third of a fire per day) will probably find it worthwhile to have more than one fire engine. To make a sensible decision about service capacity, the town needs to know not simply the average rates of service demand, but also the distribution of that rate. How often will the community have one fire in a 2-hour period, two, three, four, and so on? Or, to ask an equivalent question, what is the probability distribution of the time interval between fires? If a fire breaks out now, what is the likelihood that the next fire will erupt in 10 minutes, an hour, 5 hours, a day? Only if we know the probability distribution of these "arrival" times can we make useful predictions about waiting times for service.

To see how we would actually construct a queuing model when

---

[1] Specifically, we assume that arrivals are completely random; one arrival has no effect on the probability of another arrival.

[2] For these people waiting time is in effect infinitely long, for they don't get served at all. That is why we calculated average waiting time only for those eventually served.

customer arrivals are unpredictable, let's suppose we are planning the remodeling of a walk-in clinic for the detection of high blood pressure. The question is how many examining stations to install. To keep things simple, we will assume that all patients require the same amount of service time; the examination always takes 10 minutes. We know from past experience that an average of 12 people per hour come in to be examined. Fortunately, although visits are random within each hour, no particular hour is likely to be worse than any other. The clinic is open from 9 A.M. to 3 P.M. every day. At 3 o'clock the doors are locked and the patients then waiting are examined. If people only arrived at regular 5-minute intervals, say by appointments rigidly scheduled and religiously observed, two stations would do the job exactly. No one would have to wait for service, no stations would ever stand idle. But patients don't arrive regularly; sometimes they come in bunches and have to wait. At other times no one turns up for quite a while and some of the stations and their attending personnel go unutilized. In order to decide on the appropriate number of stations, we need answers to a range of questions such as: "If we install two stations, what is the chance that a patient will have to wait more than 10 minutes? More than 20 minutes? What will happen to waiting times if we add another station? What percentage of the time will a station stand idle? How will waiting times respond to changes in service time?" These are the kinds of questions that a queuing model can answer.

As a first step in developing the model of the clinic for detecting high blood pressure, we will need data on actual arrival frequencies, in other words, on how the actual random arrivals of patients tend to occur. This information might be collected on the spot by keeping track of patients' behavior over a period of time. (If this is impossible, as in the case of a totally new facility, the analyst must search for facilities that can reasonably be expected to exhibit similar patient behavior.) Let's suppose that the clinic has records going back for several years that include the arrival time for each patient. The analyst tabulates arrival intervals to determine the number of times that one patient has arrived immediately after another, the number of times that a patient has arrived, say, from 1 to 5 minutes after the previous patient, and so on. The length of the intervals to be used depends of course on the data and the analyst's judgment. In this example we use rather long intervals because it's simpler, but in a real analysis we would use shorter intervals, and hence more of them. In practice, intervals should be short enough so that using the midpoint to represent the whole interval provides a sufficiently good approximation. The analyst then employs the frequency table thus developed as his estimate of the probability distribution for arrival times. Suppose this procedure has been carried out and the resulting probability distribution is that shown in Table 5–1, which shows the probability p that one arrival will occur m minutes after the previous arrival.

This table indicates that if a patient walks in the door of the clinic, there is a 20 percent chance that the next patient is right on his heels, a 50 percent chance that there will be a delay of from 1 to 5 minutes, and so on.

Table 5–1

Minutes m	Probability p
0	.2
1–5	.5
6–10	.2
11–27	.1

Note that with this probability distribution, over the long run, on average one patient will arrive every 5 minutes.

The next step is to construct a model that utilizes this probability distribution for times between arrivals, the time that it takes to service each patient, and the number of stations under consideration. (In the next chapter we actually build the model.) With this model we then put the clinic through an imaginary day and see what happens. Perhaps it will be a very bad day, in that people arrive more irregularly than usual so that waiting times are longer than they normally are. Or perhaps it will be an average or an exceedingly good day. The latter might occur if on a particular day people arrived far more regularly than they do on average. Observing that days at the same clinic with the same arrival frequencies can be good, bad, or indifferent, we see that the performance on one day tells us little. We need to see what happens over many days—20, 30, perhaps even 100. Only by tabulating the results over many days can we be confident in a prediction that, say, the probability is .3 that a patient will have to wait longer than 30 minutes with a particular configuration of service capabilities. One primary output of the model will be in the form of still another probability distribution for patients' waiting times. The model will yield information on how many patients are likely to be served and how much of the time the examination facilities will not be used. It can also be set up to investigate the effect of changes in service times.

The final step is to write the program that tells the computer what to do: how to calculate, for a hypothetical day, the number of people who will not have to wait at all, and the numbers who will have to wait 1–5, 6–10, . . . minutes. Having done this, we ran the program 100 times on the computer, first for two stations and then for three, and averaged the outcomes. The resulting probability distributions for waiting times, patient loads, and idle times are shown in Table 5–2. We found that the two-station operation yielded unacceptable waiting times and three stations resulted in a great deal of idle capacity. In the latter case the three technicians who man the examining stations would just sit around almost a third of the time, which was sure to make trouble with the overworked mammography people next door.[3] So we decided to see what would happen if we scheduled consecutive one-hour lunch breaks for the three technicians. The results are included in the table.

This model is so simple that in a pinch it could be worked out by

---

[3] One of the pleasures of making up examples out of whole cloth is that it gives us a free hand with corroborative details.

Table 5-2
Probability That Patient Will Have to Wait w Minutes.

w = Waiting time for patient (minutes)	Two stations	Three stations	Three stations and consecutive one-hour lunch breaks
0	15	54	32
1–5	09	25	17
6–10	13	14	15
11–15	11	05	10
16–20	09	01	07
21–30	15	01	10
31 and over	28	00	10
Average number of patients served per day	72	72	72
Average idle time (minutes) for each station	25	123	67
Average waiting time (minutes) per patient	20	3	11

longhand; we demonstrate the method in the next chapter. But at best it's tedious work and should be left to the computer, which can run through many days in the life of the hypertension clinic in just a few seconds.[4]

The Essential Features of Queues

In the real world, queuing systems are of course likely to be much more complex and to involve several different kinds of random events. In principle the problem is still likely to be straightforward, although programming the computer may become more of a chore. It's useful to keep in mind a checklist of the types of random events and complications that can occur in a queuing system. These fall under three main headings:

1. *Arrivals.* Arrival intervals may be independent of one another, or the fact of one arrival may influence the probability as to when the next occurs. The latter will be true whenever customers are likely to arrive in groups, as at an airport customs station. The arrivals in the Registry of Motor Vehicles example were independent, on the assumption that a driver's license expires on the holder's birthday. In contrast, 20 percent of the hypertension clinic patients arrived in groups of two or more, reflecting the greater likelihood that people would choose to make joint trips to the facility. It is also possible

---

[4] On rare occasions it is possible to find an analytic function that fits the observed frequency distributions for arrival and service times, so that the whole problem may be solved as a mathematical exercise without resorting to the computer. Such techniques are discussed at length in operations research textbooks, but are most unlikely to be useful in actual practice. [See for example, Russell L. Ackoff and Maurice W. Sasieni, *Fundamentals of Operations Research* (New York: Wiley, 1968.)]

that the arrival pattern might vary with the time of day, or with the number of people waiting for service. (Some people would rather come back another day than take their place at the end of a long line.) So if we wished to make the model more sophisticated, we could relate patient arrival frequencies to the number of patients waiting. We might, for example, use one frequency distribution when fewer than 5 people are waiting, another when 5 to 10 are waiting, and so on. In this way we would recognize the influence of service characteristics on arrival behavior. It's more work to program the computer for the fancier model, but conceptually the problem is no more difficult.

2. *Service times.* Different people may require different service times. Further, the service time for one person may be affected by the number waiting or by the nature of the services rendered those who preceded him. (If one wants a cautious, leisurely haircut, he should not go at lunchtime.) Again, such embellishments on the basic model make the programming more burdensome, and it would be necessary to develop data on the frequency distribution for service times. But no fundamental changes in the model are required.

3. *The "queue discipline."* The way in which the queue forms and moves may not be a straightforward begin-at-the-foot-of-the-line-and-get-service-at-the-head-of-the-line process. There may be more than one line; line jumping may be permitted; perhaps people who receive service must then get in another queue for a second service. With the hypertension clinic's lunch breaks, we introduced the possibility of a variable number of service stations. There may be bumping or other priority procedures. For examples, the VIP may get seated first at the restaurant, the heart attack victim moves ahead of the patient with a broken arm in the emergency room. As above, additional frequency distributions and a longer computer program are needed to accommodate these complications, but the basic model remains the same.

Note that changes in the quality of service will show up as changes in queuing behavior only if arrivals or service times or the queue discipline are affected. Service quality as such need not appear independently in the model.

Using a Queuing Model in Making Policy Changes

In making an actual decision, the information produced by a queuing model is of course only one input. Before formulating a policy we must ask two classes of questions about costs, costs in the broadest sense of the term. First, how much will it cost to increase service capacity? Such increases may take the form of more stations, or may require using more or better resources per station to shorten service time. Second, what values should we attach to different lengths of waiting times?

For example, suppose you are the director of the hypertension clinic, which is currently limping along on two stations. You have observed that waiting times are unpleasantly long on average, and the technicians perennially hungry. You must decide whether to install a third station, and if so, whether to schedule lunch breaks. Your comptroller computes that it costs $10 per workday plus the technician's salary to operate and maintain a station. The technicians' contract gives them $30 per day if they get a one-hour lunch break, $36 per day if they must eat on the run. For simplicity, patient waiting time is valued at $3 per hour. The costs of the three alternatives are summarized in Table 5–3.

Table 5–3
Daily Clinic Costs

	Two stations	Three stations	Three stations and lunch breaks
(1) Operating and maintenance ($)	20	30	30
(2) Technicians' salaries ($)	72	108	90
Total expected waiting time (minutes)	72 × 20 = 1440	72 × 3 = 216	72 × 11 = 792
(hours)	24	3.6	13.2
(3) Value of waiting time ($)	72	10.80	39.60
Total costs of service per workday ($) = (1) + (2) + (3)	164	148.80	159.60

The policy makers were surprised. It was true that three stations with lunck breaks were better than two without, but three stations without lunch breaks were better still. Could four be even better? A quick check revealed that a fourth station would never be worthwhile. Eliminating all waiting time would be worth only an additional $10.80. The additional cost of that fourth station would be $10 for operating and maintenance and $12 for salaries (four technicians with lunch breaks as against three without, or $120–$108) for a total of $22. This additional cost is well in excess of $10.80.

One aspect of the three-station, no-break solution troubled the directors. As Table 5–2 shows, each of the three technicians would be idle for an average of 123 minutes each day, more than a third of the time, whereas giving each technician a lunch break would reduce the idle time to 67 minutes. It was decided that for the time being the effects on morale in mammography could safely be ignored; spending an extra $10.80 a day ($159.60 − $148.80) for lunch breaks was not warranted. The directors agreed to reevaluate this decision after one month. Lunch breaks could easily be instituted if it then seemed desirable, or perhaps the hard-working mammmographers could be given perquisites.

For the hypertension clinic, with cost estimates available, we were thus able to determine the best configuration for the clinic. We assumed that 1 minute of waiting time was exactly as costly to the person waiting as every other minute. This of course is an oversimplification. A 30-minute wait may be more than three times as onerous for a particular person as a 10-minute wait. It may be more costly than 5-minute waits for six different people. Clearly, different people will value waiting time differently. More probing assessments of waiting costs would thus be needed. Another important consequence of waiting should be taken into consideration: some patients may be deterred from using a facility if lines are permitted to grow too long. Estimates of all types of costs are a necessary input to the decision process; the queuing model merely describes the physical choices that are available to us.

Waiting Time as a Deadweight Loss

Making people wait is one way to ration a scarce commodity or service, but it is a woefully inefficient procedure. A critical factor to understand about queues is that no one derives any benefit from the waiting costs that are borne by those who stand in line. In a freely functioning private market long lines are understood and accepted as a signal that prices should be raised. But we frequently are reluctant to follow this principle in providing public services.

In order to highlight the literally useless costs that waiting entails, let's consider a retirement community that maintains a municipal golf course for its citizens. The Recreation Board, assuming that the marginal cost of an additional golfer is zero, has directed that the use of the course shall be free to citizens who are members. Membership costs the nominal amount of $75 per year; all 1000 golfers in the town join. At most 150 golfers can play in one day. We saw in the Registry of Motor Vehicles case that if arrivals are irregular, the average waiting time increases dramatically as more people demand service. The municipal golf course is no exception to this rule. Indeed, as capacity is neared, the waiting time for some zooms toward infinity, for they never get to tee off at all.

Curve SS in Figure 5–3 describes how the average wait responds to the number who demand service. Naturally, the longer people have to wait, the smaller the number who will want this nonessential service. Curve DD in Figure 5–3 shows how the number demanding service responds to the length of time they will have to wait. In this example, we assume that the demand is a simple linear function of the waiting time. The equation underlying curve DD is $N = 235 - (5/2)W$, which, of course, may also be written $W = 94 - (2/5)N$; N is the number of people wanting to play golf, and W is the waiting time in minutes.[5] Point E (at which curves SS and DD intersect) is then a stable equilibrium, slightly different in nature from the equilibria we encountered in the previous chapter. If

[5] The demand curve is, strictly speaking, merely an approximation, because the golf club doesn't admit fractional members. The resulting discrepancies are, however, very small.

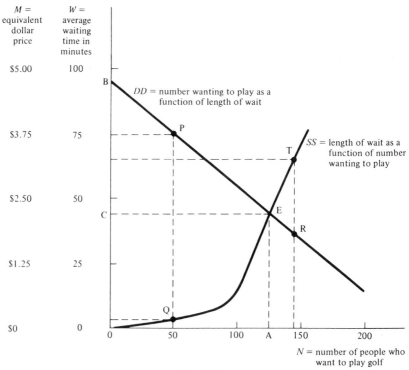

M =
equivalent
dollar
price

W =
average
waiting
time in
minutes

$5.00 100

$3.75 75

$2.50 50

$1.25 25

$0 0

DD = number wanting to play as a
function of length of wait

SS = length of wait as a
function of number
wanting to play

N = number of people who
want to play golf

Fig. 5–3

people expect to wait on average, say, 74 minutes, *DD* tells us that 50 people will want to play golf, as point *P* shows. But with no more than these 50 demanding services, *SS* indicates that the average waiting time will be only 3 minutes (as at point *Q*). As the good word spreads, more people will want to play and the waiting time will therefore increase. On the other hand, if people expect to wait 36 minutes, then 145 people will turn up. (Point *R* represents this outcome.) Waiting time will skyrocket to 65 minutes (see point *T*). This wait will be substantially longer than many of the golfers will tolerate, and they will no longer come. Ultimately, an equilibrium will be established, at point *E*, where the number of people demanding service, 125 of them, results in an average waiting time (44 minutes) that causes just 125 people to demand service. Only at that point is there no incentive for anyone to change his decision to wait or not to wait, for at point *E* expectations match reality.

For simplicity, we assume that everyone values his waiting time at $3 per hour. No one cares whether he "pays" for his golf game in dollars or waiting time or a combination of the two; it's only the equivalent dollar amount that matters. Naturally some golfers are more eager than others and consequently are willing to pay a larger combined amount. We can construct an alternative dollar scale for the vertical axis, to show the equivalent dollar prices, *M*, that a person in effect pays for service when he waits in line. This dollar scale, also shown in Figure 5–3, is $M = \$.05W$; every minute of waiting in effect costs $.05.

At point E, the average wait of 44 minutes is worth $2.20 for each person waiting. This indicates that the marginal golfer—the golfer who would not play at all if he had to "pay" any more—would just pay $2.20 in hard cash to play if he faced no wait at all. Many golfers would pay much more. The golfer with the highest value would pay up to $4.70 to tee off without a wait. With the demand curve shown, the person with the next highest value would pay two cents less; the one hundred first would pay $2.70. Since the demand curve is linear, it is very easy to add up the maximum amounts of time or money that each of the 125 who now play golf would pay. The total value of golfing activity on a day is thus calculated to be $431.25. (This amount can also be represented by the area $OAEB$ in Figure 5–3.) The total amount "paid" for the use of the golf course is $2.20 × 125 = $275.00 (or area $OAEC$). Hence the course produces daily a net value or surplus of $156.25 (area CEB). This quantity is often referred to as "consumers' surplus"; it is discussed further in Chapter 9.

Now someone proposes to the Recreation Board that it would be nice if they could work out a way to reduce the 45-minute wait. One board member suggests that tee-off times be scheduled, but the citizens find that unacceptable for two reasons: if they want to play golf on a particular day, they want to play; they do not want to be told that all the slots are taken. Further, one of the advantages of retirement is that you are no longer required to be at a certain place at a certain hour. Still, the Recreation Board feels something must be done. Having investigated the subject of queues, they recognize that waiting time is a deadweight loss. Were a golfer to pay a money fee, the funds would go to the town treasury or the recreation department. But a time fee is just wasted; the resources are lost.

Following this logic, the Recreation Board proposes a $2.00 greens fee for a round of golf, with the proceeds to be used to reduce the present membership charge. With this $2.00 fee, golfers naturally will not be willing to wait as long. Their willingness-to-wait curve can now be shown by the curve $D'D'$ in Figure 5–4 that is $2.00 or 40 minutes below the old curve DD. The new waiting equilibrium is at point F. At that point, 100 people wait on average 14 minutes to tee off for an average time cost of $.70, and pay a $2.00 fee as well. The average golfer's effective payment is thus the amount represented by the point G, or $2.70. The total "price" has gone up by $.50. What is significant, however, is that the waiting time charge, the deadweight loss associated with each golfer's price, has diminished by 30 minutes or $1.50.

The golf course now takes in 100 × $2.00 = $200 per day, which works out to be about $50,000 per year, given days of rain, snow, or winter cold. The recreation department uses the $50,000 to cut the annual membership fee by $50 for each of the 1000 members, and almost everyone hooks and slices happily every after. To be sure, about 25 fewer people play golf each

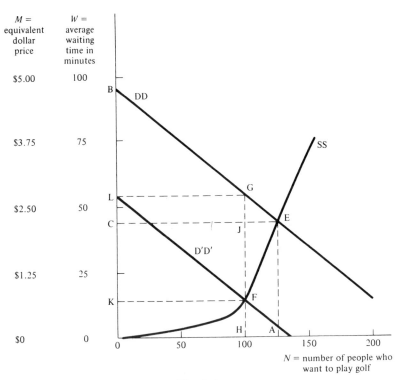

Fig. 5–4

day. But note that (1) they are the golfers who valued their games the least; (2) the net value they lose is partially offset by the reduction in membership fee; (3) the total gain to all the golfers in the community far outweighs the small losses to these golfers. The geometry of the diagram enables us to make this comparison precisely. The fees received by the recreation department correspond to the area *KFGL* in Figure 5–4. Over and above these fees, the golfers reveive net benefits of area *LGB*: that is, collectively they would be willing to pay up to that amount for the privilege of golfing at a fee of $2.00 per round. The net value produced by the golf course is thus area *KFGB*. This is obviously greater than area *CEB*, which is the net value when no fee is charged and the equilibrium is at point *E*. The gain from going to the fee system is area *KFJC* minus area *EGJ*.

Finally, we should note that the $50 cut in dues is like an increase in income for the members. They can use the money for whatever purpose they choose. Some will doubtless use part of it to play more golf, in which case the demand curves *DD* and *D′D′* will shift up somewhat. Observe that even if this happens, a tremendous amount of deadweight loss will have been eliminated. Moreover, these results are perfectly general. Net efficiency is always increased if waiting time charges for a service are replaced with dollar charges.

Why then do we tolerate long lines for public services? Why haven't we long since resorted to pricing to reduce these wasteful impositions? Frequently lines arise because we misestimate the demand for a facility, or overestimate its capability to meet demands; the price cannot be immediately adjusted. But in some instances lines are foreseen, yet accepted as a natural consequence of bureaucratic procedures. A variety of explanations may be offered. Some policy makers do not recognize the deadweight costs associated with lines. Long lines are usually justified—when people question them at all—on distributional grounds. It is contended that access to certain public services should not be limited by one's ability to pay for them, or that long lines serve a redistributional purpose because the poor value their time less highly than the rich. (Such arguments do not apply in cases like the golf course, where the service fees go back to the clientele.)

Waiting lines are an exceedingly inefficient means for redistributing income. The poor, after all, do not receive the value of the waiting time of the rich. Moreover, it is by no means clear that the poor necessarily place a low value on their own time. The working poor, for instance, may find it far more difficult to take time off from work to wait in line than the well-to-do. If political realities prevent reliance on prices as a rationing mechanism for public services, some more imaginative alternatives might be tried. For example, if parallel services were established, one free, one priced, the money collected from those willing to pay for quick service could be used to subsidize better service for those who would rather wait than pay. Such a system would be worth investigating for the hypertension clinic.

In short, time spent waiting in line is a deadweight loss, for the time expended benefits no one. Public decision makers should be urged to seek ways to eliminate rationing by waiting wherever possible.

A Note on Inventory Models

Queuing and inventory models are similar in nature. In fact, they are almost opposite sides of the same coin. In a typical queuing situation, the policy maker is confronted with arrival rates and service times that are given to him; he controls the service capacity and hence the exit rates from the facility. In the inventory situation, by contrast, the decision maker finds the exit rates—the way goods or supplies move off the shelves—given to him. He controls the arrival rates of those goods on the shelves through his decisions about when and how much to reorder. Inventory problems arise in the public sector in such contexts as the stocking of spare parts at defense installations and the maintenance of drug inventories at health clinics or blood stocks at blood banks. Queues are a more pervasive problem in the public sector than inventories, for by their very nature governments and nonprofit organizations are more likely to be involved in the delivery of services to people than in the delivery of goods. If you understand the general principles behind queuing models, inventory models will give you no trouble.

A Perspective on Queues

Beyond their intrinsic interest, queuing models have a wide range of applications in public policy. Queues simulate well; rudimentary models to be run on a computer are easy to construct, fun to play with, and can frequently lend great insights into a problem. In the following chapter we'll take a closer look at the hypertension clinic model and give you a taste of how the computer would tackle it. Despite all the pedagogical virtues of queues, we will not go further into the subject here. You have already learned the main things you need to know about queuing theory—that modeling is a useful tool in this area, that waiting times can behave in surprising ways, that optimization procedures that trade off waiting time against additional service capacity can be readily conducted, and that money pricing is an efficient means to reduce waiting time.

In any practical situation, of course, you may want to consult an expert; you may well want to secure access to a computer. Your task as a policy analyst or policy maker is to recognize when queuing problems have arisen or are likely to arise, and what alternative means there are for dealing with them. Whether your concern is with accused criminals awaiting trial, applications pending before the SEC, people waiting for service at a clinic, or cars jammed up at an intersection, a knowledge of queuing models should provide beneficial insights.

6 Simulation

The policy arena, the true world of affairs, is not always hospitable to the straightforward use of analytic methods. The analyst may be confronted with problems that are too intricate to solve directly. He can write down equations that describe the workings of a system, and this may be a useful discipline in itself. But given the complex interactions within the system, even modern mathematical techniques are not powerful enough to predict the consequences of any policy choice.

In such a case, we can try to construct a laboratory model of the system. The model can be physical; frequently ship or plane designs are tested on scale models in water tanks or wind tunnels. It may be highly abstract; military strategies are sometimes tested by reproducing battlefield conditions on what is essentially a game board. If alternative predictions are made as to how individual encounters between elements of the opposing forces will be resolved, the board representation enables army strategists to consider the overall outcome of many simultaneous encounters. Models of this sort are also helpful to transportation planners who must predict traffic flows, say to determine the benefits of a new bypass. Behavioral equations are employed to predict, for instance, how motorists' decisions will respond to traffic density—how they will change the timing of their trips, or the routes, or the destinations. Other equations predict traffic density in terms of motorists' choices. Since thousands of motorists may be involved, with trips originating in dozens of locations, the system rapidly becomes too unmanageable for an analytic approach. The only recourse in such a circumstance is to feed the whole mess of equations and relationships into the computer. With its swift operating capacity, the computer can in effect reproduce the decisions of thousands of travellers and trace out their responses to the patterns of congestion generated by those decisions. A simulation thus attempts to reproduce a system in what is the equivalent of a laboratory setting.

In carrying out a computer simulation, the analyst first builds a mathematical model of the system he wishes to study, using equations to describe the essential relationships in the system. Although these equations may in some cases be rather sophisticated, frequently they involve nothing more than an instruction to the computer to count bodies or measure elapsed time. The equations are then programmed and run on the computer. In this way a case history is generated. Many periods of history may thus be compressed into a few seconds.

Sometimes we wish to examine the histories that may result from alternative policy choices. For example, suppose a number of different pollutants are discharged into a river at several places along it. A model can be constructed to relate water conditions at various points downstream to the levels of these discharges. This model of the river basin could then be used for studying the effects of regulatory discharge levels. Any number of policy choices in the form of possible combinations of discharge levels may be investigated, and their performance assessed.[1] The simulation is in effect a machine; the policy instruments are dials that can be set to particular values, in this case various levels of permitted discharges. The exceptional speed of the computer enables us to examine the implications of a great variety of dial settings.

At other times we wish to investigate the implications of changes in certain key parameters. A river, for example, has an extraordinary ability to cleanse itself—provided pollution does not exceed certain levels. Even though it is polluted over an upstream stretch, the river may be relatively free of pollution at its mouth. Perhaps the volume of municipal sewage discharges is critical for this regenerative capacity. A computer simulation permits us to study the sensitivity of pollution levels to changes in such discharges and in other parameters. In addition, sometimes estimates of important numbers are not always firm. A computer simulation will indicate how sensitive a policy outcome is to these estimates.

Simulations directed to random situations (such as those usually encountered in queuing problems) generally run through a great number of histories to provide a feel for the frequency distribution of outcomes. For the hypertension clinic described in the previous chapter, we ran 100 simulated histories to see what waiting times would look like with a particular choice of examining stations. The input was in probabilistic form, as was shown in Table 5–1. Simulations with probabilistic inputs are sometimes called Monte Carlo models, for they bring to mind the random outcomes of the roulette wheel at that fabled gambling resort. If we run a large number of trials and if our original probability assessments are reasonably accurate, we can expect that the average distribution within our simulated outcomes will approximate that of the real world over the long run. The distributions shown in Table 5–2 are the output of such a process;

---

[1] See, for example, Bruce Ackerman, Susan Rose-Ackerman, James Sawyer, Jr., and Dale Henderson, *The Uncertain Search for Environmental Quality* (New York: The Free Press, 1974), for a discussion of models of the Delaware River Basin.

the total computer time required to run all 300 histories was less than 7 seconds, and the cost less than $1.

Although we normally turn to the computer for simulations, frequently this is more a matter of convenience than of necessity. The model we used to study the hypertension clinic's queuing problem is extremely simple, as you will shortly see. The entire problem could have been worked out by hand, without even a hand calculator, had we a few days to spare.

An Example of Computer Simulation: The Hypertension Clinic

The first point to understand about a computer simulation is that there is nothing mysterious about it. The computer will not do anything that you can't do yourself, provided you have enough time. To make this clear, we will work out the model for a simple simulation of the hypertension clinic the hard way—by longhand.

To refresh your memory, the clinic is open for 6 hours a day; patients waiting at the end of that time are seen but no more are admitted. The test takes 10 minutes; the probability p that one arrival will occur m minutes after the previous arrival is shown in Table 6–1, which replicates Table 5–1. For simplicity we assume there are only two examining stations.

Table 6–1

Minutes m	Probability p
0	.2
1–5	.5
6–10	.2
11–27	.1

In order to model the behavior of the queues that form at the clinic, we simulate the patient arrivals by using *random numbers*. A random number is just what you would expect—a number drawn completely at random. Suppose you take 10 poker chips, number them from 0 through 9, and put them in a container. If you draw a chip blindly, note the number, replace it, draw another, and so on, you will generate a sequence of random numbers. If you continue this process for a long time, you will find that each number is drawn very close to 10 percent of the time, but over the short run some numbers may be drawn more often than others.

How can we use such a sequence to simulate the arrivals of hypertension patients? We see from Table 6–1 that the probability that one patient will arrive 0 minutes after the previous patient is .2. We therefore specify that if we draw either of the chips labeled 0 or 1, we are to take it that a patient has arrived 0 minutes after the last patient. This guarantees that, over the long run, one patient will arrive immediately after another 20 percent of the time. Similarly, the probability of an arrival interval of 1 to 5 minutes is .5; we therefore specify that drawing a chip labeled 2, 3, 4, 5, or 6 means that the patient arrives 3 minutes (the average for the interval) after the previous patient. (Note that we assume that using the average value for each time interval—3 minutes for the interval 1 to 5 minutes, and so on—

gives us a good enough approximation for that interval. If this is not the case, we can eliminate the difficulty by using shorter intervals.) Following this procedure we can expand Table 6–1 to include all possible arrival intervals, as shown in Table 6–2.

Table 6–2

m	p	Average m	Random Numbers
0	.2	0	0,1
1–5	.5	3	2,3,4,5,6
6–10	.2	8	7,8
11–27	.1	19	9

We are now ready to set up a worksheet—which is simply a log for the clinic—and grind out the results. That log is shown in Table 6–3. Suppose we open the two-station clinic at 0 hours. (This might be 9 o'clock or 9:30 or 10—it doesn't matter.) We reach into our container and draw out, say, the chip numbered 7; this is recorded in column 2 of Table 6–3. Consulting Table 6–2, we record in column 3 that the first patient arrives at 08 minutes. He of course is serviced immediately. We arbitrarily assign him to Station 1 and note in the log that service begins at 08 minutes and ends at 18 minutes. We also record that he waits 0 minutes. Finally, we note in the log that each of the stations has been idle for the 8 minutes before his arrival. (It may be that you don't care how busy the stations are, in which case you would need a less comprehensive log.) The next random number drawn is, say, 2; we therefore take it that the second patient arrives 3 minutes after the first, at 11 minutes. He too is serviced immediately, beginning at 11 minutes and ending at 21 minutes. But until he arrives Station 2 is idle; therefore its cumulative idle time is 11 minutes. The third drawing

Table 6–3

Patient number	Random number	Arrival interval	Arrival time	Station 1 service	
				begins	ends
1	7	8	08	08	18
2	2	3	11	—	—
3	4	3	14	18	28
⋮	⋮	⋮	⋮	⋮	⋮
77	0	0	347	409	419
78	2	3	350	—	—
79	4	3	353	419	429
80	8	8	361	closed	

All times are in minutes.

	0	1–10
Data for run shown above:		
Frequency of waiting times	11	8
Relative frequency of waiting times	.14	.10
Data for 100 computer runs:		
Relative frequency of waiting times	.15	.22
Average number of patients served—72		
Average idle time per station—37		

of a random number yields, say, 4; the third patient thus arrives at $11 + 3$ = 14 minutes. But both stations are busy; he cannot be serviced until 18 minutes. Thus he has a 4-minute wait; he is finished at 28 minutes. We continue to draw random numbers and to record times until we reach an arrival time of 360 minutes. At 360 minutes the doors of the clinic are locked; once a drawing takes us past 360, the drawing is discontinued. The patients then waiting are processed. We complete the log by tallying up the results. This is simply a matter of counting the number of patients served, recording the frequency distribution of waiting times, and so on, as shown at the bottom of Table 6–3.

In this way we have simulated the essential features of one day's activity at the hypertension clinic. But we cannot be sure that this is a typical day—one day's sequence of random numbers may not on any particular day follow the known arrival frequencies very closely. It may be a busy day or a quiet day or just an average day; we can't be sure which. We can eliminate this uncertainty by simulating many days' activity and averaging the results for each type of information. We can then be much more confident that the predicted values for, say, the distribution of waiting times are reasonably accurate. The averages for 100 computer runs are also shown at the bottom of Table 6–3; we see that our particular day was extraordinarily busy.

Simulating 100 clinic histories would of course be much too tedious and take much too long if we had to do it by the above method. Once programmed, the computer can do the job in a few seconds. It can generate a random number virtually instantaneously whenever one is needed. The recommended procedure is to hand over to a computer programmer the table of arrival frequencies and a typical log sheet to indicate how the queuing system operates. Tell him what you want in the way of output—for

Station 2 service		Patient's waiting time	Accumulated idle time	
begins	ends		Station 1	Station 2
—	—	0	8	8
11	21	0	8	11
—	—	4	8	11
⋮	⋮	⋮	⋮	⋮
—	—	62	29	42
412	422	62	29	42
—	—	66	29	42
closed		turned away		

11–20	*21–30*	*31–40*	*> 40*
8	10	6	36
.10	.13	.08	.46
.20	.15	.10	.18

example, the frequency distribution for waiting times, average wait, total idle time for all stations, number of patients served, or whatever information the model can produce. If he is on his toes—and sympathetic to what you're trying to accomplish—he will ask you which of the input variables you may want to change for later runs. He will also ask you which of the parameters are likely to be soft estimates, so that he can check out the sensitivity of the results to these estimates. He will then be able to feed in the new values without reprogramming, while you simply sit back and wait for the output.

A Diffusion Model: Simulation of an Epidemic

One of the earliest simulations of a public health problem is the epidemic model developed by Reed and Frost of Johns Hopkins University.[2] The model is kept deliberately simple so that its ramifications will be intuitively clear.

The disease is spread directly from infected individuals ("cases") to others in the population who are not immune to it ("susceptibles") by a certain kind of contact ("adequate contact") and in no other way. Thus there are three kinds of people in the population: active cases, susceptibles, and immunes. Immunity is acquired only by having the disease.

At the start of the epidemic we have a population of P_0, consisting of C_0 cases and $S_0 = P_0 - C_0$ susceptibles. (We exclude those already immune from the group because they are of no interest to us.) The individuals in the group are wholly segregated from others outside the group. Each individual has a fixed probability p of coming into adequate contact with any other specified individual in the population within one time interval; this probability is the same for every member of the group. Any susceptible, after such contact with a case in a given time period, will develop the infection and will be infectious to others only within the following period, after which he is wholly immune. In other words, the number of susceptibles who make adequate contact in one period becomes the number of cases in the next period. The size of the epidemic is simply the sum of all the cases in all the time periods, beginning with the first case and ending when the number of cases drops to zero. Figure 6–1 shows the

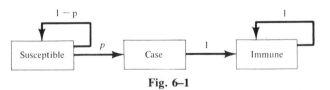

Fig. 6–1

[2] See, for example, Philip E. Sartwell, "Memoir on the Reed–Frost Epidemic Theory," *American Journal of Epidemiology*, 103, no. 2 (February 1976): 138.

flow diagram for one susceptible individual when there is a single case of this disease. In period i, the computer will send the susceptible individual through the flow diagram C_i times, or until he becomes a case.

The only element in this model that calls for simulation is the random occurrence of adequate contact between a case of the disease and a susceptible individual. This is the way the computer proceeds. Suppose we start with a population of 100, with one case and 99 susceptibles ($P_0 = 100$, $C_0 = 1$, $S_0 = 99$); we also take $p = .02$. At this point the size of the epidemic is $E_0 = C_0 = 1$. In the first period, the computer starts by investigating what happens to the first of these 99 susceptibles. It does so by calling for a two-digit random number between zero and one. (Note that probabilities involving two or more digits present no problem; $p = .3476$, for example, merely requires that we call a four-digit random number.) If the random number is 00 or 01, it is deemed that adequate contact has been made, and this particular susceptible becomes a case in the next period. If the random number turns out to be greater than 01, no contact has occurred and the susceptible continues as a susceptible in the next period. The computer then proceeds to the next susceptible, calling another random number. This process continues until all the susceptibles have been investigated.

The computer keeps a running total of the number of people who will be susceptible and cases in the next time period; these numbers become S_1 and C_1. Those who were cases during the past period become immune and are dismissed from further consideration. The size of the epidemic is now $E_1 = C_0 + C_1$.

In the second period, there are S_1 susceptibles and C_1 cases to deal with. The computer again starts in on the first susceptible, but now there are C_1 cases with whom the susceptible may make adequate contact. Therefore a total of C_1 random numbers are called to determine whether or not he makes adequate contact with any of the cases. If any of these C_1 random numbers is 00 or 01, the susceptible makes adequate contact and becomes a case in the next period. Otherwise he remains a susceptible. The computer then proceeds to the next susceptible and calls another batch of C_1 random numbers to determine his fate. When all the susceptibles have been processed, it again tallies the results to obtain S_2 and C_2, and calculates $E_2 = C_0 + C_1 + C_2$.

The computer continues with subsequent periods in a similar fashion until either everyone has had the disease or the epidemic dies out. The final size of the epidemic is the sum of all the cases in all the periods; only that number appears in the printout.

In this fashion we generate a history of an epidemic, starting from a model of how an epidemic might occur. We won't always get the same history because the random numbers won't always produce adequate contact exactly 2 percent of the time. But we know that if we carry out this same experiment many times, adequate contact will occur very, very close to 2 percent of the time on the average. This means that if we run the simulation many times, the average epidemic size will be very close to what we would arrive at if we were able to solve the problem simply by manipulating the equations.

As an example of the kinds of results to be expected, 10 computer runs with $P_0 = 100$, $C_0 = 1$, and $p = .02$ produced the following epidemic sizes: 84, 81, 63, 75, 79, 88, 81, 55, 1, 88.[3] The average for 100 runs was 64.27. When the population was cut to 50, the average epidemic size for 100 runs fell to 5.08, a substantial reduction indeed. If you were a public health official faced with decisions as to immunization and/or quarantine in communities of varying size, the policy implications of this finding would be most instructive. You would probably want to investigate also what happens with a slight upward adjustment in p, the probability of adequate contact. For an epidemic that presents a greater danger, such as the threatened swine flu epidemic of 1976, health officials would use more complex models to explore various possibilities for contact, transmission of the disease, and probability of serious illness or death.

Macroeconomic Simulation

In the last quarter century, computer simulations of the United States economy and indeed of the world economy have come into increasing prominence. These models use large numbers of equations to predict the behavior of key variables in the economy—investment, consumption, employment, imports and exports, government expenditures, and the like—over the next few quarters or years. A typical model might relate consumption in year t, for example, to wages and profits in the same year, and investment in year t to profits in years t and $(t - 1)$. Originally something of an academic exercise (getting the model to work at all was considered a real coup), some of the better known models now play a major role in both public and private decisions. Government economists trying to determine the optimal level of government spending and corporate planners trying to determine the optimal level of investment rely on them. To a degree, the models build in an element of self-fulfillment as decision makers respond to their predictions.

Similar macroeconomic models are now used to try to predict future world use of certain vital resources, especially oil. *The Limits to Growth*[4] used a complex model of the world economy to predict the exhaustion of many of our natural resources in the foreseeable future. Needless to say,

---

[3] An epidemic size of 1 is quite possible. It will occur whenever no one makes adequate contact with the initial case. The chance of this is $(.98)^{99} \approx .135$. In other words, better than 10 percent of the time, this epidemic will never materialize at all.

[4] Meadows, Meadows, Randers, and Behrens (New York: Universe Books, 1972).

many people disagree strongly with the assumptions and conclusions of the model.[5]

Simulation as a Analytic Tool

Analysts recognize that there are many problems in formulating informative simulations and usually employ them only as a last resort. The difficulties encountered in building the model can be formidable; frequently independent verification of the accuracy of the model is impossible. In addition, probabilistic output, the usual output of a simulation, is susceptible to misuse, particularly if some of the information is not presented. For example, suppose the average epidemic for a population of 100 people turns out to be 5 cases. This average could have resulted from epidemic sizes of 4, 7, 3, 5, 6, and so on, year after year. Or it could conceivably conceal the fact that no epidemic occurs 19 years out of 20, but then everyone is laid low at once; the average epidemic is still 5 cases. Obviously this information could be misleading; as a precaution, the analyst should insist on seeing a sampling of complete runs as well as the final averages. Despite these risks, in many situations simulation is the appropriate recourse for the analyst. Used wisely, it is an indispensable tool for predicting the outcomes of alternative policies.

---

[5] See, for example, H. S. D. Cole, Christopher Freeman, Marie Jahoda, and K. L. R. Pavitt, *Models of Doom*, (New York: Universe Books, 1973), and William Nordhaus, "World Dynamics: Measurement without Data," *Economic Journal* 83, no. 332 (December 1973).

7 Markov Models

Simple models sometimes yield compelling conclusions. Such models are worthy of study if their basic elements reappear in a variety of situations. Markov models are among these models;[1] an understanding of them yields insights into a number of policy issues. Pollutants moving through the biosphere, mentally ill individuals moving from one level of functional capability to another, heroin users moving from addiction to treatment to abstention and back again—all can be illuminated by casting them in a Markov framework.

Consider the following situation, which we will describe with the aid of a Markov model. New Kent has a labor force of 10,000 people. In any month, each of these 10,000 people is either employed (E) or unemployed (U). At present, 3000 are unemployed. As things now stand, 90 percent of those employed in one year are still employed the following year, while 40 percent of the unemployed find jobs and are employed in the next year. These proportions hold true year after year. New Kent's employment situation is summarized in the following table or matrix. This type of matrix is called a *transition matrix* because it describes how changes take place from one period to another.

		Next period	
		E	U
This period	E	.90	.10
	U	.40	.60

The first row of numbers tells us what proportion of the people who are employed in the first period will still be employed in the next, and what

---

[1] Markov was a Russian mathematician noted for his work in probability theory. He died in 1922.

proportion will be unemployed. Thus the .90 in row E, column E, means that of the people who are employed in the first period, .90 or 90 percent will be employed in the next period. The second row gives us the same information about those who are unemployed in the first period. We might also have labeled the two periods "y" and "$y + 1$," since it is stipulated that the proportions don't change from year to year.

We could have used a set of difference equations to set forth the information contained in the transition matrix:

$$E_2 = .90E_1 + .40U_1$$
$$U_2 = .10E_1 + .60U_1$$

The main advantage of the matrix notation is its simplicity, in writing and especially in manipulation. This becomes much more important as the number of different categories increases.

The situation we have just examined is an example of a Markov system. In this case we have considered movements within an entire population, New Kent's labor force, from employed or unemployed in one period to employed or unemployed in the next period. When we observe the probabilistic movements of a single individual, the process is called a Markov chain. The arithmetic for the two situations is identical.

Markov Chains

Let's consider an individual—we'll call him Smith—who is either well (W) or sick (S). Moreover, if Smith is well one day, he has an 80 percent chance of being well the next day. If he is sick, he has a 50 percent chance of being well the next day. These probabilities depend only on his condition today, an assumption that is crucial; his previous history doesn't matter. Smith's health is completely described by the following transition matrix, which defines a Markov chain:

		Period 2	
		W	S
	W	.80	.20
Period 1			
	S	.50	.50

Customarily we assign a label, let us call it P, to this matrix and write it simply as

$$P = \begin{pmatrix} .8 & .2 \\ .5 & .5 \end{pmatrix}$$

These probabilities for the state of Smith's health hold for any two consecutive periods.

What are the properties of a transition matrix that define a finite

Markov chain?[2] First, there must be a finite number of well-defined categories or states, such that the individual falls in one and only one state in each period; the mathematician's phrase is "mutually exclusive and collectively exhaustive."[3] This means that the system is closed—the individual always stays within it and does not move to some state outside the system, which is equivalent to stating that the numbers in each row of the matrix must add up to 1. Somtimes this inclusiveness requirement may be satisfied by enlarging the matrix, in other words by adding states so that all possibilities are accounted for. For example, suppose Smith, when he is well, has an 80 percent chance of remaining well and a 15 percent chance of being sick in the following period. He also has a 5 percent chance of dying and hence moving out of the two-state system. We may keep him in the system by adding "dead" as a third state.

A second property is that the probabilities in the transition matrix must be the same for any two consecutive periods. A third property is the so-called Markov condition: the probabilities must have no memory. It doesn't matter whether Smith was well or sick yesterday; the probability of his being well tomorrow depends only on how he is today. Suppose you find that the probability of his being well tomorrow, given that he is sick today, depends on how long he has been sick, and not just on whether he's well or sick in this period. Perhaps that probability is 50 percent if he has been sick one day, but only 30 percent if he has been sick longer. At first glance this presents insurmountable difficulties, but if only a few periods of history matter we can cope with the situation. In this particular set of circumstances, we replace the state "sick" with two states, "sick for one day" ($S1$) and "sick for two days or longer" ($S2$). The matrix Q would then represent a Markov chain:

		Period 2			
		W	$S1$	$S2$	
	W	.80	.20	0	
Period 1	$S1$	.50	0	.50	$= Q$
	$S2$	.30	0	.70	

If the number of states that the chain "remembers" is finite, it is possible to satisfy the Markov requirement by redefining the states in this manner.[4] A fourth property of a Markov chain is that time periods must be

---

[2] We will not consider transition matrices in which the number of states is infinite.

[3] Suppose, for example, we have four attributes that may describe Smith: well, sick, employed, and unemployed. These categories, though collectively exhaustive, are not mutually exclusive, for Smith could be sick and unemployed at the same time. The states must be defined as well and employed, well and unemployed, sick and employed, and sick and unemployed. Only then are they both mutually exclusive and collectively exhaustive.

[4] To check your understanding of this point, consider the following situation: Smith's possible states of health are well, sick, and very sick. Moreover, his chance of going from sick to very sick depends on whether he was well or sick in the period before last. (Before reading further, try to define the states so that the Markov property holds.)

We need to define four states for Smith: well (W), sick for one day ($S1$), sick for two days

uniform in length. This may seem to be a superfluous requirement, as here they are automatically defined that way. But now and then it can give trouble. Generations, for example, are a very difficult time unit to work with. Moreover, with longer periods we have to pay attention to moves out of and back into a state within a single period. If these conditions—inclusive states, constant and memory-less probabilities, and uniform period lengths—are satisfied, then we have a Markov chain.

Long-Term Analysis Using Markov Chains

Given the Markov chain defined by the transition matrix P above, what is the probability that Smith will be well the day after tomorrow? To put it more broadly, we may be interested in what the two-period transition matrix looks like:

		Period 3	
		W	S
Period 1	W	?	?
	S	?	?

(We could have labeled the periods d and $d+2$, for the day-to-day probabilities remain the same over time.)

We could work this out the hard way by complete enumeration, if necessary, and it's worth doing once: we note that someone who is well today and well the day after tomorrow has two ways of getting from well to well. He can proceed from well to well to well, or from well to sick to well. The probability of the first path is $.8 \times .8 = .64$, and that of the second $.2 \times .5 = .10$; hence the total probability of being well the day after tomorrow, given that Smith is well today, is $.64 + .10 = .74$. You should proceed in this fashion to calculate the other three entries and get the complete matrix:

		Period 3	
		W	S
Period 1	W	.74	.26
	S	.65	.35

---

or longer ($S2$), and very sick (VS). The following matrix suggests some plausible numbers. (The zeroes, in fact, are more than plausible—they're indisputable.)

	W	S1	S2	VS
W	.8	.15	0	.05
S1	.5	0	.3	.2
S2	.3	0	.4	.3
VS	.2	.2	0	.6

If, fortuitously, you are familiar with matrix operations (and if you aren't, don't worry about it) you will recognize that we could have found the two-period matrix directly: it is simply $P \times P = P^2$.[5] The three-period matrix, P^3, is

Period 4

		W	S
W		.722	.278
Period 1				$= P^3$
S		.695	.305

Following this procedure, we may find $P^6 = P^3 \cdot P^3$:

Period 7

		W	S
W		.714	.286
Period 1				$= P^6$
S		.714	.286

We might have gone on to display P^{10} and P^{20}, but have not done so because the elements of these matrices are the same as those of P^6 to three decimal places.

---

[5] Matrix multiplication is actually straightforward but messy. We demonstrate it for 2×2 matrices, and illustrate with an example.

Let $A = \begin{pmatrix} a_{11} & a_{12} \\ a_{21} & a_{22} \end{pmatrix}$ and $B = \begin{pmatrix} b_{11} & b_{12} \\ b_{21} & b_{22} \end{pmatrix}$

Then $A \cdot B = \begin{pmatrix} (a_{11}b_{11} + a_{12}b_{21}) & (a_{11}b_{12} + a_{12}b_{22}) \\ (a_{21}b_{11} + a_{22}b_{21}) & (a_{21}b_{12} + a_{22}b_{22}) \end{pmatrix}$

A^2 is simply

$\begin{pmatrix} (a_{11}a_{11} + a_{12}a_{21}) & (a_{11}a_{12} + a_{12}a_{22}) \\ (a_{21}a_{11} + a_{22}a_{21}) & (a_{21}a_{12} + a_{22}a_{22}) \end{pmatrix}$

For example, suppose we want to find the two-period transition matrix for the transition matrix

Period 2

		Well	Sick
Well		.9	.1
Period 1				$= T$
Sick		.4	.6

In other words, we wish to find $T \cdot T$. Applying the $A \cdot B$ formula above,

$\begin{pmatrix} .9 & .1 \\ .4 & .6 \end{pmatrix} \cdot \begin{pmatrix} .9 & .1 \\ .4 & .6 \end{pmatrix} =$

$\begin{pmatrix} (.9)(.9) + (.1)(.4) & (.9)(.1) + (.1)(.6) \\ (.4)(.9) + (.6)(.4) & (.4)(.1) + (.6)(.6) \end{pmatrix} =$

$\begin{pmatrix} .85 & .15 \\ .60 & .40 \end{pmatrix} = T \cdot T$ or T^2

Leonard E. Fuller, *Basic Matrix Theory* (Englewood Cliffs, N.J.: Prentice-Hall, Inc., 1962), is an excellent introduction to matrix operations.

The Long-Run Equilibrium Probabilities

Not only are the matrices P^6, P^{10}, and P^{20} almost the same, but the individual rows are practically identical as well. This suggests that the chances of Smith's being well or sick on any given day, provided that that day is far enough in the future, are quite independent of whether he is well or sick today. And this is in fact the case.[6]

This is a very important result, so important that it's worth restating. The long-run probabilities for Smith's being well or sick on some day far in the future do not depend on his condition today, i.e., the initial conditions do not matter. Furthermore, the long-run probabilities also tell us directly how much of the time (over the long run) Smith can expect to be well, in this case 71.4 percent of the time. Be sure you understand that we are not suggesting that Smith stops moving from one state to another after many periods have passed, but merely that if we look a long way ahead, the probability of his being in a particular state at that time does not depend on his health today.

We may extend this result to New Kent's unemployment problem. What is the likelihood that a representative worker in New Kent will be unemployed two years from now, given that there is known to be 30 percent unemployment today? The transition matrix, which we'll label R, was given as

Period 2

		E	U	
	E	.90	.10	
Period 1				$= R$
	U	.40	.60	

The two-period transition matrix is

Period 3

		E	U	
	E	.85	.15	
Period 1				$= R^2$
	U	.60	.40	

Consequently, two years hence we expect that 15 percent of those now employed (70 percent of the population) will be unemployed. Also, 40 percent of those now unemployed (30 percent of the population) will be unemployed. Hence $(.70)(.15) + (.30)(.40) = 22.5$ percent of the population will be unemployed. Over the long run this will drop to 20 percent, the equilibrium value. You may feel that the New Kent matrix doesn't accurately represent the unemployment situation; perhaps you argue that some people are temporarily unemployed whereas with others the condi-

---

[6] Those with a knowledge of matrix algebra can calculate the long-run probabilities directly by solving the equation $aP = a$, where a is the row vector of these long-run probabilities. For this particular Markov chain, $a = (5/7, 2/7)$.

tion is chronic. We return briefly to this matter of differences among individuals later in the chapter. In the meantime we stick to simple cases where all individuals face identical probabilities, in order to illustrate the mechanics.

The values for the infinitely long-run probabilities are known as the equilibrium probabilities of the system. (The concept of equilibrium was discussed in Chapter 4. Recall that it carries no favorable or unfavorable connotation; it is merely a mathematical property.) If we are considering the movements of an entire population, these probabilities may be thought of as an equilibrium distribution that the population will approach in the long run, no matter what its initial distribution may have been. For New Kent this equilibrium is 20 percent unemployment. In the case of an individual, in this case Smith, the equilibrium tells us the long-run probability that he will find himself in each of the possible states, regardless of the state he is in at present. Moreover, the equilibrium also indicates what proportion of his future time, on average and over the long run, Smith can expect to spend in each state.

Can we generalize these statements about the long-run probabilities for Smith to all Markov chains? In other words, will a transition matrix always lead in the long run to a stable probability distribution? The answer is no. Without delving into all the mathematical nuances, we can get an intuitive grasp of when a Markov chain will eventually reach an equilibrium and when it won't. Our conclusions will hold equally well for Markov processes that involve entire populations.

Essentially there are three kinds of Markov chains: (1) *regular chains*, like the ones we've already looked at; (2) *absorbing chains,* which have one state or a group of states in which the individual may become trapped; and (3) *cyclical chains*, in which the individual passes through all or some of the states and back to his starting point.

Regular Chains

In a regular chain, all states communicate with one another; it is always possible to go from any state to any other, although it may take more than one period to do it. In other words, there is some n for which the multiperiod transition matrix P^n has no zeros. For example, matrix Q on page 100 (with states well, sick for one day, and sick for two days or longer) has three zero entries:

		Period 2		
		W	$S1$	$S2$
	W	.80	.20	0
Period 1	$S1$	.50	0	.50 = Q
	$S2$	.30	0	.70

But the two-period matrix has no zeros:

		Period 3			
		W	*S1*	*S2*	
	W	.74	.16	.10	
Period 1	*S1*	.55	.10	.35	$= Q^2$
	S2	.45	.06	.49	

Thus the two-period matrix tells us that Smith could not go from sick two days to sick one day in one period—but that he could do it in two periods. Therefore, this particular chain is regular.

As noted above, regular chains will lead eventually to an equilibrium distribution. This property may be especially useful when we are predicting the behavior of entire populations rather than the probabilistic movements of a single person.

Absorbing Chains

With an absorbing chain, there are one or more absorbing states that the individual cannot leave once he has entered; it must also be possible to go from every state to an absorbing state, although not necessarily in one step.

To get an idea of what we mean by an absorbing state, look again at Smith's well–sick matrix, *P*, which is an example of a regular matrix. What happens if we decide to be more realistic and add a third category, dead (*D*)? Suppose the new transition matrix is *S*:

		Period 2			
		W	*S*	*D*	
	W	.80	.19	.01	
Period 1	*S*	.50	.47	.03	$= S$
	D	0	0	1	

(The alert reader can work out for himself why the numbers in the third row are what they are.) This is not a regular matrix—there is no way that Smith can go from dead to well or sick, no matter how much time we give him. Death is termed an absorbing state, because once an individual has entered that state it is impossible for him to leave it. Death is not the only absorbing state one encounters in analyses of public policy. Immunity is closely analogous. A pollutant may be transformed into a permanently harmless and hence benign absorbing state. On the other hand, another pollutant may be unrecoverable once it escapes containment; the absorbing state is then to be avoided.

The opposite of an absorbing state is a transient state. A person may possibly spend a number of periods in a transient state, but there is a zero probability that he will be there after a sufficiently large number of periods.[7] Sick and well are transient states in Smith's three-state health chain. A chain with a single absorbing state reaches an equilibrium of a sort, though it is not very interesting: everyone ends in the absorbing state.

Cyclical Chains

Sometimes the individual moves systematically through the states. For example, a mayor rotates his once-a-week open office hours among four little city halls. North is followed in turn by east, south, and west. The matrix is

		Period 2			
		N	E	S	W
	N	0	1	0	0
	E	0	0	1	0
Period 1					
	S	0	0	0	1
	W	1	0	0	0

---

[7] If there is only one absorbing state, we may calculate the long-run probabilities. As you might guess, for S they are 0, 0, and 1, for well, sick, and dead, respectively. The n-period matrix for large n is:

		Period $n + 1$			
		W	S	D	
	W	0	0	1	
Period 1	S	0	0	1	$= S^n$
	D	0	0	1	

In such a case we are more likely to be interested in what the transition matrix looks like for, say, 10 periods, in other words, how fast the system is converging toward its equilibrium probabilities.

The quick diagnostic for an absorbing chain is a 1 on the diagonal, i.e., on the line from the upper left to the lower right. Purists should note that if two or more states can be combined to give a 1 on the diagonal, the chain is also absorbing. For example, the matrix

		Period 2		
		W	S	VS
	W	.8	.2	0
Period 1	S	0	.8	.2
	VS	0	.5	.5

can have its categories aggregated to yield

		Period 2	
		W	S or VS
	W	.8	.2
Period 1			
	S or VS	0	1

which is clearly absorbing.

Sometimes the entire matrix will describe such a cyclical process. Sometimes only a part of the system will rotate, but once the individual is trapped in the rotation he cannot escape. In either situation, there is no equilibrium; the rotation continues indefinitely.

Using Regular, Absorbing, and Cyclical Chains

In sum, with regular Markov chains we may draw two conclusions about the long-run probabilities: (1) for the long run, the probability of being in a particular state approaches an equilibrium value that is independent of the state that the individual is in initially; (2) these equilibrium probabilities may be interpreted as the percent of time spent in each state over the very long run.

With absorbing chains, the equilibrium is frequently uninteresting. We are more likely to want to know how many periods an individual can be expected to spend in each state before he is absorbed, or how quickly he is likely to get trapped. If there is more than one absorbing state, we may be interested in knowing what the probability is that the individual lands in each.

The fully cyclical chains tell us no more than what is intuitively obvious. The rotation continues perpetually, and where you are at any particular time depends on where you started and how many periods have passed. With a partially cyclical chain, the individual will become trapped in the rotation eventually, but if we know where he started, we will at least be able to estimate the expected number of periods that will pass before he is caught up in the rotation.

Before we go further, you may be wondering how long the long run is. The answer is, "It all depends." If there is very little movement between states and if there are a large number of states, the system will be slow to converge toward its equilibrium probabilities. For example, consider the following well–sick transition matrix:

Period 2

		W	S
	W	.99999	.00001
Period 1			
	S	.00003	.99997

The equilibrium probabilities for this system are .75 and .25 for well and sick. But this is scant comfort for a sick man, whose chances of getting well quickly are slim. Contrast this with our earlier well–sick matrix, where the long-run probabilities weren't quite as favorable (.714 and .286), but which converged to the equilibrium probabilities much more rapidly. If there are a large number of states, rather than just two, and period length is, say, one week, the system may take years to come close to equilibrium.

A Practice Problem: The History of an Infection

Consider an infection that, once contracted, can never be entirely eliminated from one's system. The initial infection is acute. Subsequently it
becomes dormant, but acute periods may recur. During acute periods the
victim is uncomfortable; when the infection is dormant he is free of
discomfort. The probabilities for each state are described in the following
transition matrix:

		Period 2		
		No infection	Acute	Dormant
	No infection	.999	.001	0
Period 1	Acute	0	.6	.4
	Dormant	0	.1	.9

What are the long-run implications of this situation for an individual who
has not yet become infected?

As a practical matter, if you are the individual in question, and
assuming no medical advances are possible, you would probably like
answers to two questions:

1. What are the chances I'll catch it in the next 10 or 20 (or whatever)
   periods?
2. If I catch it, how much of the time will it be acute?

The answer to the first question is straightforward. No infection is a
transient state—once out of it you can never return. Therefore your
chances of continuing to escape for n periods are simply $(.999)^n$. If a period
is one month and you're wondering about the next 10 years, then your
chances of permanent escape are $(.999)^{120} \approx .887$. In fact, even if you
survive for another 57 years, you still have better than a 50–50 chance of
escaping altogether.

As for the second question, note that the states acute and dormant are
jointly absorbing. Once you enter either, you must always be in one or the
other. This means that when formulating a prognosis for an infected
individual we can work with the reduced matrix:

		Period $n + 1$	
		Acute	Dormant
	Acute	.6	.4
Period n	Dormant	.1	.9

The two-period transition matrix is

Period $n + 2$

		Acute	Dormant
Period n	Acute	.4	.6
	Dormant	.15	.85

The three-period matrix is

Period $n + 3$

		Acute	Dormant
Period n	Acute	.3	.7
	Dormant	.175	.825

If we continue this procedure we will find that the matrix converges very rapidly toward:

Period $n + m$
(m very large)

		Acute	Dormant
Period n	Acute	.2	.8
	Dormant	.2	.8

In other words, you can expect that on average the infection (once it hits you) will be acute 20 percent of the time.

Markov Processes

Markov processes are useful for policy analysis because they enable us to study entire populations. Whereas the Markov *chain* deals with an individual who moves in a probabilisitc manner through a set of states, a Markov *process* describes the movements of members of a population through a set of states. The same probabilities are applied simultaneously to each member. By the Law of Large Numbers, if the population is sufficiently large (and 100 is fairly large), the proportions of members moving will be close to the probabilities.[8] For example, with New Kent's labor force, the entries in the transition matrix tell us what proportion of those who are in the states employed and unemployed in one period move to each of these two states in the next period. As with Markov chains, we require mutually exclusive and collectively exhaustive states, uniform time periods, and

---

[8] More strictly, the larger the population, the more closely we would expect the observed proportions to approximate the true probabilities.

unchanging probabilities, which on a population basis approximate proportions. We must also require a fixed population. That is, there must be neither entry to nor exit from the system. And again, as with Markov chains, it is frequently possible to satisfy these requirements through careful redefinition of the states.

What happens in the long run? As with a Markov chain, if the transition matrix is regular, or if there is only one absorbing state, or only one absorbing group of states, the proportions will approach long-run values that are independent of where the system starts. These long-run values are the equilibrium values of the system. Again, we emphasize that this does not mean that individuals in the population necessarily stop moving from one state to another, but rather that the proportion of the population that is, say, unemployed approaches a constant level.

Let's go back to New Kent and its unemployment problem, which persists despite the fact that the Help Wanted sections of the *New Kent Gazette* are full of openings for skilled and semiskilled workers. For convenience, we repeat the transition matrix R:

$$
\begin{array}{ccc}
 & \text{Period 2} & \\
 & E \quad\quad U & \\
E & .90 \quad\quad .10 & \\
\text{Period 1} & & = R \\
U & .40 \quad\quad .60 &
\end{array}
$$

Assume you are a consultant to the New Kent City Council, which is trying to decide how to attack the unemployment problem. A Markov model can help you formulate your prescription. It will tell you where the council has the most leverage on the problem, in other words, what kinds of policy changes will be the most helpful. Perhaps your alternatives involve the allocation of federal funds to improve the job security of those already employed, or to establish training programs for the unemployed, or to attract new industry through tax concessions, or to increase unemployment compensation. How much employment is gained by following each of these paths? Each of these possible programs can be described in terms of the new transition matrix it produces.

The long-run equilibrium for New Kent, given the original situation described by the transition matrix R, is 80 percent employed and 20 percent unemployed. This means that if the problem is left to itself and nothing happens to change the situation, there will eventually be 2000 unemployed in New Kent. (It is, of course, straining reality to assume that so simple a model can describe such a complex situation.) And in fact by this time next year there will be only 2500 unemployed. This is a considerable improvement over the present 3000 level.

It is believed that the measures that can be taken to improve job security will produce the following new transition matrix R':

Period 2

		E	U
	E	.95	.05
Period 1				$= R'$
	U	.40	.60

The equilibrium proportions are 8/9 and 1/9, or 1111 unemployed; this approach looks promising.

You then wonder about instituting a training program, rather than working on job security. What will happen under a program that increases the percent of unemployed who find jobs each month from 40 percent to 50 percent? This time the transition matrix is R'':

Period 2

		E	U
	E	.90	.10
Period 1				$= R''$
	U	.50	.50

The equilibrium proportions for this sytem are 5/6 and 1/6, or 1667 unemployed. This is better than doing nothing, but not nearly as good as you had hoped and (perhaps surprisingly) not as good as the proposed improvement in job security.

Finally, what about persuading a large corporation to build its new assembly plant in New Kent? This would bring in 1000 new jobs, which would be filled from the ranks of the New Kent unemployed. This would immediately cut the unemployment level from 3000 to 2000. But unless there are accompanying changes in the job market, such that the probabilities in the transition matrix are also changed, that would be the limit of the improvement, for the long-run equilibrium of the system would remain at 2000 unemployed.[9]

Naturally, there are many more policy options available than we have mentioned here, and they must be evaluated in the light of many factors, including their cost and the likelihood of their bringing about other changes in the system. But even with this simple model we now know more about what is going on and what the implications of various policies might be. You should think about other uses for a Markov model. Consider, for example, how you might employ one to compute the cost of extending unemployment benefits from a 6-month maximum to an 8-month maximum.

---

[9] It is possible, of course, that favorable changes would take place in the transition probabilities. But it's also conceivable that the new plant would attract new potential workers, and ultimately aggravate the unemployment problem.

And we may easily move to more sophisticated models. We have already explored the possibility of creating additional states to refine the model. Earlier in this chapter we mentioned that you might feel that the New Kent matrix fails to give a true picture of the situation because, although some of the unemployed are only temporarily in that state, others appear to be incapable of holding a job for very long. To attack such situations we should develop two or more different transition matrices, one matrix to represent the experiences of each group of people. Similarly, disaggregation of this sort is frequently valuable in health applications, where two types of patients may respond quite differently to treatment. In all such cases, the policy implications for the groups may differ sharply, although whether we can apply the policies on a selective basis will depend on our ability to distinguish between their members.

An Example: Drug Rehabilitation

A state corrections system has established a new drug treatment facility for first offenders. The center has a capacity of 1000 inmates.

Inmates may leave the facility in either of two ways. In any period there is a 10 percent probability that an inmate will be judged rehabilitated, in which case he will be released at the beginning of the following period. There is also a 5 percent probability that an inmate will escape during each period. Rehabilitated addicts have a 20 percent chance of relapsing in each period; escapees have a 10 percent chance of being recaptured each period they are on the lam. It has been decided that both escapers and recidivists will be returned to the facility, and that these offenders will be given admissions priority over new offenders.

In describing this facility, we will wish to depict the flows within the system. For example, if the facility opens at full capacity, how many of the original inmates will be resident in the facility 10 periods hence? How many new offenders can be admitted in each of the next 2 periods? What happens if we modify the model to allow for a small possibility of death, or for a change in the probability of relapse after the first period following release?

This is a situation that lends itself well to a Markov model, for we have drug addicts moving through a variety of states. You may find it helpful to start your analysis of the problem by drawing a diagram to depict the flows. In Figure 7–1 and the matrices that follow, we use I to denote inmates, R for inmates who have been rehabilitated, and E for inmates who have escaped.

The transition matrix is:

		Period 2			
		I	R	E	
	I	.85	.10	.05	
Period 1	R	.20	.80	0	$= T$
	E	.10	0	.90	

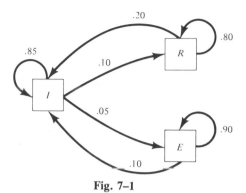

Fig. 7–1

In order to answer the first question, we need the 10-period transition matrix, T^{10}:

Period 11

		I	*R*	*E*	
	I	.527	.268	.199	
Period 1	*R*	.535	.321	.144	$= T^{10}$
	E	.412	.144	.444	

This means that 527 of the original inmates will be resident in the facility 10 periods hence, although many of these will have spent time outside in the meantime. [If you wonder how many have stayed put, it's $(.85)^{10}(1000) = 197.$]

To ascertain how many new inmates can be admitted in each of the next two periods, we start with the initial 1000 inmates; we also assume (although it isn't necessary) that in Period 1 no recidivists or escapers are lurking somewhere out there. I.e.,

$I_1 = 1000$

$R_1 = \quad 0$

$E_1 = \quad 0$

Applying the one-period transition matrix to these numbers we get:

$I_2 = .85(1000) + .20(0) + .10(0) = 850$

$R_2 = .10(1000) + .80(0) + \quad 0(0) = 100$

$E_2 = .05(1000) + \quad 0(0) + .90(0) = \quad 50$

Denote the number of inmates admitted in the second and third periods by X_2 and X_3. Then immediately we have:

$X_2 \leq 1000 - 850 = 150$

Once X_2 new inmates are admitted, the total inmate population in Period 2 becomes $850 + X_2$. We then have, for Period 3:

$I_3 = .85(850 + X_2) + .20(100) + .10(50) = 747.5 + .85X_2$

Hence we must have

$$X_3 \leq 1000 - (747.5 + .85X_2) = 252.5 - .85X_2$$

In particular, if 150 inmates (the maximum possible) are admitted in Period 2, no more than 125 can be admitted in Period 3.

With this matrix, it is impossible to establish a fixed number of new admissions for each period. The number of spaces available will vary. In the long run all former inmates will spend half their time inside the facility. No matter how few inmates are admitted each year, eventually the number needing beds will exceed 1000 and there won't be beds enough.

We may modify the model to allow for a small possibility of death (D), as for example in the following transition matrix:

		Period 2			
		I	R	E	D
	I	.84	.10	.05	.01
	R	.20	.79	0	.01
Period 1					
	E	.10	0	.89	.01
	D	0	0	0	1

Now the matrix is absorbing, and it will be possible to find a number that will permit equal admissions every year. (However, it doesn't absorb very quickly, so it is doubtful that this would be an optimal strategy.)

If we want to allow for a change in the probability of relapse once the rehabilitated offender gets past the first release period, we must add another state. $R1$ indicates the first release period, $R2$ all subsequent periods. The following is a plausible transition matrix:

		Period 2			
		I	$R1$	$R2$	E
	I	.85	.10	0	.05
	$R1$	.20	0	.80	0
Period 1					
	$R2$	.10	0	.90	0
	E	.10	0	0	.90

Now the equilibrium values are .42, .04, .33, and .21 for I, $R1$, $R2$, and E, respectively. This implies that more new offenders can be admitted from year to year on a short-term basis but it will still be impossible to set any fixed number of new admissions for the long run.

8 Defining Preferences

How should outcomes be valued? That question must be answered whenever a policy is chosen on a rational basis. The descriptive models we have been studying can only predict what outcomes may be expected; in the language of the economic model of choice, they can only locate the possibility frontier. Even if a decision maker has determined as accurately as possible what consequences will flow from each alternative action, he still needs to formulate his preferences if he is to have a basis for choice; he must, in terms of the choice model, lay out his preference function.

In some choice situations, the structure of preferences may be so simple that there is no need for systematic thought. If Sunshine City is purchasing a thousand stop signs and if all stop signs are identical, the sole element in the preference function should be cost. Sunshine City should then pick the lowest cost supplier. Unfortunately, most policy decisions involve more than the purchase of a homogeneous product. Let's suppose Sunshine City is instead purchasing a municipal recreation building. Even if the site for the building has already been determined, there will be a wide choice of possible structures. The Park Commissioner is pulled in many directions. He likes space; he wants a beautiful building; he wants it to be appropriate for indoor sports such as basketball or even hockey, yet adaptable to smaller scale crafts and activities. And he naturally is concerned about costs, both for construction and for annual maintenance. Already it should be evident that to make a wise decision, much more than a simple "minimize cost" criterion is required. The decision maker for Sunshine City, we suggest, would be well advised to spend a few hours thinking explicitly about the structure of his preferences for the recreation building. This chapter looks at some techniques that may aid his thinking.

In subsequent chapters we investigate several prescriptive models for public decision making, models that combine predictions of alternatives and statements about preferences in order to indicate the best choices. Chapter 9 reviews procedures for evaluating alternative public projects, and introduces the important and widely employed method of benefit–cost analysis. Chapter 10 takes up the persistent problem of valuing benefits and costs that stretch over periods of time, a problem that Sunshine City encounters, for example, if it accepts higher initial construction costs so as to save on annual maintenance.

Linear programming, the subject of Chapter 11, is a technique for putting together a descriptive model and a particular type of preference function to select a preferred alternative. Chapter 12 considers decision analysis, an extensively developed technique for making choices in the enormous class of situations where uncertainty is a key consideration. Sunshine City might find, for example, that it is difficult to predict with any degree of precision how much it will cost to maintain the various proposed recreation buildings. Decision analysis should help in such uncertain situations.

Public decision making is a perpetual exercise in the reconciliation of conflicting interests. Almost without exception, a public policy choice will involve the demands of several competing groups. Perhaps it's a mundane conflict. Sunshine City's recreation building decision, for example, could develop a gloomy spot of dissension if the parents of teenagers pushed strongly for a gymnasium type of structure, while those active in adult education argued that the building should contain classrooms suitable for crafts and continuing education, and those with little interest in community recreation insisted that the tax dollars be put to another purpose altogether. Often, unfortunately, the conflicts are more monumental, as prolonged controversies over busing plans and nuclear power plants illustrate. The unhappy decision maker must ultimately weigh the competing claims of the opposing groups, however painful the task. How to make tradeoffs between the welfare levels of different individuals and groups is more a matter of philosophy and judgment than of methodology. Chapter 13 reviews possible approaches to this problem.

Enough of an overview; let's get back to the public decision maker, and the issues he is likely to confront in defining his preference function. He is not in the fortunate position of the individual consumer, who can merely take an introspective approach in deciding which bundle of commodities he wishes to purchase, and who most of the time has a background of experience on which to base his judgments. First, since the public decision maker is choosing on behalf of others, looking inward would be a rather poor guide to assessment. Second, his choices will frequently involve complex combinations of consequences, and rarely will he be able to rely on the society's past experiences in "consuming" these combinations of consequences. In short, he will have a difficult time defining the equivalent of his indifference curves. This chapter argues that the public decision maker will usually find it beneficial to be explicit, at least with himself, in deciding what he is trying to accomplish in making his choices.

The Multiattribute Problem

If the assortment of possible outcomes of a policy choice is measured in terms of a single attribute, such as dollars, it isn't difficult to decide that more is better than less (or worse, if you're talking about costs) and then determine directly the best choice. The trouble is that most policy proposals (intentionally or otherwise) serve a variety of objectives, and their outcomes are described in terms of more than one characteristic, some of which may be unfavorable. These characteristics we call *attributes*. Except by extraordinary good luck no one outcome will be best with respect to all attributes. Which of the combinations of attributes is preferable is rarely self-evident, and at times it is hard to make an intelligent comparison between even two alternative actions that have complex arrays of attributes. Nor is there any mechanism ready at hand for reducing all attributes to a common denominator. It is this ubiquitous problem, termed *the multiattribute problem,* that makes it tough to determine our preferences among outcomes. The crux of the problem is that it is impossible to optimize (an all-purpose word for "maximize or minimize, as the case may be") in all directions at once.

We mentioned Sunshine City's dilemma in balancing space against aesthetics, an open structure against one that is suitable for small groups, and all of these against immediate and continuing costs. We would not expect any proposed building to surpass all other proposals on all these dimensions; the world doesn't operate that way. Somehow the Park Commissioner must decide just how much and where to compromise, how much he is willing to sacrifice, for example, in space and funds in order to have a more beautiful building. In other words, he must determine what his subjective tradeoffs are among the valued attributes. The discussion below describes a number of techniques to help the decision maker organize his thinking about preferences among such multifaceted outcomes.

Throughout this chapter (and in subsequent chapters as well) we will refer to the decision maker's preferences. This is in part shorthand, for we all know that in the final analysis the preferences at stake are those of the individuals that the decision maker represents. But it is more than just shorthand, for it serves to remind us that although the values of a society are ordered by its political processes, the results of those processes must be interpreted and translated into specific guidelines for choice.

Defining the Attributes

The first step in thinking systematically about the multiattribute problem is to define the attributes, to spell out the valued consequences, good and bad, of a policy alternative. To do this we need to know first what we are trying to accomplish, what the objectives of the policy proposal are, and second, what outcomes are predicted for each policy choice. In other words we need to think about both what we want in the way of attributes and what we are likely to get.

Since the set of attributes that is employed in a problem may ultimately determine which choice is made, considerable care should be exercised in selecting the attributes. Taken together, the set of attributes should be comprehensive. That is, there should be no gain (or loss) in well-being that is not reflected by an improvement (or worsening) on at least one attribute. If we are thinking about speed limits as a means to reduce accidents and limit gasoline consumption, we also must include effects on travel time and air pollution.

If we are concerned about air pollution in New York, then the policy objectives might be posed as fostering the health and promoting the economic well-being of the city residents. Unfortunately these objectives, although lofty and impressive, are totally unmanageable in an actual decision context. We need to break them down further, to a level of specificity where they will be useful to a decision maker. In short, we must decide which attributes we will use to measure the policy's performance in fostering health and economic well-being. At the same time, we must take care to ensure that the list of attributes reflects all the likely impacts of the proposed policy. If the pollution control program includes restrictions on parking within the city, the attributes must measure the possible ill effects on retail trade as well as the good effects on air quality. Every element in an outcome that has a bearing (favorable or otherwise) on the society's well-being must be included in the list.

Comprehensiveness may require some precision as well as completeness. For example, in dealing with the consequences of accidents, we might start by listing repair costs, fatalities, and injuries. But the last category may be too broad, since accidents can be of varying degrees of severity. Perhaps we should have different attributes for serious and minor injuries. At some point, the pursuit of comprehensiveness mires the analyst in detail. Moreover, the attributes may start to overlap one another. There is no magic solution. The key is to understand that defining attributes is a difficult and important problem, one that merits careful attention from any policy maker.

What should individual attributes look like? We should like them to be important. Just as we draw up a family budget under large and important categories such as food, clothing, and recreation, so when we confront a public decision we should make sure that we rely on categories that are truly significant. Enhanced life expectancy, improvements in health, days of recreation, dollar savings, numbers of new jobs—all are important attributes. An attribute's importance in a particular decision context depends on the extent to which it is affected by the choices at hand. Thus threats to life expectancy are hardly likely to figure prominently in Sunshine City's recreation building decision.

An attribute should be measurable, where possible. To be most useful it must serve as a yardstick that tells us how much we are accomplishing. Some quantities can be neatly measured in understandable units, dollars of repair cost, square footage available, days lost to illness. To be sure, many of the supposedly objective numbers given to us are subject to a variety of interpretations. Unemployment figures are an example; so too is the efficiency rating for the town incinerator. Frequently we must recognize that measurability as normally understood cannot be achieved. For example, suppose you have received several job offers. Your choice will no doubt depend on attributes such as salary, hours of work, colleagues, location, working conditions, and so on. Salary and hours can be readily quantified. We could quantify location, indeed give its precise latitude and longitude, but that would probably not be a good indication of what you value about a particular location. Some people would quantify it by measuring the driving time from a good ski slope. Perhaps you might want to develop a more general index or grading scheme; some locations rate an A, others a B or worse. And on some attributes—the nature of one's colleagues, for example—you may have to give up on measurability. The best course then is simply to write out a paragraph or two of description that is to be carried along throughout the analysis to make sure the attribute does not get overlooked or overshadowed by the more readily quantified variables.

The choice of attributes may depend in part on who is the client of the policy analysis. In some situations the analysis is undertaken for a single client or client group, possibly yourself, perhaps the residents of North Baltimore. In others, several clients are involved but their interests converge sufficiently so that they may be viewed as a unit. In contrast, consider a policy decision for a hospital: are the true clients the staff, the patients, or the community served by the hospital, or indeed all of them? This is the sort of question that cannot be answered in any general way. It must be considered anew in every analysis and the answer will bear heavily on the selection of appropriate attributes.

A philosophical problem arises in defining the outcome of a policy choice. Is it legitimate to exclude the process of decision making from the list of attributes, or is the process itself an attribute that is an intrinsic part of the outcome? For the truly unitary decision maker, the process of arriving at a decision is likely to be extraneous to the decision, although decision making costs may not be negligible and must always be included in the outcome. For group decisions, or public agency decisions where the interests of many groups must be considered, the process itself may achieve significant value as an attribute. To the extent that this is true, the process must be regarded as an integral part of the outcome and hence must be listed as an attribute. The criminal justice system provides outstanding examples of the importance of procedures for making decisions. So, in fact, does the majority rule procedure or indeed our entire democratic process. In many areas in public life we sacrifice efficiency, as narrowly defined in terms of our valuation of physical resources, for what might be considered a more desirable choice process. Indeed, sometimes the greatest need is for improved decision making processes, rather than improved decisions.

Finally, attributes should be formulated in an open-minded way so as not to prejudge a policy choice. They must be ends, then, and not means. (And if, as mentioned above, we believe that the decision making process is an end in itself as well as a means, so be it.) If we are interested in air pollution in New York, the valued attribute is not the number of scrubbers on smokestacks but rather the cleanliness of the air. (Indeed, the probing analyst might delve deeper and ask about the health consequences of clean air, or the ultimate link to human happiness.) If we list scrubbers as the valued attribute, we may miss a superior alternative, perhaps involving different fuels or different in-plant processes. Moreover, we would doubtless find it difficult to think about our preferences with respect to scrubbers; it's what they accomplish that matters to us, and not how many we have of them. If we were dealing with the criminal justice field, we would not want increases in average sentences to be an attribute; rather, what we value is a reduction in crime. After conducting the analysis we may conclude that increased sentences are a good way to reduce crime, but we should not prejudge the situation by the way we structure the attributes.

When we have tallied our objectives and attributes, what might the final result look like? Figure 8–1 shows a listing of the valued attributes for New York's air pollution control program.

We have accomplished a great deal once we have defined the set of

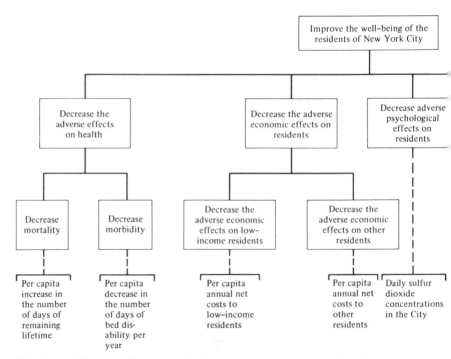

Fig. 8–1. *The complete set of objectives and attributes for choosing an air-pollution control program for New York City.**

---

* Ralph L. Keeney and Howard Raiffa, *Decisions With Multiple Objectives* (New York: 1976) John Wiley and Sons, p. 362.

attributes for a problem. We must next find a way to make difficult comparisons between alternatives, one of which may be superior on some attributes, and another on others. We start by deciding what it is we want more of, then we go further to describe the tradeoffs we are willing to make among valued attributes. In short, we try to get our preferences straight.

Ways to Attack the Multiattribute Problem

In principle, the preference-sorting problem may be attacked from either of two directions. We may first see what the outcomes of possible actions are and then find a way to compare these outcomes. Or we may first determine what our preferences are, regardless of the available options, and then see which of the feasible actions is best according to this preference schedule. The latter approach is essentially that laid out in the discussion of the fundamental model of choice in Chapter 3. We noted there, and it bears repeating, that it sounds like the consumer's indifference map of economic theory, and indeed it almost is. However (and this is a large however), no economist would ever suggest that a person constructs his indifference map and then acts in accordance with it. Rather, he would be careful to say that

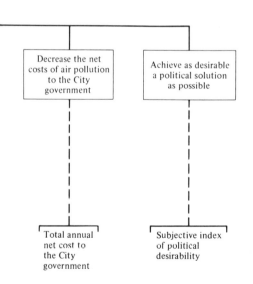

if the map accurately depicts the individual's preferences, the individual acts *as if* he were following the map. The indifference map of economic theory is revealed by observed choices; it does not determine them. What is proposed here is actual construction of relevant parts of the map, which will then be used as part of a prescriptive model to provide a guide to the best choice. This more general approach is likely to be most useful for thinking about decisions that must be made repeatedly or must be delegated to an agent, or where there are continuous variables. In effect, a formalized decision rule is provided.

If hard thought were costless, a decision maker would sketch out his whole preference function, worry conscientiously about its structure, and test its acceptability by determining what choices it would lead him to in a great number of actual situations. Such a procedure is hardly feasible. It would be time-consuming, which means that it would be far from costless. In practice, then, the decision maker looks for shortcuts, or rules of thumb, or approximations that require much less than a full sketching out of an indifference map. Such procedures can be justified if, as he should, the decision maker thinks of his objective as taking the action that yields the preferred outcome when decision making costs are taken into account. Economists sometimes jibe at each other about the marginal utility of not thinking about marginal utility. Rational decision makers can quite appropriately talk about the rationality of not attempting to make decisions by following a showcase model of rationality.

In any case, whether we follow the first route and simply look at specific outcomes to see which we like best, or the second route and build up a complete map of our preferences, the concept of transitivity is central. The assumption that preferences are transitive is implicit in both approaches.

Transitivity

Preferences are said to be transitive provided that if A is preferred to B (written $A > B$) and B preferred to C, then it necessarily follows that A is preferred to C. Further, if one is indifferent between A and B (written $A \sim B$) and one is also indifferent between B and C, then one is necessarily indifferent between A and C. Transitivity would also require, for example, that if one is indifferent between A and B, and B is preferred to C, then A must also be preferred to C. The mathematical shorthand is as follows:

If $A > B$	If $A \sim B$	If $A \sim B$
and $B > C$,	and $B \sim C$,	and $B > C$,
then $A > C$.	then $A \sim C$.	then $A > C$.

Alternatively, $A > B$ may be written $B < A$. The symbols $>$, $<$, and $\sim$ used in conjunction with preferences are analogous to the symbols $>$, $<$ and $=$ used for mathematical quantities.

We assume that for rational people preferences are transitive. It is plausible, then, to carry the transitivity assumption over to public decision makers. For example, suppose the mayor states that he prefers to build a park rather than a commercial arcade along the waterfront, and that if he is forced to a choice between the commercial arcade and an industrial complex, he would select the arcade over the complex. It then seems reasonable to assume that if the decision comes down to the park or the industrial complex, the park will be preferred. We expect our public decision makers to employ preference functions that display transitivity.

While we're at it, we should add one further piece of terminology. Preferences are said to be completely ordered if either A is preferred to B, or B is preferred to A, or one is indifferent between A and B, for all possible outcomes A and B, and if in addition such preferences are transitive. In other words, given any pair of outcomes, A and B, it must be possible to compare them and determine that either you prefer one to the other or else you are indifferent between them. The public decision maker need not devote many hours to defining his choices between all possible pairs of options, but he should be prepared, whatever means he employs to define his preferences, to make choices between the alternatives that turn out to be genuine contenders. Sunshine City's park commissioner must be prepared to choose between the two or three recreation buildings that are finalists. Paying attention to preference functions helps prevent decision makers from being frozen into quandaries of indecision and inaction.

We now review several techniques and shortcuts that might prove helpful in defining preferences.

Comparing Specific Outcomes of Possible Actions

We noted above that some choice procedures do not formalize the decision maker's preference structures, but instead rank outcomes by first seeing what the possible outcomes are and then finding some way to compare them. We'll look at five of these methods, not because they're so very clever, but because any one of them may be a useful device in a particular situation, or may at least offer a framework for thinking about a difficult problem.

Pairwise Comparisons

The most direct way to determine which of several alternatives is best is to make pairwise comparisons. Outcome A is compared in its entirety to B. The better of these two is then compared to C, and so on, until all alternatives have been examined and one is left as the best. The obviousness of this method may underwhelm you. But it is of more than passing interest. Much real-world policy making operates this way, with new alternatives always seeking to replace the status quo. Consequently it's useful to take a careful look at the weaknesses of this approach.

When King-of-the-Mountain, as this procedure is called, can be readily employed, its simplicity will make it attractive. Analytic methods will have little additional to offer. But King-of-the-Mountain has serious drawbacks and limitations. It assumes that if you have only two alternatives to choose from, you can readily decide which one is better. If the decision process is time-consuming and costly, and in a complex situation this is quite likely, you will hardly wish to proceed in this fashion. If you have a lot of alternatives, King-of-the-Mountain can prove exceedingly cumbersome. Similarly, if some of your choice variables are continuous, as in deciding how much to spend on a project, the procedure offers no guidance unless you work step-by-step along a dollar scale. It provides no information in case you want to delegate a choice, for the decision process is completely internalized. It ordinarily does not produce a complete ordering of preferences. We know only which choice is best when we get through; the entire procedure must be repeated if we wish to determine which is next best.

It is sometimes argued that this seat-of-the-pants method of choosing has the advantage that by considering the outcome as a whole, it all its richness, the intangibles are not left out, or downgraded because they are hard to quantify, or wrongly emphasized because the interactions among them are complex. We argue that it is more likely that important considerations will be overlooked or misevaluated in viewing the consequences of an action as a whole than if the decision maker sits down and conscientiously tries to make a complete list of all the valued attributes. It's all part of the process of getting things out of the back of the analyst's mind and onto a piece of paper.

"Satisficing"

Sometimes a decision maker may simplify a problem of choice by deciding on satisfactory levels for some (but not all) attributes of an outcome. This stipulation might take the following form for Sunshine City's recreation center: "The cost of construction can't exceed $200,000." In a quite different context we might have: "The infant care training program must include 200 mothers." The choice is then made among all options satisfying these conditions. This two-step process is known as "satisficing." Frequently the term is used to mean that satisfactory levels for all attributes except one are determined. Almost all choices, however uncomplicated, contain elements of satisficing, for by implication the levels of attributes excluded from consideration are acceptable. And the more successful decision makers are those who develop an instinct, within their own fields of competence, as to which attributes one should be content to satisfice on and which should be treated to a further examination.

If none of the available alternatives is good enough to meet the preset acceptability requirements, you must go back to the drawing board for a more modest estimate of the minimum requirements. On the other hand, you may be pleasantly surprised by the levels attained by the nonsatisficed attributes. (In the recreation center example, these were maintenance costs, available space, and aesthetic characteristics.) In that case you may wish to reconsider whether to upgrade some of your original aspiration levels. Satisficing approaches, it should be understood, are rule-of-thumb

able way to deal with the limited information-processing capabilities of the methods. They simplify some of the exceedingly complex problems one encounters in defining a preference function. If a quick check reveals that the shortcut does little harm, satisficing is exceedingly useful. Some observers have suggested that whatever the merits of the satisficing approach, many real-world decision makers employ it. It is a not unreason-human brain.[1] The alternative, of course, is to develop methods that do not require the decision maker to make simultaneous tradeoffs among all valued attributes.

Lexicographic Ordering

Satisficing carried to an extreme becomes what is known as lexicographic ordering. The term is derived from the process of alphabetizing. In a dictionary, all the words beginning with q precede all the words beginning with r. No "improvement" in the letters after the first will alter this arrangement; a word beginning with the letters "qz . . ."—if such a word existed—still precedes all the words that begin with "ra . . . ." In short, no tradeoffs are possible, and this is as good a way as any to define lexicographic.

Specifically, lexicographic ordering ranks alternatives *with regard to one attribute* at a time. If and only if Alternative I is equally as satisfactory as Alternative II with respect to the most important attribute, will the next most important attribute then be considered as relevant in the ordering of overall preferences.

Suppose a deposit is to be made in bank A or bank B. The outcome of each of these choices is described in terms of three attributes, X_1, X_2, and X_3, which are respectively the quality of the bank's services, the dollars earned by a deposit, and the convenience of its location. The depositor's preferences are ordered in a completely lexicographic fashion; X_1 is deemed more important than X_2, and X_2 than X_3. Then only if the two banks provide services perceived as being of exactly the same quality will the interest rate be considered at all. And only if, in addition, they pay the identical rate of interest will their location become a factor in the decision.

Lexicographic ordering is rarely appropriate except for "administrative ease"—but administrative simplicity is an important attribute and cannot be ignored. Hence we should not be startled to observe cases where lexicographic orderings are employed. It is sometimes argued that when a policy decision involves risking lives, preferences become lexicographic. In other words, the best outcome is that posing the smallest threat to people's lives. Intuitively this may be an appealing notion to some, but in fact it hardly squares with observed behavior. If people really felt this way, seat

---

[1] Organization theorists at Carnegie–Mellon University have observed that in practice many decisions are made by choosing the first good alternative that appears. In other words, the decision maker satisfices with respect to all attributes. Many families, especially those who are subject to frequent business transfers, buy houses this way. Frequently it is the most sensible approach, particularly if the costs of delay are high.

belts would always be buckled; indeed, no one would ever drive a car or cross a street or undergo cosmetic surgery.

Reducing the Search to Nondominated Alternatives

A number of methodological developments now make it possible to make policy choices directly through the use of analytic procedures. Although we would not be so naive as to assert that these methods are employed in a majority or even a sizeable minority of policy choice situations, an understanding of them will facilitate the process of policy choice.

A first principle of analytic policy choice is to eliminate clutter and complicating factors whenever they will not affect the preferred final choice. This suggests, for example, that alternatives that will clearly not be final choices should be eliminated forthwith from the competition. Sometimes this removal process is rather straightforward.

As a starter, all dominated alternatives should be removed. Alternative A is said to dominate alternative B if A is better than B in at least one respect and no worse than B in any respect. Consider again the problem that Sunshine City faces in constructing its new recreation building. Suppose, for the sake of simplicity, that all buildings cost the same, both for construction and for maintenance, and all are equally attractive. They differ only with respect to suitability for athletics and crafts. The park commissioner studies five proposals; he ranks each of these, first according to suitability for athletics and then according to suitability for crafts, with the results shown in Table 8–1. Here "1" indicates the building most preferred.

Table 8–1

	Rank	
Proposed building	Suitability for athletics	Suitability for crafts
I	4	4
II	1	2
III	3	5
IV	2	1
V	5	3

Note that we have said nothing about strength of preferences. These are purely ordinal rankings; in any particular case the margin of superiority may be large or small. We see that buildings II and IV are preferable to I, III, and V in both respects; the latter three are said to be dominated choices. We might diagram this situation as shown in Figure 8–2, which shows a diagram for which only ordinal numbers are available. The numbers run "backward" from the origin because we are accustomed to diagrams where things get better as we go to the right or to the top of the page. All points lying north and east of any point, including those due north and east, dominate that point. In this diagram we see immediately that I, III, and V are dominated, but we have no basis for choosing between II

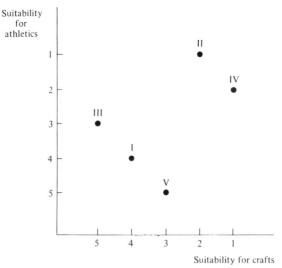

Fig. 8–2

and IV. Although no single alternative is dominant, the choice problem has been appreciably narrowed. Choices II and IV are termed efficient, because it is impossible to find a different choice that improves matters in any respect without making them worse in some other respect. Choices I, III, and V are inefficient because by choosing II or IV Sunshine City can have a building that is better both for athletics and for crafts.

Comparison Through the Computation of Equivalent Alternatives

In a complex multiattributed situation, recourse to mere intuition cannot eliminate alternatives. Still it is a help to be able to rule out some of them by inspection for dominance. Suppose you are choosing among five alternative jobs. A significant characteristic, of course, is the salary. Other important attributes are leisure, working conditions, characteristics of colleagues, and location. You rank the jobs on each of these attributes, assigning an *A* to the best performer, *B* to the next best, and so on. If there is a tie on a particular attribute, both jobs are assigned the same rank. The grades for the five jobs are shown in Table 8–2. On the basis of this matrix, you rule out jobs I, III, and V. Jobs I and III are dominated by II; V is

Table 8–2
Systematic Ranking of Alternatives

Characteristic	Job				
	I	II	III	IV	V
Salary	B	A	C	B	B
Leisure	C	C	D	A	B
Working conditions	C	A	B	C	C
Colleagues	C	B	B	A	A
Location	A	A	A	B	B

dominated by IV. This is as far as you can go with the dominance procedure, but the decision has been greatly simplified by limiting the number of contenders to two alternative jobs.

The choice has now come down to II or IV. What can we do? Job II offers a better salary, working conditions, and location, but less leisure time and less appealing colleagues. We can suggest one way to make this comparison in a systematic manner. Obviously, mere ordinal rankings will no longer be enough. We must start with a more thorough description of the performance of the two alternative jobs on the different valued attributes. The table below gives the relevant information. W_{II} and W_{IV} are paragraphs of description of working conditions. (W_{IV} might read "Little direct contact with clients, assignment to a single type of work, half a secretary, and an inside office.") C_{II} and C_{IV} are paragraphs of information about colleagues on the job, and L_{II} and L_{IV} give locations. Thus L_{II} might be "industrial area outside of Philadelphia." The comparison is shown in Table 8–3.

Table 8–3
The Initial Comparison

Attributes	Alternative jobs	
	II	IV
Salary (in $000)	20	18
Leisure (in waking hours per day)	5	8
Working conditions	W_{II}	W_{IV}
Colleagues	C_{II}	C_{IV}
Location	L_{II}	L_{IV}

First ask yourself how much of the $20,000 salary offered by job II you would give up in return for 3 additional hours of leisure per day. You decide, say, that you would give up $3000. In other words, you can define a new job, Alternative II′, that has 3 more hours leisure, or 8 hours total, and $3000 less salary, or $17,000. And II′ is exactly equivalent to II because you have so defined it. You can therefore now work with a new comparison table, Table 8–4.

Table 8–4
Equalized Leisure

Attributes	Alternative jobs	
	II′	IV
Salary (in $000)	17	18
Leisure (in waking hours per day)	8	8
Working conditions	W_{II}	W_{IV}
Colleagues	C_{II}	C_{IV}
Location	L_{II}	L_{IV}

Repeat this process with the next attribute, working conditions. According to Table 8–2, the working conditions of II were superior to those of IV. Ask yourself how much of IV's $18,000 you would be willing to give up if the working conditions could be the same as under Alternative II or II'. Say you decide $2000 is about right. Making the appropriate exchange, you get Alternative IV'. The comparison table now becomes Table 8–5.

Table 8–5
Equalized Leisure and Working Conditions

| Attributes | Alternative jobs | |
	II'	IV'
Salary (in $000)	17	16
Leisure (in waking hours per day)	8	8
Working conditions	W_{II}	W_{II}
Colleagues	C_{II}	C_{IV}
Location	L_{II}	L_{IV}

This process is continued with C and then with L so that all attributes except salary have been equalized. Those next two tables might be Tables 8–6 and 8–7.

Table 8–6
Equalized Leisure, Working Conditions, and
Colleagues

| Attributes | Alternative jobs | |
	II''	IV'
Salary (in $000)	15	16
Leisure (in waking hours per day)	8	8
Working conditions	W_{II}	W_{II}
Colleagues	C_{IV}	C_{IV}
Location	L_{II}	L_{IV}

Table 8–7
All Attributes Equalized Except Salary

| Attributes | Alternative jobs | |
	II''	IV''
Salary (in $000)	15	14
Leisure (in waking hours per day)	8	8
Working conditions	W_{II}	W_{II}
Colleagues	C_{IV}	C_{IV}
Location	L_{II}	L_{II}

In this last table everything has been equalized except salary. We have made tradeoffs to reach II'' in such a way that you are indifferent between it and original alternative II. Similarly, you are indifferent between IV and IV″. But since II″ is by inspection preferred to IV″ (or, using our earlier notation II″ > IV″), we can conclude that II is preferable to IV.

Merely through the process of making pairwise tradeoffs among valued attributes, we have discovered one alternative to be superior to the other, although initially there was no apparent basis for making a systematic comparison. This method is perfectly general. Any decision maker who is willing to proceed with these pairwise tradeoffs, and can do so in a consistent manner, can use this procedure to select his preferred alternative from any set of multiattribute alternatives. You might want to take a moment to consider how Sunshine City's park commissioner might pick a recreation building using this procedure.

Note also that this method of equivalent alternatives can frequently be employed to eliminate even undominated alternatives as final contenders. If, for example, there had been an Alternative VI that was identical to IV except that it offered a higher salary and worse working conditions, a one-step comparison could have generated VI′, indifferent to VI and identical to IV except for salary. If the salary of VI′ were below that of IV, VI would be eliminated. If it were above, VI would be the contender and IV would be dropped out.

In the job choice example, we had two quantitative variables and three that involved descriptions. All that the process requires is that there be one quantitative variable whose value can be manipulated up and down incrementally so as to produce equivalent alternatives. In policy decisions, the cost of the project would be the most likely candidate for this equilibrating role. In any particular circumstance, a quite different variable may suggest itself. It could be the level of unemployment, an index of air quality, or the number of physicians in an area. All that is necessary is that the decision maker be willing and able to make explicit tradeoffs between that variable and others of value.

This tradeoff procedure provides a means to compare any two points without sketching the whole preference function. In principle nothing more than this approach is ever necessary, but sometimes it may prove easier to determine the preference function itself.

Determining the Entire Preference Structure: Objective Functions

All of the foregoing methods involve merely the comparison of the alternatives under consideration. These methods never require the sketching of the decision maker's entire preference structure. A complete, formalized depiction of a decision maker's preferences is called an objective function. It can be described by a geometric diagram in the form of the indifference curves we discussed in Chapter 3. Alternatively, and considerably more frequently in real choice situations, the objective function is expressed in some analytic or mathematical form.

An objective function is an explicit statement of how each attribute that is a consequence of a particular choice situation contributes to a single overall index of that choice's desirability. Quite simply, it is a formal assignment of weights to these attributes. It therefore constitutes an immediate and definitive decision rule. For example, suppose Sunshine City's park commissioner, having had some experience with tough decisions, wants to allocate playground space between tennis and basketball courts in a high-density, high-demand area. For any facility, the playgrounds can be expected to be in continuous use during daylight hours. A tennis or basketball court takes up the same area; any combination of three courts is feasible. The director observes that a tennis court, T, serves 4 people at a time, whereas a basketball court, B, serves 10. If his objective is merely to maximize total recreation hours, H, his objective function will be

Maximize $H = (4T + 10B) \times$ number of daylight hours per week.

He would choose to install three basketball courts.

In practice, the commissioner is likely to have a more sophisticated objective function that takes account of the diversity of recreational needs and interests in the community. He might classify recreational users by age, say under and over 25, and/or by sex, and value the hours going to any particular group on a declining basis, the first 100 hours they receive being valued more than the second and so on. An objective function that values the monthly recreation hours going to each sex according to the square root of those hours would satisfy this condition. The equation

$$V = \sqrt{H_m} + \sqrt{H_f}$$

where the subscripts m and f refer to male and female, is such an objective function.

To use the objective function in practice, the commissioner would have to predict the recreation hours that the two groups would enjoy for each playground configuration. The men will be the overwhelming users of whatever basketball courts are available; the commissioner's projections (summarized in Table 8–8) show that the use of the tennis courts will be more or less evenly divided between the sexes. Thus, the park commissioner would choose to install one tennis court and two basketball courts.

Table 8–8

Number of basketball courts	3	2	1	0
Number of tennis courts	0	1	2	3
Total hours of use by males, H_m	1770	1300	830	360
Total hours of use by females, H_f	30	140	250	360
$V = \sqrt{H_m} + \sqrt{H_f}$	47.5	47.9	44.6	37.9

In this problem, the commissioner has nothing concrete to rely on in formulating his objective function. He should therefore probe the form of the function by testing whether it makes sense in simple situations where the choice is intuitively clear. The objective function formulated above suggests, for example, that the first 100 hours of recreation enjoyed by a group not presently enjoying recreation at all are worth just as much as an increase of 300 hours for another group whose present level of recreation is 100 hours. Or the commissioner might confront himself with the hypothetical choice between *A* and *B*, as shown in Table 8–9. If he feels comfortable

Table 8–9

	A	B
Hours to males	400	100
Hours to females	0	100

in choosing *B*, but thinks the choice is close, then at least for these values his objective function represents his preferences well.

Often, fortunately, the decision maker will have much more information to rely on. Sometimes, as we will see in more detail in the following chapter, attribute values may be expressed in dollars and simply added. In such cases the valuation problem assumes paramount importance. In many circumstances decision makers willl have to rely on processes of deduction and estimation in deciding how much one attribute is worth relative to others. Suppose, for example, that reduced air pollution is valued because it improves health, provides aesthetic benefits, and cuts cleaning costs. The decision maker may value its reduction by first assessing what gains he can expect along each of these three attributes. He might then try a variety of ways to value the gains, a complex matter we address at great length in the next chapter. Ultimately he will develop an objective function that assigns a specific value to the various possible combinations of the outputs of air pollution control strategies. Those outputs are health (H), aesthetic benefits (A), cleaning costs (C), and the costs imposed by the control strategy (I). The objective function will be of the general form

Maximize $V = f(H, A, C, I)$.

[Recall that the functional form $f(H, A, C, I)$ is used to indicate that V depends, in some manner unspecified in this general formulation, on H, A, C, and I.]

We have come a long way from our earlier problem of choosing a building or picking a job. In those examples, the decision maker directly chose the consequences. In our recreation and air pollution examples, he chose among actions that in turn generated consequences. The prediction of those consequences may well require modeling efforts of the type considered in this volume. Air pollution concentrations, for example, are frequently described with the aid of Markov models. Measurement may also present a problem; the decision maker may have to create his own scales, as he would in measuring aesthetic benefits. It is essential that the selection of the criteria—determining which attributes should be scaled for measurement—be viewed as a separate process from the formulation of the objective function. The purpose of this whole procedure is to enforce systematic thinking about which outputs are valued and how the valued outputs are to be traded off against each other.

For a simple one-shot choice, formulating the objective function is hardly a procedure to be recommended. But there are many types of recurring situations where the effort to construct this valuable tool is justified. Perhaps similar decisions must be made frequently; many business firms use objective functions in allocating productive capacity or determining minimum cost inputs. Sometimes decisions must be delegated to agents; a federal agency might well establish objective functions to serve as guidelines for its local offices. For example, the Environmental Protection Agency, a federal organization, might develop an air quality index to be used by cities and states to determine whether particular quality levels are being achieved. Still other situations exist where a once-and-for-all and very important decision is to be made, and the objective function is used as a definitive test for choosing the best of a wide range of possible actions. The choice of a particular configuration of dams for a combination flood control and irrigation project is a likely case in point. In addition, it is frequently helpful in a bargaining context to try to reconstruct the other party's objective function, or rather the objective function that he would define if he bothered to be systematic about it. Specific examples of objective functions will be studied in the chapter on linear programming.

The formulation of an objective function, properly carried out, imposes a strict discipline on the decision maker. He must analyze his preferences systematically and make explicit his tradeoffs among attributes. He must be prepared to defend these tradeoffs, and if he is a public decision maker the demand for accountability is magnified. The major drawback is that the objective function demands careful specifications of all attributes, a quantitative description being the most frequent format; in some cases this is more trouble than it's worth. Nevertheless, even when the decision maker does not go so far as to formulate the objective function explicitly, it remains an invaluable framework for thinking about a problem of choice.

9 Project Evaluation: Benefit–Cost Analysis

Benefit–cost analysis is the principal analytical framework used to evaluate public expenditure decisions. This approach requries systematic enumeration of all benefits and all costs, tangible and intangible, whether readily quantifiable or difficult to measure, that will accrue to all members of society if a particular project is adopted. Such a description ordinarily produces the reaction, "Well, naturally. What else would you expect public policy analysts to do?" Yet benefit–cost analysis is a relatively recent development. It was originally employed in analyzing water resource projects in the 1930s and has come into widespread use only since World War II. It is a typical prescriptive model, in that it incorporates a description of the total outcomes of various projects and a rule for choosing among them in accordance with the decision maker's preferences.

Benefit–cost analysis is sometimes described as the public household's version of a profit and loss statement. The analogy is strained; benefit–cost analysis examines all impacts of a project, internal and external, whereas a private business is presumed to look only at those that affect its own welfare. Moreover, profit and loss are *ex post* concepts; they describe, after the fact, what has happened. Benefit–cost analysis is *ex ante*; it attempts to evaluate a project before it is undertaken to decide in what form and at what scale it should be undertaken, and indeed whether it should be undertaken at all.

The rationale for benefit–cost analysis is economic efficiency; it aims to ensure that resources are put to their most valuable use, including the significant possibility of leaving them in private hands. As a practical matter, benefit–cost analysis is most helpful in assessing well-defined projects. It would be of great assistance in choosing among alternative pollution-control systems for a particular river system, or in deciding whether road repairs in a community should be made with a new, more weather-resistant asphalt. For wide-ranging programs, such as the War on

Poverty of the 1960s, benefit–cost analysis is most useful as a paradigm. A detailed quantitative analysis of such programs would be impossible, but thinking about the way such an analysis might be carried out forces policy makers to think hard about categories of benefits and costs, to define their expectations about outputs, and to pay attention to the tradeoffs that are implicit in their decisions.

Indeed, the harder the decision problem is to define and the more amorphous its goals, the greater will be the value of training in the systematic procedures of project evaluation. In its opening months, the Carter administration was confronted with just such a policy choice. A decision was necessary as to how strongly to push public as opposed to private employment opportunities. The debate centered on such questions as "Should we spend $2 billion on public works projects? Or $5 billion on tax cuts?" Rarely do we encounter such barebones questions about how much it costs society to achieve a valued objective.

Our general approach to benefit–cost analysis is positive and enthusiastic. But it would be unfair to praise the merits of project evaluation techniques without identifying their liabilities as well. Benefit–cost analysis is especially vulnerable to misapplication through carelessness, naiveté, or outright deception. The techniques are potentially dangerous to the extent that they convey an aura of precision and objectivity. Logically they can be no more precise than the assumptions and valuations that they employ; frequently, through the compounding of errors, they may be less so. Deception is quite a different matter, involving submerged assumptions, unfairly chosen valuations, and purposeful misestimates. Bureaucratic agencies, for example, have powerful incentives to underestimate the costs of proposed projects. Any procedure for making policy choices, from divine guidance to computer algorithms, can be manipulated unfairly. Since project evaluation techniques have been widely used in the past, it is no surprise that they have also been misapplied in some circumstances. But they are also somewhat less susceptible to manipulation than the more informal approaches to decision making, for they are designed to highlight the ingredients that go into a choice. If presented in a professional manner, they lend themselves to the introduction of alternative sets of assumptions that enable the policy maker and his critics to see whether different conclusions would emerge. Thus an important contribution of benefit–cost analysis is the information it provides to the political process.

Project evaluation techniques have proven themselves in a variety of arenas. In the defense gap scare of the early 1960s, they changed military thinking by demonstrating that a Russian army division in Europe was far from equivalent to a NATO division. They were vital in showing that many of the well-intentioned programs of the Great Society were not accomplishing their stated missions. In the energy field, early project evaluations, unfortunately not heeded, showed that we should be pursuing a diversified set of nuclear energy options. Benefit–cost analyses provided the first conclusive evidence that supersonic passenger flight would be economically wasteful, at least for the 1970s. Recently, benefit–cost and cost-effectiveness studies have been applied to a wide range of medical procedures, helping doctors to determine, for example, which patients should be routinely screened for hypertension and how they should be treated.

The Procedure

In principle, the procedure followed in a benefit–cost analysis consists of five steps.

1. The project or projects to be analyzed are identified.
2. All the impacts, both favorable and unfavorable, present and future, on all of society are determined.
3. Values, usually in dollars, are assigned to these impacts. Favorable impacts will be registered as benefits, unfavorable ones as costs.[1]
4. The *net benefit* (total benefit minus total cost) is calculated.
5. The choice is made. Criteria for making this decision are discussed in a later section of this chapter.

Benefit–cost analysis is a tool, indeed a most sophisticated set of tools. The mechanical elements of benefit–cost analysis are decision rules to determine whether a project or projects should be undertaken, and if so at what scale of activity. These decision rules do not spring into existence by some magical process; rather they are carefully designed to ensure that public decisions accurately reflect what it is that the society wants to accomplish.

The formal rules for benefit–cost analysis use as inputs estimates of the benefits and costs of the projects. But a knowledge of these rules is only the beginning of wisdom for the decision maker. He must confront such matters as:

1. Deciding which rule is appropriate for use in any particular circumstance;
2. Placing a complex problem in a benefit–cost framework;
3. Computing estimates of benefits and costs; and
4. Deciding at what level of detail and sophistication an analysis should be conducted.

We will first review the formal rules for selecting projects. Then we will look at the complications that arise when the rules are applied.

---

[1] In this chapter we follow our usual practice of taking on one complication at a time; we assume that all impacts occur immediately. Chapter 10 is devoted to the question of how to value impacts that take place over time. The methods laid out there can be immediately incorporated in benefit–cost analysis.

Benefit–Cost Criteria: The Fundamental Rule

Let's suppose for the moment that we have already determined the benefits and costs, and hence the net benefits, of several proposed projects. How do we choose among them? In other words what should the decision rule be? All benefit–cost analyses hinge on the *Fundamental Rule*:

> In any choice situation, select the alternative that produces the greatest net benefit.

It is possible, of course, that all projects produce net benefits that are negative. In that case, the best alternative is "Do nothing," which at least produces a net benefit of $0. The fundamental rule guarantees that the benefits of any project undertaken will be large enough so that those who gain by the project *could* compensate those who lose, with everyone thus made better off.[2] Moreover, the rule further guarantees that the project actually chosen is superior to all others in this respect. For example, suppose we have a town with two citizens, Bill and John. They are trying to decide whether to build a new fire station in the north end or south end of town, or whether to stick with the present fire station. The net benefits of each alternative are shown in Table 9–1.

Table 9–1

	Present fire station	North end	South end
		Changes in net benefits	
Bill	$0	−$120	$330
John	$0	$250	−$140
Total	$0	$130	$190

If the station is built in the north end, John *could* give some of his gains to Bill so that both would wind up better off than under the present situation. For example, if he gave Bill $175, Bill would be $55 better off than with the present station and John would still be $75 to the good. If the fire station is built in the south end, even larger net benefits are available for *potential* redistribution; hence both can be made better off than under the north end option. Bill *could*, for example, pay John $230; John would wind up $90 ahead of the game and Bill still $100 ahead. Both would be better off than under the redistribution scheme suggested for the north end option. In short, if the project is chosen according to the fundamental rule, it will always be possible to find a pattern of side payments such that both Bill and John *would* be better off than under any other alternative.

---

[2] The criterion that benefits of a project must outweigh costs is formally known as the Kaldor–Hicks criterion. Its implications are discussed in Chapter 13.

The abundant use of italics in these statements has been purposeful: it is not required that the compensation *actually be carried out*, but only that the *possibility* of such compensation should exist. Consequently, a project may actually leave some people worse off than before it was undertaken. Benefit–cost analysis, in its traditional form, does not address distributional issues. Yet it can be of vital assistance in structuring effective policies when distribution is an important consideration. We give special attention to distributional issues later in this chapter. In the meantime, we will assume that distribution is not a matter of consequence, as it is not for most small-scale policy choices.

Following the Fundamental Rule: Subsidiary Choice Criteria

The application of the Fundamental Rule of benefit–cost analysis is most easily understood in the context of practical examples. We will discuss the hypothetical choice problems of an official concerned with conservation management. The four choice situations we consider are:

1. Accepting or rejecting a single project.
2. Choosing one of a number of alternative projects, when the choices are (a) discrete or (b) continuous.
3. Accepting or rejecting a number of projects, subject to a constraint on a resource. (The most frequent constrained resource is the total initial expenditure, but it could be total expenditure over time, or managerial hours, or acre-feet of water.)
4. Accepting or rejecting a number of projects, and choosing as well a level of operation for each, with the whole process subject to a resource constraint.

One suggestion before turning to our examples: we discuss choices that relate to the administration of a conservation area. Later we provide examples involving solid waste disposal for you to practice on. You should understand that the cases we consider may be extrapolated to a wide range of contexts; we hope that as you read through this chapter you will make a deliberate effort to relate the concepts and criteria to policy problems in your own field. It matters not whether the problem involves health, housing, or highways; the principles of effective policy choice remain the same.

Applying the Fundamental Rule: Four Examples

Case 1: Accepting or Rejecting a Single Project

Suppose the project under consideration is a new headquarters building for a large tract of conservation land. The Wildlife Management Authority, which operates the area, has one particular building in mind; funding and other inputs are not a problem. The initial cost of the building is estimated at $175,000; benefits in the form of net savings over the years on energy costs are calculated to be worth $150,000. (These savings over the years have been converted into a single current dollar figure.) The savings on maintenance costs that will result from more up-to-date headquarters are estimated to have a value of $75,000. (The analyst would doubtless have had to work very hard to develop these estimates.) The net benefit is:

$150,000 + $75,000 − $175,000 = $50,000

In this example the Authority must make a simple yes–no decision, between building the new headquarters with an estimated net benefit of $50,000 or not building with a net benefit of $0. Following the Fundamental Rule, net benefits are maximized if the Authority builds; $50,000 is larger than $0. But if net benefits were less than $0, the Fundamental Rule would tell us not to build. Thus in the straightforward yes–no case, the Fundamental Rule becomes "Adopt the proposal if net benefits are greater than $0."

Case 2a: Choosing One of a Number of Discrete Alternative Projects

Suppose that rather than a single proposal for a new headquarters building, the Wildlife Management Authority has before it eight alternative proposals for its capital construction program, ranging from minimal storage facilities to a complete operating plant with laboratories and hatcheries. Again, funding and other inputs are not a problem. The costs and benefits of the eight alternatives are summarized in Table 9–2. Project B promises the largest net benefit, $750,000, and should therefore be chosen.

Table 9–2

Headquarters	Initial cost	Savings on energy costs	Savings on maintenance costs	Total benefit	Net benefit
A	100	100	500	600	500
B	500	400	850	1250	750
C	200	200	600	800	600
D	75	25	150	175	100
E	150	50	325	375	225
F	200	150	250	400	200
G	50	75	100	175	125
H	150	175	275	450	300

(All figures are in thousands of dollars.)

Case 2b: Choosing the Appropriate Scale for a Project

The eight alternatives posed in Case 2a were mutually exclusive and quite different alternatives. Sometimes, however, alternatives are mutually exclusive because they involve alternative sizes of what is essentially the same proposal. This case explores that situation.

Suppose that the forest manager for our conservation area wants to make an informed decision on how much fertilizer to use on the area's nursery of tree seedlings. Fortunately, the experts at the state Forestry Experiment Station have extensive data on the benefits of fertilizer and also on what these benefits are worth in dollars for a tract of this type. The information provided may be expressed in the form of a graph, as shown in Figure 9–1. The forest manager's estimates of the cost of fertilization, including the cost of the fertilizer itself, are also shown in Figure 9–1.[3] In

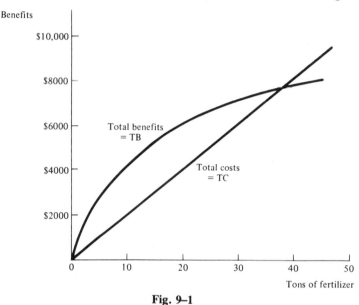

Fig. 9–1

Figure 9–2, net benefit = (total benefit − total cost) is shown. Net benefit reaches a maximum at about 15 tons. Hence 15 tons of fertilizer should be applied to the seedling forest.

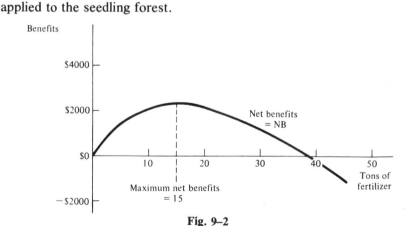

Fig. 9–2

---

[3] In actually solving a problem such as this, an analyst would ordinarily not rely on a graphical solution. Rather he would attempt to describe the relationships by equations, which would permit a more precise answer to be determined. Graphs are superior for expository purposes because they allow us to visualize what is going on.

This example is worth a further look because it gives us a chance to explore another version of the decision rule for determining the optimum scale of a project when project size is continuously variable. You will somtimes see the Fundamental Rule in this form: "Expand the size of the project to the point where marginal benefit equals marginal cost," or to put it another way, "Expand the size of the project to the point where marginal net benefit is 0." For the fertilizer case, these rules may be translated as "As long as the benefit from adding one more ton of fertilizer is greater than the cost of that addition, keep on adding fertilizer. When the additional benefit drops to the point where it just equals the additional cost of one more ton, stop right there." A crucial assumption is buried in this statement: eventually a stage is reached at which each additional ton of fertilizer will contribute less to total benefit than the preceding ton. This is the law of diminishing returns. It is of course not a physical law, but it does describe accurately a wide range of real-world phenomena. To rephrase the rule, as long as marginal benefit is greater than marginal cost, expanding the size of the project yields more than it costs; therefore you should expand. Net benefit is at a maximum at the point where it just stops paying to expand.[4]

An important point to remember about a marginal curve is that it provides no information in addition to that contained in the corresponding total curve. It is simply a different way of expressing the same information; either curve may be derived from the other. If you are to apply benefit–cost analysis, you had best get familiar with the process of transferring from total to marginal terms. To clarify the procedure, let's work through the exercise of deriving marginal curves from total curves. We start again with Figure 9–1, which shows total benefits and costs of fertilizer use. Columns (1), (2), and (3) in Table 9–3 were read directly from the graph. Net benefit is shown in column (4); it is simply total benefit (2) minus total

Table 9–3

(1) Tons	(2) TB	(3) TC	(4) NB	(5) MB_F	(6) MC_F	(7) MNB_F	(8) $MNB_\$$
5	2.5	1.0	1.5	.50	.2	.30	1.50
10	4.1	2.0	2.1	.32	.2	.12	0.60
15*	5.3	3.0	2.3	.24	.2	.04	0.20
20	6.1	4.0	2.1	.16	.2	−.04	−0.20
25	6.7	5.0	1.7	.12	.2	−.08	−0.40
30	7.2	6.0	1.2	.10	.2	−.10	−0.50
35	7.5	7.0	0.5	.06	.2	−.14	−0.70
40	7.8	8.0	−0.2	.06	.2	−.14	−0.20
45	8.0	9.0	−1.0	.04	.2	−.16	−1.00

* The optimal choice
TB, TC, and NB are in thousands of dollars.
MB_F, MC_F, and MNB_F are in thousands of dollars per ton of fertilizer.
$MNB_\$$ is in dollars per dollar of expenditure.

[4] For a case of increasing returns, look again at Figure 3–5; there the legal staff could perform more efficiently as it handled more and more cases of a single type.

cost (3). Marginal benefit per ton of fertilizer (MB_F) is obtained from columns (1) and (2) and is shown in column (5). For example, the marginal benefit per ton when 10 tons of fertilizer is used is the increase in total benefit over the last reading, or $4100 − $2500 = $1600, divided by the size of the increment, 5 tons. Therefore the marginal benefit when 10 tons of fertilizer are being used is $320 per ton.

Marginal cost and marginal net benefit per ton of fertilizer (MC_F and MNB_F, respectively) are derived in the same manner and are shown in columns (6) and (7). [Note that MNB_F could also have been computed by subtracting column (6) from column (5).] These numbers are approximations, of course; the smaller the tonnage intervals, the better the approximation and the smoother the resulting marginal curve.

It is important to observe that these marginal benefits decline as the amount of fertilizer used is increased. This is what we would expect, in the light of the law of diminishing returns. It is important to observe also that marginal quantities are always defined with respect to one particular input, here tons of fertilizer. We might have instead derived, say, the marginal net benefit per dollar of expenditure. This has been done in column (8). For example, the marginal net benefit per dollar of expenditure when total expenditures are $2000 is ($2100 − $1500)/($2000 − $1000) = $.60 per dollar of expenditures. To graph this, we would plot column (8) against column (3).

This long digression on marginal quantities might not be worth the trouble if the applications were limited to benefits and costs. In fact, situations where this type of marginal analysis is advantageous permeate the physical and economic world.

Sometimes projects are lumpy or "indivisible," in that they may be of one size or another but not of intermediate sizes. Continuous variation is impossible; marginal analysis is not applicable. Perhaps we can install one, two, or three turbines at a dam but not $2\frac{3}{4}$, or construct a building to a height of three, four, or five stories but not $4\frac{1}{4}$. Indivisibility situations require careful attention, but a commonsense application of the Fundamental Rule will still produce the correct decision. For example, if fertilizers were available only in 4-ton loads, the forest manager should apply 16 tons.

Case 3: Accepting or Rejecting a Number of Projects, Subject to a Constraint on a Resource

Suppose now that the eight alternative projects are not mutually exclusive. Instead they are proposals for a new headquarters for each of eight separate wildlife refuges. Suppose also that the Wildlife Management Authority's capital outlay funds for such facilities are limited to $500,000. Even if an additional $100,000 expenditure would yield $200,000 in net benefits, the Authority doesn't have the money to spend. Which of the new headquarters buildings should be built? The Fundamental Rule tells us to choose projects so that we get the maximum net benefit for the outlay of $500,000. We might tackle this in an ad hoc fashion by playing put and take with the projects, but since there are eight projects, each of which can be included or excluded, there are $2^8 = 256$ possible packages. Fortunately, there is an easier and more systematic way to go about it. Because initial cost is where the shoe pinches, calculate the net benefit per unit of initial cost and rank the projects according to this index. Then select projects from the top of the list down, until the $500,000 is used up. This calculation is shown in Table 9–4, with the projects ranked accordingly.

Table 9–4

Headquarters	Initial cost	Net benefit	Net benefit/ initial cost	Cumulative initial cost, all projects
A	100	500	5.0	100
C	200	600	3.0	300
G	50	125	2.5	350
H	150	300	2.0	500
E	150	225	1.5	650
B	500	750	1.5	1150
D	75	100	1.3	1225
F	200	200	1.0	1425

(All figures are in thousands of dollars.)

Now projects *A, C, G.* and *H* should be chosen, thereby exhausting the $500,000 budget. Proposal *B*, which we found to be the best when funds were unlimited, has been axed in favor of other projects that make more effective use of the constrained funds.[5]

We were fortunate this time to meet our budget constraint exactly. What happens when we have lumpy projects and things don't come out even? Suppose that Proposal *H* is replaced with *HH*, which has double the benefits and double the costs. The net-benefit/initial-cost ratio remains at 2.0, but now if we go ahead with *A, C,* and *G* there won't be enough money in the till to build *HH* as well. As this example is constructed, these are indivisible projects; there is no way to scale down any of them. If the budget cannot be stretched, and if budgetary procedures are such that unused funds cannot be carried forward to the next fiscal year, the list of projects to be accepted will have to be revised so that the largest possible total net benefit is achieved. In this case, *E* would replace *HH*.

In thinking about the problem of evaluating public policy proposals, it is only natural to slip into the habit of assuming that if there is a constraint, it is likely to be on dollar outlay. But this is not always the case, especially if the proposed project is relatively inexpensive, or if the funds required are only a small portion of a much larger budget. The problem may be that, although funds are ample, the desired input cannot be freely purchased on the market. On occasions the constrained input is land; we have 10 acres and cannot buy more. Or it may be a particular type of skilled labor; three

---

[5] If Project *B* is chosen, total net benefits will be $750,000. If *A, C, G,* and *H* are chosen, total net benefits will be ($500,000 + $600,000 + $125,000 + $300,000) = $1,525,000. Thus the limitation on initial expenditures completely changes the picture.

doctors are assigned to a clinic, or two GS–16s to a federal agency, and no more can be made available. For a developing country foreign exchange is likely to be constrained. Sometimes we find two or three constraints. In running a bicentennial celebration, for example, hotel rooms, mass transit, stadium capacity, and dollar expenditures may all be constrained; multiple constraints are discussed in the chapter on linear programming. For many policy proposals there is for all practical purposes no constrained input at all; everything required can be bought at a price, and the total expenditure does not exceed permissible outlays. For example, when the Environmental Protection Agency selects a set of pollution control regulations, its choice problems are matters primarily of prediction and valuation rather than limits on resources.

Where there is a constraint, we may be interested in finding out what that constraint costs us in terms of forgone opportunities. For example, perhaps one more dollar of initial expenditure beyond a constrained budget would permit an increase of $1.50 in total benefits. We say that the "shadow price" imposed by the initial cost constraint is $1.50 per dollar of initial cost. Shadow pricing is covered as well in the chapter on linear programming.

Case 4: Accepting or Rejecting a Number of Projects, and Choosing as Well a Level of Operation for Each, with the Whole Process Subject to a Resource Constraint

Suppose that the seedling situation is somewhat more complicated. Now we will assume that there are two tracts of different sizes, with different kinds of trees and soil conditions. If there are no constraints on resources of any type, the decision is straightforward. Each tract may be considered separately, and fertilization of each should be carried to the point where net benefit is a maximum. But suppose for some reason there isn't enough fertilizer to carry both of these projects to their optimum sizes. (Perhaps all of the fertilizer was purchased at the beginning of the year.) The Fundamental Rule says that the choice should be made so as to maximize net benefits, given the constraint on fertilizer. How should we go about this? As before, the Extension and Forestry Services provide total benefit and total cost data for each tract. From this data we can calculate net benefits and marginal net benefits. The marginal net benefits curves for the two tracts are shown in the left and middle diagrams of Figure 9–3.

Now we wish to allocate some fixed amount of fertilizer between the two tracts so that total net benefits from the two will be at a maximum. A moment's thought should convince you that each succeeding ton must be used on the tract where it will do more good, and that this means that the marginal net benefit produced by the last ton of fertilizer used must be the same for each tract. Otherwise total net benefits could be increased by reallocating some of the fertilizer from the tract with lower marginal net benefits to that with higher. Furthermore, we can calculate the quantity of fertilizer needed to achieve any level of marginal net benefit on the tracts by adding together the quantities represented on the individual marginal net benefit curves, MNB_1 and MNB_2 to get MNB_{1+2}, the right-most diagram. For example, if the level of marginal net benefits achieved on each tract is M, this requires using A tons on tract 1 and B tons on tract 2, or $A + B$ tons on tracts 1 and 2 together. Figure 9–3 thus also tells us the optimum level of marginal net benefit for each tract for whatever total amount of fertilizer is to be used. Once the amount of fertilizer is known, the appropriate amount for each tract may be determined by reversing the process and working leftward from curve MNB_{1+2} in Figure 9–3 to curves MNB_1 and MNB_2.

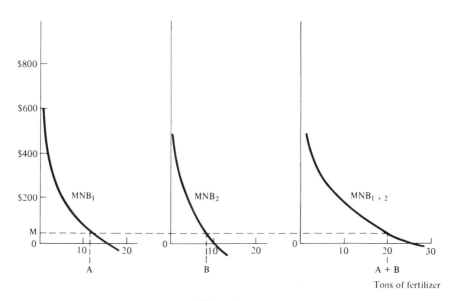

Fig. 9–3

In practice, the data for a problem such as this may be difficult to assemble; the relevant curves may not spring to view. Still the fundamental principles remain unchanged: allocate resources so as to maximize net benefits; allocate a constrained resource so that marginal net benefits are equal in each use. Even though information may be hard to monitor, we should still do our best to meet this condition. School boards and recreation departments, mayors and the Congress engage in this marginal equilibration process all the time, at least implicitly, in their procedures for choosing among competitors for funds. (Granted, they almost certainly call the process by another name.) When $100,000 has to be cut from the budget, they search for the place where it will hurt the least. Conversely, the school board's argument for spending more on textbooks in preference to field trips is that the books will provide greater benefits. And they will continue to spend more on books until the marginal net benefits for books and trips are perceived, however informally, as equal.

A Digression: Benefit/Cost Ratios

From time to time you will probably encounter a reference to a "benefit/cost ratio." Typically a project will be recommended because its benefit/cost ratio (i.e., its total benefits divided by its total costs) is greater than 1, or rejected because the ratio is less than 1. Or you will find that a project is adopted because it has the largest benefit/cost ratio among competing projects. In many circumstances the benefit/cost ratio criterion will lead to the same choice as the maximize-net-benefits criterion. But when choices must be made among mutually exclusive projects or when resources are constrained, the two criteria may lead to inconsistent choices. Although it is now generally recognized that the benefit/cost ratio is not a satisfactory criterion for choice, the old usage dies hard.

To see how the benefit/cost ratio can mislead us, suppose a local policy maker is considering alternative uses for a particular parcel of land. Budget constraints are not a consideration. Benefit–cost analysis produces the estimates shown in Table 9–5. In this situation, Project I has a higher benefit/cost ratio; Project II has larger net benefits. Since funding is not a problem, Project II should be selected.

Table 9–5

Project	Benefits	Costs	Net benefits	Benefit/cost ratio
I	$10,000	$1,000	$9,000	10
II	100,000	25,000	75,000	4.0

We should also note that the benefit/cost ratio is sensitive to how we choose to define benefits and costs. A municipal marina project costing $1 million might, for example, produce recreational benefits of $4 million and cause environmental damage of $2 million. Depending on whether that damage is regarded as a positive cost or a negative benefit, the benefit/cost ratio is 2 or 1.33. The maximize-net-benefits criterion is not susceptible to this ambiguity.

Practice in Applying Benefit–Cost Criteria

You are an analyst who is advising the city of Glenwood on solid waste disposal. You face the following decisions:

Decision 1. You must decide whether or not to recommend building a new incinerator. The incinerator would cost $100,000 a year to operate; this figure includes the amortized capital costs of initial construction. It is estimated that it would save $120,000 annually in alternative waste disposal and landfill costs. However, the citizens of Glenwood would be willing to pay $50,000 a year to avoid the air pollution that the incinerator would generate. Should the incinerator be constructed?

Decision 2. You must choose which of two types of incinerators to recommend for the city. Type *A* has virtually no pollution controls. It would cost $100,000 a year to build and operate. It is estimated that it would save $200,000 a year in alternative waste disposal and landfill costs, and would generate pollution that the citizens would pay $50,000 a year to avoid. Type *B* is equipped with an advanced scrubber. It would cost $140,000 a year, would save $200,000 a year in alternative waste disposal and landfill costs, and would eliminate all perceptible air pollution. Which incinerator should be built?

Table 9–6

| | | Costs | | |
Plant number	Land takings	Construction	Pollution	Benefits
1	60	100	70	300
2	70	100	50	260
3	80	100	85	360
4	120	100	100	400
5	40	100	40	220
6	20	100	30	200

Decision 3. You are considering a number of different incinerators for different parts of the city. The city may build as many as it wishes, but the total expenditure for land takings and construction is limited to $610,000. (Glenwood has a line-item budget, so other waste disposal funds cannot be allocated to incinerator expenditures.) The cost and benefit data (in $000) are shown in Table 9–6. Which incinerators should you recommend? (Answers will be found at the end of the book.)

Estimating Benefits and Costs

Failure to apply proper decision criteria, though it is an error to be avoided, is not a fault of many benefit–cost analyses. Difficulties in assigning values to benefits and costs, however, frequently present serious problems. Moreover, some of the consequences of a proposed policy measure may be overlooked altogether. We turn now to two elements that are critical in estimating benefits and costs, prediction and valuation.

Prediction

For each alternative project we must predict the inputs that will be employed and the outputs that will be achieved. This means that all impacts, favorable and unfavorable, must be identified. Suppose, for example, that the project to be analyzed is a proposal for a municipal incinerator to replace a suburban town dump. Some of the impacts (such as outlays for construction and maintenance) are immediate and obvious. The new arrangements may provide more (or perhaps less) satisfactory services to the dump's former patrons. Some of the second-order effects come quickly to mind: dump operating costs will be eliminated, as will the need to acquire more land for dump purposes, always a sticky issue in suburban towns. Other impacts may be inherently uncertain. For example, it is possible that policing illegal dumpers from across the town line will be easier, and this might in turn reduce substantially the volume of refuse to be handled. Even more problematical are the possible impacts on community health or on wildlife. By now it probably occurs to you that various types of descriptive models may be helpful in carrying out the analysis, which is one reason we spent so much time on models in earlier chapters and will spend a bit more in material to come.

One of the disturbing features of benefit–cost analysis is that, as history unfortunately shows, it offers no automatic protection against heroically bad assumptions. One of the authors of this book was asked to review a benefit–cost analysis of a project to eliminate the mosquitoes that carry dengue fever in the Western Hemisphere. The analysis, which had been prepared for the Pan American Health Organization, assumed that the reduced incidence of fever in areas where the mosquitoes are endemic would be proportional to population. But although the mosquitoes are prevalent in the southeastern United States, virtually no dengue fever is found there. This mistaken assumption led to a dramatic overstatement of dollar benefits, since the value of lost workdays was scaled to income levels and the United States has by far the highest per capita income in the mosquito-infested region.

Analysts should be aware that important side effects may be entirely neglected. The recent history of catalytic converters illustrates this oversight problem. It has been charged that although these devices substantially reduce emissions of carbon monoxide and hydrocarbons, emissions of sulfates are significantly increased. This is a cost of the new technology that was not foreseen by analysts in the Environmental Protection Agency and therefore was not included in the original analysis.

In other situations a benefit–cost analysis may find that total benefits justify total costs—without taking a careful look at what is going on at the margin. For example, an analysis may conclude that investing a requested sum in a particular piece of biomedical research is worthwhile, and ignore the important question of whether we should spend 10 percent more or less.

Hanke and Walker, in reevaluating the Bureau of Reclamation's proposed Nebraska Mid-State project, found many substantial errors in estimating the predicted benefits and costs. Ignored altogether were the negative impacts that would be felt downstream if the flow of water in the Platte River were reduced. The instream fishery would be destroyed and the central flyway disrupted; several endangered species—whooping cranes and bald eagles among others—would be further jeopardized. Moreover the opportunity cost of Platte water, now used by municipalities and industry, was overlooked.[6]

---

[6] This is only a partial catalogue of the analytic sins committed by the Bureau. For a full discussion, see Steve H. Hanke and Richard A. Walker, "Benefit–Cost Analysis Reconsidered: An Evaluation of the Mid-State Project," *Water Resources Research* 10, no. 5: 898–908.

Obviously, predicting outcomes is a difficult task; foolproof techniques for forecasting unforeseen consequences are by definition nonexistent. Even foreseen consequences that are of uncertain magnitude can be predicted only on a probabilistic basis. But analysts can take a few precautionary steps. They can think deliberately and explicitly about possible unexpected side effects, and about how to elicit expert testimony about them. They can check their conclusions to see how sensitive they are to small changes in the input data. They can try to choose strategies that permit sequential decision making as more information becomes available.

Valuation

Given these predictions of favorable and unfavorable impacts, we must next attach values to them. Unfavorable impacts will be registered as costs, favorable ones as benefits.[7] The usual measuring rod is money—the unit, dollars.

How can we quantify the benefits and costs of a project? One obvious method is to value the benefits and costs of a project by referring to the market values of the resources that it consumes and the goods that it produces. Thus, in a recreation program, the salaries the swimming instructors are actually paid are a good measure of costs. In assessing a housing project, benefits should be valued at the normal rental prices of equivalent units. Although this market value approach is simple in concept, we may encounter serious difficulties when we get around to actual measurement. In fact market prices will rarely be a satisfactory measure for all of the benefits and costs of a public project. For example, we need municipal parks and incinerators because, for understandable reasons, the private sector does not provide them in sufficient quantities; hence no market price exists for the services of these facilities. Environmental regulations have become necessary because we have no market in which rights to clean air can be bought and sold; hence there is no market price for clean air. A market price—even if available—is not an appropriate indicator of value if the project is so large that it will alter relative prices in the economy. A large power plant in an isolated area might have such an effect on the price of electricity. Other situations where market prices are unsatisfactory guides to value are discussed at length in Chapter 14 under the headings "Externalities" and "Market Power." In the meantime it is more relevant to turn to other methods for valuing benefits and costs.

Willingness-to-Pay as an Appropriate Measure of Benefits

Consider the case of a new parking garage at a state university. Before the garage was built, parking was very inconvenient; people parked in a distant lot owned by the university. Now they pay $1 a day to park in the garage, although many would be willing to pay more. What is the total value of the new garage to the users?

---

[7] We noted above that an unfavorable impact may sometimes be treated as a cost, sometimes as a negative benefit, and that for the procedures recommended here it doesn't matter.

Assume that demand for parking spaces responds to the price that is set as shown by the demand curve in Figure 9–4. A $1 charge then results in 1000 cars parked. If we use the market price to estimate the value of the garage to users, the total benefit is $1000 per day. But many of the users— in fact all but the "last" one—would have been willing to pay more than $1; the demand curve indicates that some 500 of them would have paid as much as $2, and one would pay almost $3. If the university could extort from each parker the maximum amount he would be willing to pay, while keeping its minimum charge at $1 per car, it would collect a total amount equivalent to the shaded area, an amount considerably greater than $1000. This amount is the value or total benefit of the garage to those who would use it if the fee charged were $1 per car. A quick glance at the diagram (and a little arithmetic) suggests that the total value of the garage to its users is thus $2000. Parkers would pay only a total of $1000. We say that the *consumers' surplus*—the value of purchases of parking to consumers over and above what they pay for it—is $2000 − $1000 = $1000.

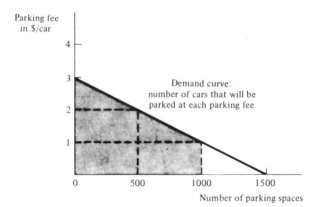

Fig. 9–4

Moreover, even when no market price at all is available because none exists, this concept of what people would be willing to pay guides us to an accurate valuation. In principle, the benefits of a project may be regarded as the total amount that individuals are willing to pay rather than go without the project. Earlier in this chapter we posited a town with two citizens, Bill and John; suppose they have made their fire station decision and now contemplate constructing a park. The benefits of the park are the sum of the amounts Bill and John are willing to pay rather than go without it. Thus if Bill would be willing to pay up to $300 and John $200, we say that the park will produce benefits of $500.

Willingness-to-pay, it should be stressed, is the maximum amount an individual would pay if his contribution would make the difference between adopting and not adopting the project. It is not the amount he may in practice be forced to pay, nor the amount that he has been observed to pay—it is what he would pay if the chips were down. (If he dislikes the project and is willing to pay some amount to prevent its being undertaken, then the negative benefit of the project to him is the minimum payment to him that would make him prefer project-plus-payment to the status quo.)

Willingness-to-pay calculations are often employed—in principle, at least—to determine whether a particular good should be publicly provided; Bill's and John's town park is a prime armchair example. Frequently, government agencies use market surveys to estimate public demand for proposed projects, although the surveyors must be on guard against those who for strategic reasons overstate their liking or distaste for the project. The National Academy of Sciences study of air pollution employed still another approach, extrapolating from housing prices and wage differentials in areas with differing pollution levels to estimate people's willingness to pay for reduced tailpipe emissions.[8]

One of the great virtues of the benefit–cost approach, as informed by willingness-to-pay calculations, is that the interests of individuals who are poorly organized or less closely involved are counted. (This contrasts with most political decision making procedures.) Even when pushed by powerful interest groups, projects whose benefits do not outweigh their costs will be shown to be undesirable. The benefits and costs accruing to all—to the highway builders, the environmentalists, the "little people," the users and providers of services, the taxpaying public—will be counted on a dollar-for-dollar basis. Benefit–cost analysis is a methodology with which we pursue efficiency and which has the effect of limiting the vagaries of the political process.

Measuring the Costs of a Project

At first glance, we might think that the costs of a project are easier to quantify than the benefits. And to the extent that costs may be regarded simply as the monetary value of the resources devoted to the project, this is true. But in some situations the market prices of these resources may be an inaccurate guide to the true costs. For one thing, large-scale government intervention in a market may bring about a substantial price change. When we initiate national health insurance, for example, we may well find that the prices of doctors' services are bid up. Income will be transferred to doctors, but the real quantity of services supplied and resources employed may show little change.

In considering whether to replace the suburban dump with an incinerator, for example, the initial construction cost could be directly ascertained, at least approximately, because incinerator construction is regularly bought and sold on the market, and in relatively small quantities. On the other hand, estimating the cost of the land to be used may not be as simple as it appears. The true cost to the town is not what was paid for the land, or even its current market value—the true cost is the value of the land to the town in its best alternative use. This value is known as the *opportunity cost*. The concept is so important that we'll take the trouble to pin it down

---

[8] *Air Quality and Automobile Emission Control,* Volume 4, prepared for the Committee on Public Works, U.S. Senate, September 1974.

more precisely. Suppose that the land the town plans to use for the incinerator was purchased 25 years ago for $20,000. The only alternative use contemplated for it is as an extension to the high school athletic complex. The net benefits over time of this extension are estimated at $200,000. Then the real cost to the town if the parcel is used for the incinerator is $200,000, even though it would bring much less if sold on the open market, for $200,000 is the amount of net benefits forgone if the athletic complex cannot be extended. If the town has no use for the land other than as an incinerator site, then the opportunity cost is the selling price. Opportunity cost is a decision making rather than an accounting concept. Corporations don't use it in preparing their tax returns, and the Internal Revenue Service wouldn't accept it if they did. But a corporation that fails to consider opportunity cost in making decisions will base those decisions on the wrong inputs. For example, the true cost to a company of using one of its scientists on a particular research project is not her salary, but the value of the research she would produce on the best alternative project. If there is no alternative project and the scientist's salary must be paid whether she works or not, the opportunity cost is $0. Opportunity costs are most likely to be ignored when the decision-making unit contemplates using a resource it already has on hand. For example, a town that owns a tract of conservation land may not take the value of the land into account in estimating the costs of the highway it proposes to build through it. Such an error can result in a sizeable overstatement of the net benefits of the highway project.

Frequently, of course, costs will occur in the form of unfavorable impacts, in other words as negative benefits. In the chapter on queues we discussed the deadweight losses of making people wait in line. In another context, how would we value the negative benefits of converting a historic building to a bus depot, or of extending Route I–93 through New Hampshire's Franconia Notch at serious risk to the Old Man of the Mountain and other unique features of the Notch? The willingness-to-pay approach still holds: the true costs of unfavorable impacts are the total amount that people would be willing to pay to avoid them.

The intangible costs of the proposed incinerator would be difficult to quantify. If in building the incinerator the town will seriously encroach on a valuable swamp, the resulting wildlife and flood control costs will be inflicted on all citizens of the area. But little market experience will be available to guide estimates of what people would be willing to pay to avoid those costs. Some form of survey or perhaps statistical extrapolation from related data might be helpful. Matters become considerably more complex when we trace through to second-order effects. Plants and animals will be affected; this will lead to consequences higher up the food chain. Here too we urge that a willingness-to-pay measure be employed to quantify what otherwise might be unquantifiable values. Even if for political or other reasons we can't ask questions directly, it is wise to keep this point in mind, asking yourself, for instance, how much people would probably pay to avoid the intangible costs of the incinerator. It is a tough question, but an essential one.

We should not underestimate either the complexity or the importance of estimating intangible costs and benefits. How do we feel about the 100 brown pelicans that are killed by hot water discharges from a nuclear power plant? People's valuations will reflect not only the worth of the pelicans, but also their opinions about man's attitudes toward nature and their suspicions that the death of the pelicans may be a signal that something more serious is going on. These are very delicate values indeed.

In some cases, it may be best to avoid quantifying some intangibles as long as possible, carrying them along instead in the form of a written paragraph of description. Maybe we will find that the intangible considerations point toward the same decision as the more easily quantified attributes. Maybe one or a few of them can be adequately handled by a decision maker without resort to quantification. We will find no escape from the numbers; they should be dealt with as honestly and accurately as possible. Ultimately the final decision will implicitly quantify a host of intangibles; there are no incommensurables when decisions are made in the real world.

Cost Effectiveness

In some situations the purpose of a government expenditure is specific and well understood, yet benefits and costs are hard to compare directly. In defense or health protection expenditures, it is often difficult to measure benefits in dollar terms. If the Department of Defense desires a given amount of transport capability, alternative systems may be investigated to determine which of them is the lowest cost method of providing that capability. The County Health Department may proceed in a like manner in choosing among alternative means for providing prenatal checkups for a given number of pregnant low-income women.

A related situation—in fact it's more or less the other side of the coin—arises when the total expenditure for a given purpose is fixed and alternative projects are evaluated to see which is most effective in achieving that purpose. If a Town Meeting appropriates $100,000 for a municipal swimming pool, the Recreation Commission will simply compare alternative pools directly, in whatever metric they decide is appropriate, rather than trying to convert the benefits of the various options into dollars. In any such case of a fixed sum to be spent, the benefits need not be expressed in dollars, for the alternatives can simply be compared against one another in whatever units we choose to measure the benefits.

These truncated versions of benefit–cost analysis are known as cost-effectiveness analysis. They are characterized by the measurement of costs and benefits in different units, with no need to search for a common metric. To put the matter briefly, cost-effectiveness analysis is applicable when (a) costs of alternative projects are identical and hence only benefits need be compared, which relieves the analyst of the need to convert benefits to dollars, or (b) when benefits are identical and hence only costs need be compared.

We can illustrate the principles of cost effectiveness with a simplified analysis of rodent control. Two alternative methods are available for eliminating the rats. Method A involves sending in an extermination team; it costs $100 per apartment visited and is 90 percent likely to be successful in any particular apartment. Method B involves sending workers to put poisons in places where the rats are likely to find and devour them. It costs only $40 per apartment, but is only 50 percent likely to be successful. The Rat Control Agency has $10,000 to spend. Five hundred apartments are believed to be rat infested.

First, it is clear that neither method could be applied to all the apartments; even the cheaper treatment would cost $20,000. The question is which program will achieve more for the $10,000 the city can spend. We can calculate the answer in a straightforward manner. Method A could be applied to $10,000/$100 = 100 apartments; on average it would relieve 90 of them of infestation. (We assume that the apartments are chosen at random and that success in one apartment is independent of success in another. The latter is, of course, a dubious assumption; a more realistic model of the extermination process could readily be incorporated in the analysis. We also assume that distributional considerations can be neglected; that is, we don't care whose apartment is freed of rats.) Method B could be applied to $10,000/$40 = 250 apartments; it would on average eliminate the rats in 125 of them. Method B is therefore preferred.

This result can be related directly to the Fundamental Rule for benefit–cost analysis, which we set forth on page 137, in any choice situation select the alternative that produces the greatest net benefit. In cost-effectiveness analysis, the rule is parallel: select the alternative that produces the maximum effectiveness. Method A produces .9 apartments freed of rats for every $100 spent; its effectiveness is .9/$100 = .009 apartments per dollar. Method B produces .5 apartments freed for $40 spent; its effectiveness is .5/$40 = .0125 per dollar.

The Rat Control Agency will surely go to the mayor and argue that it must have funds enough to cover all the apartments. Indeed, it will claim that Method A should be applied to all of them. A 90 percent chance of eliminating the rats from an apartment for the expenditure of a mere $100, they argue, will more than pay for itself in the future vermin control expenditures saved—leaving aside altogether the benefits in the form of reduced costs of health care. But the City Council is unmoved, and the Rat Control Agency determines that, given its limited budget, it gets the most for its money by following Method B.

Here, with only two treatments possible, each of which can be applied to as many apartments as funds permit, the calculations are easy. Matters are more complicated if a third method is also available. Method C is an area-wide approach to vermin control. It could be used only on the 50 apartments down near the docks and would cost a total of $3000. The chance of success is 80 percent. Its effectiveness is therefore $(.80 \times 50)/\$3000 = .0133$ apartments per dollar. If the Rat Control Agency could apply its whole budget to Method C, 167 apartments would be protected with 80 percent probability of success, for an expected protection level of 133 apartments. But Method C can be used for the 50 waterfront apartments only. Consequently the agency should use Method C to the extent possible, spending $3000, and then spend the remaining $7000 on Method B. Table 9–7 summarizes the necessary information.

Table 9 7

Method	Number of apartments to which applicable	Cost per apartment	Number of apartments that can be treated	Probability of success for each apartment	Effectiveness: apartments freed per dollar of spending
A	500	$100	100	.9	.009
B	500	40	250	.5	.0125
C	50	60	50	.8	.0133

Sometimes a method of control will work better for some apartments than for others. In that case it should be treated as two separate methods, with the number of apartments to which each is applicable apportioned accordingly.

Occasionally an extension of cost-effectiveness analysis is useful for investigating alternative budgetary allocations for a public purpose. The analyst may then be asked to measure benefits and costs in different units, detailing the maximum benefit that can be achieved for each amount of expenditure, and leaving the final choice of amount to higher level decision makers.

Because benefits and costs are measured in different units, cost-effectiveness analysis provides no direct guidance when we are unsure whether the total benefit from an undertaking justifies the total cost, or when we are trying to select the optimal budget level for a project. But if we know what we have to achieve, or what we are allowed to spend, it is an appropriate criterion that reduces the complexity of choice.

Benefit–Cost Analysis and Redistributional Objectives

We noted earlier that benefit–cost analysis, in its traditional form, does not take income distribution into account. This does not imply that policy makers who rely on this tool are not concerned about distribution. Indeed, politically astute policy makers cannot ignore the distributional implications of proposed projects. Rather, it reflects a view that the choice of public projects should not be a primary means for accomplishing distributional goals. It is usually suggested that the major distributional weapons in our arsenal of policies should be the tax system and transfer programs.

(Transfer programs are those that give funds directly to people, such as Social Security, welfare programs, and unemployment compensation.) Using public projects to achieve redistributional goals is criticized as inefficient; the poor can be made better off, at less expense to the rest of society, by direct means.

Whatever the merits of these arguments, the benefit–cost framework lends itself well to analyses that do wish to make redistribution an explicit consideration, and in recent years it has frequently been employed to do so, mostly in evaluating alternative welfare reform plans. The most general (though most difficult) procedure is to classify the benefits and costs on a person-by-person or group-by-group basis. For example, suppose a decision maker must choose between housing program A, its competitor B, or neither. Net benefit estimates for A and B are shown in Table 9–8; if no program is undertaken, the net benefits are of course $0.

Table 9–8
Net Benefits ($000) to Group in Society

	Program A	Program B
Elderly poor	180	0
Poor families with children	0	220
Middle-class taxpayers	−200	−250
Net benefits to society as a whole	−20	−30

Total net benefits—which might more accurately be labeled net efficiency benefits now that we have redistributional benefits in mind as well—for both programs are negative. Yet we often undertake programs that yield zero (or even negative) net benefits because we believe they achieve redistributional objectives that for one reason or another cannot be pursued directly. We regard the loss in efficiency as more than offset by the distributional gains. If our strongest concerns are for the elderly poor, project A may seem attractive. If, however, other relatively inexpensive means are available to transfer funds to the elderly poor, we may prefer direct transfers and no housing program.

From time to time you may see references to redistributional benefits of programs that outweigh the loss in efficiency. The basic approach is that just outlined; benefits to different groups are distinguished and tallied up. But where do we draw the line? How do we know redistributional benefits outweigh the loss in efficiency? Making the statement implies that somehow we have found a way to measure redistributional benefits. And measuring redistributional benefits is a tricky business.

One method of attacking the problem is simply to measure the net efficiency benefits that the "deserving" group receives. Let us say we wish to redistribute income from the landlords to the peasants; two projects are available. Table 9–9 shows the benefits and costs that will accrue to each group under each project.

Table 9–9

	Benefits	Costs	Net benefits
	(all amounts in $000)		
Project I			
Landlords	100	90	10
Peasants	30	20	10
Whole society	130	110	20
Project II			
Landlords	40	80	−40
Peasants	40	10	30
Whole society	80	90	−10

Which project should we choose? Project I is superior in terms of efficiency benefits, Project II in terms of redistributional benefits. But we cannot add together these two different types of benefits, any more than we can add together kilowatt-hours of electricity and gallons of water. Efficiency benefits are not commensurate with redistributional benefits once again we encounter the familiar problem of competing objectives. We would have no difficulty in choosing a project if one of them offered the greatest efficiency as well as the greatest redistributional benefits. Unfortunately this will rarely be the case.

Our problem would be easier if the decision maker could state his preferences in such a form as "In my opinion, $3 in redistributional benefits are worth $1 in net efficiency benefits." Such a preference function, however, may be complicated and hard to formulate; the trade-off rate may depend partly on the levels of benefits that are obtained. In principle one possible approach is to construct the decision maker's entire indifference map, with the two types of benefits measured on the axes. This would point directly to the best choice. But most decision makers would find it exceptionally difficult—and perhaps politically suicidal—to define their indifference maps. In practice, a public decision maker is likely to be a satisficer of a sort. A minimum level of redistributional benefits that he wishes to achieve is set, and the maximize-net-benefits rule is then applied to all projects that satisfy this condition. The philosopher-king who makes all public choices for the landlords and peasants might announce, for example, "I will choose the project that maximizes net efficiency benefits provided it results in at least a $25 net benefit for each peasant." In our own society, we find that project choices are frequently subject to the constraint that the poor shall not be made worse off, or sometimes that the rich shall not be made better off. The rhetoric, however, is more powerful than the reality; constraints that are sacred when choosing among proposed projects are often ignored, for instance, when tax or regulatory policies must be determined. U.S. airline regulations, for example, mandate more frequent service than is required to serve all who wish to travel. A convenience is thereby provided, benefiting mainly the well-to-do, that results in higher fares for all—a tradeoff that most of us, and the poor in particular, are probably unwilling to make.

Finally, even though narrow efficiency criteria may be overridden for redistributional reasons in choosing among projects, a benefit–cost analysis will highlight the nature of the choice and make explicit the price we pay to promote equity.

Benefit–Cost Analysis in Perspective

We end this discussion by reiterating an initial point: benefit–cost analysis is an approach to decision making and not a cut-and-dried formula. Many times an understanding of benefit–cost analysis will provide insights into public choice problems, even when the techniques themselves are not employed. Benefit–cost analysis is a framework for keeping our thinking straight in evaluating projects, a framework that demands explicit attention to determining the impacts of a proposal and assigning values to these impacts. But it is no more than a tool; it cannot provide a ready answer to either of these determinations, for they are ultimately matters of judgment. It does force the judgments out into the open so that they can be subjected to public scrutiny and constructive debate.

10 The Valuation of Future Consequences: Discounting

Many decisions made today will have repercussions next year and in the years thereafter. Some decisions will have effects that stretch for decades. Up to now in this volume we have tacitly assumed that all the consequences of a policy choice are felt immediately, a simplification that was useful for purposes of discussion. At this point we drop it, for it is obviously totally unrealistic. We must now find a method for comparing the desirability of outcomes that include consequences occurring at different times in the future. How, for example, should we evaluate proposals to support research on fusion power, an energy source unlikely to be commercially available until the 21st century? Should we proceed with a tidal power project in Passamaquoddy Bay between Maine and New Brunswick, which would require a heavy initial expenditure for construction but would produce electric power at a low operating cost for many years? How should we value investments in human resources? When we assess manpower training programs, for example, we must recognize that they provide a stream of benefits and costs stretching into the future. In exchange for training expenses and loss of students' earnings while they are in training, we hope to provide an individual with the ability to earn more for many years into the future. On a more down-to-earth level, how should we choose between two techniques for filling potholes? Those filled with material A stay filled on average two years. Those filled with more expensive material B have a life expectancy roughly twice that long.

If we are to make difficult choices among actions that yield streams of benefits and costs stretching into future years, we must extend the model of choice to enable us to make systematic comparisons between costs and benefits that are incurred and realized at different stages in time. Usually we are asked to compare streams of costs and benefits that have been converted into dollars. Consider a choice between two proposed projects, X and Y. Project X is built in one year at an initial cost of $10,000. It then yields a declining stream of benefits over a five-year period. Project Y takes two years to build. Initially costs are $10,000 in the first period and $5000 in the second period. It then yields a level benefit stream for its remaining four-year life span. The complete streams are shown in Table 10–1.

Table 10–1

Project	Year					
	0	1	2	3	4	5
X	−10	+5	+4	+3	+2	+1
Y	−10	−5	+6	+6	+6	+6

(All figures are in thousands of dollars.)

Which of these two streams is preferable? Most of us find it hard to compare them intuitively. And even if we come up with an ad hoc preference in this situation, we can have no confidence that we will make consistent choices over many such situations. This choice problem is faced repeatedly by governments, taxable and nonprofit corporations, and individuals, for all must make decisions that take future costs and benefits into account. Consequently it is not surprising that a standard procedure, called *discounting*, has been developed for handling the matter of valuations over time.

The essence of discounting is that it reduces a stream of costs and/or benefits to a single amount, termed the *present value*, by using the method of compound interest. The calculation of present value is thus a calculation of net benefit that takes explicit account of the timing of costs and benefits. The benefit–cost criteria that were developed in the last chapter may then be applied, with the term *net benefit* understood to mean "the present value of the discounted stream of net benefits."

The basic rationale is this: everyone, under almost any circumstances, would prefer $1 now to $1 a year from now. A sum of money in hand is worth more than a promise of the same sum at a specified time in the future, because the money may be invested so as to produce earnings in the intervening time. This is true whether the money is to be invested by an individual or by a business, or by a government that must raise the necessary funds through taxation or borrowing, although to be sure the uses for the money will differ. Take the simplest case, that of an individual. Suppose Mrs. Robinson is to be paid $100 a year from now. There is some lesser sum that she can invest today, for instance by depositing it in a savings bank, that will accumulate to $100 by the time the year has passed. This lesser sum is the present value of the payment a year hence of $100.

Note carefully that we are not saying anything about risk; we assume no risk is involved here and that Mrs. Robinson's $100 is as certain as anything can be. Rather, we are saying that having to wait for payment means forgoing the income that could be earned on the money in the meantime. In other words, waiting carries a cost in the form of a lost opportunity. This is not to suggest that risk should be ignored in analyzing a project—far from it—but merely that this is not where it enters the analysis. The problem of decision making under conditions of risk and uncertainty will be considered later in this book. In the real world, uncertainty and pure waiting are often entangled; it is important that we understand that they are separate phenomena.

Although the calculation of present value ordinarily involves flows of dollar amounts, the method is applicable to any stream where all the returns are measured in the same units. (Thus, we could discount recreation days or acre-feet of water, or additions to food stocks.) We discuss below both the actual mechanics of the calculation and the theoretical and practical problems that arise in the choice of a discount rate.

The Mechanics: The Arithmetic of Present Value

We have just seen that waiting involves an opportunity cost; naturally the question is "How much?" What is the present value of a payment one year from now of $100? Clearly it depends on our assumption about what return a sum of money invested today will earn over the coming year. Suppose it will earn 5 percent; if we invest $100 today, it will accumulate to $105 by a year from now. If we invest $90 now, we will have $94.50 then. And there is some amount X that we can invest today at 5 percent interest that will give us exactly $100 a year from now:

$$X(1 + .05) = 100,$$

or

$$X = \frac{100}{1.05} = 95.24.$$

We say that $95.24 is the *present value* of $100 payable a year from now at an annual *discount rate* of 5 percent. If the rate that could be earned were 10 percent, the present value would be:

$$\frac{\$100}{1.10} = \$90.91.[1]$$

At this point you may ask, "What is this discount rate? It looks like an interest rate!" Indeed it does; interest rate and discount rate are different names for what is arithmetically the same thing. It is customary, however, to use the two terms in different contexts. When we start with a sum of money and calculate the earnings on it forward into the future, we speak of the interest rate. When we start with a given sum at some time in the future and calculate back in time to the present to determine the present value, we speak of the discount rate. As far as the arithmetic is concerned it's almost a distinction without a difference. We saw in the section on

---

[1] For simplicity, we assume an accounting period of one year. The implications of shorter or longer periods were discussed in the section on difference equations.

difference equations that when we compute compound interest we write

$$S_1 = (1 + r)S_0$$

where S_1 is the sum of money after one year, r is the rate of interest, and S_0 is the initial sum. When we discount, we simply move the discount factor $(1 + r)$ over to the other side of the equation and write:

$$S_0 = \frac{S_1}{1 + r}$$

Although r is still a rate of interest, we now call it the discount rate.

There is good reason to continue to use both terms. The interest rate, or to be more exact the whole complex of interest rates, including rates paid by savings banks on deposits, rates paid by homeowners on their mortgages, rates paid by businesses on commercial paper and on long-term loans, and rates paid by governments on their debts, is determined in the capital markets. As far as we are concerned, it is given to us exogenously. The discount rate, on the other hand, is deliberately (but not arbitrarily) chosen by the person performing an analysis. He may be making this choice according to very strict guidelines, and the various interest rates currently available in the market will bear heavily on his choice. Nevertheless it is a choice, and a very sensitive one at that, as we shall shortly see. Consequently it is useful to preserve the parallel terminology, and you should soon find yourself comfortable with it.

To get back to the main thread of this discussion, it should be clear that the general formula for the present value (PV) of a sum of money S_1 payable a year from now, assuming a discount rate r, is

$$PV = \frac{S_1}{1 + r}$$

And after all our work on difference equations you should expect the present value of a sum S_n payable n years from now to be

$$PV = \frac{S_n}{(1 + r)^n}$$

This implicitly assumes that if PV_0 is the present value today of a future payment, and PV_1 is what the present value of that payment would be if we were to figure it one year hence, then

$$PV_0 = \frac{PV_1}{1 + r}$$

In other words, we can treat a present value calculated as of some time in the future exactly as if it were a payment occurring at that time.

Furthermore, we don't care whether the sum is payable *to* us or *by* us. The formula still holds. You might think a little about the implications of this. It means that if we owe money, we would prefer to pay later rather than sooner, because the later we pay, the less will be the present value of the amount paid. If we are owed money, the opposite will be true. Extending this idea to public projects, it means that all other things being equal, we should prefer a project with early benefits and deferred costs to one where the reverse holds.

Ordinarily, public projects do not result in a single benefit at some time in the future. Rather, a stream of costs and benefits is generated over time. The present value of such a stream is simply the sum of the present values of the individual items. We may illustrate this with the two projects X and Y that were mentioned at the beginning of the chapter. For convenience, here they are again:

Table 10–1

Project	Year					
	0	1	2	3	4	5
X	−10	+5	+4	+3	+2	+1
Y	−10	−5	+6	+6	+6	+6

(All figures are in thousands of dollars.)

We need two pieces of information in order to calculate the present values of these projects: (1) When within each year does each of these payments occur? Clearly it makes a difference whether the payment takes place at the beginning or end of each year.[2] We will follow convention in assuming that in this case all payments are made at the end of the year. (2) More important, what discount rate is appropriate? A later section will consider this choice. For now we will specify several arbitrary discount rates and see how they work out.

Suppose we apply a discount rate of 5 percent. Project X will yield a net benefit (in thousands of dollars) of −10 immediately, and the present value of this is simply −10. At the end of the first year there is an additional yield of +5, with a present value of $5/1.05 = 4.76$. The present value of the second year flow of +4 is $4/(1.05)^2 = 3.63$, and so on. The total present value of X, PV_X, is

$$PV_X = -10 + \frac{5}{1.05} + \frac{4}{(1.05)^2} + \frac{3}{(1.05)^3} + \frac{2}{(1.05)^4} + \frac{1}{(1.05)^5}$$
$$= 3.41 \text{ or } \$3410$$

---

[2] We dwelt at considerable length on this period problem in the chapter on difference equations and won't go into it further here except to wave one yellow flag. Beware the word *now*. Sometimes it truly does mean right now—but then again sometimes it means one year from now.

"Many financial problems involve sequences of equal payments made at intervals of one year; the first payment being made one year from now, the last payment being made n years from now. . . . [T]he stream will be said to *start now* and *last n years* even though the first payment does not actually occur until the end of this year." (Harvard Business School, "Time Value of Money," 9–172–060, p. 3.)

There is no sure way to handle this confusing terminology, other than to be on the lookout for it.

Similarly,

$$PV_Y = -10 - \frac{5}{1.05} + \frac{6}{(1.05)^2} + \frac{6}{(1.05)^3} + \frac{6}{(1.05)^4} + \frac{6}{(1.05)^5}$$
$$= 5.50 \text{ or } \$550\upsilon$$

If it is indeed appropriate to employ a discount rate of 5 percent, we should prefer project Y.

What would these present values look like with some other choices of the discount rate? If we carried out the calculations we would find results as shown in Table 10–2. These results are then plotted in Figure 10–1.

Suppose X and Y are competing proposals. We see from the graph that if the discount rate is between 0 and about 13 percent, project Y is preferred because it has a larger present value. If it is between 13 and 20 percent, project X should be chosen. And if it is greater than 20 percent, both X and Y have a negative present value and neither should be carried forward.

The proposed Passamaquoddy tidal power project offers a compelling demonstration of the significance of the discount rate in choosing appropriate projects. This project had long been advocated as a promising Canadian–American joint venture. An early benefit–cost analysis was completed in 1959. Using the same benefit and cost figures, the U.S. analysts (the Army Corps of Engineers) recommended adoption of the proposal while their Canadian counterparts recommended rejection. The project would have required a heavy initial capital investment; the flow of benefits

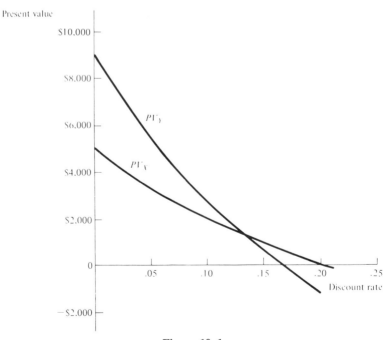

Figure 10–1

Table 10-2

Discount rate	PV_X	PV_Y
0	5.00	9.00
.02	4.33	7.50
.04	3.71	6.14
.06	3.13	4.90
.08	2.59	3.77
.10	2.09	2.74
.12	1.64	1.81
.14	1.20	.95
.16	0.78	.16
.18	0.41	−.56
.20	0.05	−1.23

(PV$_X$ and PV$_Y$ are in thousands of dollars.)

would have stretched far into the future. The source of the disagreement was the choice of discount rate. The U.S. analysts used a rate of 2.5 percent, which produced a positive present value, while the Canadian choice of 4.125 percent resulted in a negative present value.

The choice between thermal and hydroelectric power plants provides another illustration of the importance of the discount rate. For a thermal plant, initial capital outlay accounts for about 35 to 40 percent of the cost per megawatt of output.[3] For a hydroelectric plant, the initial outlay runs to 80 or 85 percent of the unit cost of power. A high discount rate thus favors the thermal plant because more of the costs are postponed. As the discount rate falls, it becomes less and less advantageous to delay expenditures as long as possible, and at some level of the rate the hydroelectric plant will become more economical.

The Internal Rate of Return

Sooner or later you are sure to encounter the scientific-sounding term *internal rate of return*. Hence you should know what it means and understand its implications. The discount rate at which the present value of a project becomes zero is known as its internal rate of return. By looking at the graph in Figure 10-1, we see that the internal rate of return for project X is about 20 percent; for project Y, about 16.5 percent. For a yes–no decision on a single project, the choice criterion associated with this concept is: "Undertake a project if its internal rate of return is greater than the appropriate discount rate." Thus if the choice is between carrying out project X and doing nothing, we should proceed with the project if the appropriate discount rate is less than 20 percent. The criterion is based on the intuitively appealing assumption that a project should be undertaken if it offers a rate of return greater than the rate at which money can be

---

[3] These are pre-OPEC numbers, based on 1970 oil prices.

borrowed, or than whatever interest rate the decision maker feels to be appropriate. It is thus directed only to those situations in which there is an initial outflow of funds, followed by a stream of positive returns.

The corresponding criterion for choosing among competing projects is: "Choose the project with the highest internal rate of return." Much of the time this is a valid decision rule, but it can't always be counted on to produce the correct decision. Note that if we are comparing two competing projects such as X and Y above, X has a higher internal rate of return. Yet if the appropriate discount rate is in the 0 to 13 percent range, Y should be preferred. Adopting the rule of choosing the highest rate of return may also cause the decision maker to overlook the possibility that doing nothing is better than carrying out any of the proposed projects. If the discount rate is about 20 percent (which is most unlikely, to be sure), projects X and Y are both inferior to doing nothing. In another situation, doing nothing might become the preferred choice at a more plausible discount rate.

Table 10–3

Project	Year				
	1	2	3	4	5
Z	−21	+10	+30	+20	−40

(All figures are in thousands of dollars.)

It is sometimes proposed that in evaluating a single project the decision criterion should be: "Proceed if the internal rate of return is greater than, say, 10 percent." This rule too can cause trouble, for we might encounter a project with a time stream such as that shown in Table 10–3. This particular stream of costs and benefits produces a present value curve that changes direction as the discount rate is increased. The curve is shown in Figure 10–2. Now there is more than one internal rate of return, and the proposed decision rule leaves us nowhere.

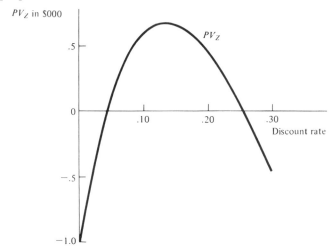

Figure 10–2

It is now widely (but not yet widely enough) realized that the present value criterion and the internal rate of return criterion lead to accepting and rejecting the same projects only if there are no budgetary limitations, if projects do not preclude one another, and if streams of net returns are first negative and then positive. Unfortunately, most public policy decisions must be made in the face of budget constraints. The government planner cannot simply float another bond issue or increase taxes whenever an appealing new project comes along. Moreover, projects frequently are mutually exclusive, as when they compete with one another for the same site. In short, because it is applicable in all situations in which the appropriate discount rate can be determined, even though projects compete or budgets are limited, the proper criterion is: "Choose the mix of projects that offers the highest present value."

Payback Periods

You may run across other rules of thumb for selecting projects when net benefits are a flow received over time. Businesses frequently employ the concept of the payback (or sometimes payout) period. They compute how long it will take before a project pays for itself. The project with the shortest payback period is then preferred. Or if many projects can be selected, they may, say, choose all that pay back within five years' time. The payback criterion is fine if all other things are equal, for example if the streams of benefits within the period is the same for all projects. But other things may not be equal. For example, consider the projects shown in Table 10–4. Project J has a payback period of three years, and project K of four years. Yet most businessmen would prefer project K.

Table 10–4

Project	0	1	2	3	4	5	6
				Year			
J	−100	35	35	35	0	0	0
K	−100	30	30	30	30	30	30

The point you should take away from this discussion (and the discussion of the internal rate of return) is that there are many criteria for making choices among projects that extend over periods of time. Most of them will work out in most circumstances. But only one of them works out virtually all of the time, indeed whenever an appropriate discount rate can be identified. That criterion requires us to select from among the feasible packages of alternatives the one that offers the highest present value.[4]

---

[4] Incidentally, in the business world the present value is also known as the "discounted cash flow." That term will be avoided here. It is appropriate for businesses but not for governments, since most governments do not calculate depreciation on their fixed investments.

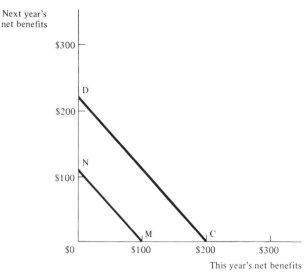

Next year's
net benefits

Figure 10–3

Discounting and the Fundamental Model of Choice

In discussing the criteria for making optimum decisions when costs and benefits occur as dollar flows over time, the connection with the fundamental model of choice, set forth in Chapter 3, may not have been evident.

How can we relate discounting to the fundamental model? Suppose we start by diagramming what the discount rate implies for making choices among alternative streams of net benefits. As usual, we keep it simple by sticking to two dimensions. Hence we consider the two-period case; net benefits occur this year and next year, and that's it. In Figure 10–3 we plot this year's benefits along the horizontal axis and next year's along the vertical axis. Then what does it mean in terms of this diagram to say that the discount rate is 10 percent? It means, for example, that the two streams—(*M*) $100 this year, $0 next; and (*N*) $0 this year, $110 next—are equally satisfactory. And so is the combination $50 this year, $55 next—and all the other combinations on the straight line joining points *M* and *N*. Similarly, all points on the straight line joining (*C*) $200 this year, $0 next, and (*D*) $0 this year, $220 next, are equally desirable. In fact, we may construct a whole preference map, consisting of parallel straight lines, with each line more desirable as we move north and east from the origin.

Now let's consider a choice between the projects in Table 10–5. Which of the two projects is preferable if the discount rate is 10 percent? In Figure 10–4 we reproduce the preference map we have already constructed. Points *A* and *B* are then plotted on this diagram; they are a noncontinuous possibility frontier. For a 10 percent discount rate, we see that project *B* is preferred. Moreover, we can in theory read the present value of each project directly off the graph, for the horizontal intercept of each of the

Table 10–5

	Net benefits ($000)	
Project	Year 1	Year 2
A	$200	$200
B	$150	$275

preference lines is the present value of every point along that line. (We say "in theory" because in practice we couldn't draw the graph accurately enough.) In other words, the discount rate is in principle a very special kind of preference map that permits us to compare alternative streams of net benefits by reducing all such streams to a single number, the present value. In practice, however, one would never bother to draw a graph at all.

Note that this preference map for the government decision maker, as we have drawn it, consists of straight lines, implying a willingness to trade off present for future benefits at a constant rate. For benefits and costs that are small relative to the total assets of the decision making unit—as is the case with most public projects—this assumption is reasonable. But as the amounts in question grow larger, we would expect to see the straight lines

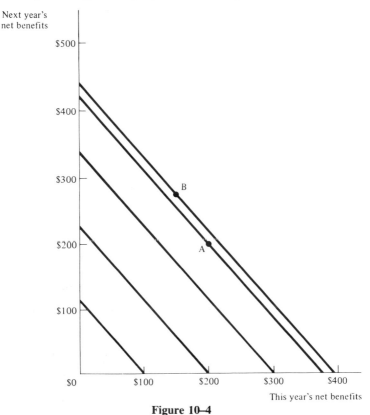

Figure 10–4

gradually become convex to the origin, as with the conventional indifference map.

The Choice of a Discount Rate

At a number of junctures we have referred to the "appropriate discount rate." We saw that the present value of a stream of payments is likely to be extremely sensitive to the choice of the discount rate. Consequently, it behooves us to think carefully about what is the appropriate discount rate for public projects.

The funds expended for a government project are not funds that would otherwise stand idle. They are obtained by the government from the private sector, either by taxation or by borrowing, or from the government itself by diverting funds from other purposes. If left in the private sector, they will be put to use there, and in that use will earn a rate of return that measures the value that society places on that use of the funds. If the funds are diverted to government use, the true cost of the diversion is the return that would otherwise have been earned. This cost (as we noted in the previous chapter) is known as the *opportunity cost*. The opportunity cost is the correct discount rate to use in calculating the present value of a proposed project. If the present value is positive, the project uses the funds to better advantage than they are currently being used in the private sector. If the present value is negative, it doesn't. It's as simple as that.

For example, suppose that the federal government, alarmed by an increasing number of oil barge and tanker accidents in coastal waterways, contemplates a project to improve the charting and marking of marine hazards. For simplicity, assume that this project is to be financed entirely by a tax on upper incomes, and that the individuals hit by the tax will pay it by reducing the amounts they save. If they are currently earning 8 percent interest on these savings, then the opportunity cost of the funds for the project is 8 percent. The estimated stream of costs and benefits from the project should therefore be discounted at 8 percent, and if this arithmetic produces a present value of net benefits greater than zero, the project should be adopted. If the present value is negative, it should be rejected. Pursuing it would in that case mean using funds in a way that society values less highly than the alternative use in the private sector.[5]

Throughout this chapter we have chosen to simplify the discussion by referring to the funds used for a public project. Those trained in economics will recognize that these funds are only the medium of exchange, and that what happens in real terms is that real resources—land, labor, raw materials, plant and equipment, and so on—are diverted from one use to

---

[5] This of course leaves aside distributional considerations. These were discussed separately in the last chapter.

another. Money is merely the vehicle. The displacement of investment may in fact be a complex process. If there is slack in the economy and the Federal Reserve is following an expansionary policy, little private investment will be crowded out of the market. If credit is tight, or if real resources are scarce, the impact will be immediate. For our purposes, however, the restriction of the discussion to financial resources is legitimate, since ordinarily the additional amount of funding for an individual project is small relative to the total size of a government's budget, and real inputs for a public project will be bought and sold on the market in quantities small enough relative to the total market that others' purchases of them will not be affected. The most likely exception is the case where a public project can be built on one site only, and will thereby displace a prospective private project. In such a case the appropriate discount rate is the return that would have been earned on the private project.

We saw earlier that, in general, the lower the discount rate, the more favorable it is for projects with early costs and late benefits. As the rate rises, it becomes more important to delay paying out and to get a quick return. This makes sense in terms of the state of the economy. A low discount rate implies that the marginal opportunities for investment in the private sector are not particularly promising, so it isn't surprising that public projects that are slow to pay off or that don't offer particularly high rates of return may look attractive by comparison. On the other hand, a high discount rate means that it is easy to find a good rate of return in the private sector. In that case, a public project must show a good or quick return in order to compete.

While this opportunity cost approach provides an accurate theoretical answer to the discount rate question, it doesn't offer much practical help. Because of imperfections in the capital markets, rates of return vary from one type of investment to another. How on earth could anyone ever identify the spending displaced by the adoption of a particular project? In the real world, government taxation and borrowing displace consumer spending, consumer saving, and business investment, in some cases directly, in others indirectly. And at times government spending may displace other government spending. The appropriate discount rate for any period is a weighted average of the rates of return for all the displaced uses of funds. The weights are the fractions of the total funds derived from each source. Needless to say, the correct weights are extremely difficult to determine in practice.

You may wonder how we would go about estimating the rate of return on consumer spending when that return takes the form of satisfaction, not dollars. For those consumers who both spend and save, the rate of return on spending must be the same at the margin as the rate of return on saving. If it weren't, they could increase their satisfaction by altering their spending–saving habits. We can't make any such simple statement about those who don't save, but at least we can establish a lower bound. It is obvious that the rate of return on savings is too low to tempt them.

Therefore their rate of return on spending must be higher than the going rate of interest on savings deposits.

Ideally, the weights used in figuring the appropriate discount rate should be separately determined for each individual project, for the mix of sources of the funds may differ. This implies that the government should sometimes reject some projects while accepting others with equal costs but lower payment streams; the latter may draw funds from sources with lower opportunity costs. Furthermore, if funds for a project are drawn from a source other than the beneficiaries of that project, separate discount rates should in principle be used for costs and benefits. Determination of appropriate weights may be possible in certain rare cases, such as a specific bond issue for a specific project, but for the most part the funds obtained by taxes and borrowing all end up in the same pot. Analysts must then rely on a discount rate that is at best an approximation. This is nevertheless a considerable improvement over past practices where discount rates have usually been unrealistically low, have varied widely from one agency to the next, and have occasionally been ignored altogether.

When we get down to discussing real numbers, most of the voluminous discount rate literature becomes suddenly vague. Some writers suggest qualitative estimates. Others confine themselves to describing what the discount rate is not. Still others proceed to set upper and lower bounds for the rate. This may in fact be a valuable exercise. Often an analyst is able to say, "I don't know what the right discount rate for this project is, but fortunately it doesn't really matter. It surely is well above 3 percent, and the analysis shows that for any discount rate greater than 3 percent the project looks absolutely rotten. Therefore it should be dropped forthwith." Moreover, we always have at hand as a convenient lower bound the interest rate on long-term government bonds, for certainly a project should not be undertaken if it cannot yield a return as large as the cost to the government of borrowed funds.

Most economists who are concerned with determining the appropriate discount rate for public projects would probably come up with a 1977 figure of about 10 percent. Given the kinds of budget constraints most governments operate under, the 10 percent rate will give a good result in most situations. But for very long-term considerations, a more accurate assessment of the proper rate is required. We mentioned the Passamaquoddy analysis, where a discrepancy of 1.625 percent in the choice of discount rate led to opposite conclusions as to the feasibility of the project. That was a very long-term project indeed, with benefits stretching out over decades.

An illustration of the crucial nature of the rate choice is provided in the nuclear energy field. Should we rely mainly on the light water reactor for electricity generation in the 1990s or should we concentrate our efforts on the development of the fast breeder reactor? The benefit–cost analysis of these alternatives favors the light water reactor if the discount rate chosen is as high as 10 percent, the fast breeder reactor if it is as low as 7.5

percent. The indeterminate results in the 7.5 to 10 percent range are due mainly to differences among energy experts as to the probable future cost of high-grade uranium ore.

Related Issues and Reservations

There are additional practical and theoretical issues in the choice of a discount rate that we can merely touch on here. Discounting is employed to assess projects whose benefits and costs stretch over many years. Frequently (and quite naturally) these yearly payoffs, particularly those further in the future, will be highly uncertain. It is occasionally proposed that the discount rate should be adjusted upward to compensate for this element of risk. That approach is now widely agreed to be not only incorrect conceptually, but also likely to result in significantly inferior choices. Raising the discount rate in effect changes the tradeoff rate between payoffs in different periods, yet there is no inherent reason why uncertainties about the amounts of future payoffs should affect the way we are willing to trade off one year's payoff against the following year's. The correct analytical approach is to separate the question of the risk-free discount rate from the question of how we value risky outcomes. Chapter 12 addresses the latter question.

In a more philosophical vein, it is argued that, given the present income distribution, no observed rate of return can provide an accurate reading of the intertemporal preferences of the society as a whole. Moreover, a lower discount rate may result in pursuit of projects that benefit lower income groups at the expense of those with high marginal tax rates. In this view, the discount rate should instead be a conscious value judgment as to the rate at which society wishes to trade off future for present resources. In other words, the choice of a discount rate should be used deliberately to apportion costs and benefits among income groups and among present and future time periods, and hence generations, according to the values held by society. To be sure, rates of return currently obtaining in an economy provide information as to the needs and attitudes of the people in the society, and should be considered in choosing a discount rate. These arguments seem most valid when applied to underdeveloped countries, where the capital markets are likely to be rudimentary and the income distribution leaves few people willing to save anything at all voluntarily.

As a further—and perhaps stronger—argument for explicit value judgments about the appropriate discount rate for a society, it is sometimes pointed out that ultimately the very size of the public sector will be determined by the discount rate. Proponents of an explicitly set social rate of discount claim that decisions about the size of the government sector should not fluctuate in response to changed conditions in private capital markets.

Although this value judgment approach seems on the surface to be entirely different from the opportunity cost approach to the choice of a discount rate, the difference is likely to be more ideological than practical. The opportunity cost approach instructs us to choose the discount rate on the basis of rates of return observed in the economy, corrected insofar as possible for what are judged to be imperfections in the market system. The social time preference approach instructs us to make a deliberate choice of a discount rate to reflect our preferences about providing for future generations, and this choice is to be enlightened and informed by observing actual rates of return in the economy. Thus the opportunity cost advocates start with observed rates of return and correct these according to their social values, while the social time preference advocates start with a value judgment but rely on observed rates of return to inform this judgment. From opposite ends of the spectrum they move toward one another, and in some cases there may be little disagreement as to the appropriate discount rate for a public project.[6]

It is indeed true that if we do wish to benefit future generations at our collective expense, and moreover to do so by means of increased government investment, the discount rate is a possible mechanism. But it seems clear that in the United States at least, there is no such consensus in favor of the future. If per capita income continues to grow as it has over the last two centuries, our children's children will be far better off financially than we are. Any sacrifice for the benefit of future generations would be made by the not-very-poor for the benefit of the even-less-poor. The truly poor who are among us today might well question our collective values. This is not to say that we should ignore the needs of future generations, who are represented in the marketplace only by their predecessors, particularly when it comes to the exhaustion of valuable natural resources or the irreversible destruction of all kinds of amenities, from scenic vistas to the ozone layer. But the way to handle these issues analytically is to identify all the benefits and all the costs of a project, and to estimate and assign probabilities where appropriate, not to resort to a second-best juggling of the discount rate.

One of the difficult current issues in discounting is what to do about inflation. As long as the rate of inflation was low this was not considered to be a serious problem. (As a matter of fact, it wasn't considered at all.) But over the past few years we have experienced inflation rates that have been high enough to raise serious questions about appropriate discounting procedures. We frequently hear it said today that people's expectations about inflation have become incorporated in the interest rate. To the extent that this is true, inflation is less of a problem as far as the choice of a

---

[6] For excellent discussions of these approaches to the choice of a discount rate, see William J. Baumol, "On the Discount Rate for Public Projects," in R. Haveman and J. Margolis (eds.), *Public Expenditures and Policy Analysis* (Chicago: Markham, 1970); and United Nations Industrial Development Organization, *Guidelines for Project Evaluation* (New York: United Nations, 1972), Ch. 13, "Intertemporal Choice: The Social Rate of Discount."

discount rate is concerned. In addition, there is in principle no reason why the same discount rate should be used for all future periods, any more than the same rate should be used for discounting both costs and benefits.[7] As policy analysis becomes more sophisticated we can expect to see more disaggregation of the discounting process, with respect to both time periods and income groups.

What about discount rates for state and municipal governments? The same reasoning applies as with federal projects: the flow of costs and benefits from a proposed use of funds should be discounted at the opportunity cost of the funds. These governments are usually external borrowers in that they borrow mainly outside their own tax jurisdictions. They ordinarily operate under a balanced budget constraint, New York City's predicament notwithstanding, so that amortization of loans must be considered in the analysis. The ramifications are complex, but the principle of opportunity cost still holds.

The case of the private nonprofit sector is more difficult. These institutions get their funds in part from governments, in part from user charges, and in part from charitable gifts. Voluntary giving, however, is sensitive to the givers' perception of the use to which the funds are put. Hence decisions of this type are essentially interactive, and not a matter simply for a unitary decision maker.

People sometimes wonder if there ever is an occasion to use a negative discount rate. When is it desirable to trade more present resources for fewer in the future? It is not easy to devise an example, and economists usually fall back on decomposing hardtack in a lifeboat. Shipwrecked sailors are presumed to value some fraction of a piece of hardtack received tomorrow more highly than a whole piece today. A farmer who annually has a surfeit of water in the spring and a drastic shortage in late summer will spend money to build a reservoir to store water, even though he will lose much of it through evaporation. In effect, he uses a negative discount rate in trading more water now for less later to decide whether the reservoir is worth the cost. Under certain circumstances Swiss banks charge interest on savings deposits rather than paying it, yet people continue to deposit funds in these accounts. In general, negative discount rates are applicable when people have no recourse but to rely on highly imperfect stores of value, that is, on commodities that are expected to deteriorate over time.

All of this discussion has been couched in terms of the discounting of dollar flows. It is arguable that ordinary discount rates are not appropriate for discounting flows that consist of intangibles such as pain and suffering, or improved health, or especially changes in the risk of death. Such goods are not exchanged in the market; forward and backward flows through time

---

[7] For a discussion of real and nominal discount rates, see S. Hanke, P. Carver, and P. Bugg, "Project Evaluation During Inflation," in the 1974 issue of *Benefit–Cost and Policy Analysis,* edited by R. Zeckhauser et al. (Chicago: Aldine, 1975).

will not be in accord with market interest rates. This issue is still very much up in the air. Some economists and analysts have in the past preferred not to discount such streams; others discount routinely at going rates. A few are beginning to think seriously about this enormously perplexing problem.

Finally, although we are left with no magic number for the appropriate discount rate, it is reassuring to know that a good approximation will usually produce good results, especially if it is applied consistently throughout all the decision making agencies in the government. Above all, it will weed out the abysmally unjustifiable projects. And that is a giant step forward.

11 Linear Programming

Linear programming is a technique for allocating resources when the supplies of these resources are strictly limited. It is a straightforward prescriptive model of widespread applicability that has the additional pedagogic virtue of laying bare the general structure of optimal resource allocation. It can be an invaluable aid for making policy choices that range from allocating the budget for a small library to selecting the components for a gigantic hydroelectric plant. A linear programming model of the entire Ganges–Brahmaputra river system takes into account flood control, power production, irrigation, navigation, and salinity control.[1] In another large-scale analysis, linear programming models are used to explore alternative sources of fuel for meeting U.S. energy demands over the next half century or so.[2]

Of the various types of operations research, mathematical programming, and linear programming in particular, is the most highly developed and widely used. Programming is a means of optimizing; i.e., it is concerned with choosing the best levels for various activities in situations where these activities compete for scarce resources, or with choosing the minimum-cost method of producing required outputs. This breed of problem pervades all levels of all societies; it is relatively immune to ideological differences in interpretation. The corporation manager must allocate factory space among competing product lines; so must his counterpart in the Soviet Union. The producer of animal feeds must meet an assortment of nutritional requirements while minimizing costs; so must the hospital dietician. The police commissioner must develop a work schedule that uses officer time efficiently. A church finance committee must determine expenditure levels for

---

[1] Peter Rogers, "A Game Theory Approach to the Problems of International River Basins," *Water Resources Research* 5, no. 4 (August 1969): 749–60.
[2] Alan S. Manne, "What Happens When Oil and Gas Run Out?" *Harvard Business Review* (July–August 1975): 123.

various activities. A legal aid office must allocate lawyers' time among types of cases. (Note that there are difficult problems of evaluating the outputs of some of these organizations. Perhaps you should stop here and think for a few minutes about what the inputs and outputs of a legal aid office or an urban health clinic might be. If you feel that they are intangible or difficult to measure, you might ponder what surrogates you would be willing to employ as indicators of input and output levels.)

These are all situations where mathematical programming, whether used as a formal technique or as a guide to thinking, is enormously helpful. In some cases it can give us an outright solution, say an assignment of the police officers. In others it offers a solution only if we are able to make certain value judgments; perhaps we can assign weights to the cases the legal aid office might handle. At still other times no immediate answers are forthcoming, but greater insights may be gained by trying to structure the problem in a programming format by thinking carefully about the limited inputs available, the outputs desired, and the relationships among them. With such a problem we are still a long way from a decision, but at least we are asking better questions.

What do all the problems enumerated above have in common? In all of them we are looking for the best values of certain variables, which we will refer to as the control or decision variables. These variables represent the activities the decision maker can control, either directly or indirectly; they are the variables subject to decision. But in determining the levels of these activities, certain side conditions, called constraints, also have to be met. The factory manager cannot exceed his plant capacity. The feed producer must maintain his advertised nutritional levels. The police commissioner must cover his stations without violating the union prohibition against split shifts. The church finance committee has to worry about the budget and also about negative feedbacks to income if some of the church programs are curtailed. The legal aid office is confronted with a limited budget and legal staff and a variety of political, social, and institutional constraints.

In some contexts these constraints take the form of equalities—$100,000 must be spent, 360 police hours must be assigned—but more often they are in the form of inequalities. For example, the manager of the animal feed factory wants to minimize the cost of the ingredients he uses, but at the same time he must be sure his product contains certain minimum levels of proteins, carbohydrates, and vitamins. He need not achieve these minimum levels exactly; he is willing to exceed some of them if that is necessary to minimize costs. (You should be able to convince yourself that it may sometimes be less expensive to exceed a minimum requirement. For example, if you are looking for a car that among other requirements gets at least 20 miles to the gallon, you may find that the best choice, all things considered, gets 25 miles.)

Because these constraints are in the form of inequalities, the usual mathematical methods of computation, which involve the calculus and Lagrangean multipliers, will not work. It was not until 1947 that George

Dantzig developed a method for solving such problems.[3] Carrying out the computations is tedious at best, especially if there are more than three or four variables. Fortunately, most high-speed computers are routinely programmed to perform this kind of calculation. We need only to formulate the problem in appropriate form.

Allocations determined by means of linear programming are made under conditions of certainty. The choice of a diet to meet certain nutritional requirements at the least possible cost was an early application through which linear programming gained fame. In this case, the assumption of certainty implies that we know how much a pound of beans or carrots costs, and how much each contains of the various nutritional elements. Obviously this is a simplification. But if one pound of carrots is enough like another, and if price variations are sufficiently narrow, we can use average values and be confident that the solution for our certainty problem will serve as a quite satisfactory solution for the uncertainty problem that really pertains.

Philosophers and some physicists, concerned more with pure theory and less with practical choice, would see this matter differently; they would stress the uncertainty that remains. As we have emphasized in our earlier chapters on descriptive models, when analysts and policy makers choose to rely on optimization techniques under certainty, they recognize that nothing is 100 percent sure. Rather, they view certainty as a good approximation conveying substantial benefits at little cost.

The examples of linear programming that we will use to describe the method involve concrete situations and hard numbers. These are the obvious cases where linear programming applies directly and with great practical success, and consequently they are the best way to gain an acquaintance with the technique. But they are not what we are driving at in this volume. In most organizations, someone with substantial familiarity with mathematical techniques has primary responsibility for such specific problems. The aim here is rather to impart an understanding of how linear programming optimizes the allocation of scarce resources so that when you are faced with an allocation problem, however intractable, you will have at your command a framework for analyzing it. Many administrators have developed such a framework through long experience. Indeed, we might look at the choice of contents for this chapter as a programming problem. Our objective is to maximize your understanding of the structure and concepts of linear programming. The activities we can control are your exposure to (1) analytic techniques, (2) philosophical discussion, and (3) concrete problems. The principal constraint is the number of pages allocated to this chapter.

One of the major virtues of an understanding of analytic models and

---

[3] At the time, Dantzig was working on techniques for planning the diverse activities of the U.S. Air Force. Actually, the Soviet mathematician Leonid Kantorovich solved the same problem earlier and published his results in 1939, but his work went unnoticed—even in Russia—for a quarter of a century.

methods, as we have stressed, is that it gives insights into many situations where direct application of the methods may not be possible or desirable. Here is a further example to encourage you to think in this fashion. Suppose you are a campaign manager advising a political candidate how he should allocate his time among various parts of the electorate, or his funds among different types of advertising. Can you use the method of linear programming, if not to arrive at a solution, at least to think more intelligently about the alternatives, the limitations, and the outcomes? It is our contention that when confronted with such a choice situation you will find it helpful to consider how you would formulate this sort of situation as a programming problem.

The Elements of a Linear Programming Problem

Our discussion will be largely confined to linear programming. The linear case assumes, first, that all relations between variables are proportional. If we double the inputs, we will double the outputs as well. Thus, if we need 1 widget and 2 gadgets to make 1 bobbin, we will need 2 widgets and 4 gadgets to make 2 bobbins. Economists refer to this property as "constant returns to scale." Second, we assume that all variable inputs and all outputs are infinitely divisible: fractional bobbins and gadgets cause us no problems. Third, we also assume that processes can be added together. For example, suppose the bobbin factory can make 5000 bobbins in a day, *or* 8000 spindles. Then it can instead make 2500 bobbins *and* 4000 spindles.

Anyone who understands linear programming can readily comprehend the basic ideas behind the more complicated types of mathematical programming. Our assumptions of constant returns, divisibility, and additivity are purely for expository reasons; none is critical for the kind of use that we wish to make of mathematical programming.[4]

The best way to acquire an understanding of linear programming is by doing some. More important, we hope that working through a linear programming problem and actually getting a solution will give you a better understanding of what is necessarily involved in the optimal allocation of scarce resources.

The Technique of Linear Programming: The Transit Authority Repair Shop

We illustrate the technique of linear programming with an example adapted from Dorfman's classic expository article on the subject.[5]

---

[4] The approach here will be intuitive and nonrigorous; students desiring a more mathematical discussion should consult any of the standard texts on operations research. See, for example, Harvey M. Wagner, *Principles of Operations Research,* 2nd ed. (Englewood Cliffs, N.J.: Prentice-Hall, Inc., 1975).

[5] Robert Dorfman, "Mathematical or Linear Programming: A Nonmathematical Approach," *American Economic Review* 43 (December 1953): 797–825. The original adaption was the Sherman Motor Company case (Harvard Business School 9–107–010).

The Transit Authority maintains a repair facility that engages in two activities. One of the activities is the refurbishing of vehicles; the other is the refitting of various mechanical parts in a vehicle. Either of these activities can be sent out to commercial firms. Indeed, though there has not been an exact costing of internal procedures, a recent watchdog report presented fairly conclusive evidence that the commercial firms can do either job more cheaply than the repair facility. There is, however, no thought or prospect of closing down the Transit Authority's repair shop, or indeed of even reducing its capacity. The question for policy choice is how to utilize the facility to save the Transit Authority the most money.

The repair shop conducts its operations in four departments: testing, disassembly–reassembly, paint and upholstery, and machine shop. Monthly production in each department is limited. The entries in Table 11-1 give the maximum number of vehicles that can be handled, assuming that each department devotes full time to one type of repair.

Table 11–1
Monthly Capacities (Number of Vehicles)

Department	Type of repair	
	Refurbish	Refit
Testing	25	35
Disassembly–Reassembly	$33\frac{1}{3}$	$16\frac{2}{3}$
Paint and Upholstery	$22\frac{1}{2}$	—
Machine Shop	—	15

That is, the capacity of the testing department is sufficient to conduct necessary tests for 25 refurbishings or 35 refittings if it devotes full time to either operation. The department could also devote part time to each. It could, for example, test $12\frac{1}{2}$ refurbishings and $17\frac{1}{2}$ refittings monthly if it were to divide its time equally.

The Transit Authority has a long-term contract with a number of private repair shops. These shops charge \$3000 per vehicle for refurbishing; a refitting costs \$3500. In either case, whether the repairs are done in the Transit Authority's shop or externally, the Authority pays for all parts used. Each month on average 60 cars need refurbishing, 30 refitting. The variability from month to month is relatively small, so that even if all the repair shops were turned over to a single activity, there is no chance of running out of cars to refurbish or refit. The Transit Authority could, of course, contract out all its repair work, but since it must operate the repair facility anyway, it can realize substantial savings by doing as much of the work as possible in its own shop. The question is how the repair facility should allocate its capacity so as to maximize these savings.

In using linear programming to attack this problem, we must formulate mathematically what we are trying to accomplish and what the limitations imposed on us are. Once these steps have been taken, the solution is a matter of mechanics.

To set up the problem in this way, we must first determine what it is we are trying to maximize. Here we have a straightforward dollars-and-cents problem. We are told that we are trying to maximize savings; each in-house refurbishing saves $3000 and each refitting $3500. Next we must determine what activities the Transit Authority has control over, in other words, what the control or decision variables are. In this case the answer is obvious: the Transit Authority has control over how many vehicles it refurbishes and how many it refits. Therefore, if we let S = total savings, X_1 = number of refurbishings, and X_2 = number of refittings, we may formulate our objective mathematically:

$$\text{Maximize } S = 3000X_1 + 3500X_2 \qquad (11\text{--}1)$$

The expression in equation (11-1) is known as the *objective function*; it defines what the choice is intended to accomplish.

Now we turn to the capacity restrictions. We see that if the testing shop devotes itself entirely to testing refurbished cars, it can handle 25 cars a month. In other words, each refurbishing requires 1/25 of the total monthly testing capacity. By the same reasoning, each refurbishing also requires 1/33.33 of the disassembly–reassembly capacity. Similarly, each refitting requires 1/35 of testing capacity and 1/16.67 of disassembly-reassembly capacity. Since no department can operate at more than 100 percent of capacity, the Transit Authority repair shop is limited in the following ways:

$$\left(\frac{1}{25}\right)X_1 + \left(\frac{1}{35}\right)X_2 \leq 1 \qquad (11\text{--}2)$$

$$\left(\frac{1}{33.33}\right)X_1 + \left(\frac{1}{16.67}\right)X_2 \leq 1 \qquad (11\text{--}3)$$

Thus we have expressed mathematically the limits on testing and disassembly-reassembly. Alternatively, you might have noted that each refitting requires 5/7 as much testing as a refurbishing. This leads to the constraint equation

$$X_1 + \frac{5}{7}X_2 \leq 25 \qquad (11\text{--}2a)$$

which comes to the same thing as (11-2) above. A similar formulation is possible in place of (11-3) above. There is no reason to prefer one version to the other; you should use whichever you find easier.

We are also told that because of limits on the paint and upholstery department and machine shop, our solution must satisfy these conditions:

$$X_1 \leq 22.5 \qquad (11\text{--}4)$$

$$X_2 \leq 15 \qquad (11\text{--}5)$$

Our formulation of the problem is almost complete—except for one thing. It seems obvious to us that X_1 and X_2 cannot be negative, that is, there is no process of unrefurbishing or unrefitting a subway car whereby we can create additional capacity. But this physical requirement of nonnegativity is not at all obvious to a computer, or to an analyst who has not been briefed on the context of the decision and is asked only to solve the mathematical problem. So we must add two final constraints:

$$X_1 \geq 0 \tag{11-6}$$

$$X_2 \geq 0 \tag{11-7}$$

To recapitulate, we have formulated the Transit Authority's optimization problem as a linear programming problem with an objective function and six constraints:

$$\text{Maximize } S = 3000X_1 + 3500X_2 \tag{11-1}$$

subject to:

$$\left(\frac{1}{25}\right)X_1 + \left(\frac{1}{35}\right)X_2 \leq 1 \tag{11-2}$$

$$\left(\frac{1}{33.33}\right)X_1 + \left(\frac{1}{16.67}\right)X_2 \leq 1 \tag{11-3}$$

$$X_1 \leq 22.5 \tag{11-4}$$

$$X_2 \leq 15 \tag{11-5}$$

$$X_1 \geq 0 \tag{11-6}$$

$$X_2 \geq 0 \tag{11-7}$$

If this were a complicated problem with lots of control variables, we would at this point hand it over to a computer or someone who knows how to run a computer for solution. In fact this is the recommended procedure for most linear programming problems, however simple.[6] Not only is it quicker and easier, but in addition the computer is usually programmed to give useful information about the problem beyond the immediate solution. It is useful, however, to work through the diagram of a linear programming problem once to see what is going on inside the computer and what is the nature of a solution to the problem.

Because the Transit Authority repair shop is a two-variable problem, we can plot it on a graph. In Figures 11-1 and 11-2, X_1 is measured on the horizontal axis and X_2 on the vertical axis. The first constraint, identified above,

$$\left(\frac{1}{25}\right)X_1 + \left(\frac{1}{35}\right)X_2 \leq 1 \tag{11-2}$$

---

[6] If you're going to be doing a lot of linear programming, you ought to work through a few simple problems by hand. This will give you a much better understanding of what the computer does. W. J. Baumol, *Economic Theory and Operations Analysis* (3rd ed.; Englewood Cliffs, N.J.: Prentice-Hall, 1972), is very clear on the procedure, which is known as the Simplex Method.

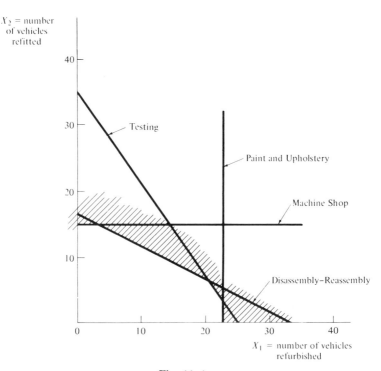

Fig. 11–1

imposes upper limits on the values X_1 and X_2 can jointly take; the boundary line it establishes for feasible points is given by the equation

$$\left(\frac{1}{25}\right)X_1 + \left(\frac{1}{35}\right)X_2 = 1$$

This is the equation of a straight line; we plot this line in Figure 11–1; it is labeled *Testing*. All points to the north or east of this line are unattainable.

The next three constraints, (11–3), (11–4), and (11–5), may also be plotted as straight lines on our graph. They too are shown in Figure 11–1.

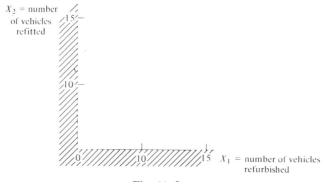

Fig. 11–2

The shaded areas in this figure violate one or more of the constraints and hence are unattainable. Similarly, the nonnegativity constraints provide boundaries on the down side, as shown in Figure 11–2. Combining these results in Figure 11–3, we are left with a polygon of attainable combinations of X_1 and X_2. This is called the *feasible set*; it is still another version of the possibility frontier set forth in Chapter 3.

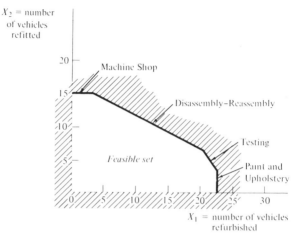

Fig. 11–3

The next step is to find the best possible point in this feasible set. The best point depends on what we are trying to maximize, and this takes us back to our objective function. How can we show this objective function on a graph? We have

$$S = 3000X_1 + 3500X_2$$

but we can't plot this because we don't know what the value of S is—we know only that we want it to be as large as possible. What we *can* do is to try different values of S and see what this exercise tells us.

Suppose we let $S = 70,000$. We plot the equation

$$70,000 = 3000X_1 + 3500X_2$$

in Figure 11–4. This is the equation of a straight line. It gives the combinations of X_1 and X_2 that will produce savings of exactly $70,000. A segment of this line lies within the feasible set; hence the Transit Authority repair shop could save $70,000 per month. But we also see that the Transit Authority can do better than that: all points in the feasible set that lie north or east of this $70,000 line are both preferable and attainable. What about $S = 105,000$? If we plot this equation in Figure 11–4, we see that it is a line parallel to the $70,000 savings line, but it falls entirely outside the feasible set. If we were to continue with this procedure, we would find that each line showing the combinations of X_1 and X_2 that yield a given amount of savings is parallel to every other such line, and that the savings generated by the repair shop get steadily larger as we move out to the northeast.

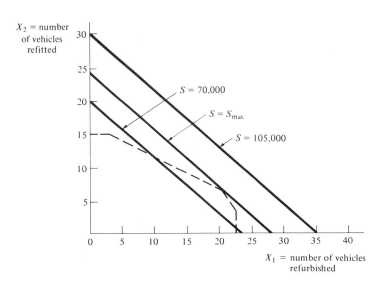

Fig. 11–4

This should be enough of a hint, especially if you recall the basic principles outlined in the fundamental model of economic choice. The largest savings that the repair shop can generate will be achieved by selecting the set of activities represented by the point where the feasible set just reaches the highest possible profit line. This is shown in Figure 11–4 as $S = S_{max}$. Any smaller savings can be improved upon by moving to the north and east, and any larger is unattainable. In this problem we can see that this point occurs where the testing and disassembly–reassembly constraint lines intersect. We may locate this point exactly by treating those two constraint lines as a pair of simultaneous equations.

$$\left.\begin{array}{l} \left(\dfrac{1}{25}\right)X_1 + \left(\dfrac{1}{35}\right)X_2 = 1 \\[2mm] \left(\dfrac{1}{33.33}\right)X_1 + \left(\dfrac{1}{16.67}\right)X_2 = 1 \end{array}\right\}$$

Solving, we find that these constraints intersect at the point

$$\left.\begin{array}{l} X_1 = 20.37 \\ X_2 = 6.48 \end{array}\right\}$$

Output at these levels yields monthly savings of

$$(3000)(20.37) + (3500)(6.48) = \$83,790$$

The fractional vehicles may be conveniently viewed as carrying over into the next month.

The solution itself is not very important for us, although it certainly would be for the Transit Authority. We are more concerned with the general principles that we may deduce from this solution.

First, we usually expect to find the best possible combination of outputs at a corner of the feasible set, for this is the inevitable result of the tangency condition and the shape of the possibility frontier. As we introduce more variables the feasible set becomes impossible to graph or even to visualize. Although "corner" is then no longer an obvious notion, the idea remains valid, and the best solution will still occur at a point where some of the constraints intersect.

You may wonder what happens if the maximum attainable savings line coincides with a segment of one of the constraint lines. This means simply that all the combinations of output along that line segment are equally good.

The observation that the solution to the problem will be found at a corner provides a clue as to how the computer finds that solution. Following a routine known as the Simplex Method, it searches systematically and efficiently among the corners of the feasible set to find the best point. It is interesting that although generations of mathematicians have known how to formulate linear programming problems, this knowledge was of no practical use because solving the problems was too difficult. Now that solution methods have been developed, we regard that aspect of linear programming as routine. But formulating the problems becomes more arduous as we try to apply the technique to a broader range of situations.

Second, the values of the decision variables in the solution are not affected by constant terms in the objective function, although the value of the objective function itself is. For example, suppose we want to maximize the actual monthly savings generated by the repair facility. The facility costs $95,000 a month to run, let us say. The objective function will be:

Maximize $S = 3000X_1 + 3500X_2 - 95,000$

The best production combination will still be found at the same corner of the feasible set, because the slope of the profit lines will not change. However, S itself will be changed from its earlier value. It is now in fact negative. Assuming that closing or scaling down the facility is impossible, the best the Transit Authority can do is "save" $83,790 - $95,000 per month. That is, its minimal monthly loss is $11,210. Quite apart from the geometry, you should convince yourself that adding or subtracting a constant from the objective function never changes the best choice of inputs. A similar observation holds if the coefficients in the objective function are multiplied by a constant. Suppose that rather than our original objective function we have:

Maximize $S = 6000X_1 + 7000X_2$

Again S is a maximum for the same values of X_1 and X_2, but the value of S is changed. In other words, the decision does not change, but the value of the outcome does. This may be particularly important when we are uncertain as to the coefficients in the objective function.

Finally, the solution to a particular linear programming problem may not be very sensitive to nonproportional changes in the coefficients of the objective function. For example, suppose the costs of outside refurbishings and refittings go to $4000 and $3750. If we solve the repair shop problem with the new objective function, we will find that best course is still to produce at $X_1 = 20.37$ and $X_2 = 6.48$. The choice remains the same; only the amount of the savings changes.

Shadow Prices

The solution of a linear programming problem provides us with an additional useful piece of information. Frequently we would like to know how much it would be worth if we could relax one of the constraints. For example, what would it be worth to the Transit Authority if it could add one unit to its Testing capacity? In this example we have measured capacity in terms of percentage of utilization. Hence we may take a unit increase as being a 1 percent increase in capacity. How much would this 1 percent increase add to the savings generated by the repair shop? We could recalculate the problem with the first constraint now reading:

$$\left(\frac{1}{25}\right)X_1 + \left(\frac{1}{35}\right)X_2 \leq 1.01$$

Actually this recalculation isn't necessary; most computers are routinely programmed to give us the additional information.[7] The number that the computer finds is known as the "shadow price" for Testing capacity. It tells us what that particular capacity constraint costs the Transit Authority, per unit, in the way of forgone savings. Here the shadow price for 1 percent of Testing capacity is found to be $486.

A more general way to put this is: "The shadow price tells us what it would be worth to relax a particular constraint by one unit." This version has the advantage that it allows for the possibility that a constraint is in the form of a lower limit. Thus if a constraint reads

$5a + 2b \geq 17$

relaxing it by one unit implies

$5a + 2b \geq 16$

Several points should be made about shadow prices. First, the shadow price for an input not used to full capacity is $0. Thus the Transit Authority would gain nothing by increasing its Paint and Upholstery department or its Machine Shop, since it is using neither of these facilities fully.

---

[7] They do it by solving a counterpart problem known as "the dual." Anyone interested in pursuing linear programming further will have to come to terms with the dual, and the sooner the better; see any operations research text. Others should let sleeping dogs lie.

Second, a shadow price is valid only so long as you don't run into another binding constraint. For example, each increase of 1 percent of the original capacity in the repair shop's Testing department is worth \$486 in additional monthly savings—but only up to the point where the shop is refurbishing 22.5 vehicles and refitting 5.41 vehicles. This is shown in Figure 11–5. Beyond that point there is no possibility of increasing the number of refurbishings, there being no unused capacity in the Paint and Upholstery department. The shadow price for Testing would then become \$0, and the shadow price for Paint and Upholstery capacity would move from \$0 to a positive amount.

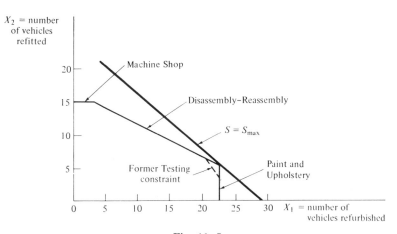

Fig. 11–5

Third, because a \$0 shadow price may become positive as other constraints are relaxed, you should not leave nonbinding constraints out of consideration. A change in the situation may make them binding.

Fourth and most important, comparison of shadow prices with costs of eliminating or modifying the relevant constraints may point decision makers toward expansion of one type of capacity rather than another. Or it may suggest a strong research and development effort so that the constraint may eventually be circumvented. Or perhaps it turns out that the shadow price for a political constraint is very high. Take the case of a municipal cemetery department engaged in the grave task of preparing next year's budget. For political reasons, no nonmanagerial employee can be transferred from one cemetery to another, in spite of improvements in equipment and changing land-use patterns that have left some cemeteries overstaffed and others short-handed. Sometimes administrators who have been close to this kind of dilemma for a long time become blind to it. They come to accept the constraint as a permanent fixture and lull themselves into believing that it doesn't cost all that much. Indeed, in the short run the department's hands may well be tied. But disclosure of the high shadow price would spotlight the extraordinary cost of this constraint and suggest a long-run change in hiring and attrition policy, plus a dose of public education.

Sensitivity Analysis

Most computer programs will automatically provide you with information as to how sensitive the results obtained are to changes in the input data, which is particularly useful when you are uncertain as to the accuracy of the data, or when you expect changes over time. This process is known as *sensitivity analysis*.[8] In effect, the computer solves the problem for slightly different values of the parameters. For example, the Transit Authority might be doubtful that it can continue to purchase outside refurbishing at $3000 per vehicle. Sensitivity analysis would disclose whether a rise in this cost should alter the decision on the mix of activities. Similarly, we could explore the implications of the estimates of, say, test capacity.

More Examples of Linear Programming Problems

Now that you have read through and thought about the Transit Authority problem and have begun to develop an understanding of linear programming, you may want to try a few problems on your own. Here are four exercises for you to practice on.

The city government of Burtonville faces several difficult allocation problems, among them the four situations described below. Formulate them as linear programming problems. You should try to write down only the objective function and the constraints; don't worry about working out the final answers. We will take you through the process of setting up the equations, step by step, in the answers section at the end of the book.

1. *Incinerators and Pollution Control.* Burtonville burns 3000 tons of trash per day in three elderly incinerators. All three have antipollution devices that are less than satisfactory. Their emission profiles differ, as is shown in Table 11–2. At present all three incinerators are operating at full capacity. The remainder of the city's trash,

Table 11–2

Incinerator	Capacity in tons/day	Emissions per ton burned	
		Units of sulfur dioxide	Units of particulate
A	1,200	250	20
B	800	150	30
C	1,000	220	24

---

[8] Strictly speaking, determination of the shadow prices is a type of sensitivity analysis, but because of their particular analytical significance and special importance, they have a name of their own.

another 1500 tons per day, is dumped in a sanitary landfill area. This is a much more expensive method of disposal. The state's Environmental Quality Commission has brought suit against the city; the Superior Court has issued a temporary restraining order under which sulfur dioxide emissions must be limited to 400,000 units per day and particulate emissions to 50,000 units per day. What is the most economical way to make the necessary cutbacks?

2. *Police Shifts.* Burtonville has minimum requirements for the number of patrolmen on duty during each 4-hour period, as shown in Table 11–3. There are no part-time patrolmen, and union regulations prohibit split shifts. Hence each policeman works eight consecutive hours. Work out a daily schedule that employs the fewest policemen.

Table 11–3

Time of day

12 noon	to	4 P.M.	100
4 P.M.	to	8 P.M.	250
8 P.M.	to	12 P.M.	400
12 P.M.	to	4 A.M.	500
4 A.M.	to	8 A.M.	200
8 A.M.	to	12 noon	150

3. *Assignments to Hospitals.* The director of the Burtonville Civil Defense Agency has been ordered to draw up a disaster plan for assigning casualties to hospitals in the event of a serious earthquake. For simplicity, we will assume that casualties will occur at two points in the city and will be transported to three hospitals. It is estimated that there will be 300 casualties at point A and 200 at point B. Travel times from point A to hospitals 1, 2, and 3 are 25, 15, and 10 minutes, respectively; from point B they are 20, 5, and 15 minutes. Hospital capacities for emergency cases are 250, 150, and 150 patients. How should the victims be assigned to minimize the total time lost in transporting them?

4. *Electricity Generation and Pollution Control.* The Burtonville Municipal Power Company must produce 2000 megawatt-hours (mwh) of electricity each hour. Air pollution ordinances require it to keep emissions of pollutants below 2800 pounds per hour. (For purposes of this exercise we ignore interesting phenomena like weather and load fluctuation.) The company must decide how to do this at least cost. It can switch to low-sulfur fuel, use stack filters and either

Table 11–4

Method	Results	Cost/mwh
Use present fuel	Pollution = 10 lbs/mwh	$3.50
Use low-sulfur fuel	Pollution = 1.2 lb/mwh	$5.00
Use stack filters	Pollution reduced by 90%	$.80
Import power	No pollution on Burtonville	$4.00

high- or low-sulfur fuel, or import power from elsewhere. The relevant characteristics of these options (as well as the company's present method) are given in Table 11–4. The company can import only 200 mwh per hour. What should the company do?

Attacking the Right Problem

Although all four of the Burtonville exercises are mathematically solvable, it is by no means clear that the existing institutional structure will guarantee that the solutions will be socially desirable. It may be, for instance, that the decision making process does not take into account the well-being of all those who are affected by the decision.

Consider, for example, the electricity pollution problem above. The Burtonville Municipal Power Company was concerned about pollution only to the extent that it met the constraint. What if pollution could be reduced below the constraint level at very little additional cost? The company might not be overly concerned, but the state's Director of Environmental Quality might be very interested. He would want to know how much it would cost to reduce pollution still further, or alternatively, how much could be saved if the emission regulations were less stringent. What he really is after is the shadow price for pollution reduction, to tell him how much we are paying at the margin to eliminate pollution. If he found that price to be very low, he might push for stricter controls. If he found it high, he might reconsider whether all the improved air quality was worth the cost. Nothing in our formulation of the problem addressed the shadow price issue.

We shall not delve further into this matter. Among the lessons to be learned is that just getting a problem to the stage where it is complete, in that it contains a descriptive model and a representation of the decision maker's preferences, does not insure that we are solving the correct problem, or are operating within ideal institutional structures. Yet it may be advantageous to push problems to the stage where they are complete; they frequently become more transparent, so that the appropriate structuring is more clearly perceived.

There is a countervailing danger, of course. A neatly formulated problem acquires a touch of majesty. Analysts and critics may hesitate to question clear mathematical formulas, whereas the language that sets forth the underlying assumptions might more readily be criticized.

Linear Programming as a General Approach

In considering how you are to use linear programming in thinking about an allocation problem, you must have clear the basic elements of such formulations. Any linear programming problem has five analytic components: (1) the available activities, (2) the criterion for overall performance or output according to which the choice will ultimately be made, (3) the coefficients in the objective function, which are the weights that measure the effectiveness of each of the activities in enhancing total output or overall performance, (4) the coefficients telling how much of each resource is employed in each activity, and (5) the constraints on total resources that can be used. In the Transit Authority repair shop problem, the activities were refurbishing and refitting. The criterion for performance was total savings; the weights in the objective function therefore were the commercial prices per unit of refurbishing and refitting, $3000 and $3500. Both the coefficients and constraints were fully described by the entries in Table 11–1. The entries in this table were expressed in more traditional form in equations (11–2) through (11–7), with the coefficients lined up on the left-hand side, and the constraints on the right.

Public Issues and Objective Functions

For many public issues, it will be more difficult to define and weight the objectives than it was for the Transit Authority, which was interested only in dollar savings. Public decision makers are likely to encounter problems for several reasons. They normally must take into consideration the welfare of many people who may have divergent preferences for outcomes. They frequently find no convenient way to measure the things the government provides or uses, for many of these inputs and outputs have no market prices. Sometimes the final outputs that are desired of a public project are unambiguous, but they may not be subject to direct attack. For example, a suburban community is the beneficiary of a large trust fund. The donor has stipulated that the fund is to be used for the construction and maintenance of a health facility. If you were one of the trustees of this fund, where would you begin? (This example is taken from an actual Massachusetts case.) Your goal is improved health for residents of the town, but this isn't much practical help. Instead you must focus on intermediate goals, such as reduced infant morbidity or improved dental care for school children, more frequent Pap tests for women or better nutrition for senior citizens—the list of possibilities is endless. And as you think about the problem, you may decide that even such laudable aims as these are too vague to serve as working objectives, and that you need to be still more specific. In other words, you must decide what surrogate goals you can use as practical substitutes for whatever it is that you are trying to optimize. This may seem rather abstract, yet you would probably agree that most of our immediate objectives, both personal and public, are really more or less satisfactory surrogates for other, less tangible, goals.

Furthermore, in the real world the relation between action and outcome may be so remote that the ultimate goal provides but scant guidance to specific action. Hard thinking may be necessary to determine even proximately what tangible objectives are appropriate. Examples of this abound in the public welfare field, where particular programs are likely to become ends in themselves and remain so long after we have lost sight of the original purpose, or in education, where the goals of the educational process provide better fuel for debate than guide to policy. In short, the choice of an objective is by no means a cut-and-dried affair. It may require the kind of explicit thinking that a linear programming approach enforces.

In defining the activities of your programming problem, you should be careful not to restrict yourself to too literal an interpretation of "activity." It may be simply an ingredient that is to be used. If we think of a metaphor in which choosing policies is in effect running a machine, the control variables are the dials for setting the levels of the various activities. We cannot slide over the word *level* too swiftly: it implies that we are talking about activities than can be measured and controlled, however crudely.[9]

For the Transit Authority, the available activities are the two maintenance operations on the subway cars. Their levels of operation are indicated by the quantities X_1 and X_2. In the classic diet problem the activities consist of using certain foods, in amounts to be determined. A political campaign manager has the considerable task of deciding just what activities on the part of the candidate and his staff are relevant and controllable. Various types of advertising and possible uses of the candidate's time come to mind immediately, but these are only the beginning. In addition to considering all the possible activities, he must also find ways to measure them. He might well measure advertising in dollars and candidate's time in hours; measuring the use of volunteers would be much stickier.

Suppose you are facing an even less tangible problem. For instance, you are a member of a commission that is charged with making recommendations for the improvement of criminal justice. Here the decision maker, whether the individual or the group, is confronted not only with the difficulty of choosing a practicable objective but also with determining what the specific activities of a criminal justice system are, and if and how they can be measured. What should be valued positively and what negatively? How should you handle factors that are obviously important yet may be ambiguous indicators of value? Fewer arrests, for example, might mean less crime, or less efficient police, or greater protection of civil liberties. These key conceptual problems, however difficult, must necessarily be dealt with when you formulate a problem well.

Finally, what of the weights to be attached to the objectives? Quite simply, these weights indicate how effective each activity is, relative to the others, in propelling you toward your objective. We have already seen how important these weights may be in benefit–cost analysis. For the Transit Authority, in-house refittings save more than refurbishings. The Authority knows this because its long-term contracts yield precise figures as to savings. The campaign manager should know how effective various uses of the media and of the candidate's time are. If he hasn't thought about the

---

[9] It is possible to have variables that take on only discrete values. In formulating a dam problem for example, we may find that a sluice gate must be either open or closed, i.e., that the variable must take the value 1 or 0.

matter and tried to come up with reasonably good estimates, the candidate needs a new manager. Some of the activities at his command will give him more trouble, but the fact is that he can't avoid making decisions and he must try to bring the best information to bear on these decisions.

As a further example, a River Basin Authority may be deciding where to locate dams to enhance four types of benefits: electricity generation, recreation, flood control, and the environment. (For the environment, the objective may be to limit losses.) Assuming that this situation could be represented by a linear programming problem, which would relate the outputs of benefits to the type of dam at each location, it would still be most difficult to assign weights to the four types of benefits. What is the relative value of recreation benefits for upstream fishermen as opposed to downstream boaters? How are recreation benefits to be weighed against the benefits from flood control? What is it worth to prevent floods in marginal areas that may not be developed for human habitation? These are tough questions. A linear programming approach (or more generally, an analytic approach) cannot supply answers; it can only force us to face up to the questions.

For the more abstract problems, the assignment of weights thus requires careful thought about the nature of the possible activities, how they are to be measured, and how they contribute to the objective.[10] It is sometimes argued that it is impossible to make such a determination of appropriate weights. The counterargument is that whenever a decision is actually made to pursue one activity more intensively than another, the decision maker has implicitly assigned relative weights to these activities (or has at least assigned boundary values to them)—even though he has not done so consciously.

For example, a recreation commission, in choosing to expand its expenditures on park maintenance at the expense of playground equipment, has implicitly determined that additional dollars spent on maintenance contribute more to its objective (whatever that may be) than those spent on equipment. The maintenance variable (measured in dollars of maintenance) has a larger coefficient than the equipment variable (measured in dollars of equipment). In practice it may be possible to perform some sort of rudimentary sensitivity analysis to see just how sensitive the decision is to the estimate of these coefficients.

Moreover, it is sometimes useful in a complex situation to attempt a process of backward induction. We can ask ourselves what kind of objective function actual observed choices of activity levels must imply, and whether this objective function is consistent with the overall goal. This exercise has the advantage that it may highlight side effects, desirable and otherwise.

---

[10] This should remind you of the multiattribute problem that we discussed earlier. That was essentially a stripped-down version of a programming problem, where we were constrained by a finite number of discrete and specific choices.

Public Issues and Constraints

So much for the elements of the objective function. We turn now to a similar consideration of the other basic component of a linear programming problem, the constraints. Constraints are usually easier to deal with than the objective function. This really isn't very surprising—we ordinarily have a clearer idea of what we can't do than of what we want to do and how we can do it.

There are several types of constraints. First are the restrictions that certain variables (and frequently all of them) may not be negative. Second are the constraints that arise out of the technology of the situation; they define the limits that the various activities cannot exceed, or relationships that must exist among some of the activities. Third, there may be political, social, economic, or other institutional limits on the values that some of the variables may take.

The nonnegativity constraints are self-explanatory. Once pointed out, they become obvious. Constraints of the second type, those that operate through the technology, describe the action and interaction of the various activities in competing for scarce inputs or in producing the required outputs. Thus the repair shop's two maintenance activities compete for Testing and Disassembly–Reassembly capacity and are further limited by the capacities of the Paint and Upholstery department and the Machine Shop. The police commissioner assigns men to produce the required complements on each shift without resorting to split shifts. The political candidate's campaign activities cannot add up to more than 24 hours in any one day, nor more than around 18 on the average. On the other hand, a park manager may be able to put his facilities to different uses at different times. In other words, these constraints describe how one activity is forced to give if we push too far with another.

Political, economic, social, and institutional constraints usually place direct limits on levels at which the activities may be used. For example, in the diet problem we might wish to achieve a taste balance as well as a nutritional balance. A typical set of budget constraints for an institution might require that no program receive less than last year, nor more than a 10 percent increase over last year. Or it might specify that the ratio of the amounts expended on two programs remain within certain limits. In all these cases we are, in a sense, establishing subsidiary objectives for certain activities. The Transit Authority does not maximize refurbishings because its overall objective is savings. But it might demand a certain minimum level of refurbishings if it felt that over the long run the failure to refurbish might cost it that capability. This could be disastrous if commercial refurbishing were to become much more expensive. Subsidiary objectives of this sort are related to what is known as "satisficing," which was discussed briefly in Chapter 8. Constraints of this third type are more in the nature of self-imposed limits, given the environment, whereas those of the second type are more a matter of the technological facts of life.

If this last statement sounds a little imprecise, it is because it would be more misleading than helpful to make it precise. We can't always establish this kind of fine distinction between technological and other constraints, for in some sense they are all imposed by the environment of the problem. Oftentimes the dividing line will be blurred and the categories will overlap. But it is useful to keep in mind that you must think about all possible sources of constraint in formulating your problem. Paradoxically, although the taxonomy of constraints may be less clear-cut than that of the objective function, the facts relevant to constraints are usually clearer.

The Limitations of Linear Programming

The foregoing should give you the impression that the programming approach will have many beneficial applications to policy decisions. Still, all is hardly clear sailing. We should now back off and look at some of the difficulties that you may encounter.

First, some of the relationships may be nonlinear; some of the variables may take only integral values. As an example of nonlinearity, suppose the State of California contemplates building a mental health facility on a certain parcel of land. The building will be subject to setback and sideline requirements, height limitations, and restrictions on the percentage of total area covered. If the aim is to maximize the cubic feet of usable space made available, the objective function will be at worst a complicated variant of

maximize $V = lwh$

where V = volume, l = length, w = width, and h = height. This is a nonlinear equation, but the same principles apply as for linear programming. Fortunately it is comparatively easy to locate a computer program that will handle a problem such as this one.

To be strictly accurate, the Transit Authority repair shop is an integer problem for any one month—there is nothing to be saved by half refurbishing a subway car. But we chose to ignore this because the error was small relative to the total number of cars involved, because it was clear that the capacity numbers were best estimates rather than certainties, and because in this case the half-finished work would be completed in the following month. (Why stop with one good reason when you can find three?) If we had been considering, say, the one-shot manufacture of small numbers of large generators, we would have had to specify that only integral solutions were possible. Interestingly enough, it is ordinarily more difficult to write an integer program than a nonlinear program.

A second possibility is that the constraints are such that no feasible solution yields acceptable scores on the objective function. In that case, one possibility is merely to do the best we can with the onerous set of constraints. Alternatively, we can go back and see if the original problem can be respecified. Perhaps when the lack of acceptability of outcomes is pointed out to the individuals or agencies that imposed the constraints originally, they will agree to some degree of relaxation. The police chief may petition the City Council for additional clerical support. The director of a community health center may go back to his Board of Trustees and state that he absolutely must have another X-ray machine to carry out the center's normal duties.

A third possible difficulty is that it may prove impossible to reconcile conflicting objectives. For example, in specifying the criteria for the design of an incinerator, the City Council may require that maximum capacity be achieved at minimum cost. This reflects insufficient attention to the task of formulating objectives, for the Council can't have both at the same time. What it really wants to do is to find some optimal mix of the two, trading off the objectives of holding down costs and increasing capacity against each other. If it can't decide what tradeoffs it is willing to make between these, no objective function can be formulated.

This matter of defining the objective function is not to be taken lightly, especially in public sector decision making where the social and political opinions of constituents may diverge widely. When the decision maker finds it impossible to resolve conflicts among objectives, he may find it practical to resort to satisficing. This involves setting acceptable levels for some objectives, thereby converting these objectives into constraints, and then optimizing with respect to the remaining objectives. Satisficing is an approximation, a way of doing reasonably well without getting into extraordinary complexities.

Finally, the most obvious problem is that some parts of a system may not be readily quantifiable. This is all too frequently the case, in fact.

We have all heard the admonition, "You can't put numbers on everything," or "Beware of quantifying the nonquantifiables." Certainly it is very difficult to articulate political issues, much less to quantify and measure them. But even if one could measure them, the public official would often be reluctant to do so. Such openness would not only leave him vulnerable to criticism but would eliminate much of his maneuverability.

Since the subjective components of a decision analysis are by nature more debatable than the objective components, adversaries concentrate on these aspects when attacking an analysis in an attempt to discredit the results. This has the effect that "hard" facts and data tend to outweigh "soft" subjective information in formal analyses. The consequence is that too much emphasis is placed on economics and efficiency and not enough on social and political implications.

One solution is to do two types of analyses: a private and a public one. But this proposed solution, as we indicated earlier, has severe societal penalties and goes to the heart of the public mistrust of its social institutions. We are on the horns of a dilemma. The public wants more attention paid to subjective considerations, wants more honesty and openness, but is not sophisticated enough to withstand the rhetoric of those advocates who stand ready to demolish any nonobjective arguments. Certainly this calls for the development of standardized procedures for quantifying that which is truly quantifiable, and we suspect that much more is quantifiable than the public realizes. After all, GNP is an awfully abstract concept that has taken on a tangible meaning of its own. Perhaps the public can also learn to internalize the meaning of other social indices of our quality of life.[11]

The real trouble is that nonquantifiability doesn't let you off the hook—you can't for this reason simply duck making a choice. Somehow you have to come up with a decision, and when you do you will have implicitly quantified the unquantifiable.

It is our opinion that societal problems demand the consideration of subjective values and tradeoffs. The question, as we see it, is not whether subjective elements should be considered, but rather whether they should be articulated and incorporated into a formal, systematic analysis. The choice is between *formal analysis* and *informal synthesis*, and this metadilemma does not have an obvious solution.[12]

The Role of Linear Programming in Decision Making

In Chapter 1 we laid out a five-step approach to policy analysis, starting with the definition of the problem and ending with the choice of an action. Linear programming is just one of the many optimization techniques in which the general approach outlined in that chapter is followed. It forces us to find out and formulate what we're trying to accomplish, what ways there are to go about it, how effective these activities are relative to one another, and how the choices among them are limited. In particular, we saw that the problem faced by the Transit Authority repair shop could be crisply formulated along these lines, with the result that it was much easier to address than many of the vast range of policy issues.

Linear programming is no magical black box that churns out answers to hitherto impenetrable questions. If a problem is incorrectly formulated, no solution technique, however sophisticated, can be expected to provide the optimal solution. Regardless of how firm and reliable the numbers may be, the problem must be correctly posed by a thinking human being who understands the alternatives, the objectives, the constraints, and the behavioral relationships that define the situation requiring a policy choice. Like all the techniques described in this book, linear programming is an aid to decision making, not a substitute for it.

---

[11] R. Keeney and H. Raiffa, "A Critique of Formal Analysis in Public Decision Making," in A. Drake, R. Keeney, and P. Morse, eds., *Analysis of Public Systems* (Cambridge, Mass.: MIT Press, 1972), p. 72.

[12] Ibid., p. 64.

Although it is formally applicable only if certain rather formidable conditions are met, many of the issues that must be confronted by public sector policy makers are clarified by casting them in a linear programming format. Allocating limited resources among competing uses is, after all, a ubiquitous problem. Even though the analysis is not carried to the point of quantifying the variables, trying to structure the problem in this fashion requires the analyst to refine his thinking about what is valued and what the alternatives are. Thus linear programming not only provides numerical answers to an important class of fully quantified problems, it also helps structure an entire approach to less tractable problems. The latter may well be its main contribution to improved decisions.

12 Decision Analysis

Many policy problems are hard to sort out. A situation may require a sequence of interrelated decisions that is more complex than the mind can readily encompass. More often it is difficult to decide what is the best choice because the outcomes that result from the required decisions depend in part on chance events; the decision maker is not in full control. Perhaps the uncertainty stems from nature; he does not know, for example, the level to which the spring runoff will carry the river. Perhaps he cannot be sure how many people will take advantage of a new job-training program. Like it or not, he cannot foresee the future; he must take his chances. Since the early 1960s, businessmen have increasingly used a method of analysis called *decision analysis* for tackling problems where decisions must be made sequentially and where uncertainty is a critical element. The application of decision analysis to problems in the public sector lagged by about a decade, mainly because the estimation of probabilities and the valuation of outcomes proved difficult. But decision analysis has increasingly become a valuable tool for analyzing and formulating public policies. It has been employed to address such diverse problems as prescribing appropriate treatment for a sore throat, choosing the site for a new airport for Mexico City, and deciding whether the U.S. should proceed with commercial supersonic flight.

Decision analysis in effect provides us with a road map for picking our way through confusing and uncertain territory. Equally important, it gives us a technique for finding the best route. Without further ado, let's look at the bare bones of the method, so that you will have a general understanding of what decision analysis is all about and how it works. We will then gradually introduce variations on the basic model that will greatly expand the range of situations to which it can be applied.[1]

---

[1] A lucid introduction to the field is Howard Raiffa's *Decision Analysis* (Reading, Mass.: Addison-Wesley, 1968). We strongly recommend it to those who desire a more comprehensive treatment of decision analysis.

The Decision Tree: A Descriptive Model

Most of the public policy issues for which decision analysis is useful are complex, far too complex to use in introducing the subject. Consequently, we will start with a deliberately trivial problem, culled from the 1974 sample examination for Administrative Officers of the U.S. Foreign Service:

> The officer in charge of a United States Embassy recreation program has decided to replenish the employees club funds by arranging a dinner. It rains nine days out of ten at the post and he must decide whether to hold the dinner indoors or out. An enclosed pavilion is available but uncomfortable, and past experience has shown turnout to be low at indoor functions, resulting in a 60 per cent chance of gaining $100 from a dinner held in the pavilion and a 40 per cent chance of losing $20. On the other hand, an outdoor dinner could be expected to earn $500 unless it rains, in which case the dinner would lose about $10.

(Where this damp and dismal post might be located escapes us.)

The first step in using decision analysis to attack the officer's problem is to diagram the sequence of decisions and chance events that he faces. The particular type of diagram that is used is called a decision tree. In Figure 12–1 we have drawn the decision tree for this situation; you may want to try to figure it out for yourself before reading on.

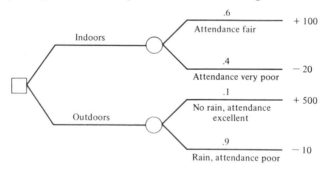

Fig. 12–1

To understand the tree, we begin, quite logically, with the first decision the officer faces: Should he hold the party indoors or outdoors? At the left we draw a square, or *decision node*, to indicate that at this point a decision must be made. We then draw two lines branching out of the decision node to show his two possible choices, and label them *Indoors* and *Outdoors*. Next we ask "What happens if we follow along the upper branch, in other words, if he holds the dinner indoors?" The answer isn't much help: "It all depends." In fact, we are told that it all depends on chance, on how well people turn out for the dinner. Hence at the end of the Indoors branch we draw a circle or *chance node*, to indicate that at this point an uncertainty must be resolved one way or another. At this chance node there are two possibilities: The party may be moderately successful ("attendance fair"), or it may be an utter disaster ("attendance very poor"). Hence we draw two branches for these possible results, and label them accordingly. Moreover, for this decision problem we know the probabilities of these possible outcomes, for we are told that there is a 60 percent chance of the former and a 40 percent chance of the latter. These numbers are recorded along the appropriate branches. Finally, we are also told that the gain from a moderately successful dinner is $100, while very poor attendance will result in the loss of $20. These are the ultimate outcomes or *payoffs* for each possible combination of choice and chance; they are shown at the tips of the branches.

Similarly, the two possibilities for an outdoor affair, their probabilities, and their payoffs are shown emanating from the lower chance node. The tree thus summarizes all the essential information that is available. Note very carefully the order in which events occur: the decision must be made before the decision maker knows what the weather will be. Hence the decision node must precede the chance nodes. The appropriate sequencing of decision and chance nodes always requires close attention when a decision tree is drawn.

The problem as set forth has obviously been drastically simplified; the officer might have additional options, including doing nothing, or other weather possibilities, such as "threatening." He could try to secure a long-range weather forecast, or even pay some extra amount for the option of delaying his decision until a few hours before the affair. It is the formulation and diagramming of the problem that we are concerned with now, not realism.

A decision tree is, then, a flow diagram that shows the logical structure of a decision problem. It contains four elements:

1. *Decision nodes,* which indicate all possible courses of action open to the decision maker;
2. *Chance nodes,* which show the intervening uncertain events and all their possible outcomes;
3. *Probabilities* for each possible outcome of a chance event; and
4. *Payoffs,* which summarize the consequences of each possible combination of choice and chance.

If you fully understand these simple principles for constructing a decision tree, you have already mastered the essence of the method. Yet despite their simplicity, it would be difficult to overemphasize the usefulness and importance of decision trees. As we have found with almost every type of model, the foremost advantage is the discipline imposed by the model. It requires us to structure the problem, break it into manageable pieces, and get all its elements down on paper—tasks that appear deceptively easy. Frequently they turn out to be very difficult. And even when it is hard or perhaps impossible to assign objective probabilities to chance events or to quantify outcomes in physical units, the effort of drawing the tree correctly provides valuable insights into the complexity of a problem. A corollary advantage is that a decision tree helps us communicate assumptions and valuations to others; it is a tool that facilitates sensible policy discussion.

Some Further Clarification

Decision trees must be constructed to show *all* events that can possibly occur at a chance node, and *all* options that might be pursued at a decision node. Moreover, these events and options must be defined in such a way that they don't overlap. (The technical phrase for this state of affairs is "mutually exclusive and collectively exhaustive.") For example, if we wished to consider the weather possibilities for our Foreign Service officer less simplistically, we might add temperature categories "hot" and "cold." But it would be wrong merely to modify the chance nodes by adding hot and cold branches, as in Figure 12–2. Rather we would have to show four possibilities, as in Figure 12–3.

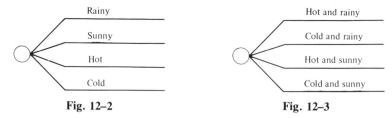

Fig. 12–2 Fig. 12–3

Alternatively, we could diagram this as the two successive chance events of Figure 12–4. Or we could put the "sunny–rainy" chance node on the tree before the "hot–cold" node. In some contexts only one version of the tree will make sense; this is particularly likely to be true when there is a well-defined, chronological sequence. In others there may be little reason to prefer one version to another and the choice will depend on whatever seems most logical in terms of the information available.

Similarly, the possibilities for action must be mutually exclusive and collectively exhaustive. As a homely example, if you are trying to decide whether to wear a raincoat or carry an umbrella, the alternatives presumably are not mutually exclusive. The correct diagram is then Figure 12–5.

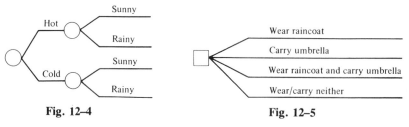

Fig. 12–4 Fig. 12–5

The above examples are deliberately commonplace, yet the point we are making is applicable to all decision problems, however complex. Decision analysis forces you to think carefully about

1. The true nature of the decision problem;

2. The role of chance; and
3. The nature of the sequential interaction of decisions and chance events.

When the course of action may be carried on at various levels, the use of a decision tree becomes more cumbersome. For example, suppose you are trying to decide what sum of money to carry with you on an extended foreign trip, and how much of it to carry as cash and how much in travellers' checks. A limitless number of combinations are possible. If you are to use decision analysis to tackle this problem, you must, as a practical matter, narrow the problem down to a finite number of discrete choices. You might, for instance, construct the relevant part of the tree as in Figure 12–6. When you are satisfied that you have determined the right branch for

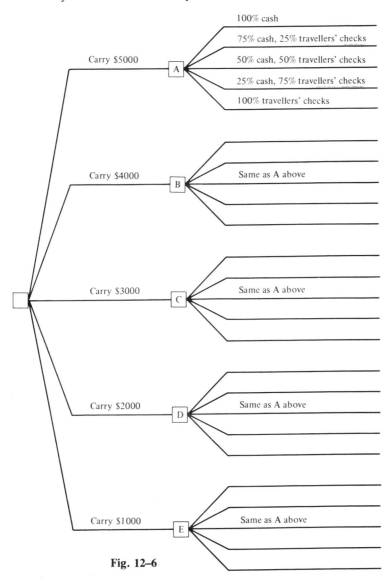

Carry $5000 — A
- 100% cash
- 75% cash, 25% travellers' checks
- 50% cash, 50% travellers' checks
- 25% cash, 75% travellers' checks
- 100% travellers' checks

Carry $4000 — B — Same as A above

Carry $3000 — C — Same as A above

Carry $2000 — D — Same as A above

Carry $1000 — E — Same as A above

Fig. 12–6

you, you may want to try an amplified version of that branch to refine your choice.

Obviously, an analyst who is determined to keep his blinders on will not find his performance improved by mindlessly sketching a decision tree. But we have discovered that with a little experience, just drawing that first square on a piece of paper encourages most people to think more systematically about the matter at hand. To be sure, the exact shape the tree should take is sometimes far from obvious, as you will discover when you find yourself up against an amorphous problem whose ramifications seem endless. Yet the more difficult it is to develop the model, the more useful it is likely to prove. A decision made without an appropriate model in mind almost certainly will reflect confusion in thinking.

A Representative Decision Problem with Testing: The Choice of Generators

Earlier in this book we considered choices among alternative dam projects, all of which generated electricity and at the same time provided water for irrigation. In the real world the performance characteristics of irrigation systems and power plants are uncertain and variable, and may change from year to year over the extended lifetime of a project. For purposes of illustration we will suppress some of the engineering facts of life and look at a much simplified problem.

Suppose that the choice among dam projects has been narrowed to a particular dam and power plant configuration that will produce a known amount of water for irrigation. The only decision remaining is the choice of generators for the power plant. Assume for convenience that at the end of a year the earth will open and swallow up the whole project.[2] The final stages of development have recently been completed on a new and much more efficient type of generator, but that type has not yet been tested in conjunction with a dam of this kind. The costs of the old type and this new one are identical. A plant equipped with conventional generators will produce electricity worth $5 million a year. Such a plant will supply only a very small proportion of the region's electricity; any excess or deficiency can be sold or bought at a constant price. The output of the new type of generator is uncertain but it is estimated that there is a .3 chance that operating difficulties will develop so that it can be run only at low capacity, in which case it will generate only $3 million of electricity per year. Correspondingly, there is a .7 chance that the new type of generator will work well, in which case it will produce $8 million of electricity. (It might be more realistic to postulate a whole distribution of outcomes, but that would further complicate the problem while offering few compensating gains in insights into the decision analysis technique.) It is possible to build and test a prototype generator at a cost of $.5 million. The tests would

---

[2] You have already studied benefit–cost analysis and discounting so you know how a stream of benefits over time would be handled in practice. How to aggregate the consequences in future time periods is a separate issue that has no bearing on the point we are now trying to make.

predict the reliability of the new technology with complete accuracy. Before reading on, you should structure this problem for the decision maker in the form of a decision tree. (Don't forget to deduct the cost of the prototype from the payoff wherever appropriate.)

We'll return to this problem shortly; at the moment we want only to give you a little practice in tree drawing. If you wish to check your work, the tree is shown in Figure 12–7. Decision nodes are indicated by numbers, chance nodes by letters. Note carefully the effect of the test on the probabilities at chance nodes C and D, and also that the cost of the test has been included in the payoffs for the appropriate branches.

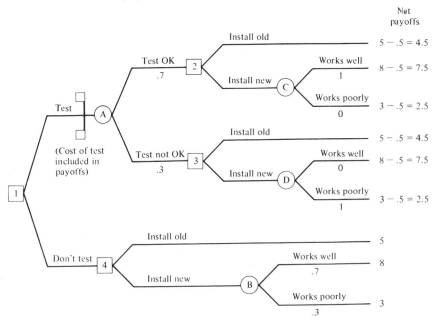

Fig. 12–7 (Payoffs are in millions of dollars.)

You will find that in many discussions of decision analysis costs are entered as "tolls" at the point where they occur. This is one logical way to handle them, and it certainly helps us visualize the problem more accurately. We follow this practice only in part. The symbol ⧈ is entered on the tree to show the point in the decision process at which an additional cost is incurred; the dollar costs are subtracted to give the net payoffs, which appear on the right at the tips of the branches. It is never wrong to carry the costs out to the tips of the tree in this manner, and in situations where the decision maker is not risk neutral (a matter we'll get to shortly) all costs *must* be carried out to the tips. It therefore seems simpler in this abbreviated treatment of decision analysis to establish uniform rules.

Used as descriptive models, decision trees have great intuitive appeal, for they are easy to understand, readily discussed, and applicable to almost every choice we face in the real world. Trees are also an invaluable normative model, for whenever it is possible to assign values to probabilities and payoffs we can use the tree to determine the preferred course of action. We turn now to consideration of decision analysis as a normative tool that facilitates effective choice.

Decision Analysis: Folding Back and Choosing the Preferred Course of Action

The decision tree lays out the decision process for us so that we may visualize it in its entirety; it does not directly define the preferred course of action. If we try to reach a decision by working along the tree from left to right, following the logical sequence of choice and chance, we can hardly get started. Indeed, beginning that way would undo much of the value of drawing the tree in the first place. The embassy officer can't decide whether to hold his party indoors or out, because he doesn't know how to evaluate the uncertain consequences of either choice. For the same reason, the designers of the power plant can't decide whether or not to test the new generator. To evaluate the choices facing either decision maker, we must start at the right, with the tips of the trees, and work backward along the branches. This process is easier to understand (or at any rate it's easier to describe) if we work through some concrete examples first and talk about general principles afterward.

Working Backward Under Certainty: The Land Bequest

Let's start with a decision problem that has the simplest structure possible. Suppose you are the mayor of a small city. You are trying to decide what to do with a parcel of land recently bequeathed to the city. One group of citizens contends that the land should be used for recreation, another that it should be sold for residential construction. City planners who have studied the situation recommend three alternative recreational uses: (1) as a wildlife refuge; (2) as a municipal pitch-and-putt course; (3) as a public park with tennis courts and a softball diamond. If the parcel is sold for housing, the possibilities are (1) single-family houses; (2) condominiums; (3) mixed-income, federally subsidized apartment buildings. A majority of the City Council is docile and will follow your recommendation, but you find it difficult to make up your mind as to what is the best course for the city. The decision tree is shown in Figure 12–8.

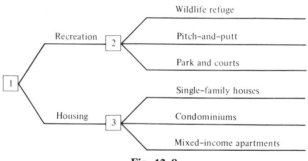

Fig. 12–8

In situations like this, the choice between recreation and housing is clearer if you follow the "work backward" system. Assume for the moment that you will recommend using the parcel for recreation and that you are therefore at decision node 2. You then consider what is the best recreational use for the land. Let's say that you decide that the park and courts are best. Turning next to decision node 3, you decide that if the land is to be used for housing, the best choice is mixed-income apartments. Ordinarily such apartments are not attractive to builders, but several builders have assured you that they are willing to undertake the project, given the sizeable federal subsidy. Your choice is thus narrowed to two contenders, the park and mixed-income apartments. In effect the decision tree has been pruned to that shown in Figure 12–9.

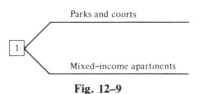

Parks and courts

1

Mixed–income apartments

Fig. 12–9

Clearly there is nothing very startling about this process or its end result, and indeed deterministic decision trees such as this one hardly set one's normative blood aboil. Ordinal preferences, which merely provide rankings of alternatives, are always sufficient for finding the best choice.

Folding Back With Uncertainty: The Hospital Lawn

The more interesting and valuable applications of decision analysis are those in which chance plays an important role in the outcome of a decision. This is the case with the embassy official's decision problem described earlier. Let's look at another deliberately simple problem. A hospital administrator—we'll call her Harriet—must let a contract for reseeding the hospital lawn. She can give the contract to company A, which has agreed to do the job for $1500 provided that the weather is good over the next month; the charge will escalate to $2400 if the weather is bad. (Bad weather is defined as less than one or more than four inches of rain.) Or she can give it to company B, which has submitted a flat bid of $2000. Meteorological records indicate that there is a 15 percent chance there will be less than one inch of rain and a 25 percent chance of more than four inches. Thus there is a 60 percent chance that the weather will be good. What should Harriet do? The decision tree is shown in Figure 12–10.

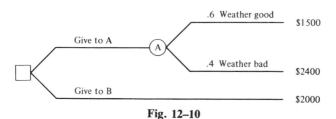

.6 Weather good $1500

Give to A   A

.4 Weather bad $2400

Give to B $2000

Fig. 12–10

Again we start to work backward from the tips of the tree, or rather Harriet does. Right away she comes to chance node A, shown in Figure 12–11. Now if Harriet could pick an outcome, she would choose to have company A do the work in good weather for $1500. But she cannot simply choose that outcome since nature is in control. If she gives the contract to company A she will have to take whatever comes in the way of weather; in effect she must accept a lottery. This means that she must find a way to assign a value to this node *as a whole*, a measure of what it's worth to her to be in a position where she faces a lottery with a 60 percent chance of spending $1500 on the lawn and a 40 percent chance of spending $2400.

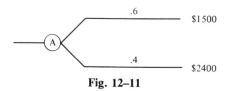

Fig. 12–11

One way she might do this is to determine some sort of an average value for chance node A. What do we mean by the average value of a lottery? It is what the average outcome of the lottery would be, in the long run, if the lottery were played again and again. This long-run average is aptly termed the *expected value*. In this case, where dollars are at stake, we usually refer to the *expected monetary value* or *EMV*.

The expected value may be calculated directly. It is found by multiplying the value of each of the possible outcomes at a chance node by its probability and then summing these products. For chance node A, we calculate

$$EMV_A = .6(\$1500) + .4(\$2400) = \$1860$$

The expected value if Harriet gives the contract to company B is, of course, $2000. The decision tree, thus, in essence reduces to Figure 12–12. If Harriet is willing to play the long-run averages, she should choose the action that offers the best expected value. In this case we're talking about costs; therefore the best EMV is the lowest and Harriet should give the contract to company A. A double line (//) is used to indicate that the choice "Give to B" has been eliminated.

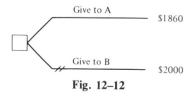

Fig. 12–12

A decision maker who bases his actions on expected values is said to be *risk neutral*. It is reasonable to assume that Harriet is risk neutral, for the amounts at stake in reseeding the hospital lawn are not large, at least not relative to the budget of a hospital in this expensive age. For the time being we will suppose all our decision makers to be risk neutral: this will keep the exposition simple. Later on we'll have more to say about the decision maker who is not risk neutral. In the meantime it may reassure you to know that, even then, the use of expected values usually provides a good first cut at a problem.

Anyway, if Harriet feels the hospital should be risk neutral with respect to the particular lottery it faces, that it should treat a $400 risk the way she herself would treat one for $5, her decision is clear. She gives the contract to company A and since hoping is free, if ineffective, she hopes for good weather. Some of you may wonder which path Harriet should follow if the outcomes achieved by following the two paths are equal. This point has been adequately covered in the literature.

"Would you tell me, please, which way I ought to go from here?"
"That depends a good deal on where you want to get to," said the Cat.
"I don't much care where—" said Alice.
"Then it doesn't matter which way you go," said the Cat.
　　　　　　　　　　　　—Lewis Carroll, *Alice in Wonderland*

Before returning to the more complex generator problem, let's summarize what we have been doing. Essentially we have assumed that the decision maker is risk neutral, that is, willing to proceed on the basis of expected value. We have then relied on two procedures in working backward from the tips of the tree to the initial decision:

1. At each chance node, we have assigned a value, the expected monetary value or EMV, to the node as a whole.
2. At each decision node, we have chosen the action with the best EMV (the highest or lowest, whichever is appropriate for the case at hand) and have eliminated other possible courses of action.

Howard Raiffa refers to this whole process of working back along the branches of the tree as "averaging out and folding back."

As a check on your understanding of EMV and its use, assume that the embassy officer of Figure 12–1 is risk neutral. Where should he hold the party?[3]

Folding Back with Uncertainty and Learning: The Choice of Generators

Earlier in this chapter we asked you to try to draw the decision tree illustrating the choice between two types of generators for a power plant. We are now ready to go back and determine the preferred choice. The tree was shown in Figure 12–7. We can now average out and fold back from

---

[3] $EMV_{Indoors} = .6(100) + .4(-20) = 52.$ $EMV_{Outdoors} = .1(500) + .9(-10) = 41.$ Therefore he should hold the party indoors.

those payoffs to the initial decision. We strongly urge you to try this for yourself before reading on.

If you do indeed stop to work the problem out, you probably will start with the top branch. Working back from its payoff of 4.5, you come to decision node 2—where you can't make a choice until you know the EMV at chance node *C*. Fortunately, that EMV can be determined by inspection to be 7.5, which is entered above the node. The choice at node 2 is then between an outcome of 4.5 with old generators and an expected value of 7.5 with new. Since these are positive payoffs, the preferred choice offers the larger expected value and the old generator branch is crossed out. The same procedure is followed for the other branches; eventually the choice is reduced to Figure 12–13. The decision is clear; all that remains is to cross out the inferior choice, "Don't test." The completed tree is shown in

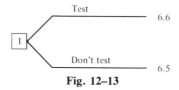

Fig. 12–13

Figure 12–14. The best strategy is to test; if it passes the test, the new type of generator should be installed. If not, the old type should be chosen.

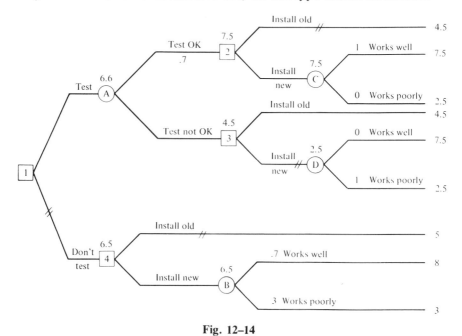

Fig. 12–14

Note that this tree describes a situation where the decision maker must make a first decision, then wait to acquire further information before making a second decision. In other words, he waits until he finds out how the probabilities break, until he knows along which path chance will lead him.

Decision trees thus do more than systematically lay out the opportunities for action and the uncertainties that will affect outcomes; they portray as well the gains from gathering further information. They induce, indeed almost force, the decision maker to consider sequential strategies, where further action will depend on the information observed to date. A major problem with government programs is that once started they are hard to stop, or even to modify. If policy makers used a decision tree at the outset, they might be modest about their ability to predict outcomes and would then be more likely to build information-gathering feedback loops into the decision process.

For example, suppose that you, an educational planner, must determine which of two reading techniques will be the subject of a three-year trial. You discover quickly that you have the option of using one in some classrooms and the second in others. Moreover, you can revamp the trial during its course as information on the two techniques begins to accumulate. An accurate representation of the situation requires drawing the tree so as to reflect *all* the various possibilities for setting up and revising the experiment. In this way decision analysis forces you to structure your choices so that you can react to information as it becomes available. In other words, it emphasizes flexibility in contrast to the construction of an immutable master plan.

Note also, if you haven't already, that although the value at each chance node depends on *all* the possible outcomes, the value at a decision node is the value of the preferred outcome only.[4] This, of course, reflects the fact that the decision maker is in control at a decision node, whereas he must accept whatever fate deals him at a chance node.

Before turning to variations on the basic model, let's look at a more complicated problem of a sort that occasionally appears in the press.

Using a Decision Tree to Structure a Complicated Problem: The Fish Ladder

A hydroelectric power plant on the Connecticut River has been ordered to build a fish ladder so that salmon can swim upstream beyond its dam. Three firms have submitted designs and cost estimates for the ladder.

Design *A* is the most expensive; it will cost $8.4 million and will take three years to build. A ladder of this type is already in successful operation in Oregon.

Design *B* is apparently similar, although it cuts a few corners to save construction time and money. It will cost $7.4 million and will take two years to build. We say "apparently" because although to the human eye it appears to capture the essential design features, the ichthyologists are reluctant to guarantee absolutely that the salmon will agree; they (the

---

[4] This is another of those points that are so obvious we're embarrassed to mention them. Yet experience has shown that students unfamiliar with decision analysis are likely to trip themselves up on just this point.

ichthyologists, that is) estimate the probability of success at .9. If for some reason the fish refuse to climb the ladder, the problem will become obvious by the end of the first year of operation. Modifications that will unquestionably satisfy the salmon can then be carried out at an additional cost of $2.8 million and a further delay of a year.

Design C is an altogether different type of ladder; the ichthyologists believe that it has only a .7 chance of success. It is far less expensive—$5.6 million—and will take only a year to build. It will take an additional year to determine whether or not it works. If it does not work, it will have to be abandoned and a ladder of type A or B will then have to be built. Although no fish ladders of type C are now in operation, one is currently under construction in New Brunswick, and by a year from now it will be known whether or not it is successful. If it works there, we can confidently expect it to work here.

Environmental and recreational benefits from a successful ladder are estimated at $1 million a year, whichever type of ladder it may be.

The design of the ladder must be approved by a state agency. The agency quite reasonably decides that its goal should be to minimize total cost, on the theory that costs to the utility will eventually wind up on the

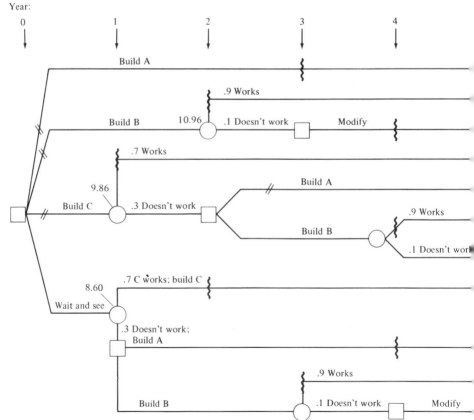

Fig. 12–15 A, B, C are costs ($ million). Subscripts indicate time at which incurred.

consumers' bills by way of rate increases, and the losses in environmental and recreational benefits due to construction delays will be borne by substantially the same group. The agency discounts both costs and benefits at 8 percent per year. It is anticipated that construction costs will rise at the rate of 10 percent per year.

Assuming that the three ladders will last equally long, and that the agency is risk neutral, what is the agency's best course of action? (For convenience, assume that construction costs are incurred when a ladder comes on line.)

This problem is typical of a situation where the decision maker desperately needs to keep track of what's going on and where he is in the process. It is, of course, an armchair case, with all the loose ends tidied up. But it hints at several problems that would be encountered in the real world, in particular the evaluation of intangibles (environment and recreation), allowance for the passage of time, and the possibility of acquiring further information. The probabilities are not more than "best guesses"— but if this is the best information you have, you should use it.

The decision tree for the fish ladder is shown in Figure 12–15, but before you turn to it you should try to formulate the tree and work out the

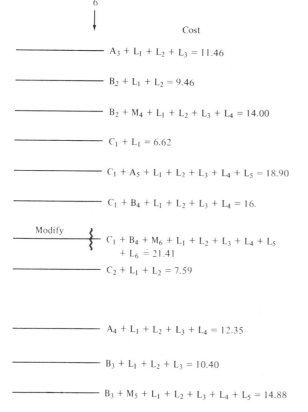

6

Cost

$A_3 + L_1 + L_2 + L_3 = 11.46$

$B_2 + L_1 + L_2 = 9.46$

$B_2 + M_4 + L_1 + L_2 + L_3 + L_4 = 14.00$

$C_1 + L_1 = 6.62$

$C_1 + A_5 + L_1 + L_2 + L_3 + L_4 + L_5 = 18.90$

$C_1 + B_4 + L_1 + L_2 + L_3 + L_4 = 16.$

Modify

$C_1 + B_4 + M_6 + L_1 + L_2 + L_3 + L_4 + L_5 + L_6 \doteq 21.41$

$C_2 + L_1 + L_2 = 7.59$

$A_4 + L_1 + L_2 + L_3 + L_4 = 12.35$

$B_3 + L_1 + L_2 + L_3 = 10.40$

$B_3 + M_5 + L_1 + L_2 + L_3 + L_4 + L_5 = 14.88$

L is loss of environmental benefits for subscripted year.

preferred choice for yourself. A new feature has been added, and we suggest that you incorporate it in your tree: the entire tree is put in a time frame, partly for clarity of exposition and partly because it makes it easier to figure the time lost along each route. A zigzag line ($\}$) is used to indicate the point at which a fish ladder comes on line.

Allowing for Risk Aversion

If this were as far as decision analysis could take us, it would still be valuable as a conceptual framework for thinking about decision problems, as well as a direct guide to choice whenever the decision maker operates on an expected value basis. Fortunately, decision analysis also points us toward a systematic approach to situations in which the decision maker will not be risk neutral. In this section we take an intuitive look at this approach.

We saw above that it was plausible to assume that Harriet, the hospital administrator, was risk neutral, for the amounts involved were not large. But let's look at a more dramatic example. Suppose an individual—let's call him Henry—is compelled to make a decision that in effect amounts to choosing between the two lotteries shown in Figure 12–16. If he is risk neutral, he will choose lottery A because it has a larger EMV, despite the fact that he could lose a bundle—$10,000, to be exact. At this point you

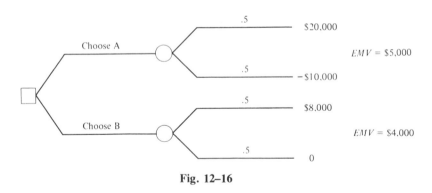

Fig. 12–16

may feel that risk neutrality is fine for Henry if that's the way he wants it, but it's not your cup of tea. In fact, the structure of your preferences is quite different. This is indeed a sensible reaction. Most people who are risk neutral when relatively small amounts are at stake are *risk averse* if the sums involved are large enough. If you prefer lottery B to A, you too are risk averse; most of your friends would probably react the same way. Yet the same people may on occasion exhibit *risk seeking* behavior. Anyone who has spent $1 for a raffle ticket that gives him a one-in-a-thousand shot at a $500 television set has been a risk seeker, although one might argue that the thrill of the game is an additional positive consideration.

A Problem That Introduces Risk Aversion: The Desalinization Plant

In our examples thus far, we have relied on expected value, in other words on the long-run averages, to see which of the available alternatives we should undertake. Let's take a closer look at what this implies. Consider the problem faced by the government of a small island that has insufficient fresh water. A desalinization plant is to be built, with a choice of technologies available. Technology E is well established; it will produce 6 million gallons of fresh water a day. Technology A is more advanced but less certain. There is a 50–50 chance that it will work well, in which case it will have an output of 10 million gallons a day. If it works poorly, the output will be 3 million gallons. The decision tree is shown in Figure 12–17.

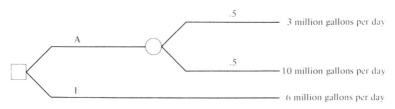

Fig. 12–17

If the government is interested in the greatest expected number of gallons, then it should choose Technology A. Indeed this would be the sensible action if, whatever the outcome, the island will be regularly purchasing additional supplies from some convenient source such as a pipeline from the mainland. (Thus far, this decision problem sounds like the electricity-generating problem discussed earlier.) The number of gallons at risk with the advanced technology may then be translated directly into dollars at risk should an additional purchase be necessary. That dollar amount will presumably be small relative to the total budget for the island. An expected value or averaging process would therefore be reasonable.

But what if this desalinization plant is to be a primary source of water for the island (and this is where this example departs from the generating plant example), and if additional water can be brought in only by an expensive process, say, by tanker? Then we will need to adopt a different approach. Although there will certainly be gains in producing 10 million gallons a day rather than 6, the uses to which the last gallons are put will be less valued than earlier uses. Perhaps the last million gallons a day will be used on lawns and fairways. In contrast, a drop to 3 million gallons a day would mean curtailing much more valuable uses of the water, such as irrigation of vegetable crops.

Suppose, for example, that experience with droughts in the past indicates that the first 3 million gallons to be produced by the plant will be worth $10,000 to the islanders, a supply of 6 million gallons will be worth $18,000, and one of 10 million gallons is worth a total of $25,000. The decision tree now becomes Figure 12–18. Looked at in this light, the traditional technology is superior. In other words, the loss in value if output is reduced from 6 million to 3 million gallons a day is $8000, which is greater than the gain of $7000 that would result from an increase in output from 6 million to 10 million gallons a day. Therefore the average dollar value achieved by pursuing Alternative *A* is less than the average dollar value achieved by pursuing Alternative *E*. With average dollars as our criterion of choice, Alternative *E* should be chosen. Moreover, if the island government is in addition risk averse with respect to money lotteries, the strength of this preference for Alternative *E* would be increased, for Alternative *E* is a sure thing.

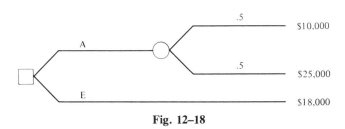

Fig. 12–18

This example shows that relying on the average output of some quantity such as gallons per day may be inappropriate. The gains from the same gallon increment may not be the same across different ranges of values. In this case it was legitimate to convert gallons to dollar equivalents and to use expected dollars as our criterion of choice. The islanders were willing to be risk neutral with respect to dollars, at least for the magnitude of dollars involved, but they were not willing to be risk neutral with respect to quantities of water.

But just as the value of gallons may diminish as we get more of them, so too the real worth to us of a dollar may not be the same at all dollar levels. Suppose you are offered a choice between $10,000 for sure, and the flip of a coin to determine whether you get $0 or $25,000. You might well prefer to receive $10,000, despite the fact that the lottery offers an expected dollar value of $12,500. The simple lesson is that when a gamble may substantially alter one's endowment of a vital commodity, whether dollars or gallons of water or health or environmental amenities, it may be inappropriate to use expected values in making a choice.

Economists and decision theorists have developed methods for handling situations where expected dollars are not a suitable criterion for choice because there is a substantial variation in the value of dollars achieved under alternative outcomes. The basic approach involves converting dollar outcomes to an artificially constructed scale of values called utilities. The methodology is called *utility theory*. It can appear deceptively simple, but in fact the scaling process is rigorously defined and ensures that the individual will be risk neutral with respect to lotteries that are expressed in terms of these utilities. As we converted gallons to dollars in the desalinization plant example, so utility theory converts dollars, or any other measurable unit, to utility units. We shall not deal with utility theory here; it is left to an appendix at the end of this chapter. The lazy reader will take comfort from our confession that we have encountered few actual public policy analyses where utility theory was explicitly employed, though some might claim that its use is implicit in structuring a graduated income tax. The budding decision analyst will master that appendix, hoping perhaps to be among the first to apply this important technique to the assessment of critical policy issues. One major application of the utility theory approach, was addressed to the appropriate location of the new Mexico City airport.[5] It had a significant impact on the Mexican government's ultimate policy choice.

The Value of Information

We return again to the problem in which a decision maker was required to choose between two types of generators for a power plant. The output characteristics for the old type of generator were known with certainty; for the new they were not. The decision maker also had the option of acquiring accurate information about the new technology by having a prototype built and tested. We found that the latter was the best choice, with the final decision relying on the results of the test. (The complete decision tree is shown in Figure 12–7.)

Is it always advisable to gather additional information before making a decision? If you think for a minute, the answer clearly must be no. First and most simply, it may be that the information, whatever it is, cannot possibly change the decision. Second, even when a decision might be altered, the cost of acquiring the information in terms of resources and delays may be more than the information is worth. For example, the director of the dam project would not have found it worthwhile to spend $2 million to test the prototype generator, because the expected value of the "Test" branch would then be only $5.1 million, significantly less than the $6.5 million EMV of the "Don't test" branch. Just how much should the decision maker be willing to pay?

We can work this out using our decision tree. Let T be the cost of the test in millions (we will get back to specific values of T in a moment). Then the payoffs (reading from the top of the tree down) are $5 - T$, $8 - T$, and so on. If we average out and fold back, the tree reduces to Figure 12–19. Note

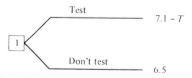

Fig. 12–19
(All payoffs are in millions of dollars.)

[5] See Ralph L. Keeney, "A Decision Analysis with Multiple Objectives: The Mexico City Airport," *Bell Journal of Economics and Management Science* 4 (1973): 101–17.

that we don't need to know the value of T in order to make a choice at decision node 2. The choice is between "Install old" for a payoff of $5 - T$ and "Install new" for a payoff of $8 - T$. Whatever the value of T, "Install new" is better. But at decision node 1, the choice depends on what T is. Clearly the decision maker should choose "Test" as long as the cost of the test is less than $.6 million; if it is greater than $.6 million, he should install the new type of generator without testing. Thus for any amount up to $.6 million, the test is a good buy; anything more would be a mistake. Hence the test is worth $.6 million to the decision maker. We call this amount the Expected Value of Perfect Information, or *EVPI*. A decision maker who can undertake a costly perfect test should be willing to pay up to his EVPI for it. In general, the EVPI is the difference between the EMV of the "Test" branch for a perfectly accurate test and the EMV of the next best branch.

Another Illustration of the Value of Information: The Metropole Subway System

Metropole, a large subway system, is considering the installation of automatic train-speed controls on its new branch. The savings in personnel costs will be significant. Two types of controls are available. The type sold by Venerable Engineering has been thoroughly tested in use. It will cost $14 million. A much cheaper alternative is produced by Innovative Technology. Unfortunately, it has not been proven in practice. Metropole believes that it is 60 percent likely that Innovative's controls will work. If that system is purchased and it then fails, all payments made to Innovative will be refunded. But Metropole will have to fall back on a nonautomated system for six months while the Innovative controls are removed and the Venerable system installed. Extra personnel costs during these six months will amount to $3 million. Innovative Technology is eager to pull off a sale to a big subway system and offers its speed controls to Metropole for $10 million. The decision tree (for pedagogic simplicity, we ignore discounting considerations) is shown in Figure 12–20.

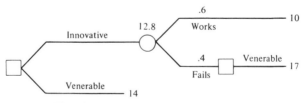

Fig. 12–20
(All payoffs are in millions of dollars.)

Note that in this decision problem we are seeking to minimize expected costs, and hence should choose the lowest expected value at each decision node. If Metropole is risk neutral, and we shall assume that it is on gambles of this size, then it should adopt the Innovative system.

Another possibility is available. A simulated system could be developed to create the equivalent of a field test for the Innovative controls. Metropole has not yet received firm bids for this field test. (Before it does, you might want to work out how much it should pay at the most.) Assume that the test could be run in the next few months, that it is completely reliable, that if it succeeds the Innovative system will be installed on schedule, and that if it fails the Venerable system will be available at the time it is needed. The decision tree has now acquired another branch. Before looking at Figure 12–21, try to work out for yourself how much Metropole should be willing to pay for the test.

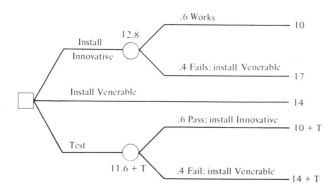

Fig. 12–21

The EMV of the "Test" branch is $11.6 million plus the cost of the test, T. The EMV of the "Don't test" branch is $12.8 million. Therefore the EVPI is (12.8) − (11.6) = 1.2 million dollars. Metropole should be willing to pay up to that amount for the test.

Perfect information is rarely to be had through a straightforward expenditure of dollars; we can acquire it, if at all, only by waiting, and waiting carries its own costs, costs that must be considered as part of the test costs. For example, in our subway example, if the conditions were different, the test might have delayed the installation of automated speed controls by one month. This then would have added $.5 million in personnel costs to the system, whatever the outcome of the test. Even when they occur in intangible form, it is usually helpful to think about information costs and how much the information is worth.

Drawing Inferences from Imperfect Tests

It was easy to trace the implications of the tests we considered for the prototype generator and the speed control system, for we assumed that the tests were perfectly accurate. The real world is usually less cooperative, and is less precise about revealing the true situation. Our devices for gathering information turn out to be tests that are imperfect in a variety of ways. Must a test be wholly reliable in order to be of value? Any test whose results may change a decision has some value. (Poker players make mighty efforts to catch the slightest clue or hint of information from their fellow players.) Naturally, the more imperfect the test, the less we should be willing to pay for it. The EVPI serves as an upper bound for testing costs; if information is not completely reliable, we should pay at a maximum somewhat less than that amount.

Let's stick with our Metropole example a bit longer; we now assume that the simulated field test is imperfect. If the test result is "Fail," the controls will surely fail in operation. But "Pass" is less reliable. The controls are expected to pass the test 80 percent of the time, but the pass result is accurate only 75 percent of the time; one time in four when the controls pass the test they will fail in practice. This implies that the controls will work in practice 80 percent × 75 percent = 60 percent of the time. How much should Metropole be willing to pay for this imperfect test?

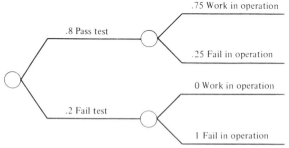

Fig. 12–22
(All payoffs in millions of dollars; IT is the cost of the imperfect test.)

We can summarize the test information in an *event tree*, as in Figure 12–22. (An event tree has only chance nodes; such trees have been used notably in studies of nuclear reactor safety.) This minitree is then incorporated in a full decision tree, as is shown in Figure 12–23. Working backward from the tips of the tree, we immediately see that "Install Innovative without testing" has an EMV of 12.8, and "Install Venerable " an EMV of 14. These figures are the same as in the earlier version of the problem. As before, Venerable controls are eliminated from further consideration because the expected cost is higher than for Innovative. The "Test Innovative" branch is more complicated, but if we average out and fold back we find that its EMV is $12.2 million plus the cost of the imperfect

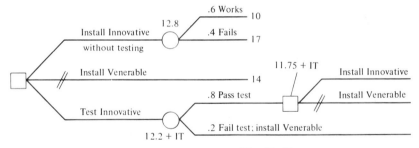

Fig. 12–23

test, *IT*. Metropole should be willing to pay up to $.6 million for the imperfect test.

Putting Imperfect Test Information into Usable Form: Abused Children

In the example just considered, we were supplied with all the test information we needed. But frequently the information isn't as neatly arranged as this. Consider the following situation, based on an investigation of the problems in identifying abused children.[6]

School officials believe that 3 percent of a city's 10,000 school children are physically abused. Measures can be taken to help these children, but first they must be located. It is proposed to carry out a preliminary screening of all children; when evidence of abuse (such as bruises of a certain type) is found, interviews with parents will follow. Unfortunately the screening process is not entirely reliable. If a child is actually abused, the chance is 95 percent that the test used for the screening will be positive, i.e., will indicate that the child is abused. On the other hand, if the child is not abused, the chance is only 10 percent that the test will be positive.[7] School officials are most anxious to identify cases of abuse, yet must proceed cautiously given the enormous stigma that attaches to parents who are falsely accused. The tradeoffs are painful, and it is imperative that school officials understand the implications of a positive or negative test.

The difficulty is that the information is not in a shape that's readily usable. However, we have all the numbers we need; we just have to perform a few calculations and rearrange them. Figure 12–24 sets forth what we now know.

But it doesn't serve any purpose to screen a child *after* we know he is

---

[6] Richard Light, "Abused and Neglected Children in America: A Study of Alternative Policies," *Harvard Educational Review* 43, no. 4 (November 1973).

[7] For purposes of illustration, abuse and the test for it are assumed to be yes–no variables (the technical term is "binary"). We all know that this is an oversimplification; there are many degrees of abuse, and evidence of abuse varies in its degree of ambiguity. Introducing this additional complexity would cause no conceptual difficulty, though more arithmetic would be required to get the information into usable form. Note, moreover, that when it comes to taking action on behalf of abused children, both the screening test and the actual existence of abuse may well be viewed as binary. Authorities may determine that even though the results of the screening may be reported along a continuous scale, scores above a certain cutoff point will be regarded as indicating abuse and will result in direct intervention with the family.

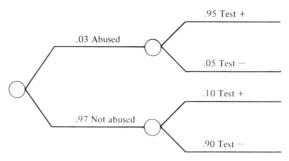

Fig. 12–24

abused. We need to know what the likelihood is that a positive test means that a child is indeed abused, or that a negative test means that he is not. In other words, we want the information in the form of Figure 12–25.

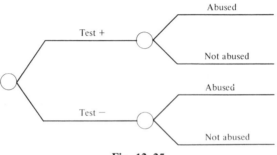

Fig. 12–25

Look again at the tree shown in Figure 12–24, and think about what it means to follow along the topmost branch: it means that the child is abused and at the same time the test is positive. The probability of this combined event—the joint probability—is .03 × .95 = .0285. It is called the *path probability* because it's the probability of following the whole course of one particular path on the decision tree. (Granted, in the interest of consistency it might be called the branch probability, but it isn't.) Look next at the topmost path in Figure 12–25; if we follow along this path it means that the child's test is positive and he also is abused. But this combined event is just the same as the combined event "is abused and has positive test"; the order is immaterial. Hence the joint probability must be the same, .0285. Similarly, each of the other paths on the second tree is the counterpart of a path on the first tree, although the order from top to bottom is not the same on both trees. The probabilities for each path are shown at the tips of the branches in Figures 12–26a and 12–26b.

Now comes the crucial step. Notice that *if* a child's test is positive it must be that either he is abused (with probability .0285 for the joint event "test positive, is abused") or he isn't (with probability .097 for the joint event "test positive, is not abused"); the total probability of a positive test is the sum of these, .1255. Similarly, we find that the probability of a negative test is the sum of the probability that the child is abused and has a

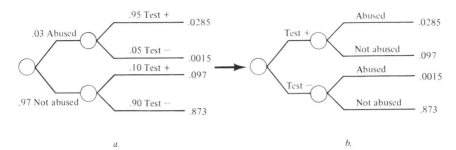

Fig. 12–26

negative test (.0015) and the probability that he is not abused and has a negative test (.873), or .8745. Entering these results on Figure 12–25's target tree, we have Figure 12–27.

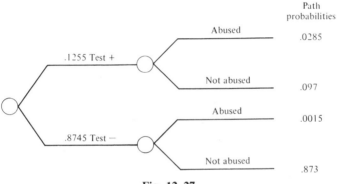

Path probabilities

Fig. 12–27

It remains only to fill in the probabilities at the final two chance nodes, and this is a matter of simple arithmetic. If the probability of a positive test is .1255, and the probability of the path "Test +; abused" is .0285, then the probability that the child is abused, *once his test is positive,* is .0285/.1255 = .2271. Following the same procedure, we fill in the rest of the tree, as in Figure 12–28.

This event tree is in a form that is of use to us; it is what we have been aiming for. The whole process is called "tree flipping", it is the intuitive version of Bayes' formula.[8] The tree flipping technique offers many advantages. It's simple; there's no formula to forget or foul up; and most

---

[8] For those who are more comfortable with formal mathematical notation we print the usual Bayes' formula:

$$p(A \mid +) = \frac{p(A)p(+ \mid A)}{[p(A)p(+ \mid A)] + [p(\text{Not } A)p(+ \mid \text{Not } A)]}$$

In this notation $p(A)$ is the overall probability (the "prior" probability) of abuse. The vertical line $\mid$ indicates a conditional probability; $p(A \mid +)$, for example, is to be read "the probability of abuse, given that the test is positive." The formula was originally set forth by the Reverend Thomas Bayes, an 18th-century English cleric. We strongly urge you to rely on tree flipping for updating probabilities.

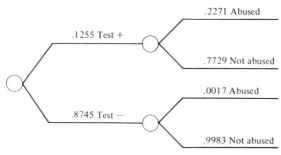

Fig. 12–28

important, it works well for more complex situations, such as those in which there are more than two underlying conditions. Suppose, for example, that the underlying conditions are no evidence of abuse, strong evidence, and ambiguous evidence, while the test reports are +, −, and ?. The formula is a mess in such cases, but the tree is crystal clear.

Practice in Tree Flipping: A Medical Test

A doctor must treat a patient who has a tumor. He knows that 70 percent of similar tumors are benign. He can perform a test, but the test is not perfectly accurate. If the tumor is malignant, long experience with the test indicates that the probability is 80 percent that the test will be positive, and 10 percent that it will be negative; 10 percent of the tests are inconclusive. If the tumor is benign, the probability is 70 percent that the test will be negative, 20 percent that it will be positive; again, 10 percent of the tests are inconclusive. What is the significance of a positive or negative test?

The information immediately available to the doctor is described succinctly in the event tree in Figure 12–29. But it doesn't serve any

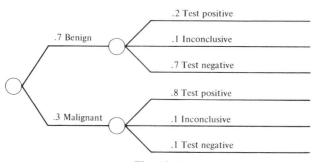

Fig. 12–29

purpose to perform the test after we know whether the tumor is benign or malignant. The doctor needs to know the probabilities for the event tree in Figure 12–30.

Try to work out the answer for yourself before looking at the complete conversion in Figure 12–31.

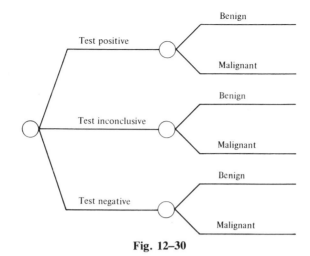

Fig. 12–30

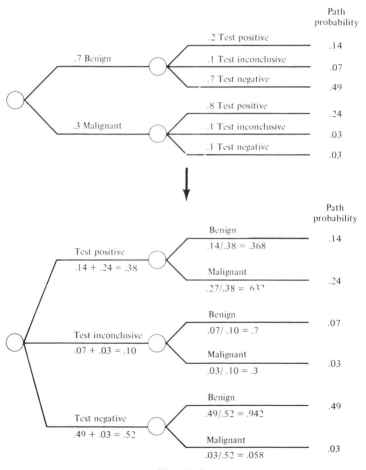

Fig. 12–31

Imperfect Tests and Intangible Payoffs

Both the child abuse and the tumor tests ultimately lead to decisions about subsequent courses of action that cannot be quantified in any clearcut fashion. Nevertheless decision analysis poses the nature of the decision maker's dilemma very clearly. For example, suppose for simplicity that good medical practice requires that a malignant tumor be treated surgically and a benign tumor left alone. Then four general types of intermediate outcome are possible: (1) the patient has a necessary operation; (2) the patient undergoes surgery unnecessarily; (3) the patient receives no treatment and none is needed; (4) the patient fails to receive necessary treatment. For each of these intermediate outcomes, the patient will have certain probabilities of recovering and dying. (In the long run, of course, the probability of dying is 1.0. We are talking about the short run.)

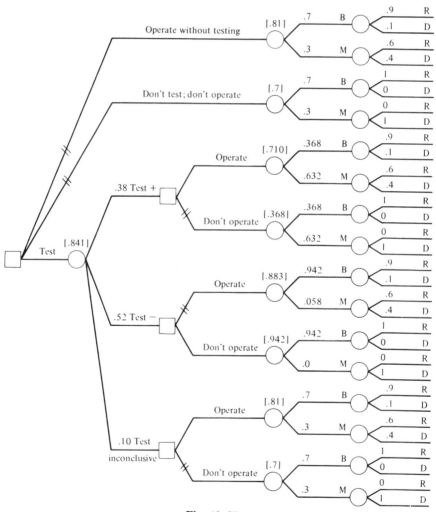

Fig. 12–32

Decision analysis cannot help the doctor determine the value of each of these outcomes. But it does remind him starkly that whatever decision he makes, given what he knows about the probability that a tumor is benign or malignant and the likelihood of recovery or death in each situation, he will implicitly set boundaries on the values he assigns to these outcomes. The decision tree is shown in Figure 12–32. The benign/malignant probabilities are transposed from Figure 12–31. If the recover/die probabilities can be estimated, the course that gives the patient the best chance of recovery can be directly determined. We have used conjectural probabilities for recover (*R*) and die (*D*) in Figure 12–32; the numbers in brackets [ ] are the resulting chances of recovery. Death of the patient due to other causes is excluded from consideration, in order to simplify the exposition; additional chance nodes could easily be added to allow for such contingencies. Similarly, "recover" is of course much too broad a category; in practice we might well insist that the prospective quality of the patient's life be taken into consideration.

The child abuse problem is similar. What should school officials do once the preliminary screening indicates that a child is abused? Perhaps their first instinct is to pursue vigorously each suspected case of abuse. The relevant part of this event tree is shown in Figure 12–33. In other words, the chances are greater than three in four that, if a suspected case is followed up, the parents will turn out to be innocent. The school department may well feel that this is hardly the way to win friends for its programs, or do good for its community. It must weigh the severe harm of permitting an occasional case of child abuse to continue against the serious costs of falsely implicating parents. In practice this analysis would probably lead the department to schedule careful follow-ups after symptoms of abuse are detected. Or if test outcomes were in the form of several gradations from negative to positive, as might well be the case in the real world, perhaps only the strongest positives would be pursued.

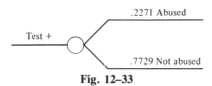

Fig. 12–33

These treat–don't treat dilemmas are encountered in many guises. Even when unnecessary treatment is not positively harmful, it is likely to be expensive and time-consuming. Utility theory offers each decision maker a way to quantify the value of these risky and intangible outcomes in terms of his own personal preferences; it is discussed in the appendix to this chapter.

Decision Analysis and a Contemporary Policy Issue

One of the most complex issues currently facing the United States is the question of how electricity is to be generated for the next half century. The choice between continued reliance on the light water nuclear reactor and development of the breeder (more accurately, the liquid metal fast breeder reactor) is one aspect of that controversy. A study of the optimal timing of research and development (R&D) for the U.S. breeder reactor program illustrates the tremendous capabilities that decision analysis offers for clarifying such a problem.[9]

The Clinch River breeder reactor, a demonstration plant located near Oak Ridge, Tennessee, is scheduled for completion in 1983, provided Congress does not cut off its funding. The next step planned for the breeder program is to build a large breeder reactor that would serve as a commercial prototype, to be followed in turn by the first commercial breeder reactor. The study examines four options: (1) concurrent development of Clinch River and the commercial prototype, with a decision to be made in 1986 as to whether we should then proceed with a full-scale commercial breeder; (2) sequential development, with Clinch River to be developed now, a decision on the prototype to be made in 1986, and a decision on the commercial breeder in 2005; (3) waiting until 1986 before making a decision on both Clinch River and the prototype, with the concurrent development route then pursued if information is favorable; and (4) stopping development now and ceasing R&D. The first stage of the decision tree is shown in Figure 12-34. The dates at the tips of the branches indicate when the first commercial prototype would come into use.

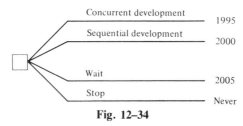

Fig. 12–34

In this analysis, several key uncertainties affect the outcome of each decision and hence are included in the complete decision tree. These uncertainties relate to the success of the initial breeders, the supply of uranium, future energy demands, capital cost differentials between the light water reactor and the breeder, the future availability of other advanced technologies, breeder R&D costs, and public reaction to the issues of nuclear safety and potential environmental damage. Benefits take the form of lower energy costs in the future.

The Atomic Energy Commission (AEC, later ERDA, the Energy Research and Development Administration), on the other hand, favors a deterministic model to investigate the ramifications of the R&D decision, using a number of possible scenarios for the future. Net benefits are then

[9] Richard G. Richels, *R & D under Uncertainty: A Study of the U.S. Breeder Reactor Program* (Cambridge, Mass.: Energy and Environmental Policy Center, Harvard University, 1976).

calculated for each scenario. The AEC thus relies on a once-and-for-all masterplan, with a commitment to an entire timetable. In contrast, the decision tree approach would permit the AEC to set up a decision process that enables it to take advantage of new information as it becomes available. As a result of the scenario approach, those opposed to the further development of the breeder have focused on the scenarios that make it look bad, while the proponents have stressed those that lead to a recommendation of concurrent development. No sense of the likelihood of each scenario emerges from the analysis, and hence no estimation of expected net benefits is possible. Both types of scenario are plausible; the debate continues.

One of the interesting features of the decision analysis study of this issue is its treatment of environmental and safety issues. Rather than addressing them directly, all such issues are subsumed under a single uncertainty, the likelihood of a moratorium on further use of nuclear power, assuming implicitly that a moratorium will be invoked when environmental and safety costs are high. This approach has several virtues. It limits the scope of the analysis; in effect it says only, "*If* we decide to go ahead with the breeder, this is the economically effective way to go." In thus separating dollar outlay and benefit questions from the crucially important intangible considerations, the tradeoffs between dollars and potential threats to safety and the environment are made explicit. Focusing on the likelihood of a nuclear moratorium also recognizes that, since the parties to the nuclear debate will never reach agreement on the safety of the breeder, the critical issue is what people believe about its safety.

Figure 12–35 shows the essential features of the complete decision tree. A programming model is used to derive estimates of the relevant costs and benefits, and probabilities are carefully assessed. The tree is then folded back and we find that if the decision is to be made on economic grounds alone, the concurrent development strategy is preferable, though not by a wide margin. Not to leave you in suspense, the expected values (discounted at a 10 percent annual rate) of the four alternatives are shown in Table 12–1.

You may argue that the analysis is all well and good, but given the political mood in this country and the widely expressed concerns about reactor safety and spent fuel disposal, the large outlay implied by concur-

Table 12–1

Concurrent development	$13.8 billion
Sequential development	$12.5 billion
Wait	$11.5 billion
Stop	$ 0

rent or even sequential development is no longer feasible. Decision analysis makes it relatively easy to evaluate altered situations; of course, it may be necessary to fold back the tree afresh. Sometimes it's simply a matter of introducing revised probabilities or refining the estimates of the payoffs. At other times whole branches must be struck off the tree. Since the nuclear R&D analysis was completed, for example, the breeder has been put on hold. Sometimes the exploration of new options will require us to add a bit of vegetation. Here again, the required revisions in the analysis

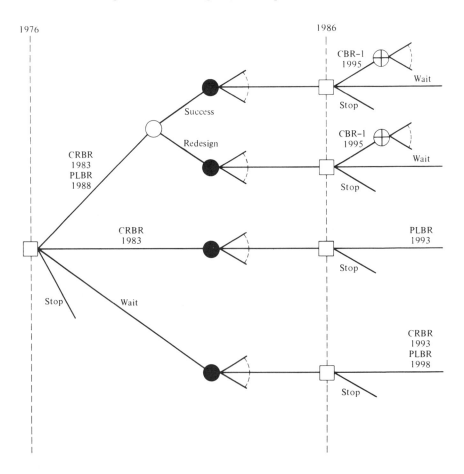

Fig. 12–35
CRBR = Clinch River Breeder Reactor
PLBR = Prototype Large Breeder Reactor
CBR–1 = First Commercial Breeder Reactor
Dates are estimated completion times.
Chance nodes:
    1. Design succeeds or redesign necessary
    2. Combined uncertainties about nuclear moratorium, demand projections, and uranium availability
    3. Combined uncertainties about capital cost differentials, availability of other advanced technologies, and more up-to-date estimates of uranium supply
    4. Still later estimates of uranium supply
    5. Combined uncertainties (at a later date than above) about capital cost differentials and availability of other advanced technologies

are straightforward. Finally, decision analysis also permits us easily to investigate the sensitivity of the conclusions reached to the quantitative assumptions made, a matter of particular interest in the nuclear debate. We turn now to a brief consideration of that aspect of decision analysis.

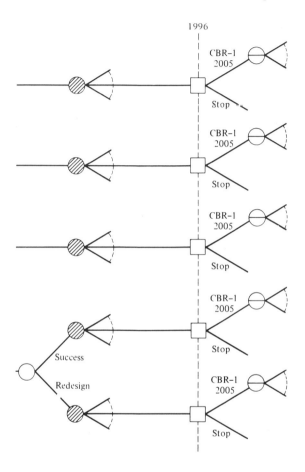

Sensitivity Analysis

Sometimes experts in a particular field object to the conclusions reached by a decision analysis. If they do, their objections should be rooted not in the methodology but in the assumptions that guided the construction of the tree. Thus an expert on energy might claim that the study of research and development strategies for nuclear power plants discussed in the preceding section neglected certain alternative strategies, such as proceeding full speed ahead to develop solar power. Perhaps some aspects of the payoffs were understated; maybe the future availability of uranium was misestimated. Or perhaps some of the probabilities were miscalculated. The estimate of the likelihood that the first design for the Clinch River breeder reactor would prove successful by 1986 was in fact much too high.

Assume for the moment that at least some of these claims are correct. Should we blame decision analysis? No, it is merely a tool. To discredit the method because it is misapplied would be equivalent to blaming the manufacturer of the architect's table and T-square for the design of an inadequate structure. Indeed, a more forceful defense can be made for decision analysis. It is particularly well suited for examining the effect of changing some of the critical underlying assumptions. This process is called sensitivity analysis.

Usually the probability distributions and payoffs used in a decision analysis are estimates rather than hard numbers. In fact, sometimes they are little more than informed guesses. Nevertheless, if this is the best information the decision maker can come up with, he should go ahead and use it. In such circumstances he naturally would like to know how sensitive his final decision is to the estimates he has used. If he finds it to be very sensitive, he should then spend more time refining the estimates. Decision analysis lends itself very well to a careful calculation of that sensitivity. Here is a very simple example.

A risk neutral decision maker must choose between two construction sites. Site preparation for Location I will cost $85,000. For Location II the cost is iffier; the decision maker thinks there is a 60 percent chance it will cost $100,000, but if he's lucky it will cost only $40,000. The tree is shown in Figure 12–36.

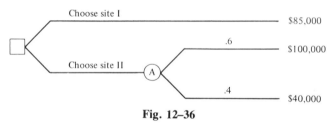

Fig. 12–36

The EMV at chance node A is $76,000, and so Site II appears to be the preferred choice. But in fact the probabilities .6 and .4 are based on limited information; the decision maker believes they could be refined significantly with a little effort. How sensitive is his decision to these probabilities? To put it another way, how different would they have to be to change his decision? He can find out by calculating the probabilities for which Location I would be preferred to Location II. As the probability of a cost of $100,000 increases, Site II will become less and less attractive, until for some probability p the decision maker is neutral between the two sites. Thereafter he will prefer Site I. Let's find the p for which he would be indifferent, for which the expected cost of the two alternatives is the same. That p will satisfy the equation

$$p(100,000) + (1 - p)(40,000) = 85,000$$

which yields $p = .75$. In other words, whenever the probability that the cost at Site II is $100,000 exceeds .75, Site I will be preferred. Now the decision maker may feel unsure that p is .6, but at the same time feel reasonably certain that no information he gathers will push it higher than .7. If this is his belief, he should proceed with Location II; no benefit will result from gathering further information even if it is costless. If the sensitivity analysis still leaves him uneasy with the decision, he can always figure out what it would be worth to get more information before proceeding. And perhaps he should reexamine his assumption of risk neutrality.

A similar procedure can be used to test sensitivity to payoff values of other critical parameters. Let's assume that at Location II getting clear title to the land will involve legal expenses. The decision maker might wish to determine just how large those expenses can be before he should choose Location I.

In discussing the operate/don't-operate decision described on page 228, we used conjectural probabilities for recovery and death. It so happens that with these particular probabilities, "test" narrowly edges out "operate without testing." If we perform a crude sensitivity analysis (i.e., take a good hard look at the numbers) we see that this result comes about because the mortality rate when the tumor is benign is 10 percent. Had we hit upon a mortality rate of 0.1 percent, the preferred choice would have been "operate without testing," for in that case an incorrect negative test presents a greater danger than the operation.[10]

In the choice of energy reseach and development strategies, a critical parameter is the discount rate. If the discount rate used is greater than 10 percent, strategies that get substantial R&D programs underway immediately look less desirable. If it turns out that the optimal R&D strategy shifts when the discount rate rises from 10 to, say, 10.2 percent, then much more time should be spent attempting to pin down the current rate. But if the preferred choice does not change until the rate exceeds 18 percent, then the objection that "things came out that way only because they picked a low discount rate" would quickly be shown to be misguided. In such a situation, we say that the conclusion is *robust* with respect to variations in the discount rate. Sensitivity analysis is thus potentially a powerful tool for policy analysis and debate.

In the breeder study, sensitivity analysis was used to check the probability assessments, and all were found to be robust with the exception of the likelihood of a nuclear moratorium. It was found that if concurrent development is ruled out for political reasons, sequential development is the preferred economic alternative provided the probability of a moratorium is less than .63. If that probability is between .63 and .86, the best strategy is to wait. If it is greater than .86, then research and development should be stopped altogether.

---

[10] Realistically, we should recognize that doctors are strongly influenced by standards of "good medical practice," by the fact that the costs of tests are usually covered by the patient's medical insurance, and by the need to practice defensive medicine in the face of possible malpractice litigation. The type of analysis set forth above enables us to assess the consequences when doctors respond to such influences.

Sometimes we can be confident that we are choosing desirable courses of action because we can formulate relatively precise assumptions about critical variables. At other times we may be in the fortunate position of having policies available that are robust with respect to a realistic range of assumptions. Decision analysis can tell us when our preferred policy choices are robust and when they are sensitive to the numbers assumed in the analysis. If they are sensitive, decision analysis will help us identify which assumptions are critical and which don't matter much. It cannot resolve debates about underlying values, but it is of great assistance when we must engage in a discussion about the implications of alternative sets of values.

The Uses of Decision Analysis

How does a decision tree fit in with the other models we have examined? Many of the analytic techniques studied earlier may be useful for estimating probabilities or payoffs, or even for determining options. The use of a tree is wholly compatible with the other techniques. Indeed, it is more than likely that benefit–cost analysis and discounting will be required in estimating payoffs, and we recognize that other models will be used to formulate probabilities.

This brief discussion of decision analysis has been aimed at convincing you of the wide applicability of the conceptual framework. Sometimes a decision appears so straightforward that it's hardly worth writing down the numbers and running them through the mill, yet defining the problem in the form of a decision tree may uncover issues and perspectives that would otherwise be overlooked. On other occasions a tree may prove helpful in sorting out a decision problem with so many ramifications that only a systematic approach can make it manageable. And the more difficult the task, the more useful decision analysis is likely to prove in comparison to the alternatives of no analysis at all or back-of-the-envelope calculations.

Appendix: Utility Theory

In the foregoing chapter we observed that expected value is frequently an unsatisfactory criterion for choice in risky situations. One example that we explored in detail involved the water supply for an island. In that case, we saw that by attaching dollar values to the water, we could get a much more accurate measure of the true value of alternative lotteries. Utility theory generalizes this procedure to any lottery, including most specifically lotteries where the decision maker is uncomfortable with a decision based on expected monetary value (EMV).

Our discussion focuses on the individual decision maker, who may be acting on his own behalf or on behalf of others; the broad principles we develop are appropriate in either situation. The policy maker who understands the central issues involved in making any risky decision is better equipped to make choices that affect the well-being of his individual constituents.

The Nature of the Problem and a Suggested Solution

Consider the very simple situation set forth in Figure 12A–1. The EMV of each of these two choices is $0, but most of us would have little difficulty in deciding quickly that we prefer Y. We say that, faced with a choice between these two courses of action, we would be *risk averse*; we would choose the less risky alternative, and we would even pay something of a

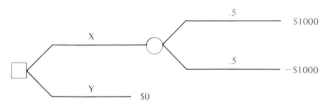

Fig. 12A–1

premium to get it rather than the risky option X. If we were to analyze the underlying reasons for our attitudes, we would probably conclude that Y appears preferable to X because losing $1000 would hurt us far more than winning $1000 would benefit us. This is an example of what economists sometimes loosely refer to as the diminishing marginal utility of money. In laymen's terms, it means that we spend our money on whatever we value most highly. Additional money, if we had it to spend, would go for something less valuable to us. Consequently, the loss of $1000 would hurt more than the gain of $1000 would help.[11]

---

[11] This principle was recognized at least as early as 1738. Daniel Bernoulli, in analyzing the famous St. Petersburg paradox, noted that expected value does not serve as a guide to action for most people. The paradox arises in the following way: you are offered the opportunity to buy a lottery in which a coin is tossed until it comes up heads. The game then ends and you

How can we find a systematic method for handling situations of this type? Suppose you are a decision maker; you are faced with the gamble shown in Figure 12A–2. You're not sure how much you like it. You may even conclude that you'd prefer to say "No thanks" and walk away, but that is not an option. The lottery is yours. However, you do have the right to dispose of the lottery to someone else, either by selling it to him or by paying him to take if off your hands. What is the ownership of this gamble worth to you? Perhaps you would say to yourself, "I can think of a dozen things I would like to do with $1000, but if the coin comes up tails and I lose $500 I will have to give up my summer vacation plans, and I certainly don't want to do that. On the other hand, the loss of $500 wouldn't wipe me out, and it *is* a favorable gamble. What if I were to sell it? I could do a lot with $300, or even with $200; how about $150? I don't think I'd sell out for as little as that. OK, if I can get as much as $200 for it, I'll take the sure $200, but not a penny less. Otherwise, I'll stick with the gamble, though frankly the prospect makes me a little nervous." We would then say that your *certainty equivalent* or certainty monetary equivalent (CME) for this lottery is $200. Notice that we refer to *your* CME for *this* lottery. The CME is the individual's subjective evaluation of a specific lottery. We will argue below that you ought to be consistent in your evaluations from one lottery to the next, and consistency of this type is the foundation on which utility theory is built.

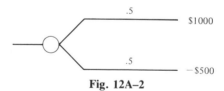

Fig. 12A–2

What have we accomplished by abandoning the EMV of a lottery in favor of a lump sum evaluation of the entire chance node? Can we still use the averaging out and folding back procedure? Indeed we can, and that is the purpose of this exercise. In working backward from the tips of the trees, the decision maker assigns to every chance node his own subjective evaluation of what the lottery represented by that node is worth to him. In effect we did just that in the last chapter in assigning dollar values to various amounts of the island's water supply. We explicitly recognized that although more is better, it is not proportionately better. Just as the

---

receive a payment of ($2)^n, where n is the number of tosses in the game. The probability of heads on the first toss is 1/2, of tails on the first and heads on the second $(1/2)^2 = 1/4$; in general the probability of $(n - 1)$ tails followed by heads on the nth toss is $(1/2)^n$. Hence the expected value of the payoff is

$$1/2(\$2) + 1/4(\$4) + 1/8(\$8) + \ldots = 1 + 1 + 1 + \ldots$$

which is an infinitely large sum. You should therefore be willing to pay any amount, however large, for the opportunity to play this game. But would you? Certainly not—and that is the alleged paradox, which is hardly paradoxical once we recognize the existence of risk aversion.

islanders would not in general be risk neutral on gambles involving significant quantities of water, most individuals are not risk neutral on gambles involving significant sums of money.

Let's see how this would work in a very simple case. Suppose that you are a thoroughly risk averse individual and are faced with the decision problem shown in Figure 12A–3. (We leave you the task of contriving a plausible story to accompany these numbers. Perhaps you have succumbed to a bizarre raffle offered by the State Lottery Commission.)

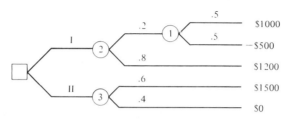

Fig. 12A–3

How do you proceed? As before, you must work back from the tips of the trees. But now at each chance node you make your own judgment as to what that particular lottery is worth to you. Your steps might proceed as follows:

1. Node 1: This is the lottery we discussed just above; you have already decided that your CME for it is $200. In other words, even though the EMV at this node is $250, you would take $200 for sure (although no amount less).

2. Node 2 is now seen to be equivalent to Figure 12A–4. You decide your CME at this node is $900.

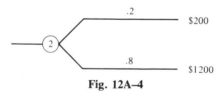

Fig. 12A–4

3. Node 3: You decide your CME is $800. Again, you would settle for a sure $800, even though the EMV of this lottery is $900.

4. The decision is thus reduced to Figure 12A–5. The best choice is then clearly Action I.

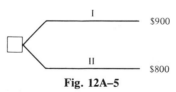

Fig. 12A–5

At this point two questions may occur to you. First, is this method legitimate? In other words, can we be confident that the decision reached by this substitution technique, which has something of an air of sleight-of-hand, reflects the decision maker's true preferences between I and II? Happily, the answer is a firm "yes"—subject to certain assumptions about the consistency of these preferences, which we believe you will find reasonable. These assumptions are discussed at the end of this appendix; right now we'd rather not interrupt the thread of the discussion.

Second, does it really help? Here the answer must be "yes, but not always directly." We have reduced the overall decision problem to a series of smaller problems, which is surely an improvement over ad hoc intuitive procedures. But the simple problems may still not be simple enough. If you can readily assign reasonably consistent CMEs to each chance node that you encounter, your problem is solved. It's relatively easy to determine your CMEs for simple lotteries like those we've just considered, each of which have only two outcomes. But suppose you are working away, assigning CMEs and averaging out and folding back at a good clip, and you come up against a chance node that looks like Figure 12A–6. What is your CME for this lottery? Even if after thorough reflection you came up with a number, would you have any confidence that it's "right," that it really

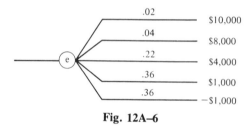

Fig. 12A–6

reflects your preferences accurately? Fortunately, von Neumann–Morgenstern utility theory provides a way out of this dilemma, a systematic method for handling such combinations. First published in 1944, it was developed by the brilliant mathematician John von Neumann, who among other accomplishments built the first working computer, and Oskar Morgenstern, a leading economist.

The Measurement of Preferences: von Neumann–Morgenstern Utility Theory

We have tried throughout this volume to deal with the more mathematical aspects of public choice on a purely intuitive level. Utility theory is the acid test for this approach.

The problem of measuring satisfaction (which is what we really mean by that awkward word *utility*) has pricked and pervaded economics for more than a century. The heart of the difficulty is this: purchases of goods and services are only a means to an end, the achievement of satisfaction. We can measure the dollars spent by the individual on these purchases, but we have no direct way to measure the satisfaction he achieves from them. Therefore, we cannot determine whether a dollar spent by one person provides him with more or less satisfaction than a dollar spent by another. It is tempting to assume that of course a rich man's last dollar offers him less satisfaction than a poor man's, because the former is less strapped for the necessities of life. But in fact we have no justification for making this assumption, for we have no meter for rating their capacities for enjoyment. A poverty-stricken misanthrope may derive less real pleasure from another $100 in income than his affluent neighbor who spends it on a case of champagne. In short, we have no way to assign an objective cardinal index to individual preferences, no basis whatsoever for making interpersonal comparisons of satisfaction, and consequently no factual basis for making judgments that rely on such comparisons. This is not to say that such judgments should not be made—they are unavoidable—but merely to recognize that they necessarily involve subjective evaluations.

We can't even find a way to assign a cardinal index to the different levels of satisfaction experienced by a single individual. We can record *whether* he prefers one outcome to another, which is more than we can do in trying to make comparisons between two different people. But we can't say by *how much* he prefers one outcome to another. Thus the statement, "I like oranges three times as much as apples," has no operational meaning—we simply cannot assign any numbers that uniquely and unequivocally reflect this statement. To repeat, we can compare outcomes for an individual and thereby establish his preference ordering for those outcomes, but we cannot assign a cardinal value to them in the way we assign cardinal values when we measure height and weight.

What does all this have to do with decision analysis? When choices are made under certainty, the decision maker's ordinal preference rankings are sufficient for determining the best course of action.[12] In fact, if the decision tree has been drawn, there is no need to work through the whole tree to determine the best course of action. The decision maker merely runs down the list of outcomes, finds the best, and then works backward from it to determine the succession of choices that will lead to it. But once uncertainty enters the picture, ordinal preferences may not provide him with enough guidance to make the best decision. Consider the following three very simple situations, where $X > Y > Z$ (outcome X is preferred to Y, which is in turn preferred to Z). If you find it easier to think about concrete situations—and who doesn't—pretend that X, Y, and Z are a town pool, six new tennis courts, and rebuilt bulkheads alongside the local dock.

If one is faced with the decision problem exemplified by Figures 12A–7 or 12A–8, ordinal preferences are sufficient for making the best choices. In Figure 12A–7, I must be preferred; in Figure 12A–8, II. But Figure 12A–9 is another story; now the choice depends on how good an outcome Y is relative to X and Z, and that is a matter on which we have been given no information.

---

[12] Remember that throughout this chapter we assume a single decision maker. Hence no problem of aggregating the divergent preferences of many people can arise.

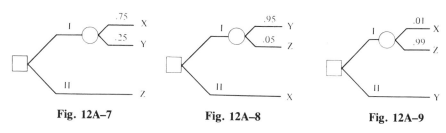

Fig. 12A–7   Fig. 12A–8   Fig. 12A–9

Or consider another pair of decisions, faced by a decision maker who is known to be risk averse (Figures 12A–10 and 12A–11). In Figure 12A–10 it is not difficult to predict our decision maker's choice. We saw early in this appendix that for someone who is risk averse, the $1000 he might gain is worth less to him than the $1000 he might lose. He will refuse the lottery. But in Figure 12A–11 we cannot predict the decision maker's choice solely from the information given. Even though we know he is risk averse, we don't know whether he is sufficiently so to turn down the actuarially favorable gamble offered him. (Actuaries, dealing with large populations, usually think in terms of expected values. Hence the term *actuarially favorable* implies a lottery with an expected value greater than $0.)

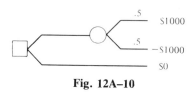

Fig. 12A–10

In short, we need a system for assigning numbers to X, Y, and Z, or to the dollar amounts in Figure 12A–11, that will somehow accurately reflect the strength of the decision maker's preferences among these outcomes. And we have just seen that apparently there is no meaningful way to devise such a system, for there is no yardstick external to the individual against which his satisfaction can be measured.

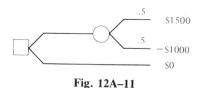

Fig. 12A–11

It was the genius of John von Neumann and Oskar Morgenstern that they found a way out of this quandary; they recognized that a full cardinal measure of satisfaction is not required for unitary decision making under uncertainty. Ordinal preferences, to be sure, aren't enough, but von Neumann and Morgenstern developed an ordering system, more than ordinal yet less than fully cardinal, that does the job for uncertain choices.

Although their approach is mathematically rigorous, our discussion of it will not be.

The core of von Neumann-Morgenstern utility theory is this observation: Consider outcomes $x > Y > Z$ and the decision problem in Figure 12A–12, where p is the (known) probability of achieving outcome X. Then the very act of making a choice, of asserting a preference between Acts I and II, conveys *fundamentally new information* about the decision maker's relative preferences among X, Y, and Z.

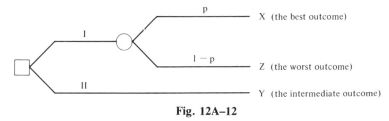

Fig. 12A–12

Thus, they perceived that the problem of choice under uncertainty, rather than being unresolvable, is precisely the case in which it is possible to measure the strength of preferences. We spell this out in detail in the following section.

An Intuitive Approach to Utility Theory

We're going to ask you to think about a highly artificial situation. It is deliberately so: we want to put you in a position where you already have all the background knowledge you need to make a decision, and where you can't solve your decision problem by simply converting your choices to their dollar values and then opting for the most valuable outcome.

Imagine you have been adrift for a week, all alone in a lifeboat that is well stocked with hardtack and water. Along comes a large yacht with a diabolical captain. He says to you, "I won't pick you up, but I will give you something to eat. In fact, I'll play a game with you. I'm going to offer you a choice between two lotteries. Each of them gives you a chance to win a steak, a bowl of mashed turnips, a tunafish sandwich, or a dish of cottage cheese. You are to decide which of the lotteries you prefer. You can then pull a random number out of this bag of numbered chips and we'll see what you win. Here are the lotteries." He tosses you the tree shown in Figure 12A–13. "Cheerio," he cries. "Think it over and decide which one you want; I'll be back in an hour or so."

What are you to do? Which lottery suits you better? If both involved only the steak and the turnips, most people would find the choice simple; they would simply opt for the lottery that gives them the bigger shot at the steak. But in this case the better chance at the steak carries with it a bigger chance of getting stuck with the turnips. In short, everything depends on how strongly you feel about tunafish and cottage cheese relative to steak and turnips. How on earth are you to quantify your preferences for those four delicacies? (We could of course have simply offered you a choice among dollar lotteries, but we think the four foods are easier to keep in mind as you work through the example.)

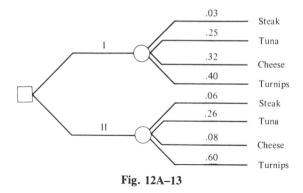

Fig. 12A–13

Von Neumann and Morgenstern approach this quantification problem in the following way. First they ask you to rank the outcomes; let's say you prefer (1) steak, (2) tuna, (3) cheese, and (4) turnips, in that order. Not everyone would accept that ranking, of course, but we have chosen a list that we think most people would agree on, only because that makes the exposition a little easier. You would then be asked to consider the fictitious decision problem of Figure 12A–14.

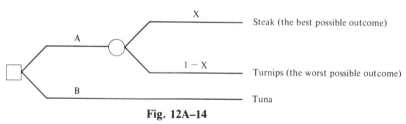

Fig. 12A–14

Here, X is the (unknown) probability of winning a steak in lottery A. You are next asked what value of X would leave you *just indifferent* between choices A and B. In other words, what would the probability of winning the steak have to be to make you *genuinely neutral* between getting the tunafish sandwich for certain and getting the steak–turnips lottery? The authors tried this question on a law school class of a hundred students; for most of them X was about .85. Think very carefully about what this means. Whenever one of these students is faced with the possible outcome "tunafish sandwich," he is willing to substitute the lottery in Figure 12A–15 for that sure sandwich.

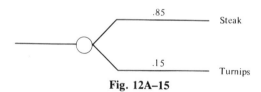

Fig. 12A–15

This point is so important it merits reiteration: he literally doesn't care whether he gets a tunafish sandwich for sure, or the lottery. They are equally attractive options and can be freely substituted for one another.

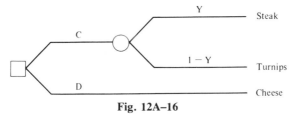

Fig. 12A–16

The law school students were next asked how they felt about the choice in Figure 12A–16. For most of them, Y was about .50. If we substitute these lotteries in the original tree—and we know we can do it because X and Y were chosen so as to make it possible—we have Figure 12A–17 for our representative students.

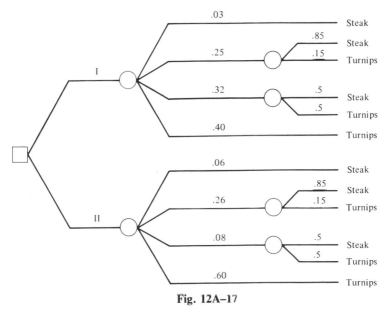

Fig. 12A–17

Simplifying the compound lotteries and adding up the chances of getting the steak and the turnips in each case, we have Figure 12A–18.

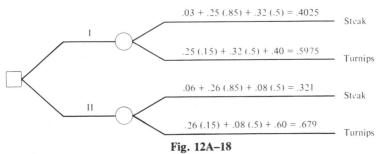

Fig. 12A–18

Clearly if we pose the decision problem in this way, choice I is preferable because it offers a larger chance of winning the steak.

Following von Neumann and Morgenstern, we call X the "utility" of tuna and Y the "utility" of cottage cheese. These utilities are expressed on an arbitrary scale that runs from turnips to steak. What about the utility values for turnips and steak? If we apply the same technique as above, we must investigate the choice in Figure 12A–19. What value of Z would leave

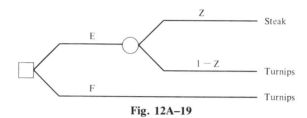

Fig. 12A–19

you neutral between E and F? Only $Z = 0$; the utility of turnips must therefore be 0. By similar reasoning, the utility of steak must be 1. Our results are summarized in Table 12A–1.

Table 12A–1

Outcome	Utility
Steak	1
Tuna	.85
Cottage Cheese	.50
Turnips	0

Observe that if we use these utility numbers as indices of value in the original decision problem, we can simply write the utility values as payoffs at the tips of the tree, as in Figure 12A–20. Then the *expected utility* for lottery I is

$$.03(1) + .25(.85) + .32(.5) = .4025$$

—exactly the expression we found for the probability of winning a steak in

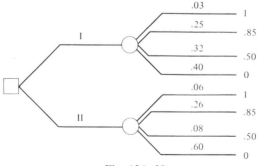

Fig. 12A–20

Figure 12A–18. In other words, if you (1) calculate your utility values by the above procedure, (2) use these utilities as indices of value for averaging out and folding back, and (3) choose the action having the largest expected utility, you can be confident that your choice is consistent with the strength of your own preferences among the four outcomes.

The crucial fact to keep firmly in mind is the fact that these utilities are nothing more than shorthand for lotteries, for lotteries of a most convenient type, with the happy property that they all have the same pair of outcomes. If the X and Y values have been conscientiously determined so that they truly reflect the strength of your preferences among outcomes, then you need not make your decision by considering the problem as a whole. You can continue to break it down and enjoy the advantages of decision analysis by considering more and simpler questions rather than fewer but harder ones.

Utility Theory and Dollar Outcomes

Our hypothetical example was developed in terms of food. More traditionally, utility theory is applied when a risk averse decision maker is confronted with choices that involve money lotteries or outcomes that are readily converted to monetary equivalents. Let's return to the chance node shown in Figure 12A–5. Suppose the decision maker is offered that lottery; should he accept it? His decision tree is Figure 12A–21.

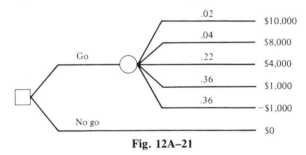

Fig. 12A–21

A risk neutral decision maker would value the lottery at its EMV, $1400, and therefore would immediately choose "Go." But if he is risk averse he may have a harder time making up his mind; $1000 is a lot to lose, and he has better than one chance in three of losing that amount. How does the decision maker proceed? How does he think systematically about this problem? The logic outlined above provides the answer. We ask him to think about simpler choices of the type in Figure 12A–22. Note that

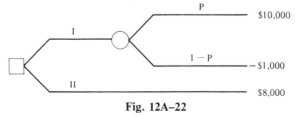

Fig. 12A–22

the fictitious lottery posed is between the best possible outcome, $10,000, and the worst, −$1,000.

For each possible intermediate amount he estimates actual numerical values for P. This is no easy task, but assume he has done it and for him the table of utility values turns out to be that in Table 12A–2.

Table 12A–2

Dollar amount	Utility
$10,000	1
8,000	.95
4,000	.7
1,000	.38
0	.22
−1,000	0

Having thus found an actual number for each P, we can assign these utility values to each outcome. The decision problem then becomes Figure 12A–23. Remember that this is no more than an abbreviated representation of the more complex formulation of the decision tree shown in Figure 12A–24.

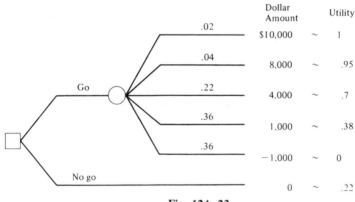

Fig. 12A–23

Returning to Figure 12A--23, directly calculating the expected values of the utilities in the lottery gives

$$.02(1) + .04(.95) + .22(.7) + .36(.38) + .36(0) = .3488$$

Go thus offers an expected utility of roughly .35, No go of .22; the decision maker should choose Go. This is the choice that is in accord with the strength of his preferences among the various dollar amounts. In other words, the additional information about the strength of those preferences that we acquired when he estimated his P values permits us to state confidently that he prefers Go.

To bring the argument full circle, the decision maker, in making what is for him the preferred choice, acts *as if* he maximizes expected utility.

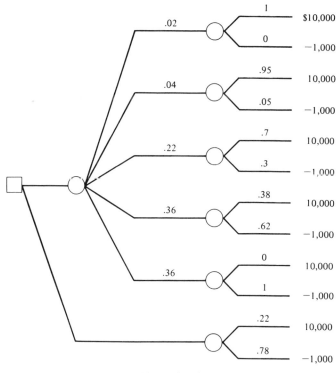

Fig. 12A–24

Once he has figured out the utility to him of each possible outcome, he need not stick around for the actual decision making. He can hand his agent a list of his utility values and go out to lunch, confident that the agent is fully equipped to act in his behalf in any choice involving lotteries among those outcomes.

Finally, what if we carry out this procedure and the decision maker says, "That's all very well, but looking at the original decision problem as a whole, I would have made a different choice." What can we say? Only that if this is the case, the decision maker is not consistent in his preferences. If he persists in this, there is nothing to be done; von Neumann and Morgenstern have little to offer the inconsistent decision maker. Nor do we; he is on his own.

One major caveat with regard to language is in order. It is very easy, in working with utility values, to slide into the error of saying "Jones prefers outcome *M* to outcome *N* because it has a higher utility." The correct statement must always be "We *assign* a higher utility to *M* than to *N because* Jones prefers *M*." (It *is* correct, however, to say, "Smith should prefer action *A* to action *B* because it has a higher *expected* utility.) It is the decision maker's preferences that truly matter; the utilities are only a shorthand description of the strength of these preferences.

A Shortcut for Calculating the Utility of Dollar Amounts

If outcomes are in dollars, the procedure can be further simplified. In the previous example, $10,000 was the best possible dollar outcome and −$1,000 the worst. Consider the decision in Figure 12A–25. Find the X that leaves you neutral between choices Act 1 and Act 2. Say you decide X is $2000. In other words, when X = $2000, the expected utility is the same for both courses of action. The expected utility of Act 1 is .5(1) + .5(0) = .5; the utility of $2000 must be the same, .5.

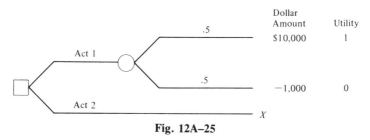

Fig. 12A–25

Repeat this process for Figure 12A–26. You decide Y is $4500. Then the utility value for $4500 must be .5(1) + .5(.5) = .75.

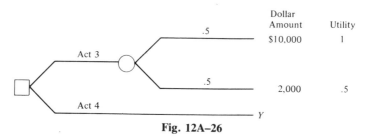

Fig. 12A–26

Next, investigate Figure 12A–27. You decide Z is $200. Then the utility value for $200 must be .5(.5) + .5(0) = .25.

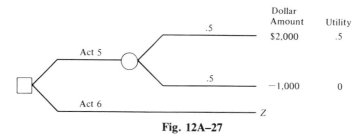

Fig. 12A–27

Figure 12A–28 shows a rough curve for the values found above. Continue this interpolative calibrating process until you have enough points to sketch an entire curve. Plot the utility values against the corresponding dollar amounts. Check for internal consistency; if the curve is not reasonably smooth, assure yourself that that is the way you really feel.

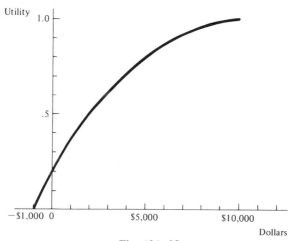

Fig. 12A–28

Government Attitudes Toward Risk

Utility theory focuses on the individual who is making decisions under conditions of uncertainty. This volume, by contrast, is addressed to policy choice. That raises a critical question: How should a policy maker make choices on behalf of others when outcomes are uncertain? The benefits and costs of his decision, after all, do not accrue primarily to him but rather to the population he serves; he is merely an agent. The preferences of the public he represents should determine the outcome. In certainty situations, we saw that this approach is a cornerstone of benefit–cost analysis. A benefit provided to an individual—one day of recreation, for example—is valued as the individual would himself value it. So too with lotteries on outcomes; they should be valued as the recipient would value them, with due regard for his attitude toward risk.

Consider a community of 1000 families that has already floated bonds for a new school. It is now proposed that a new construction technique be tried out for the school. If it is successful, an outcome that the school committee assesses to be 25 percent likely, the saving in construction costs will be $200,000; each family will get a $200 tax rebate. If the new technique fails, $50,000 will be wasted and the school must then be built by the tried-and-true construction method. Each family will be assessed an additional $50 to cover this waste. The school committee must essentially choose for each of the families between the two alternatives of Figure 12A–29.

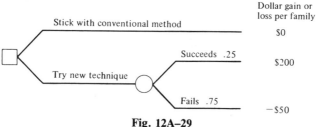

Fig. 12A–29

Using the new technique offers each family an expected value of .25($200) + .75(−$50) = $12.50. If the families are strongly risk-averse, however, their certainty equivalents for the lottery may be negative, in which case they would prefer to stick with the conventional method. The school committee should attempt to assess community feeling toward this risk before making its choice. It is of course most unlikely to be able to address utility functions directly. Rather, it can gauge the attitudes of the citizens toward risk through public meetings, referenda, surveys, and the like.

Policy choice under uncertainty is thus properly understood as a three-step process. First, the alternatives are assessed to determine what lotteries they imply for individual members of the population. Second, the attitudes toward risk of these individuals are evaluated to determine the certainty equivalents for the lotteries. Third, having estimated the equivalent monetary benefits that each alternative offers to the different members of the population, the decision maker selects the preferred outcome. If distribution is not of consequence, his choice criterion is likely to be to maximize the sum of net benefits. That is, he would choose the lottery for which the sum of the certainty equivalents is the largest.

The government may be involved in projects that require the expenditure of many millions or even billions of dollars. Yet if no significant risks are imposed on any individual it should act as if it were risk neutral. Consider a federal undertaking that can proceed through alternatives A or B. Alternative A is equally likely to cost $50 million or $100 million. Alternative B assures the same project for $80 million. It might seem that, given the vast sums of money and the known risk aversion of the population, B should be chosen. But if these costs are to be spread roughly evenly over 220 million citizens, the most serious consequences will be a loss of less than 50 cents. Over this range of payoff, individuals are likely to be almost risk-neutral. If so, it seems ill-advised to give away $5 million in expected value just to limit risk. As this example suggests, government policy makers should be relatively risk neutral unless either (1) the projects are so massive in scope that their risks are still consequential even though spread across the population, or (2) the projects concentrate benefits and costs on particular groups that are therefore strongly affected. In the first category are policy choices relating to a national energy policy, or to macroeconomic measures that attempt to influence the performance of the economy. The consequences of such policies may be so massive that even when spread across an entire population the individual risks may remain significant. Less risky alternatives, despite offering lower expected value, may be preferred. The decision whether to undertake a flood control project might fall in the second category. In the absence of the project, the risks for those who might get flooded would be substantial, so that risk aversion becomes a significant element in the decision.

To sum up, given that a policy maker is making his choice for others, he should see how those others are affected and use their preferences to inform his choice.

The Assumptions Behind Utility Theory

As we have proceeded with our description of utility theory, we have been rather casual about making whatever assumptions we needed en route. It is now time to go back and gather up these assumptions so that we may examine their validity. You should work through the following list one by one and decide for yourself whether you can be comfortable with them. It may surprise you to discover that they are not particularly hard to swallow.

1. The decision maker knows what he likes. Offer him any pair of outcomes or lotteries and he is able to state either that he prefers one to the other or that he is indifferent. He never says "I can't tell you whether I like one better than the other or not; they simply can't be compared." (Note that this implicitly includes the possibility of comparing a sure outcome with a lottery, for a sure thing is in fact the limiting case of a lottery with probabilities 1 and 0.)

2. The decision maker is transitive in his preferences. That is, if he likes A better than B and B better than C, then he is guaranteed to like A better than C. This goes both for sure outcomes and for lotteries. To our knowledge, no one has ever mounted a successful attack on the transitivity assumption. We have a standing offer of $25 to anyone who can produce a genuine nontrivial example of a unitary decision maker with nontransitive preferences.

3. If the decision maker is equally happy with either of two sure outcomes, then he is also willing to substitute one for the other in a lottery. For example, suppose he is indifferent between having a red car and a blue car. He is then given a choice between two lottery tickets. One offers him equal chances at a red car and a set of golf clubs, the other equal chances at a blue car and the same set of clubs. Bringing the golf clubs into the act has no effect on him; he is neutral between the two lotteries just as he was neutral between the two sure outcomes.

4. The decision maker will always accept a lottery between the best and worst outcome in preference to a sure intermediate outcome provided we sweeten the odds enough. We relied on this assumption when we offered the shipwrecked decision maker the hypothetical choice in Figure 12A–30, and directed him to find the X that

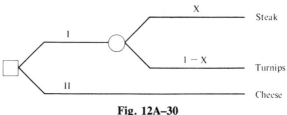

Fig. 12A–30

would leave him indifferent between choices I and II. For most types of outcome, the assumption is plausible. You might try to tell us that there is no P that would make you prefer choice I to choice II in the decision situation of Figure 12A–31. But suppose we reply, "How about $P = .9999999999$?" Are you positive that you would still take the sure million? This continuity assumption may indeed fail, however, when one of the outcomes involves severe injury or death. On the other hand, it may not—after all, people do choose to undergo elective surgery.

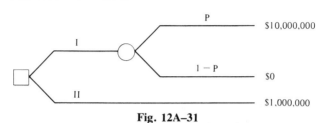

Fig. 12A–31

5. If the decision maker is offered a choice between two two-pronged lotteries with identical prizes but different odds, he will choose the lottery that offers him the larger chance of receiving the preferred prize. As we suggested earlier, this appears to be equivalent to assuming that the decision maker is in his right mind. Actually, it isn't quite as simple as that, for it demands that the probabilities themselves have no utility. The assumption fails if the decision maker is in some sense playing a game with himself and would prefer the heady possibility of winning a new watch in a 100 to 1 raffle to the better chance of winning it by the mundane flip of a coin. Presumably when serious and substantial outcomes are at stake, decision makers don't play games with themselves.

6. The decision maker is neither attracted nor repelled by the process of gambling. He is neutral between a compound lottery and the simple lottery to which it can be reduced. He would just as soon face one as the other, and the extra thrills (pleasant or otherwise) provided by a two-stage lottery are of no consequence to him. We made use of this assumption above when we converted the compound lottery of Figure 12A–17 to the simple lottery of Figure 12A–18. Of course, it fails when one gambles for the fun of it, but, again, when serious decisions are to be made, involving outcomes of major importance, it appears to be reasonable.

This description of the assumptions that underlie von Neumann–Morgenstern utility theory is, needless to say, not at all rigorous. Those desiring a mathematical treatment should consult R. Duncan Luce and Howard Raiffa, *Games and Decisions* (New York: John Wiley & Sons, Inc., 1957), Chapter 2.

Part III

Ends and Means

13 Public Choice— To What Ends?

What are the ends of public decision; what should it try to accomplish?

This question has occupied the minds of philosophers and other students of society for hundreds of years. It still makes for good conversation. We can do no more here than sketch out some conclusions that have won fairly widespread (though by no means universal) adherence, indicate what these conclusions accomplish and where they leave gaps, and explain how to proceed from agreed-upon principles to the more mundane matter of making a particular policy decision.

There is more than one twist to the discussion. To help keep you with us, we first set forth a simplified overview. We shall delineate, and in some cases argue, the following propositions:

1. The purpose of public decisions is to promote the welfare of society.

2. The welfare levels of the individual members of society are the building blocks for the welfare of society.

3. Anything that affects individual welfares therefore affects the welfare of society. Something that has no effect on individual welfare levels has no impact on the welfare of society.

4. With rare exceptions, we should accept individuals' own judgments as the appropriate indicators of their own welfare.

5. We would like to have an unambiguous procedure for aggregating the welfares of different individuals so that we can compare the welfare of society if one policy is followed with its welfare if another policy is followed. Although in some circumstances unequivocal judgments can be made, there is no universally applicable procedure. Nevertheless, significant insights about policy making may be derived by reflecting on the appropriate way to value social outcomes.

The phrasing of these five propositions suggests—correctly—that despite much work on the purposes of policy decisions, many of the conclusions that have been reached are not subject to empirical verification. But we have learned a great deal about the appropriate criteria for policy choice. What's more, we understand what it is that we do not know and perhaps never can.

In marked contrast to the earlier chapters of this book, this one is necessarily somewhat abstract. The five propositions do not translate readily into guidelines for action. But the goal of the discussion is strictly practical—helping the public decision maker find criteria for judging policies in the real world. The standards for evaluation set forth here are purely conceptual; policy makers will rarely apply them directly in a decision-making context. Frequently political factors will appear to weigh heavily. Still, most individuals who must make decisions or carry out analyses on behalf of others are more comfortable when they know they can relate their work to a firm ethical foundation, when they are confident of the philosophical underpinnings of the criteria on which they rely. This is true even when the decision maker's task is primarily one of implementing broader-gauge decisions that have been made at a higher level. The points made here underlie most present discussion in both academic and practical policy making circles on the appropriate goals for public policy.

You may find it easier to think about these matters if we pose a specific problem that illustrates the issues considered in this chapter. Suppose, for example, that you are a member of the Transportation Commission in a sprawling suburban community. Spurred on by the arguments of senior citizens without cars, tired chauffeur-mothers, and assorted energy conservationists, the town has appropriated $50,000 for subsidized bus service within the town. On what basis are you to decide between, say, establishing weekday shopping routes and weekend routes serving school athletic facilities? We choose this problem for you to keep in the back of your mind because it is relatively easy to clear away extraneous issues. While no specialized knowledge is necessary to consider it, you do need to understand the fundamental principles on which policy decisions should ultimately be made, and how they apply in the situation at hand. We hope that by the time you finish this chapter you will have a clearer idea of what underlying issues are involved when such questions are addressed.

Society: What Is It?

When we speak of the welfare of society, what do we mean by society? Surely in the United States, with its thousands of governments, government agencies, and quasi-public organizations, with many overlapping jurisdictions, any terms such as the American people or the citizens of New Mexico will incorporate numerous decision making units. Yet we need a term that includes all of the people whose interests are affected and supposedly considered when a particular decision is made. We use the word *society* to represent that concept. For some decision problems, society will be all the citizens of the country, for others the residents of a neighborhood. In the suburban transportation example, the society is most logically the residents of the particular town. The underlying assumption is that the bus schedules will have a negligible effect on people residing outside the town; thus when we speak of the welfare of society in the context of that example, we can legitimately stop at the town line. For the present, we assume a decision making unit in which no consequences spill over to affect individuals in other jurisdictions, whether those jurisdictions are defined by geography, occupational status, time period, or whatever. In the next chapter we will consider the problems that arise when decisions made by one person or organization fail to take account of the impact on others.

Correspondingly, we will use the term *social situation* or simply *situation* to mean all the arrangements that result from a particular policy choice reached by the society in question. If policy *A* is two trips a day around town on weekdays plus one trip a day on weekends, then social state *A* is the total configuration of goods, services, employment, living arrangements, and so on, for all the town's citizens, that results from the implementation of that policy.

The Well-Being of Society

In producing a good society, as in developing a fine photograph, some apparatus is essential. That is the justification for the rather technical material that makes up the bulk of this volume. But at some point we must stop and decide just what we want to accomplish. We are now at what photographers might call the esthetic moment. What are we after? What are the criteria by which we are to determine that one set of policy choices is preferable to another?

Much of the discussion in this *Primer* assumes that such profound questions are asked and answered elsewhere. Thus our public decision maker in Chapter 3 took as given that the objectives were gallons of water and kilowatt-hours of electricity. Moreover, he already knew the tradeoff rates he should accept between those two variables—that is, the society's evaluation of one objective relative to the other. We were then able to consider the more technical question of how we should pursue our objectives separately from the problem of deciding what we should value. Now, however, we turn our attention to the question that perhaps logically should have come first. What should be on the axes of a public decision maker's indifference map? What is it that the member of the suburban Transportation Commission really seeks to accomplish with the bus schedule? This is a perplexing question. Although cast in the language of the economist, it is riddled with philosophical and political implications. Still, economics can suggest useful guidelines for policy.

Indeed, most discussion within modern economics starts with the disclaimer that economists are neither the creators nor the dictators of values. They merely provide a procedure for inferring and pursuing existing values; their role is descriptive or "positive" rather than prescriptive or "normative." In a similar vein, most argue that public decision makers in a democratic society should function as servants of the people, attempting to do what is best for those they serve. This suggests that a democratic society can only be successful if it achieves a wide consensus about fundamental values. The broad goals of public policy must reflect those fundamental values, although people will inevitably differ in the way they translate values into specific objectives and ultimately into program choices. For example, broad agreement on the worth of the individual—an underlying consensus—impels most of us to believe that reducing unemployment is a desirable goal. But people quite legitimately disagree about the role of government in this process, or about how far we should sacrifice other objectives—the control of inflation, for instance—in order to push unemployment down another percent. Similarly, they will disagree about the relative importance of bus rides for the elderly and for the children of busy parents. Often the conflict will be more visible, the clash of principles more basic. Should, for instance, a farmer be forced to relinquish his homestead so that a reservoir and recreation area can be created for the cityfolk?

As these examples suggest, we must recognize that objectives are at heart personal judgments about which intelligent and well-informed people can disagree. But at the same time policy makers, who operate mostly with already established objectives, should understand that part of their job is to ensure that these proximate objectives are consonant with the fundamental values of the society. Realistically, of course, we recognize that few policy makers can afford the time to address conceptual issues as part of their daily routines. We must hope that the tools of analysis and everyday decision criteria that they employ in effect build in these fundamental values. The methods we set forth in the chapters that follow are not only consistent with the philosophy of this discussion, but in many instances are its logical product.

Differences in Prediction vs. Differences in Values

Even people who are in agreement on ultimate values may differ in the predictions they make about the performance of alternative policies. In the context of the unemployment problem just considered, one analyst may suggest that among three alternatives, spending $1 billion on public service employment will create the most jobs. Another may argue that manpower training programs will do more for the same expenditure. Still a third may strongly recommend allocating the $1 billion to wage subsidies for the private sector. Similarly, analysts' predictions about the results of alternative bus schedules may differ. Perhaps they will not agree on the likely extent of use by the elderly, or on the reduction in private trips that increased weekend scheduling will bring about.

Much policy discussion revolves around proximate or intermediate objectives rather than ultimate values. Individuals whose fundamental values roughly coincide may still differ strongly on more immediate goals for social policy if they hold different beliefs about the way the world will respond to alternative policy choices. For example, proponents of federally supported comprehensive health insurance claim that it will help control health care costs as well as providing quality care to all. Others, although adhering to the same stated objectives, bitterly oppose such insurance, believing that it will escalate costs without noticeably improving health care. Our Transportation Commission may generate similar disagreements. Suburbanites who support weekday buses for the elderly as well as those who advocate weekend routes for children may both assert their concern for energy conservation and the quality of suburban life.

Much of Part II of this volume addressed means for improving our ability to predict the consequences of alternative policies. One objective of descriptive analysis is to narrow areas of disagreement in policy disputes. Milton Friedman has argued that we should concentrate on differences in prediction as opposed to differences in values:

> Differences about economic policy among disinterested citizens derive predominantly from different predictions about the economic consequences of taking action—differences that in principle can be eliminated by the progress of positive economics—rather than from fundamental differences in basic values, differences about which men can ultimately only fight.[1]

Friedman's argument applies to the choice of a technology for electricity generation, or of a surface for the town's tennis courts, or of a bus schedule, as well as to the choice of fiscal and monetary policies for the nation's economy. Policy disagreements would lessen—and perhaps vanish—if we could predict with certainty the safety consequences of the breeder reactor, or the costs of annual upkeep of clay courts, or whether a special shuttle bus for the elderly would be heavily used.

Guidelines for Social Choice

We start then with an understanding that some of our disagreements about values will not be resolved. And even if they are, differences in predictions may lead some analysts to recommend one policy and others another. We can still provide useful guidelines for making social choices. Rather than embarking on an exhaustive philosophical discussion, we will take as axiomatic two statements about policy goals and the values that underlie them, statements that are widely (although not universally) accepted as guiding principles in most social science discussions. Our entire analysis is based on these two fundamental postulates.

1. *The well-being of society depends solely on the welfare of its individual members.* We take a good look below at individual welfare to

---

[1] *Essays in Positive Economics* (Chicago: University of Chicago Press, 1953), p. 5.

make sure what we mean by it and how we think policy makers should take it into account in their decisions. Our main point is that it's people, and only people, that count. This means that redwoods and bluebirds and Lake Baikal and the Old Man of the Mountain are worth saving only if people believe them worth saving. Abstractly considered, the rights of nonhuman entities may seem a valid criterion for policy choice. But in fact these rights are meaningless unless championed by people; neither the redwoods nor the bluebirds can speak for themselves. If this judgment strikes you as unduly hard-nosed, look at the other side of the coin. How many voices are raised on behalf of that vanishing species, the smallpox virus? And who speaks for the boll weevil? There is ample pragmatic support for an anthropocentric approach. All philosophical justifications to the contrary, unless human beings care about redwoods, the redwoods will be destroyed.[2]

2. *Tradeoffs among individuals must be made.* Most social choices require us, explicitly or otherwise, to trade off the welfares of some individuals against the welfares of others. The fundamental problem for any society is establishing and maintaining a procedure for making these painful choices. Any policy maker who has to decide anything less trivial than what color to paint the town hall trash cans will find himself in the unhappy position of making recommendations or decisions that enhance the welfare of some people and diminish that of others. Earlier kindergarten hours may be splendid for the working mother but may totally disrupt the lives of mothers caring for still younger children at home. The man who sets school hours, indeed any policy maker, is going to have to find a way to combine the costs and benefits going to different individuals so that he can judge which of the alternative proposals facing him is better for society as a whole. In the latter part of this chapter we take a closer look at this search for suitable criteria.

Individual Welfare: The Building Block for Evaluation

If we are to accept the principle that individual welfare is all that ultimately counts in making policy choices, we must make it an operational concept, one we can get a handle on and do something with. Specifically, we must understand what we mean by individual welfare, who should judge it, how we are to measure it, how it is affected by the actions of individuals and of society.

---

[2] We can't resist calling to your attention the recent debate on the fate of the Tennessee snail darter. As far as is known, this fish, slightly larger than a guppy, lives only in a short stretch of the Little Tennessee River. Its existence was first discovered in 1975. Environmentalists, realizing that the tiny fish would be wiped out by a dam now being built on the river, persuaded the Fish and Wildlife Service to place the Tennessee snail darter on the endangered species list and then sued the Tennessee Valley Authority to bar completion of the $110 million project. Although construction was already completed, a federal appeals court ruled early in 1977 that the dam could not be put into operation. The injunction will remain in effect unless the Supreme Court strikes it down or Congress takes legislative action to exempt the project or to remove the snail darter from the endangered list.

1. *What do we mean by individual welfare?* To put it very simply, we mean a person's total situation. This includes the goods and services he enjoys, the free band concerts he attends, the way he feels about the government he lives under, the way income and wealth are distributed among the population, the friendly welcome by the local Rotary Club, even the noise disturbance he suffers from his neighbor's lawnmower. In short we take an all-inclusive view of what affects the well-being of the individual. As a practical matter, most of the time it is reasonably legitimate and certainly more convenient to look at only a portion of a person's position, and to assume that other elements of his consumption bundle do not shift as the items under consideration are varied. For example, we might wish to investigate whether Smith's welfare is greater with one particular bundle of goods *X* (consisting of four morning and three afternoon bus trips) or with another bundle *Y* (three morning and five afternoon trips). We would assume in comparing his welfare when he has *X* and when he has *Y* that most of the other details of his total situation, for example his record collection, would remain unchanged. Where should we draw the line in accepting ''other things'' as equal? That may be a delicate question, but usually there is no need to go out and see if the neighbor's lawnmower is still running or if the mayor has been caught on the take. To use the terminology of the indifference curve diagram we have relied on so heavily, when we display preferences between two attributes we have implicitly tucked away in some corner a list of the other elements in the individual's consumption bundle.[3]

2. *Who shall be the judge of an individual's welfare?* In the United States we usually take the position that it is the individual's own preferences that count, that he is the best judge of his own welfare. For example, we ask whether a person is better off in one situation or another, in situation *A* or situation *B*. If he expresses a preference for *B*, or if through his market choices he reveals that he likes *B* better, then we say that he is better off in *B* than in *A*. This "criterion of individual choice" means merely that the individual's preferences are the standard by which we judge his well-being.

Some people reject the idea that individual choice is the appropriate criterion for making welfare judgments. Their arguments have a common thread: left to himself, the individual will make poor choices. "Even though he chooses *A*, *B* is better for him." Several alternative rationales may lie behind such a statement.

a. The person may be a child or a madman and unable to comprehend or evaluate the alternatives available to him. Courts in a variety of

---

[3] Sometimes, the structure of preferences is such that the tradeoffs in one area will be independent of the levels of other goods. When different areas of choice are separable, it is possible to suboptimize decisions, to make the best decision in each area without simultaneous reference to the others. This is particularly important in the public sphere. We may wish to make choices in Massachusetts without worrying about what is going on in Illinois, or make choices relating to energy technologies without simultaneously being concerned with the way we are reformulating our national park strategies.

instances make another person or the state responsible for the choices affecting such individuals' welfare.

b. We may disapprove of certain activities, such as the use of narcotics or the purchase of sex, whatever the consumer's views on such matters.

c. We may feel that the individual's ability to make good choices is limited by habit, as in the case of cigarette smoking.

d. Perhaps we believe that the individual would make a different choice if he had more information, information that is now available to others. One argument for keeping youngsters in school is that they (and perhaps even their parents) do not fully comprehend the benefits in ultimate employability they will lose if they drop out.

e. Experience or education may be a prerequisite for appreciating the merits of an alternative, which might be black olives, the music of Stravinsky, or a complex piece of legislation.

f. It may be felt that preferences have been manipulated by advertising or propaganda. By influencing taste, both private institutions and policy makers may alter the welfare evaluations made by individuals.[4]

3. *How should we measure individual welfare?* It would be helpful to have an unambiguous measure of an individual's welfare, or utility, just as we have a means to calibrate his weight and height. (*Utility* is a technical term that means welfare, or well-being, or satisfaction. It is an awkward word but it is here to stay.) In the past some economic theorists, following in the tradition of Jeremy Bentham, attempted to develop cardinal measures of individual welfare, in other words, a measure of the absolute quantity of welfare an individual enjoys. A cardinal measure would convey two pieces of information—(1) how much better off the individual is in situation B than in situation A, and (2) how much better or worse off he is than someone else—just as a scale tells us how many pounds a man has gained and how much more or less he weighs than his neighbor. In fact, we would be happy to find a more restricted cardinal measure that would merely tell us about the magnitude of local changes; it would tell us whether John's gain in welfare when we undertake a particular policy is greater than Mary's loss.

Unfortunately (but not surprisingly), neither Bentham nor his successors were ever able to make such a measurement process operational. As a consequence, discussions of cardinal utility went out of fashion and were left to those who worried about angels and pins. Therefore we confine

---

[4] Analysts do not entirely agree about the welfare criteria that should be used when tastes are changing. Surely B should be ranked over A if it is preferred both before and after the change. Some observers feel that if there is a conflict the more recent preference should be given more weight because it may be the result of a learning process. Others argue that newly developed tastes that may have been created by advertising or by social aspirations are artificial and should be discounted. In some choices, a man commits himself to actions in the future when he fears his tastes may be different. Ulysses made such a commitment when he asked to be bound to the mast while he sailed past the sirens; today people have their jaws wired together in an effort to lose weight.

ourselves to ordinal comparisons: "Is the individual better off in situation A or in situation B?" Following the criterion of individual choice, we find the answer to this question by observing the individual's own choices. If, when given a choice, he selects situation B over situation A, we say that he assigns B a higher ordinal ranking, a higher utility value. In this manner we can in principle establish the individual's ranking of all possible states.

A partial solution to the measurement problem may be reached by inferring ordinal preferences. Sometimes it is not possible to offer the individual a choice between different situations so that we can observe his selection, yet we can still, by inference, establish his preferences between them. Situations A and B may be thought of as two different sets of bundles of goods that are offered to the decision maker. For example, suppose that in situation A Smith is offered several alternative bundles of goods (where we take goods to include services, amenities, and so on) and from these he chooses one particular bundle X, consisting of, say, a tax increase of \$5 and free buses Monday, Wednesday, and Friday noons. In situation B Smith is offered a different collection of alternative bundles, one of which is the same bundle X. In situation B, Smith could still secure his preferred allocation from situation A; that is, he could still choose bundle X. This implies that Smith's welfare cannot be greater in A than in B. Moreover, if in B he chooses some bundle other than X, his welfare in A would in fact be less.

What is the practical use of abstractions like this one? Sometimes they aren't all that abstract, and can give us real down-to-earth assistance in making judgments about economic welfare. Consider the following abstraction and note its implications for policy: if we expand a person's set of opportunities to include the one he originally selected, his welfare cannot be diminished, assuming we are willing to let him be the judge of his own welfare, and that the decision-making costs of dealing with an expanded opportunity set are not significant. For example, suppose oranges are selling for a nickel apiece, and there is in addition a tax of one cent per orange, so that the price to the purchaser is six cents. Ralph chooses to buy six oranges at this price. If we accept the criterion of choice, we would agree that Ralph's welfare could not be decreased if he were instead assessed a lump sum tax of six cents and the oranges were sold untaxed for a nickel.[5] Think about it a minute. The latter situation would still allow Ralph to reach his initial position of six oranges together with a total outlay of 36 cents, and would permit other—perhaps superior—choices as well.

The important principle embodied in this example is directly relevant, for example, when a public choice must be made between cash transfers to individuals or families and in-kind transfers of goods such as food or

---

[5] Recall that we said above that in comparing two alternative situations we usually assume a large dose of "other things being equal." We of course have done so here. If in fact Ralph has a strong ideological attachment to the sales tax and abhors lump sum taxes, then everything of consequence has not been included. We might still decide to override his tax preferences, however, on the ground that if he knew more about economic efficiency and tax incidence he would have a different opinion.

housing or education that are of the same value. Provided that the donor is interested solely in the recipient's welfare, and the recipient is the appropriate judge of his own welfare, the cash transfer must be superior for both the recipient and donor.

4. *How is individual welfare enhanced?* In this country, the competitive free market is generally regarded as the primary means by which individuals enhance their own welfares. The underlying rationale for the market arrangement is that the voluntary exchange of resources and goods among individuals (or at times, firms acting on behalf of the individuals who own them) will lead to a desirable outcome. The market merely serves as a mechanism facilitating such exchanges. What then, in broad terms, is the appropriate role for government in our free exchange economy? The government should step in only when the private market will not operate satisfactorily. In the next chapter, after a review of the virtues of an effectively functioning market, we consider some factors that may impair its operation. That discussion will set the framework for considering policy formulation by the government or some other form of public organization.

In short, individuals' welfares should be enhanced through their participation in market processes, and when these processes function ineffectively, through the intervention of the government or other public or private collective institution.

A Far More Difficult Problem: Evaluating Social Welfare

We have been discussing the way individual welfare should be measured, and have underscored the ethical principle that each person should be the judge of his own welfare. Nothing beyond this principle is required for market transactions to play their appropriate role. Each individual, judging his own welfare as he wishes, engages in those transactions he personally finds to be the most beneficial.

Government policy choice requires something more than this ethical principle, for there is no "ownself" whose welfare is being promoted. Rather it is the welfare of society as a whole, or social welfare, that must be the concern of government policy makers. And these policy makers have no clear-cut criterion for choice because, in general, the government policy that is best for one is not best for all. Most public decisions require choices that are difficult—both ethically and politically—among alternative policies, with one policy best for one group and another policy best for another. In this section we set forth the nature of the dilemma and a method for depicting it graphically that will help us understand the judgments any government makes when it is forced to trade off one citizen's interests against those of another.

To make the government's choice problem evident with a painfully simple example, how should a community composed of two citizens, Bill and John, choose between policies *A* and *B*? To continue with our bus example, *A* and *B* might be alternative schedules. Suppose that Bill's and

Table 13–1
Citizens' Rankings of Social States Resulting from
Alternative Policies

	Present policy P	Proposed policy A	Proposed policy B
Bill	3rd	2nd	1st
John	3rd	1st	2nd

John's rankings of the two policies, together with the additional possibility of doing nothing, are as shown in Table 13–1. This rudimentary choice problem, masquerading in a variety of guises, has perplexed philosophers and economists for decades. No definitive answer can be expected, but insights and helpful guidelines can be generated with the aid of the apparatus we have already developed. We begin by arguing that an essential step (at least in spirit) for every policy choice is predicting the consequences for all affected parties. Bill and John have already made significant progress: they have stated their ordinal rankings for the possible outcomes. We assume that there are no difficulties of prediction associated with these policy choices. Bill and John understand how policies lead to social situations, and agree on which situations will result from each policy choice. We also assume that they both are good decision makers on their own behalf. That is, whatever policy is adopted, each will make his own decisions to spend, save, work, and allocate his leisure time so as to reach the highest possible indifference curve on his own personal preference map.

To take another example, suppose the state owns a 10-acre tract of land four miles from town. Policy A would convert this tract to an energy park that would yield a reduction in electricity rates. Policy B would develop the land as a recreation area, with user fees well below prevailing rates in the area. Either policy would give Bill more opportunities. Using the geometry of our model of choice it would swing Bill's budget frontier outward, though the pivot points for the two policies would differ. Policy A would be preferable if he were a major electricity consumer; for example, he could now purchase four kilowatt-hours if he wished, when previously two was the maximum. Policy B would be superior for him if, as is suggested in Figure 13–1, he is strongly oriented to recreation.

I_0, I_1, and I_2 are the indifference curves that Bill will reach as a result of policies P, A, and B. We may arbitrarily assign index numbers to these indifference curves, so long as the numbers get larger as preferred curves are reached. We might, for example, assign the following index numbers:

Policy P: $I_0 = 2.5$
Policy A; $I_1 = 3$
Policy B: $I_2 = 4$

Assume that we have also indexed the indifference curves that John would

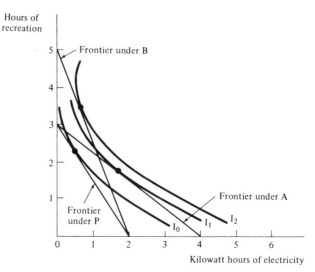

Fig. 13–1

land on for each possible policy choice. The arbitrarily assigned numbers for both Bill and John are shown in Table 13–2.

Table 13–2

	P	A	B
Bill	2.5	3	4
John	3	6	4

We are now prepared to create a geometric representation of the policy choice situation, as the diagram in Figure 13–2 indicates.

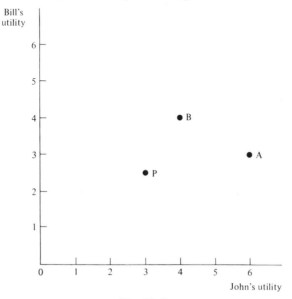

Fig. 13–2

The social situations associated with the three policies, A, B, and P, are in Figure 13.2. The horizontal coordinate gives the index value from John's indifference map; the vertical coordinate is the corresponding index value for Bill. In this limited case the utility possibility frontier consists merely of points A and B. If a continuous range of policy choices were available, the utility possibility frontier would be a continuous line, as in Figure 13-3. You should recognize that the utility possibility frontier is one application of the possibility frontier introduced in Chapter 3, and that point P, as a dominated point, is not on this frontier.

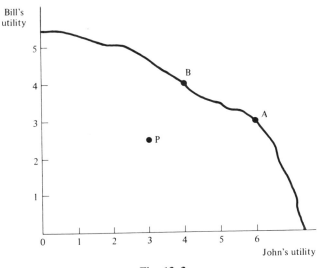

Fig. 13–3

In short, just as the possibility frontier in Chapter 3 showed the maximum output of electricity consistent with a given level of water production, the utility possibility curve shows the highest level of satisfaction that Bill can reach for each of John's possible utility levels, given the alternatives defined by the resources and technologies of society. There is, however, a significant distinction between these two types of possibility curves. We can measure electricity and water in cardinal units such as kilowatt-hours and gallons. No such convenient measure is available for individual satisfaction. We took up this matter at some length in the Appendix to Chapter 12, which dealt with utility theory. The summary conclusion from that analysis was that all a utility possibility diagram can tell us is whether one social situation lies north and east of another, that is, whether Bill prefers the first situation and whether John prefers it. Situation B lies to the north and to the west of situation A. Consequently, if given a choice between these two situations, Bill would select B and John would choose A.

You should be clear in your own mind that assigning a different set of arbitrary index numbers to the utility level curves for Bill and John will produce the same result. Suppose we pick the numbers shown in Table 13–

3. Again *A* and *B* are northeast of *P*; John will choose *A* and Bill *B*. We will make further use of this two-man community later on in the chapter when we discuss procedures for determining the preferred choice.

Table 13–3

	P	A	B
Bill	1	3	7
John	2	5	3·

In tracing the implications of alternative policies for individuals' welfares, we have engaged in the prediction exercise that is an essential first step for effective policy choice. Part II of this book laid out the basic elements of that prediction process; the ultimate output of the process, at least in concept, should be a utility possibility frontier of the type just shown. Once that frontier has been defined, the policy maker comes down to the nitty-gritty: choosing among the available combinations of individual welfares. This is the heart of the problem of public choice.

The Pareto Criterion: Making Social Welfare Responsive to Individual Welfare

What principles should guide the policy maker's choice among policies? We have already accepted the ethical belief that social welfare should depend only on the welfare levels of individual citizens. Thus at the very least our choice criterion should respond positively to an increase in the welfare of individual citizens. In the case of our two-man town, one policy choice should be preferred to another if it makes Bill better off (i.e., he is able to move to a higher indifference curve) without hurting John. This test is known as the Pareto criterion.[6] It may be stated formally as:

> Situation *Q* is preferred to situation *R* if at least one person is better off in situation *Q*, and no one is worse off.

In Figure 13–3, for example, a move from *P* to either *A* or *B* would satisfy the Pareto criterion. In Figure 13–4, a move from situation *R* to situation *Q*

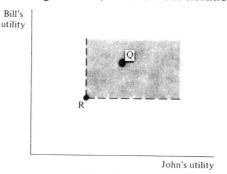

Fig. 13–4

---

[6] Vilfredo Pareto (1848–1923) was an Italian economist and sociologist.

is said to be a Pareto improvement; sometimes Q is described as Pareto superior. Any point in the shaded area (including the boundaries) is Pareto superior to R. If for situation R it is impossible to find any situation that is declared preferable by the Pareto criterion, then we say situation R is a *Pareto optimum*. In choosing among all possible social situations, we should like to select a Pareto optimum, a position in which it is not possible to make someone better off without making somebody else worse off. In the original diagram of Bill's and John's utilities, situations A and B are Pareto optimal; situation P is not. In short, all points and only those points that lie along the utility possibility frontier are Pareto optimal.

It is essential that we keep clear in our minds the distinction between a Pareto optimum and the Pareto criterion. A Pareto optimum is *any* point on the utility possibility frontier, without reference to where the society is at present; it is a static concept. The Pareto criterion says that a move north and/or east from society's present position represents an improvement in social welfare and therefore should be preferred to the present state. It is a dynamic concept. In Figure 13–5 the utility possibility frontier UU represents all points that are Pareto optimal. The Pareto criterion tells us that all points in (and on the boundary of) its shaded area are preferable to P_1 and all points in (and on the boundary of) its shaded area are preferable to P_2, where P_1 and P_2 are two possible present situations.

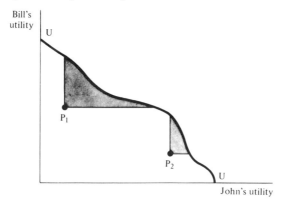

Fig. 13–5

A fundamental theorem of welfare economics, which economists have been busy proving under different assumptions since the days of Adam Smith, demonstrates that under certain ideal conditions free competition working through the price system will produce a Pareto optimum. Moreover, voluntary exchanges on competitive markets will necessarily respect the Pareto criterion: they will consist solely of Pareto improvements, since no individual would willingly trade goods or services or money in a manner that hurts his own welfare. In the next chapter we examine the logic supporting these assertions. We also examine the role of government in situations where the conditions of free competition cannot be expected to prevail. In the meantime, we continue our inquiry into what criteria should guide government choice when free markets fail to function satisfactorily.

The Inadequacy of the Pareto Criterion as a Guide for Government Decision Making

Our first thought might be that the government decision maker need merely look to the Pareto criterion as a guide to action. In fact, he would encounter two important classes of difficulties.

1. The public policy maker must often choose between the status quo and a policy change that will make some individuals better and others worse off. For example, when the decision is made to tax citizens to pay for the national defense, there is no assurance that all the citizens who pay for these government services will prefer them to a bundle containing less defense and lower taxes.[7] Thus such actions will not always satisfy the Pareto criterion; they may make some individuals worse off. On a more local level, an improvement in traffic safety will not satisfy the Pareto criterion unless compensation is paid to the body shops that lose business because of the reduction in accidents. In terms of our Bill–John diagram, a government service that fails to meet the Pareto criterion might be represented by point C in Figure 13–6. Here P is the present policy; C represents an improvement in Bill's position but a setback for John. A change in bus schedules by the Suburban Transportation Commission will be Pareto superior only if all citizens are at worst neutral, and at least one prefers it.

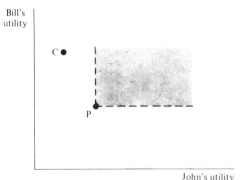

Fig. 13–6

2. Even if the decision maker can be sure that a government action satisfies the Pareto criterion, he will almost certainly encounter difficulties because the criterion falls far short of defining a complete ranking of all social states. The Pareto criterion will not help us when some individuals are better off in one state and some in another. In the Bill–John example, the Pareto criterion tells us to undertake either policy A or policy B in preference to remaining with policy P, but it does not enable us to choose between A and B, whether A and B relate to land development or bus schedules. Note the common element in these two weaknesses of the Pareto criterion: in both cases, the decision maker is forced to choose

---

[7] Witness the refusal of a number of individuals to remit portions of their income taxes that go to support various government activities that they feel are positively detrimental.

between policies that trade off one person's welfare against another's, and the Pareto criterion gives him no help. It is to the intractable problem of establishing a procedure for ranking such policies that we now turn.

Defining a Criterion for Social Choice: The Social Welfare Function

We have been trying to find guidelines that will help a public policy maker choose among possible combinations of individual welfare levels. In the specific case of the two-man community, the Pareto criterion eliminates policy P but leaves him no wiser when it comes to a choice between A and B. How is he to make this difficult decision? He might proceed on an ad hoc basis, comparing one specific outcome to another, case by case. Alternatively, following the fundamental model of choice, he could in principle construct an entire indifference map to present systematically his preferences among alternative combinations of individuals' utilities. The two approaches parallel the distinction we made earlier between simply stating which of three or four commodity bundles the decision maker likes best, and sketching out his entire indifference map.

The particular type of preference function that describes a decision maker's preferences among alternative combinations of individual utilities is called a *social welfare function*. It displays completely just how the decision maker is willing to trade off one person's welfare or utility against another's, just as the indifference maps we looked at earlier displayed the systematic tradeoffs that a consumer is willing to make between apples and oranges, or a public decision maker between electricity and water for irrigation. On the preference map for Bill–John City, for example, a particular indifference curve would connect all the points that represent

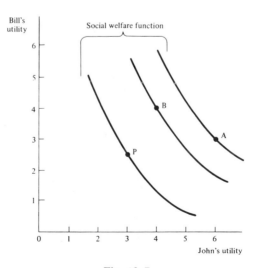

Fig. 13–7

combinations of Bill's utility level and John's utility level that are equally satisfactory from the decision maker's point of view. Figure 13–7 shows one possible preference map. According to this particular social welfare function, policy *A* is preferred. Figure 13–8 shows a continuous utility-possibility frontier and a different social welfare function; the best choice among the feasible points is obviously at *T*.

Note, incidentally, that we can draw a negative implication from our discussion of the social welfare function: it is wrong to assume that any point that is a Pareto optimum is preferable to any that is not. In Figure 13–8 for example, point *S* is preferable to point *Y*, even though *Y* is a Pareto optimum and *S* is not.

These limitations may lead you to conclude that the concept of Pareto optimality is of little value. Far from it; a policy choice that is not Pareto optimal is *a priori* known not to be the best possible choice. Moreover, the Pareto criterion itself frequently points us in a preferable policy direction, pushing us always to search for outcomes that will be superior for all. The trouble is that it does not provide a complete ordering of local states; there are some choices it just won't make for us. When a choice must be made between taxing Peter to benefit Paul and doing nothing (a course that Peter quite naturally prefers), the Pareto criterion cannot help us. The social welfare function we seek will respect, but go beyond, the Pareto criterion.

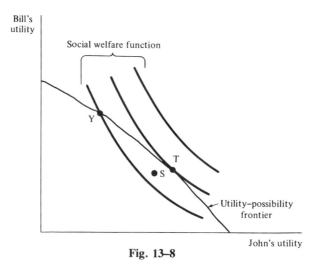

Fig. 13–8

The Inability to Construct the Social Welfare Function

We have just seen that to rank alternative social situations, none of which is Pareto superior to any of the others, we would like to have a social welfare function. Such a function must make explicit judgments as to whether a change that moves one person to a higher indifference curve and another to a curve that is lower is an improvement; such judgments are known as interpersonal comparisons of welfare.[8] How are we to go about constructing our sought-after social welfare function? The short answer is that although such a social welfare function exists in principle—indeed, it is implicit in every public choice that is made—we cannot provide a universally acceptable basis for its construction that is both logical and practical.

The fundamental problem frustrating efforts to rank social welfare is that we have no demonstrably correct procedure for making interpersonal comparisons of welfare. We have no way to attach meaningful index values to one individual's indifference curves that will enable us to make comparisons with the welfare indicated on indifference curves of another. In Table 13–2, for example, we arbitrarily assigned an index value of 4 to policy B for both Bill and John. But this is no guarantee that Bill and John reach equal levels of satisfaction under policy B, and indeed we aren't even prepared to say how we would definitively determine that they are at equal levels.

Even if we could unambiguously define welfare levels, there is no way to reach agreement as to how various distributions of welfare should be ranked. Do we (as a decision maker for society) believe that welfares should be equal for all people? Or do we believe that greater welfare should be the lot of those who show more ability, or work harder, or live longer, or behave better, or are luckier in their choice of parents? When formulating transfer programs such as the income tax, which takes resources from people, or welfare or food stamps, which distribute resources, how should we balance the need to maintain incentives for individual effort against the objective of promoting a more equal apportionment of resources? Conceivably collective agreement on these questions might be easier if no one knew whether he was to be a welfare child or the scion of a wealthy family, whether he would end up physically handicapped or athletically gifted. But most such determinations have already been made. People know who and what they are, and do not lay aside this knowledge when assessing alternative distributions of welfare. Hence universal agreement cannot be expected on how to rank welfare distributions, especially since the fundamental underlying questions do not lend themselves to logically deducible answers.[9]

---

[8] Social welfare, we have argued, should depend solely on the welfares or utility levels of the members of the community. Using the shorthand of mathematical notation, this relationship may be written

$$W = f(u_1, u_2, \ldots, u_n)$$

Here the us represent the levels of utility—that is, the indifference curves reached for the individuals in the n-member society; W is the welfare indicator, and f is the social welfare function. Those familiar with the calculus will recognize that requiring that the social welfare function respect the Pareto criterion is equivalent to the requirement that all the first-order derivatives of the function f be positive.

[9] Recently the proposals of John Rawls have excited a great deal of attention. He employs the metaphor of a "veil of ignorance"; individuals would choose the constitutional rules for their society before they knew where they would reside in that society. Rawls argues that people would then adopt as their criterion for choice: Select the set of rules that achieves the highest

Philosophers and economists have tried for two centuries to devise unambiguous procedures for measuring and combining the welfares of two or more individuals to provide a measure of total social welfare. Their quest has been about as successful as the alchemists' attempt to transmute lead into gold. The occasional flickers of hope have all been extinguished; not only have no feasible procedures been developed, none are on the horizon. Indeed, Kenneth Arrow has virtually demonstrated that we should give up the search. In *Social Choice and Individual Values*, [10] he proves that no wholly satisfactory procedure for combining individual preferences to produce a ranking for society as a whole can ever be found.

What should we do now, compelled to admit that we can never find an unequivocal and totally satisfactory measure for social welfare? One possibility is to give up the attempt to link the design of public policies directly to the promotion of social welfare. We could, for example, decide to clean up the Muddy River by imposing strict pollution controls without trying to estimate the costs of these controls or their impact on all affected people. The Suburban Transportation Commission could simply announce a bus schedule without worrying about what it would accomplish. We urge that such a know-nothing approach be dismissed. Rather, we should strike out in positive directions.

We have already developed insights about the evaluation of social welfare. We have accepted the proposition that social welfare depends only on the welfare of individuals, and we have learned that a decision maker or policy analyst should not expect to be able to construct an actual social welfare function starting with some widely agreed-upon set of basic principles. Nevertheless the concept of a mechanism for determining whether, given the decision maker's preferences, one social state is superior to another is enormously valuable. Such an ordering is implicit in any situation of policy choice, whether a government decision maker is choosing among sweeping alternatives or a private citizen is expressing his value judgments about the world around him. Thus, when the Suburban Transportation Commission finally decides on a bus schedule, it necessarily has determined—consciously or otherwise—that the schedule chosen increases social welfare more than the other possible schedules. And in so doing the changes in individuals' welfares are implicitly measured and combined to estimate the welfare of society.

Carrying the impossible dream of a social welfare function in the back of his mind gives the decision maker a valuable perspective on making actual policy choices. Understanding how he might like to construct a social welfare function, and being sensitive to the problems that he would

---

welfare for the worst-off member of society. See *A Theory of Justice* (Cambridge, Mass.: Harvard University Press, 1971). Others have argued strongly that people would not adopt the Rawls criterion. Instead they would prefer a set of rules that permits a higher average welfare level even though it leaves the man at the bottom a little worse off. The decision analysis methodology laid out in Chapter 12 is invaluable for pondering an issue such as this.

[10] New York: John Wiley & Sons, Inc. 1963. See the appendix to this chapter for a discussion of Arrow's impossibility theorem.

encounter, is likely to prove helpful when he must develop ad hoc procedures to formulate and choose among policy alternatives.

Developing Ad Hoc Procedures for Estimating Social Welfare

If we truly believe that public policy should promote the welfare of society—and we do indeed believe it—then there is no getting away from trying to assess social welfare. Despite the practical and theoretical difficulties, economists have not abandoned the attempt to develop workable criteria for determining when social welfare is increased. They observe that in the real world governments *do* make decisions, and that these decisions exhibit a degree of consistency. Analysts have accordingly tried to discover and make explicit the criteria that appear to have governed such choices, and which therefore might legitimately help guide policy makers in future decisions.

Most pragmatic social welfare tests make four types of simplifications: (1) they focus on a specified set of alternatives rather than considering all possible combinations of policies; (2) they do not concern themselves with comparisons of total social welfare but seek only to determine which policy will lead to the greatest increment over present welfare; (3) they employ a surrogate, most frequently a measure of the individual's effective income, in assessing individual welfares; quantitative comparisons employing this surrogate indicator are then possible; (4) they aggregate individual welfares to provide a measure of social welfare using this surrogate, not the welfare levels as such.

1. *Limiting the alternatives.* As a practical matter, analysts confine their consideration to a relatively small number of policy alternatives; otherwise decisions would rarely get made. The Suburban Transportation Commission would probably limit its study to motor vehicles; a monorail system is unlikely to get much attention. How this winnowing is to be carried out depends on the particular situation; it relies ultimately on the analyst's good judgment. Frequently the decision maker will refine the scope of choice, partly in response to his assessment of political constants. In eliminating proposals from further study, however, the analyst should take care not to exclude a genuinely innovative policy. He should also be alert to opportunities to gather further information; a flexible strategy is usually preferable to an immutable masterplan. Finally, all too often the possibility of doing nothing is overlooked.

2. *Considering only changes in social welfare.* Considering only changes in social welfare has great practical advantages. Frequently we are able to judge that one proposal will enhance the welfare of society more than another, even though we could never come up with an absolute measure of social welfare. For example, we know that if a newly proposed policy satisfies the Pareto criterion it will increase social welfare, regardless of the actual level of social welfare.

We will not in general be able to determine whether social welfare is enhanced or decreased merely by looking at changes in the welfare levels of individuals. For example, if our two-man town is considering a new policy that is beneficial for Bill but hurts John, we will want to know not only the magnitudes of the benefit and harm, but where the two men started off. Similarly, any comparison of weekday and weekend buses must depend in part on how well off the elderly are relative to the parents of school children.

3. *Effective income as a proxy for welfare.* Once into the actual analysis of a policy issue, most analysts take some measure of individual income as a proxy for individual welfare. They are measuring a surrogate, of course, and an imperfect surrogate at that. But the measures of income that have been developed are the best imperfect indicators of welfare found to date.

In measuring the effects of proposed programs, the analyst must therefore try to assign dollar values to the benefits and costs that accrue to individuals. If a new school costs Jane Johnson $25 per year in additional taxes and is worth $40 per·year to her (in the sense that she would be willing to pay as much as $40 per year rather than go without it), then we say that her effective income is increased by $15. If an elderly person would pay $10 for weekday bus service, his effective income is increased by $10 when such service is provided at no charge.

The "income indicates welfare" approach sidesteps the question of whether people with identical incomes may differ in their capacities for enjoyment, but then most of us are probably happy to ignore that question anyway. Even if we accept income as a surrogate for welfare, our work has only begun; the numbers are not handed to us on a platter. Numerous problems of definition, discovery, and measurement remain. In a sophisticated society income accrues to people in diverse ways; the term becomes difficult to define with precision, as anyone knows who has studied the structure of our income tax. A much more devilish problem arises in trying to place a dollar value on the benefits and costs to the individual of a proposed policy change. Many commodities that are of value to us, such as health, air quality, or the absence of crime, are not bought and sold in a market. No convenient record is made of how individuals make choices, if indeed they have the option of choice. Hence it is difficult to estimate who gains and loses, and by how much, when we raise taxes or prices to provide safer streets or purer air. Much of policy analysis gets involved in complex issues of evaluation like these, issues that are implicitly resolved whenever a decision is actually made.

4. *Aggregating individual welfares.* Even if we could unambiguously determine a satisfactory measure of effective income for every member of society, we would still have to decide whether one income pattern was superior to another. Is it better to choose a policy that yields Bill $10,000 and John $9,000, or an alternative that gives Bill and John each $9,400? Is

it better to spend $50,000 for bus service worth $55,000 to the elderly poor or for service worth $60,000 to middle-income parents? To develop workable criteria for making such choices, practical compromises must be made. The rest of this chapter considers a variety of ways to make these compromises.

One Approach: Maximizing Net Benefits

One school of thought maintains that a change from the present social state should be undertaken if the gainers from the change *could* compensate the losers in such a way that everyone would be better off, in that way satisfying the Pareto criterion. Note that the adherents of this school, which is associated with the names of two British economists, Nicholas Kaldor and Sir John Hicks, do not require that compensation be actually carried out. Basically they are saying:

> Make a change when total income increases; don't worry about how it is distributed.

This is the maximize-net-benefits approach to social policy. Gains and losses in welfare are added up for all of society and whichever policy produces the largest net increase in total effective income is chosen. If buses for the well-to-do outscore buses for the elderly poor by $60,000 to $55,000, they are to be preferred. Because the distribution of income is left aside, this approach greatly simplifies the computations. The incomes of each individual need not be determined, only the overall increases or decreases in income that result from the choice of particular policies.

To see this criterion in application, suppose that our imaginary community of two is presently at point I in Figure 13–9. A new school building, financed via the present tax structure, would move the community to II. Bill prefers II to I; John prefers I.[11] However, if construction of the new school were contingent upon a $100 side payment from Bill to John that would take them to point III, both of them would like to see this

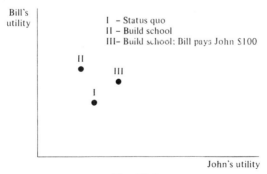

Fig. 13–9

---

[11] It is tempting to infer that Bill has a house full of toddlers and John is a childless bachelor. But those with New England town meeting experience have discovered that people's social welfare functions are not always so myopically self-centered.

option in preference to the status quo. The Kaldor–Hicks criterion requires that the school be built whether or not the side payment is made, and whether or not Bill is a millionaire or John a pauper.

Benefit–cost analysis in its most elemental form is merely a straightforward application of the Kaldor–Hicks approach. As we saw in Chapter 9, it recommends that a project be undertaken when its total benefits to all parties exceed its total costs. Obviously, if total benefits exceed total costs, there is a hypothetical pattern of compensation that will leave everyone better off if a project is undertaken. Suppose that in the school building example just cited the pattern of costs and benefits is as shown in Table 13–4. As long as the total net benefits ($70 in this example) are positive, a pattern of side payments can be found such that all citizens will benefit if the project is undertaken. Here, if Bill pays John $100 he will reap a net benefit of $50; John will be ahead of the game by $20.

Table 13–4

	Bill	John	Total
Benefits	$350	$120	$470
Costs	$200	$200	$400
Net benefits	$150	−$80	$70

The Kaldor–Hicks criterion is satisfied in many public policy decisions, especially those for which the number and scope of available choices is restricted, the programs are relatively small, and the redistributive effects are minor. However, many people have been repelled by its insensitivity to the equity aspects of policy changes, in other words, to the effects of programs on the distribution of effective income. If a policy change would give King Khalid of Saudi Arabia an additional $1 million and cost one thousand individuals of moderate means $999 each, the maximize-net-benefits criterion says that the change should be undertaken. King Khalid could pay each of the losers $999 and still have $1000 left over for himself. According to Kaldor–Hicks, the change should be undertaken even if King Khalid does not carry out this payment scheme. Hicks has justified the criterion on the grounds that over a period of time things average out. One group benefits from one change, another from a later change; thus, in the long run, the welfare position of each person is eventually improved. To which the critics snort, with Keynes, "In the long run we are all dead."

Another Approach: Attempting Interpersonal Comparisons

If it is not sufficient to "look only at net benefits," how should policy making proceed? We must develop an explicit procedure for making interpersonal welfare comparisons, for the choice of a public policy almost invariably helps one group at the expense of another. Sometimes the injured group loses absolutely. At other times, it merely loses out on the benefits it would have reaped had a different choice been made. For example, the acquisitions director of a library must constantly balance the benefits going to readers of assorted ages and interests. Similarly, lowering speed limits in the harbor benefits those who sail but restricts the power boaters. Moving a health clinic to a more densely populated location inconveniences some individuals and cuts travel time for others. How should a decision maker confront the question of whether providing an annual checkup to individual A, an impoverished person in relatively good health, is more important than an additional psychiatric visit for individual B, a disturbed elderly citizen of moderate means? Paul Samuelson points out that the ethical judgments governments make about distribution, judgments about which individuals or groups will be permitted to benefit at the expense of others, are similar to the decisions parents make when they allocate family income. Roller skates for Bobby must be compared with ukelele lessons for Susan and a hair transplant for father. In the real world, public decision makers face this type of policy choice every day. Policy makers must in effect make interpersonal comparisons of welfare, and then make judgments about the way welfares should be distributed. How do they accomplish these difficult tasks? In comparing the welfares of individuals, public policy makers rely on observation, on interviews, on conventional wisdom and current reports about attitudes, and on inferences drawn from individuals' choices and from choices that were available to them but they chose not to make.

The analyses that inform these choices usually employ, as we have suggested, some measure of effective income, an indicator of the valued resources that will accrue to the individual. In practice, proposed social changes will affect large numbers of people, so that it may not be possible to consider individuals on a one-by-one basis. Decision makers thus tend to think in terms of average or representative citizens, or of groups who are similar in essential circumstances. Such a group might be the citizens of Oakland, or all asthmatics, or the elderly of the United States.

Taking Distribution into Account

Assuming that we could identify the consequences of a proposed policy for all affected groups or individuals, what sort of distributional guidelines are available to help decision makers in such situations? The following principles are representative of what we believe to be the present consensus among most participants in and students of the policy process, although that consensus is rarely articulated precisely.

1. A program should be adopted when it will yield benefits to one group that are greater than the losses of another group, provided that the two groups are in roughly equivalent circumstances, and the changes in welfare are not of great magnitude. In the absence of other information, a librarian's discovery that new gardening books circulate on average five times a year, and new ornithology books only twice, would justify buying more gardening and fewer bird books.

2. If the benefits of a proposed policy are greater for one group than the costs for another group, and if it redresses the discriminatory effects of earlier policy choices, that policy should be undertaken. Thus, the deputy health commissioner may feel more justified in moving the well-baby clinic from one low-income neighborhood to another if the city has recently constructed a major recreation complex in the first area. Compensatory changes of this type are particularly likely to work themselves out through the tugging and hauling of various groups that are active in the political process. In the United States at least (and no doubt elsewhere), policy changes that significantly hurt particular interest groups are extraordinarily difficult to undertake, however beneficial they may be on a net benefits basis. Thus, our politicians and decision makers are always alert to packages of policies that appear to promote the welfares of all organized and readily identifiable affected parties. Unorganized groups, most significantly the taxpayers as a whole, are those who stand to lose from such logrolled packages.

3. It is not so clear whether policies should be undertaken if they will benefit some groups only by imposing significant costs on others. It is sometimes proposed that a policy change should be adopted if and only if it passes a two-part test: (a) it yields positive net benefits, and (b) the redistributional effects of the change are beneficial. This test, despite its appealing ring, encounters two major sources of difficulty: first, it presupposes that general agreement can be reached on which patterns of redistribution are beneficial.[12] Second, it is too restrictive. By requiring that both of two desirable criteria be met if a policy change is to be deemed acceptable, it prevents a tradeoff when one criterion is met but the other isn't. For example, the positive net benefits requirement would rule out all redistributional programs that entail any administrative costs whatsoever. The stipulation that redistributional effects must be "beneficial" would defeat a program that would provide $1000 in net benefits to Mary Brown even if it cost only $1 to Jane Smith who is at a slightly lower welfare level.

4. Agreement is also less clear when it comes to favorable redistributional efforts that do not pass the maximize-net-benefits test. Even if there is widespread agreement about redistributional objectives, it may be difficult to determine what level of real resource sacrifice we should accept to achieve any given level of redistribution. Thus even if all the voters in our suburban community are happy to have the Transportation Commission do something for the town's senior citizens, many of them may think that one bus a day is enough. The resolution of this type of disagreement will inevitably be worked out through the political process. Social choice criteria are unlikely to be of assistance in such a situation.

None of the social choice criteria we have outlined can be totally

---

[12] It is conceivable that a proposed policy could benefit the poor at too great an expense to the well-to-do. Efforts to redistribute must be balanced against the need to maintain incentives. The 50 percent limit on the tax on earned income is one expression of Congressional interest in this matter.

satisfactory guides to policy. Still, since there are no superior alternatives, they can be useful in a wide range of circumstances, particularly to indicate the right general direction for change. Indeed, most policy analysis in the United States rests on the maximize-net-benefits approach, which is a distillation of the Kaldor–Hicks criterion. Moreover, even when the suggested criteria are not applied directly, they may be valuable in leading us to include in any policy analysis a systematic identification of the benefits and costs for those affected. Policy choice in the United States would be much improved if it always started by identifying the consequences of choices for individual welfare, since these, as we have stressed, are the critical components of social welfare.

A Further Approach: Emphasizing the Social Decision Process

The inability to find unassailable criteria for resolving conflicts on social policy has turned many people to a search for efficient decision-making processes that will be accepted as legitimate. When we are interested in how to resolve the conflicting wishes of individuals, it is usually because they belong to a society in which choices must be made that will affect many of the members. (Remember that society is a widely inclusive term, as broad as the entire nation, as narrow as a bowling club.) In forming the society, the members have agreed, implicitly or explicitly, on a process for making these decisions. It has therefore been argued that we should stop worrying about how to combine the diverse preferences of individuals to get a measure of social welfare—which is an impossible task anyway. Instead we should simply accept the ranking of social states that is produced by the society's established decision process. Short of revolution we cannot escape from the choices made for us by past, present, and prospective elected and appointed officials; hence the idea has a lot of practical appeal. According to this argument, for example, if our duly constituted Suburban Transportation Commission votes for weekday bus routes as opposed to weekend routes, the vote is to be taken as a valid expression of the town's social preference. If a majority of the townspeople disagree, their recourse is to the ballot box; they can vote the commission or whoever appoints it out of office. When all the members of a society attach importance to a particular method of making a social choice, it is a persuasive justification for adopting as a de facto social welfare function the ranking produced by that method of decision.

Reliance on the society's established decision process implies that even when individuals disagree strongly over what decision should be made, they agree on who should make the decision and by what procedures. They believe that how a decision is made is fundamentally more important than what that decision is. Consider, for example, the following policy alternatives:

1. Traffic law *A*, prohibiting overnight parking on streets in the business district, passed by the City Council;

2. Traffic law *B,* permitting overnight parking on alternate sides of the same streets, passed by the City Council;
3. Traffic law *A,* set forth as an administrative enactment of the Police Commissioner;
4. Traffic law *B,* also an administrative enactment of the Police Commissioner.

Mr. Jones prefers traffic law *B.* He also prefers that traffic laws be passed by the City Council. Therefore he prefers alternative (2) to alternatives (1), (3), and (4). However, if the City Council votes, it will pass law *A;* alternative (2) is not available. Mr. Jones may well prefer having the decision made by the City Council to having a decision he likes better made at the expense of a change in the method of choice. In short, he may prefer (1) to (4).

In some circumstances a society will accept a general analytic principle, such as maximize-net-benefits, as a guide for policy choices, with decisions made on a rather technocratic basis. This principle has long been followed, though not without controversy, in assigning responsibility for decisions about flood control projects to the Army Corps of Engineers. In other circumstances an avowedly political process is the preferred method of choice, as when an issue is settled by fighting it out on the floor of a popularly elected legislature.

Satisfactory Processes for Social Choice

If people believe that how a decision is made is fundamentally more important than what that decision is, what makes for an acceptable method of choice?

A person's regard for a decision process may depend in part on the decisions it reaches and the outcomes thereby made possible. For simplicity we have been speaking as though a decision process is selected to make just one decision. In fact, processes are established to make many decisions over a period of time. Mr. Jones may wish to retain a process even though he may be hurt by a particular decision, because he expects to benefit on balance from the series of decisions forthcoming. But if the City Council frequently voted frivolous or punitive traffic laws, Mr. Jones might object to that method of choice. When a society continues to use a particular choice process, it suggests that people believe that on the whole the process is performing adequately, or if inadequately, the fault lies not with the process but with those administering it. To be sure, agreement on a decision process is rather like an agreement to settle a dispute by flipping a coin, in that in any particular case people are uncertain as to what the outcome will be.

Decision processes may be judged on other grounds. In accordance with our ideas about justice and good government, we may value a decision process directly for ethical reasons, paying only indirect attention to the results it produces. In short, we may wish to retain a process because we believe it is fair. Mr. Jones may in fact prefer that there be no traffic laws at all. He may realize a net loss in welfare from the decision actually taken by the City Council, yet still think it important that the decision be made in this way. Thus a process can win universal approval if each member of a society recognizes that he benefits from a stable mechanism for resolving his conflicts with others in an ethically satisfactory way.

For most organizations, majority rule is the accepted mode of decision; many people take it for granted that this is the democratic way of doing things. Yet a closer look at our decision processes reveals that we employ a wide variety of choice methods, and a great deal of thought and effort go into their design. The bylaws of the bowling club, no less than the United States Constitution, spell out who is to make what decisions and how. Even in societies where most substantive questions are decided by a simple majority vote, we are likely to find that a two-thirds vote is required for a bylaw change. The concern for process is thus affirmed. For some painful decisions, notably the question of who shall be called for military service, we at one juncture deliberately ordained that the choice should be made by a lottery, in the belief that that was the fairest procedure. Indeed, concern for process was the determining factor in the actual choice of that policy.

The process by which choices are made is an important, valued attribute in a variety of contexts. As a general rule, the further removed the outputs and inputs of a policy are from goods traded on markets, the more important the process of choice seems. Thus process may be of paramount importance in decisions involving health or criminal justice, and much less critical for choices among highway-construction techniques.[13]

Our discussion of process highlights an important lesson of this chapter: any attributes that individuals value should be weighed when public policy is determined. In the coming decade the federal government must face a number of choices about life-threatening activities; decisions about pollution, the ozone layer, and nuclear safety come immediately to mind. As such decisions become more frequent our concern with process grows, for the procedures by which such decisions are to be made are likely to be considered as important as the actual dollar numbers employed to value the lives involved.

A Summing Up

In this chapter we have stepped back from the analysis of specific situations of public choice to look at public policy from a broader perspective. We have focused on the issue that is fundamental for all of public policy: What are we trying to accomplish? Philosophers and presidents must consider this issue in depth. So too should the analyst who must recommend one dam project over another, the environmental affairs commissioner who opposes or approves a nuclear power plant, and the

---

[13] See Zeckhauser's "Procedures for Valuing Lives," *Public Policy* (Fall 1975): 419–64.

legislator who must vote on the eligibility requirements for state fellow-ships for higher education.

The objective of public policy, we have argued, should be to promote the welfare of society. Moreover, the welfare of society depends wholly on the welfare of individuals; it's people that count. Social welfare is a strange commodity. Although a social welfare function is implicit in every public choice that is made, social welfare can never be observed or measured directly. Public decision makers must work instead with surrogates and with ad hoc procedures for measuring social welfare. The major part of this book has been devoted to specific techniques for predicting outcomes and making decisions, but the broad philosophical issues we have discussed in this chapter are always in the background. The decision maker who keeps the concept of a social welfare function firmly in mind will find that he thinks more clearly and more productively about the tasks immediately at hand.

Appendix: Arrow's Impossibility Theorem

It may seem that by focusing on the procedural systems by which society settles individual issues, we can bypass the intractable problem of drawing up a social welfare function for the society. In fact, as Kenneth Arrow has shown,[14] we would only be sweeping the problem a little further under the rug, for the theoretical difficulties that plague us in trying to devise a social welfare function also confound our efforts to devise any satisfactory decision process.

Arrow suggests several ethically appealing conditions that we might reasonably demand of any procedure for combining individual preferences to provide a preference ordering for society as a whole. These conditions are applicable whether we are confronting the practical problem of electing public officials or the more theoretical problem of ordering social states. He then proves rigorously that no procedure can simultaneously satisfy these rather modest conditions. Arrow's rigor is not for us; instead we will simply indicate the essence of his conditions.

1. The voting procedure must provide a way to combine every possible pattern of individual rankings into a single ordering of the group's preferences. In particular, the social ordering must always be transitive, so that if *A* is ranked ahead of *B* and *B* ahead of *C,* then *A* would also be ranked ahead of *C.* Consider the case of majority rule. If voters must choose between two candidates only, majority rule presents no problem. But suppose we are serving breakfast to the three bears. Their preferences among three alternative kinds of cereal are shown in Table 13A–1. If we ask the bears to vote between any two cereals, we will find that two bears prefer oatmeal to grits and two prefer grits to cornflakes. Therefore if majority rule is to be transitive in this situation, it must rank oatmeal above cornflakes. But instead a majority of the bears prefers cornflakes to oatmeal. In short, oatmeal defeats grits, grits defeat cornflakes—but cornflakes then defeats oatmeal. The ordering produced by majority rule is intransitive.

Table 13A–1

Preference	Papa Bear	Mama Bear	Baby Bear
1st	oatmeal	grits	cornflakes
2nd	grits	cornflakes	oatmeal
3rd	cornflakes	oatmeal	grits

The procedural rules of most democratic bodies implicitly recognize this difficulty. The order in which amendments are voted, for example, is ordinarily prescribed by an organization's bylaws so as to prevent intransitivities from rising to the surface. The bears' voting procedures, for

---

[14] *Social Choice and Individual Values* (New York: John Wiley & Sons, 1963).

example, may specify the order in which pairs of cereals are put to a vote. Oatmeal having defeated grits, it is then compared to cornflakes—and this second vote closes the matter. Runoff elections among the leading contenders prevent intransitivities from being observed in the election process.

.2. The decision procedure must respect the citizens' unanimous choices. Suppose Andrea, Barbara, and Regina are running for dogcatcher. The voters are divided into two groups, dog lovers and dog haters; the preferences of the two groups are shown in Table 13A–2. Everyone would rather have Barbara than Regina; it would be an unsatisfactory system if Regina got elected.

Table 13A–2

Preference	Dog lovers	Dog haters
1st	Andrea	Barbara
2nd	Barbara	Regina
3rd	Regina	Andrea

This condition is related to Pareto optimality, which was discussed in the main body of this chapter. In Figure 13A–1, the axes represent the preferences of the two groups. The Pareto optimal frontier consists of Andrea and Barbara, and therefore the choice should be made from between them.

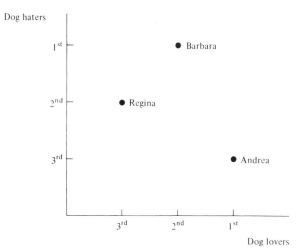

Fig. 13A–1

3. The decision process must be "independent of irrelevant alternatives." Suppose you are trying to design a voting procedure to select a joint vacation plan for Holly and Linda. Holly prefers camping in the mountains and Linda camping at the seashore. If each is permitted to cast one vote, a tie will result. Perhaps you think you can cleverly resolve the dilemma by offering them a third (hypothetical) choice, camping on a farm.

Table 13A–3

Preference	Holly	Linda
1st	mountains	farm
2nd	seashore	seashore
3rd	farm	mountains

You find that their preference rankings would then be as in Table 13A-3. Some people would argue that this additional information tells you something about strength of preferences, and that the seashore (which is at worst the second choice of both) should therefore win out. Arrow's independence requirement prohibits this attempt to gather and employ more information about the strength of their preferences for mountains and seashore than you did before. You must not have recourse to this essentially extraneous information in designing the voting procedure.

4. The decision process must be nondictatorial. For example, we could solve the problem of what to serve the three bears if we gave Baby Bear's vote a heavier weight than Mama's and Papa's combined. Then cornflakes would always win, for Baby's preferences would be decisive. This hardly seems fair.

All of these conditions appear to be desirable and plausible for democratic decision making. Consequently Arrow's proof that it is impossible to devise a voting procedure for combining individual preferences that will simultaneously satisfy all the conditions caused considerable consternation, at least among economists. Needless to say, it has not led to the collapse of democratic institutions; in practice, one or more of the conditions is abandoned.

Most frequently the condition that is dropped is the independence of irrelevant alternatives. Certain types of all-star balloting, for example, violate it. Suppose two sportswriters each rank five shortstops in order of preference; first place gets 10 points, second 9, third 8, and so on. Points are added to give the overall preference ranking for each shortstop. The results are shown in Table 13A–4. *D* wins the highest rank, with *B* second.

Table 13A–4

Player	Writer 1	Writer 2	Total
A	8	6	14
B	7	10	17
C	6	9	15
D	10	8	18
E	9	7	16

Now suppose *A* and *E* both break their legs. The new ranking, with *A* and *E* eliminated from the balloting, is in Table 13A–5. Now *B* gets the all-star nod.

It is important to note that in the framework of Arrow's theorem it is

Table 13A–5

Player	Writer 1	Writer 2	Total
B	9	10	19
C	8	9	17
D	10	8	18

impossible to take the strength of individuals' preferences into account. The social preferences must depend only on people's ranking of the alternatives. This requirement is often violated by decision rules in actual use. Benefit–cost analysis attempts to measure differences between more or less preferred alternatives by a common unit of measurement, namely dollars. Logrolling procedures in legislatures provide another means of securing outcomes that respond to strengths of preferences.

As if it were not enough that Arrow's conditions are impossible to fulfill simultaneously, a further problem is not addressed by his theorem. Suppose we have constructed a procedure for combining individual preferences into a social preference ordering (violating, of course, one or more of Arrow's conditions). In order to use this procedure, we need to know people's preferences. How do we find them out? The only way is to ask the persons themselves. But can we be sure we will be given candid answers? In general, we cannot; frequently a person may gain by revealing his preferences incorrectly.

Eliciting preferences and processing them to reach a decision are the major problems encountered in designing procedures for social choice. The purpose of a voting procedure or a social welfare function is to ensure that the groups decisions of a society reflect the desires of its individual members. Arrow has shown that the design of any such procedure will necessarily require compromises and difficult tradeoffs.

14 Achieving Desirable Outcomes

Every society employs both public and private choice mechanisms to promote the welfare of its citizens. Effective public choice, the subject of this book, requires that the decision maker pay explicit attention to a great variety of complex issues. The primary instrument of public choice in our society is the government. Government decision makers are found on the local, state, and federal levels, in the executive, legislative, and judicial branches. Quasi-public choices must be made by the decision makers in nonprofit institutions. Private choices, on the other hand, are made through the market; an understanding of the market mechanism is critical for an intelligent approach to problems of public choice.

In the modern world, *market* has several shades of meaning. To economists, the market is the market system as a whole, or sometimes the arrangements for buying and selling a particular good or service, whether apples, appendectomies, or structural steel. They speak of the operation of the market, meaning the whole system of institutional arrangements whereby goods are exchanged. Or they refer to the labor market, focusing on the mechanisms by which employers and workers coordinate their exchanges of dollars for services. In this book, when we speak of the market we will normally mean the market system as a whole, a large set of different markets.

The working of the market is extraordinarily complex; a full understanding of it may require years of study. Fortunately, private decision makers confronted with market processes, unlike their policy making public counterparts, need not understand all the details of the mechanism with which they must deal. The corporate executive, the shop owner, the shoemaker, and the housewife, four representative market participants, have probably been making effective market choices for many years, although they may well have been unaware of that fact. Anyone who sells his goods for the best price he can get or who shops around for the cheapest source of supply is operating effectively in the market.

These effective individual choices yield an impressive result if the market satisfies the ideal conditions that are required to make it perfectly competitive. A Pareto optimal outcome, an outcome that is efficient, will automatically be generated. That is, given the resources and technology of the society, no rearrangement of goods and services can unambiguously improve the welfare of society: no rearrangement of goods will lead to a higher level of welfare for some individual without reducing the welfare of at least one other. This result has been well known since the time of Adam Smith. It supplies the motivation for arguments for free enterprise, as opposed to systems in which patterns of production, indeed even patterns of consumption, are strongly (and deliberately) influenced by government.

Why a Government at All?

In view of these widely advertised virtues of the market, why might we still wish to have a government, other than to facilitate market processes by maintaining law and order, establishing property rights, and enforcing contracts? First, as we shall review in some detail in this chapter, the markets in which many goods are traded are not perfectly competitive. Hence the efficient outcome is never reached. It may then be desirable for the government to step in to deal with these situations where the market has "failed."

Second, efficiency, the main accomplishment of competitive markets, is only one contributor to social welfare. And even if the economy operates with perfect efficiency, we are assured only that we reach an allocation of goods and services such that no one can be made better off without sacrificing another's welfare. We are given no assurance as to which allocation, which point on the possibility frontier, we will actually reach. The society's social welfare function, its ranking of alternative social states, may express strong preferences among different points on that frontier. Indeed, we saw in Chapter 13 (see especially Figure 13–8) that many points inside the frontier may be preferable to points that are on it. What we have just expressed in rather technical language as a concern about the location of a point on a frontier is more conventionally discussed as a concern with the distribution of goods and services in the society, or more summarily, the income distribution.

Third, some people may regard the market process itself as unattractive, in that it rewards behavior that they feel is socially undesirable. It fosters competition and the ethic of the survival of the fittest at the expense of cooperative ventures and communitarian values. This objection is to the market system per se, however equitable and efficient the allocations of goods and services that it generates. Such an objection implies that the process by which choices are made is a valued end in itself, no different from apples and oranges, or leisure time, or freedom from pollution. Most of us agree wholeheartedly with the idea that process is important. But at the same time, if it is to serve as the basis for a telling objection to the market system, we must be able to demonstrate that there is a more attractive system for allocating resources, one whose shortfall in performance relative to a market system does not render it unacceptable. These issues, not surprisingly, form the cornerstone of the debate between proponents of centrally controlled economies and those who prefer a more decentralized system oriented toward private ownership of the means of production. When we wander from questions of logic and methodology to those of ideology, thought processes become less deductive and more reflective of personal preference and belief. Having made this disclaimer, the authors affirm their own belief that the "more attractive process" arguments in favor of collective choice are not well supported by experience.

In sum, we believe that government participation in the resource allocation processes of society can be justified on two grounds only:

1. *Equity:* A more desirable distribution of goods and services among the members of the society is fostered.
2. *Efficiency:* Efficiency is promoted in situations where the market has failed.

The Market System and Efficiency

Our focus in this volume is on government decisions. Still, it is essential that we have a feel for the way markets and the price system achieve desirable outcomes, for government choices should be viewed as complementary to those private mechanisms of resource allocation. Most public decision makers must interact daily with private markets. More important, an understanding of how prices and the market system operate will provide insights into the way government choices should be made.

The fundamental result emerging from the detailed study of the performance of markets (we repeat for emphasis) is that under certain ideal conditions free competition, working through the price system, will yield an efficient outcome, a point on the possibility frontier. This result is worth examining in some detail.

Let us start by identifying the most crucial of the ideal conditions that guarantee the efficiency of competitive markets. First, information in the market must be fully shared. Each participant must understand the nature of goods and services sold on the market. Second, exchanging goods on the market must be a costless process. Third, markets must exist for buying and selling any commodity that individuals might wish to trade. Fourth, each participant must take market prices as a given. Generally this requires that there be a large number of buyers and sellers on a market, none with too big a share, so that no one will have the ability to influence market price by distorting his behavior. Fifth, the consumption or production decisions of one individual, or more generally his actions, must not influence the welfare of another. That is, there must be no externalities;

Brown's welfare must depend solely on the goods he consumes, and not on those that Smith consumes or Jones produces. Sixth, there must be no goods such as national defense, that can be consumed only in common.

Let us assume that the market satisfies these conditions, and see then how efficiency is achieved. In Chapter 3, "The Model of Choice," we defined the best point for the individual decision maker as the highest ranked of all those points available to him. We also derived certain conditions that must hold at any such optimum. By definition, an optimal point is better than all other available points, including those immediately surrounding it. This means that no small change, in any direction, can lead to an improvement in his condition. Decisions may thus be simplified by focusing on the marginal rate of substitution (MRS), the rate at which an individual is *willing* to substitute one good or one attribute for another—and the marginal rate of transformation (MRT), the rate at which an individual is *able* to substitute that good or attribute for the other. If these two rates are unequal, then the individual can make a substitution that will move him to a position that he prefers. Moreover, if he is an efficient maximizer of his own satisfaction, he will do so.

If two people have marginal rates of substitution between two commodities that are unequal, and if both have some of each commodity on hand, then a trade can be arranged that will move each to a more preferred position. Suppose that George's marginal rate of substitution between peaches and pears is three peaches for one pear, and Peter's MRS is four for one. A trade could be arranged from which both would benefit. For example, Peter would be more than willing to give up three and one-half peaches in exchange for one pear, and George would be receiving one-half peach more than is necessary to compensate him for the loss of a pear. Because each participant in such a transaction moves to a position he prefers, each is made better off, according to the choice criterion for individual welfare. When someone is made better off without making anyone else worse off, as is the case here, the Pareto criterion says that society is made better off by the voluntary trade. At a Pareto optimum, no such improvements remain to be made. Consequently it must be that at a Pareto optimum all individuals have equal marginal rates of substitution for each pair of goods. Otherwise an exchange could be arranged that would make two people better off and no one worse off.

Not only must everybody have the same marginal rate of substitution for any pair of commodities, but this rate must equal the marginal rate at which one commodity can be transformed into the other. For example, suppose that in a two-man society Peter and George have made their peach–pear trade; now each is willing to give up one pear for three and one-half peaches. But production conditions are such that if one less pear is grown, four more peaches can be produced. Then Peter and George can both be made better off by switching some resources—land, workers, equipment, fertilizer, insecticides, and the like—from growing pears to growing peaches. In effect, a trade is made with nature. By the Pareto criterion, society is then better off. At a Pareto optimum, further such beneficial alterations in production are not possible. Outputs thus must be such that the marginal rate of transformation between any two goods is equal to the marginal rate of substitution between the commodities that is common to all individuals. In this case more and more peaches would be produced, and fewer pears. As Peter and George give up pears for peaches, pears begin to look relatively better to them. Their tradeoff rates shift, until eventually they reach a marginal rate of substitution of four peaches for one pear, the rate of exchange in production.

We need speak only in terms of relative prices. Tradeoff possibilities between peaches and pears are the same whether their prices are 5 and 20 cents respectively, or 1 and 4 Martian kronei. The tradeoffs available to a consumer are represented diagrammatically in Figure 14–1 by the line *ED*. Suppose that a man's income is sufficient to buy eight pears if he purchases no peaches. With the relative prices specified above, he could trade one pear for four peaches, and could choose any point along the budget line *ED*. With the indifference map shown, point *P* is the optimum; he buys 5 pears and 12 peaches. Everyone responds to the relative prices of the goods by adjusting his purchases so that his MRS is equal to the rate of exchange possible at those prices. Not to do so would mean that he fails to maximize his satisfaction.

Similarly, productive resources are continually transferred until the rate at which the economy can transform one good into another is equal to the rate of exchange in the market. Say, for example, that doll houses are selling for $100 each and rocking horses for $25. A toy manufacturer knows that if he manufactures one less doll house per day and uses the workers and materials to make rocking horses, he can produce an additional five horses daily. The rate of exchange in the market, one to four, is above his

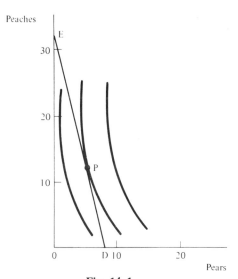

Fig. 14–1

marginal rate of transformation. As long as his own rate of transformation is less than the market rate, he should continue to transfer resources toward rocking horse production. Otherwise, he would be failing to maximize his income.

Once all individuals' marginal rates of substitution and the economy's marginal rates of transformation between all pairs of goods are brought into equality we will be at a Pareto optimum. No profitable trades between producers, between consumers, or between combinations thereof will be possible. The functioning of the price system as a signaling mechanism allows this optimal equilibrium to come about.

Our discussion has assumed that relative prices were set by some autonomous force, but of course they are set by the actions of human decision makers. Actually, in a large market economy each consumer and most producers play such a minor role that their purchases and sales have no effect on existing prices for market-traded goods. No wheat farmer can raise the price of wheat by withholding his crop from the market. Similarly, no household can affect the price of bread by boosting its purchases. Indeed, a critical assumption of the competitive model is that all participants recognize their impotence in this area. Rather than trying any such manipulations, they take prices as given.

The mass action of many consumers or producers can affect prices, however, just as the mass movement of many motorists can create a traffic jam that no individual motorist could either prevent or create. Some of you may recall Adam Smith's famous metaphor of an invisible hand at work in the marketplace. It is beyond the scope of this volume to discuss the dextrous performance of the invisible hand. But the essence of its operation can be readily understood. Say, in the example above, that the price of a pear is only twice that of a peach. Both Peter and George will choose to specialize in peach production, hoping to exchange peaches for pears on the market at the rate of two peaches for a pear—a real bargain in view of their ability to produce four peaches for each pear whose production is sacrificed. But when they come to market with their supplies of peaches, pears will be in short supply. (Remember that this is a two-man economy—if they don't grow pears, no one will.) Too many peaches are available at the going price, and not enough pears. The price of peaches will fall relative to the price of pears. They will adjust production, and eventually an equilibrium will be reached where the price of a pear is four times that of a peach.

In general, if the quoted price of a commodity is above its equilibrium value, the quantity of that commodity put up for sale will exceed the quantity demanded. The sellers with excess supplies will lower prices just a bit. This will coax out a bit more demand. The interplay of the forces of supply and demand will lead ultimately to a price for each good such that the amount offered for sale is just the amount desired for purchase. This process is the famous law of supply and demand in operation. All consumers' marginal rates of substitution for different goods will reflect the same relative prices. And these relative prices will also represent marginal rates of transformation.

All this is accomplished in the ideal circumstances where the market is functioning perfectly. No one needs to be appointed to coordinate purchases or production. The self-interest of consumers and producers, who react to the prices they encounter and make trades with each other and with nature, propels the society to a Pareto optimum. Society's resources are being used efficiently, yet no one needs to be exhorted to fulfill his obligations for the market system harnesses people's own natural inclinations.

Much of the free-market, laissez-faire ideology is based on this rosy vision of the invisible hand at work in perfectly competitive markets. The catch is, of course, in the phrase "perfectly competitive"—for in the real world such markets are rare.[1] In the next section we discuss a number of situations where the conditions for a competitive market are not met. Such situations pervade many areas of our economy. Nonetheless, it should be emphasized that in this nation the free market is generally regarded as the primary means through which individuals' welfares should be pursued, with each person maximizing on his own behalf. The success of this mechanism depends, of course, on whether conditions for a competitive market are reasonably well met or can be established.

How the Market May Fail

This brief sojourn in the competitive market should give us some understanding of its accomplishments in those situations in which it can be expected to perform satisfactorily. In such cases, the market should be permitted free rein. We would never, for example, entrust the government with the tasks of manufacturing shoelaces and ensuring that all retail outlets are supplied with them. The rationale for government intervention must be either that in particular areas the market is performing poorly or not at all, or that the society has objectives in addition to economic efficiency. A concern for the distribution of welfare is the principal additional objective. In the sections to come we review the possible causes of market failure, and then describe alternative policies that might be invoked to deal with them. We conclude the chapter with a brief discussion

---

[1] Traditional economics is frequently criticized on the grounds that its emphasis on competitive markets implies a devotion to a particular system of production, namely capitalism. Although it may have been true at times in the past that the mechanism was viewed as a justification for the ideology, this charge is no longer warranted. If anything the intellectual emphasis today runs in the opposite direction. Most economists now use the model of the competitive market for a different purpose, as a framework for examining the interrelationships among the various parts of any economic system, capitalist or otherwise. For them it is merely a convenient point of departure. For example, in this volume we emphasize the analysis not of the competitive market but of policies that may be undertaken when the market has failed. Radical economists would no doubt argue that even this use of the market framework is value-loaded.

of the income distribution issue, and of mechanisms to promote more equal distributions.

The promised discussion of market failure is lengthy. Therefore we should provide you with a plan of attack before launching into it. In the next six sections we discuss possible reasons for market failure: (1) the imperfect flow of information; (2) transactions costs; (3) the nonexistence of markets for some goods; (4) market power; (5) externalities; and (6) public goods.

The Imperfect Flow of Information

For the price system to perform its signaling function perfectly, information must be costlessly shared among all individuals, including information on the prices charged by various suppliers. Uncertainties will of course remain. No one predicts the weather with complete accuracy; no one knows for sure what technologies will be relied on in the next century. But there can be no asymmetries in the availability of whatever information exists. If an employer knows that a job entails a high safety risk, his employee must know that as well. If a particular appliance is likely to break in a few months, the customer must be as aware of its deficiencies as the manufacturer. If a paramedic has only limited experience in treating trauma, his patient must not be surprised to learn it. When a person is applying for a job, his potential employer must have access to all information the applicant himself possesses about his likely performance. Obviously, perfection is rarely achieved. The critical issue will be how consequential the asymmetries in information are.

The unhindered flow of information is essential to the market system to ensure that all participants are trading the same goods. One bushel of Number 2 red wheat may be clearly identical to another. But if different graduates of the same college are very unequal in ability and if employers cannot discern those differences, they may be unwilling to hire any of those graduates. Yet they would in fact be happy to employ perhaps the top half of them if they could gather full information on them. So, too, the prospective patient must be able to judge the expected quality of the paramedic's services, the consumer the durability of an appliance, and the worker the attributes of a job. In short, the free flow of information and the ability of people to use it is essential if the trading of commodities on competitive markets is to lead to an efficient outcome.

Transactions Costs

An efficient outcome, as we saw above, requires that there be no further beneficial trades available that are not undertaken. Besides deficiencies in information, there may be other impediments to the conduct of beneficial trades. Basically, trading may be a costly process. The costs of conducting such trades are called transactions costs; if significant, they will prevent free markets from yielding efficient outcomes.

Consider an example. A small pond borders the property of both Farwell, a farmer, and Swinburne, a swimmer. Swinburne would pay $300 to keep the pond clean and Farwell would stop dumping his animal wastes in it if he were paid $250 to do so. It would cost $100 to draw up an antipollution agreement. This transaction cost prevents the two neighbors from striking the nonpollution bargain that would be beneficial to both.

Transactions costs are generated in diverse ways. They may represent the straightforward cost of merely bringing a commodity to market. They may stem from the time that must be spent bargaining or negotiating an outcome—or even in identifying those with whom trades should be made. Sometimes, as labor strikes all too convincingly attest, transactions that both parties recognize as highly beneficial are not completed because the two sides try to get shares of the mutual gains that add up to more than is available. In an all-or-nothing, no-alternative situation the workers might accept $5 per hour, and the employer might pay $6. But in actual negotiations both may for a time choose a strike in preference to accepting $5.50. The losses to both sides that result because strikes occasionally occur represent transaction costs.

All fees for drawing up contracts are transactions costs. Most of what lawyers earn falls into this category; so too does the spread between the interest rate at which the bank will lend to an individual and the rate at which it will borrow from (i.e., pay interest on deposits to) the same type of individual. The transactions costs that prevent trades from taking place may never be observed. Consider another pond—enough larger than the last one that we can legitimately call it a lake—with 100 potential swimmers and 50 dumpers of refuse. If the swimmers would pay $300 each and if the dumpers would forgo their activity for $250 each, a no-dumping agreement would yield net gains of $(100 \times \$300) - (50 \times \$250) = \$17,500$. That figure leaves room for a lot of transactions costs. Yet an uncoordinated market would hardly be likely to achieve the no-dumping outcome. There are now 100×50 potential pairs of dumping-and-swimming negotiators, a lot of bargains to coordinate even if per pair transactions costs are low.

If transactions costs are too high, it is not possible to have a market. Even Farwell and Swinburne could not make a deal. With many people, even if the free market functions, the lake may be subject to unlimited dumping. In fact, even activities that are the most damaging and the least costly to refrain from may continue. Alas, that is why we find beer cans along the road, although the tossers reap only slight personal gain from their antisocial activities. When transactions costs are high, only the most beneficial trades are undertaken.

The Nonexistence of Markets for Some Goods

If transactions costs are sufficiently high, not only will beneficial trades be forgone, the market itself may not be established. For example, future generations can hardly compensate us now for not destroying critical wetlands or not depleting the ozone layer. Yet these future citizens might be willing to give up much more than sufficient amounts of their material resources if they could only carry out such trades with us. Or suppose by some miracle it were possible for us to pay our forebears of a century and a half ago to preserve the log cabin in which Abraham Lincoln was born. Does anyone doubt that the necessary funds would promptly pour forth? There simply is not a market for these goods.

Transactions are particularly difficult and costly to conduct when major uncertainties are present. In such cases the perfect flow of information is particularly relevant. Ideally, it should be possible to make trades that are contingent on whatever outcome occurs. For example, Oliver grows tomatoes and Andrew raises oranges. Oliver gives Andrew two tomatoes. In return Andrew promises to give Oliver five oranges but only if it rains so heavily that Oliver's next tomato crop rots. The trade thus provides Oliver with insurance. Note that neither Oliver nor Andrew has any influence over whether it rains or not.

What if the contingency is less neutral? Suppose Oliver receives the five oranges from Andrew if his tomato crop is poor for any reason, rain, worms, neglect, or whatever. Indeed, it is against just such unfavorable personal contingencies that most people would like to insure themselves. Andrew encounters two classes of difficulties if he makes this insurance trade. First, Oliver may choose to insure his crop only if he knows that his operation is somewhat marginal. Second, once Oliver is insured, he may choose to weed and fertilize with less diligence since someone else will be sharing the costs of poor production. These two problems are sometimes referred to as *adverse selection* and *adverse incentives*. The first implies that those who choose to insure will be a selected and biased sample, with worse-than-average expected performance. The term adverse incentives, also known as moral hazard, suggests that efforts to avoid unfortunate outcomes will be diminished once insurance is issued. To deal with these problems, Andrew would undoubtedly wish to inspect Oliver's farm before entering into the insurance contract, to write language into the contract requiring Oliver to make a decent effort, and then to monitor Oliver's behavior to make sure he was not slacking off. Similarly, if the payoff event were Oliver's poor health instead of his poor tomato crop, Andrew would want to subject him to a medical inspection before insuring him. And even then he would not know whether chest pains or shortness of breath went unreported. Obviously, such monitoring processes are both costly and less than totally effective. That is a major reason why there are no markets in many areas where it would otherwise be attractive to make trades that are contingent on outcomes.

Of course important exceptions can be cited. Markets for life, health, fire, and casualty insurance, for example, represent trades where the future payment depends on the contingency that occurs. But many desirable types of what might be called insurance trades cannot be undertaken efficiently on private markets. In some areas the meagerness of private markets has been especially significant for public policy. One of these is insurance against income loss; government unemployment insurance and welfare programs may be thought of as efforts to remedy this market deficiency. Another is insurance against living too long after becoming disabled or retiring and thereby using up one's savings; the Social Security system serves as a response to such needs.

Some goods, such as health, cannot be traded for technological reasons. Other types of markets—for example, those for selling votes, heroin, prostitution, or slaves—are prohibited by law, though illicit transactions may still occur. Whenever a market does not exist, for whatever reason, some exchanges that both parties would view as beneficial (whether or not the society agrees) will not take place.

Market Power

Our description of the perfectly functioning price and market system suggests that producers continually search to see if they can find a way to purchase additional inputs, convert them to outputs, and sell them at a price that exceeds the purchase cost of all the inputs. If wood for a table costs $20 and the going wage for a table maker with tools is $30 per day, and if a man can produce a table a day, then any table manufacturer will hire him if the going price of a table is above $50. The output of tables will expand. As the expansion continues, the price of wood may be bid up, as may the price of labor. Simultaneously there may be a reduction in the price of tables as efforts are made to sell the expanded output. As these changes take place the cost of buying inputs and the prices of the resulting outputs are brought into equality; the table manufacturer's profit drops to $0, and the expansion in table output slows to a halt.

If there are many table manufacturers, we can expect the market to function in this manner. A key phrase in our description, however, is "the going price"; it implies that the table entrepreneur has no influence over the currently quoted price. He takes it as given, confident that with his very small share of the market he will be able to sell whatever he produces. We observed above that the mass action of many producers does in fact affect the price, but that in a competitive market each actor believes himself to be too small a frog in too large a puddle to have any influence. The key result is that this system generates an efficient outcome. All beneficial exchanges are undertaken. So long as a consumer is willing to pay more for a table than the resource costs of producing it, it will be produced.

What if there is only one table manufacturer? If no one else is currently manufacturing tables or can go into the table business, then our entrepreneur is free to set the price of a table at whatever level he wishes, and to sell as many tables as he can at that price. He is constrained only by the demand for tables at whatever price he sets, and not by any threat that competitors will undercut his price and snatch his customers away from him. Suppose the demand conditions are as set forth in Table 14-1. The

Table 14–1

Production per day	Price at which all tables produced can be sold	Cost per table	Profit per table	Total profit
1 table	$70	$50	$20	$20
2 tables	$65	$50	$15	$30
3 tables	$62	$50	$12	$36
4 tables	$58	$50	$ 8	$32
5 tables	$54	$50	$ 4	$20
6 tables	$50	$50	$ 0	$ 0

manufacturer will recognize that he personally is an important—indeed the sole—factor in the market, and hence can influence the price of tables. (If he doesn't know it to begin with, he'll soon find out as he tries to expand production without lowering the price.) He makes the largest profit when he produces only three tables. Although he would net $8 on that fourth table, which implies that further beneficial exchanges are available at that level of production, he would reap $4 less in profit on each of the first three tables. The maximum profit outcome is far from efficient. Our prescription, remember, is that the costs of inputs required for production should just equal output value; six tables would be the efficient level of production.

This suggests that the market will fail to perform satisfactorily when a commodity is produced by only one or a few manufacturers, or in other words when monopoly or oligopoly is present. If anyone can go readily into the table business and produce tables just as cheaply as the present manufacturer, his monopoly will be impossible to sustain. On the other hand, it is impossible to compete with the monopolist if he possesses a permanent advantage that permits him to produce more cheaply than others. The potential monopolist will have just such an advantage when costs per unit fall as output increases, at output levels that represent a significant share of the total amount of a commodity that can be sold. A manufacturer of shoelaces may, for example, be able to produce his laces at a decreasing cost per pair—up to 50,000 pairs a week. Beyond that, the unit costs begin to rise again; perhaps the factory is simply not big enough to handle a larger output conveniently. If the total demand for shoelaces is 5 million pairs a week, there's plenty of room for lots of manufacturers in the market.[2] Competition among them will drive the price down. But if our shoelace manufacturer has a gigantic automated factory, in which unit costs continue to fall even when production reaches the level of 4 or 5 million pairs a week, he will always be able to underprice a smaller-scale competitor.

Decreasing unit costs at output levels that are high relative to total

[2] In the chapter on models, we mentioned long division as a possible conceptual model. Perhaps in the above example 5 million pairs a week strikes you as a lot of shoelaces. Long division of the simplest type tells us that it's only a little over one pair a year for each person in the U.S.—not so farfetched after all.

demand are a characteristic of numerous important industries. Among these are telecommunications, railroads, and automobile manufacture. The cost of an additional phone call—indeed of an additional million calls—on the Bell system is small relative to what it would cost a competitor to provide them. The Conrail system can add another train per day at a cost that is minor in comparison to the cost to a railroad that had to build its own roadbed. The enormous costs for auto manufacturing plants, together with costs such as research and development or retooling that are independent of the level of output, make it impossible for small firms to compete effectively in the market for popularly priced cars.

How can we relate the market power situation to the efficiency condition MRT = MRS that we set forth above? In a competitive market, the workings of the market will bring the marginal rate of transformation of producers into equality with the marginal rate of substitution of consumers. As long as the MRT differs from the MRS, producers and consumers have every incentive to change their behavior. Contrast this situation with the market power case history. Although the table monopolist's MRT of tables for dollars is one table for $50, he sets the price at one table for $62. Hence the consumer's MRS of tables for dollars is one table for $62. And there is no reason for the MRT and the MRS to converge toward one another. Consumers must accept the $62 price on a take-it-or-leave-it basis, and the monopolist has no fear that competitors will move in with cheaper tables to deprive him of his customers. The presence of market power thus defeats the efficient functioning of the market.

Market power may develop for several reasons. Decreasing unit costs generate conditions in which a single producer, or perhaps a handful of producers, is the most efficient mode of production. A patent, to cite another example, may give a producer market power. A labor contract may give one union sole control of the labor supply for a particular industry. The government may award an airline a monopoly for a designated route. Where monopolies or oligopolies prevail, for whatever reasons, whether they involve factors of production or final goods, market processes cannot be counted on to produce an efficient outcome.

Externalities

Assume for the moment that the price system works perfectly, in that relative prices reflect marginal rates of substitution and transformation. There may still be conditions that prevent individual actions, guided by the price system, from achieving an efficient outcome. A particularly troublesome class of problems involves what are called externalities, situations in which the actions of one individual (perhaps a person, perhaps a firm or a government) affect the welfare of another. We have discussed an externality situation already in relation to the pond. When Farwell chooses dumping in the pond from among alternative refuse disposal systems, he affects Swinburne's welfare. The efficiency loss occurs because Farwell in no way takes Swinburne's welfare into account when he makes his decision to dump.

In many situations an individual's actions provide benefits and/or costs to others. When benefits are provided, we say the externality is positive, or we call it an external economy. Imposed costs are referred to as negative externalities, or alternatively as external diseconomies. If you construct a retaining wall, you may help prevent erosion on your neighbor's land. If you allow your lawn to run to crabgrass, your neighbors may soon find that their lawns have become infested as well. If you act in your individual self-interest, you will not, in making your decisions, take into account these external benefits and costs that result from your actions unless you are compensated for doing so. Unless society has worked out such a compensation plan—and we know that transactions costs are likely to prevent private markets from accomplishing this task—we will find that self-interested behavior by each individual will not lead to actions that are optimal in terms of society as a whole. We are not arguing that the optimal situation is one with no gullies and no crabgrass. That would be clearly uneconomic if the cost of getting rid of them exceeded the total benefits to be gained by their elimination. Rather we are arguing that, in the absence of compensation schemes, society will end up with too few retaining walls and too much crabgrass. Because of the divergence between private and social (i.e., total community) returns, uncoordinated individual actions lead to less than optimal results.

Externalities, and the market failures they generate, are a major reason for government intervention in private markets. The most familiar and most widely discussed externalities relate to the environment. Given present pricing arrangements, we cannot expect market processes to yield air and water that are sufficiently pure. Although the environment comes most immediately to mind, many government activities that we now take almost for granted developed originally in response to externality problems. Zoning laws exclude the gasoline station from residential neighborhoods. Traffic control devices and personnel diminish the extent to which one driver's choices inconvenience others.

On the other hand, social arrangements sometimes create externalities where they would not otherwise exist. The elderly on Medicare spend resources for all of us when they go to the hospital or a nursing home. These private decisions quite naturally take into account only the costs to the decision maker and not the full costs to society. Hence resources tend to be overutilized when the costs of providing them are shared by others. This externality is financial, in contrast with the physical externalities of the environment; both types are costly. Public decision makers should scrutinize examples such as these. Many of our mechanisms for achieving social objectives tend to encourage individual behavior that erects new roadblocks to the efficient functioning of the market. Our taxation and welfare systems create a range of financial externalities. If an individual on welfare obtains a job and thereby becomes a taxpayer, society as a whole secures a direct benefit equal to the sum of his income taxes and the welfare payments he no longer receives. Similarly, when a productively employed person chooses to get further training and increase his productivity, the members of society reap an externality equal to his increased tax payments. But he decides how much further training to get only on the basis of the benefits that he and his family will reap. Externalities of this sort, if they remain uncompensated, lead to underinvestment in human resources. In general, self-interested market behavior produces too little of activities that generate positive externalities and too much of those that generate external costs.

In his famous article "The Tragedy of the Commons,"[3] Garrett Hardin warns of the perils that threaten when people fail to take into account the costs they impose on others. The parable of the commons is a tale of villagers who own a common grazing ground and use it for pasturing their cows. The grass is ample for a few cows, but once the number of cows rises above a certain level, the effects of overgrazing are felt. The cows grow scrawnier and the total output of meat drops. Yet each villager, seeking to maximize his own welfare, is inexorably drawn to pasturing as many cows as he can afford. All grow poorer and poorer.

The commons is an all-too-familiar model. Cars crowding an expressway, industries and municipalities dumping their wastes in a river, trawlers overfishing Georges Bank—all impose costs on others and suffer costs at the hands of those who behave in a symmetrical fashion. All use up a resource that is held in common. Yet there is no incentive for anyone to change his habits, for the benefit he can capture for himself by doing so is far less than the cost. Some mechanism must be found to induce a reduction in driving or dumping or fishing.

Public Goods

If a good delivers external economies, one person will benefit when another person or institution purchases or provides the good. To be sure, the purchaser himself receives benefits that are large enough (relative to cost) to induce him to buy it. He will, however, buy less—of retaining walls, say—than is socially optimal. With some goods, called *public goods,* the individual gets so small a share of the total benefit that it is likely that no one will be inclined to purchase the goods on his own.

In terms of externalities, public goods are the limit of a continuum. Most of the goods we regularly purchase and use are primarily private. When Nick buys new socks or new dental work, no one else gets any significant benefit from his purchases. Neither retaining walls nor efforts to control crabgrass are public goods; their external effects are of a decidedly limited nature, and private gains are enough to induce significant private action. The characteristic outputs of government, on the other hand, those

---

[3] *Science* 162, no. 3859 (December 13, 1968): 1243–48.

goods and services that affect the common interests of the citizens, are public goods. The need to provide such goods is one of the main justifications for a public choice mechanism, and indeed for the very existence of governments. Among the more obvious examples of public goods are wilderness areas, the national defense, and flood-control projects. A visitor to San Francisco may enjoy Golden Gate Park even though he does not share in its upkeep. Weather Bureau forecasts are equally available to taxpayers and nontaxpayers. Any objective that is held in common and can be achieved only in common may be thought of as a public good. If the common objective is achieved, everyone in the group benefits, regardless of how much individual effort and expenditure he has put forth.

Some public goods, information for instance, are abstract in nature; the weather forecasts are a case in point. Were it not for the strictures of our patent system, most technological developments and inventions would belong to everyone. (To be sure, a few trade secrets can be kept, even without patents; the Coca-Cola formula is perhaps the most renowned.) The more important area of scientific knowledge is in many ways a public good. That argument has led to the establishment of the National Science Foundation, with its stringent requirements that findings be widely disseminated. What is knowledge for one becomes knowledge for all, and all of society benefits.

In the past, public goods were viewed by scholars as a strictly defined class of goods, identifiable by a list of attributes. It has gradually become apparent that not everyone agrees on what attributes should be on the list, and that in any case most goods widely regarded as public possess the essential features only to a degree. Nonetheless, it is instructive to list the attributes because they do pinpoint the ways in which a public good differs from what is merely a case of rampant externalities.

1. *Nonprovision (or gross underprovision).* Individuals will not provide the good if left to themselves, even though total benefits to the members of the group exceed total cost. It would not be worthwhile, for instance, for you alone (or anyone else) to install a sidewalk from your isolated neighborhood to the village center. In fact, the benefit you would derive from the sidewalk is independent of whether or how much you contribute to its provision. If you feel sure that it will be installed without your help, you will have no incentive to make even a modest contribution toward it voluntarily. Even though the total benefits that the sidewalk would bring everyone in the neighborhood would more than warrant its installation, there will be no sidewalk unless some way is found to coordinate the financial arrangements for supplying it. To be sure, some organizations that provide goods that are clearly public in nature manage to do so on a voluntary basis. Religious and charitable organizations are in effect coalitions that rely on voluntary contributions. Their good works benefit everyone who shares in their objectives, whether he actually contributes or not, and there is no limit to the number who may thus

benefit. (Contributors, of course, gain certain private satisfactions from the services they render.) Note, however, that these organizations can function successfully only if they continue to receive a certain level of support; donors must believe they play a critical part in the organization's survival. Many ventures that are necessarily cooperative cannot achieve this level of voluntary support. They will be funded only if it is assured that *all* members of the society will contribute; some element of compulsion is essential. For example, you perhaps would not have voluntarily installed a pollution-control device on your car in the 1960s, but you might have been willing to do so if all other motorists were forced to do likewise. You may not be willing to give money to buy a quarter acre of woods for a town forest, but you might vote for a tax bill that would force all of the 1000 townspeople to contribute on a nonvoluntary basis to the purchase of a 250-acre tract. To be sure, some degree of common interest must be recognized before any method of compulsion, be it taxation or regulation, is regarded as legitimate.

2. *Nonrivalry.* One man's use does not reduce another's consumption, hence it is inefficient to exclude those who do not pay. The sidewalk is a good that will be used jointly. One walker's use of it will not appreciably diminish the quantity available for others, and hence it is inefficient to exclude those who do not help to pay for it. On the other hand, clearly there are limits to nonrivalry. At some point additional walkers do begin to impose nonnegligible burdens on others, and if the traffic is really heavy these costs of congestion become large. That is why town beaches, for example, are frequently closed to nonresidents. Still, sidewalks, roads, parks, beaches, and the like are ordinarily most usefully regarded as public goods; they are best provided jointly, even though access may be restricted.

3. *Nonexcludability.* It is impossible or impractical to exclude noncontributors. We might, of course, set up barbed wire fences and pay-as-you-go turnstyles to restrict access to the sidewalk and in that way limit it to contributors. This is hardly an attractive solution; exclusion, although feasible in other cases (as toll roads prove), is totally impractical here. Nevertheless, we must recognize that nonexcludability is a rarer phenomenon than it once was. As technology grows more sophisticated, exclusion frequently becomes feasible where formerly it was not. The standard example of a public good was once the lighthouse; it was regarded as a public good because no mariner could be excluded from its benefits even though he paid nothing toward its maintenance. Today, equipment to restrict the reception of lighthouse signals to those who have paid for the privilege could be made available at moderate cost. But it would be miserably inefficient to do so because there is no rivalry among consumers; additional users impose no additional costs on either the provider or on other users. And so the lighthouse is on other grounds still legitimately viewed as a public good.

Of these three, nonrivalry in consumption is the key attribute for identifying a public good, although we should keep in mind that publicness is a matter of degree. The important lesson for policy is that by their very nature public goods will not be produced if the task is left to individuals acting in isolation, even when it is to everyone's advantage to have them produced and hence clearly best for the group as a whole. They are, in short, a classic case of market failure. We turn now to possible remedies for such failure.

Ways to Cope with Market Failure

The market has failed. What shall we do? The answer should depend on the degree and type of failure, and on the instruments available to deal with it.

Private Mechanisms for Dealing with Market Failure

In some situations, private action may be the best way to deal with market failure. A tennis court is a limited form of a decreasing-cost product, in that most of the cost of the court must be incurred whether it is used for 2 hours or 12 hours a day. People recognize this when they set up nonprofit tennis clubs as a remedy for this not-so-consequential market failure. We noted above that private charities and voluntary organizations play very substantial roles in the provision of various public goods. Audubon sanctuaries offer significant open spaces and refuges in many areas of the nation. Numerous organizations provide material support of one sort or another for less fortunate citizens; their efforts are in effect public goods for the rest of society.

All such efforts require some degree of cooperation or coordination; many of them involve organizations with long histories of successful operation. The important point to recognize is that a considerable amount of voluntary collective behavior in our society is conducted without recourse to the government, and that such voluntary behavior may frequently be the most effective means available for dealing with a situation of market failure.

The possibility for private mechanisms suggests a negative lesson as well. Government efforts, say, the provision of tennis courts or housing for a certain target group, may displace private initiatives that would have been equally effective. When the government has already stepped in, we frequently have no opportunity to observe how well private alternatives would have performed.

The Government's Role in Dealing with Market Failure

This volume, since it focuses on public decision making, addresses one central issue: How should the government formulate effective policies to promote social welfare? It is as important for us to understand when the government should and should not play a role as it is to know how that role should be played. We have argued, quite simply, that there may be a role for government action when the market fails to work well enough.

What modes of action are available to the government? First, the government may choose to do nothing. Effective government policy must strike a balance between refraining from action when it is not called for and intervening when positive benefit can be expected.

Doing Nothing

It may turn out that doing nothing is best. We noted above that government programs that displace private initiatives may accomplish very little overall. One major difficulty is that the policies we can actually implement are likely to contrast sharply with those that in some ideal world would be best. The form of intervention that we can reasonably expect to achieve may on balance make matters worse. We are all familiar with the history of Prohibition. The consumption of alcohol generated negative externalities, which led to a government ban on its sale. The net result was a significant increase in lawlessness, accompanied by a reduction in drinking that was less than anticipated. Prohibition was abolished. We now deal with the alcohol externality through more limited devices such as taxation, age restrictions, liquor licences, and traffic laws. It is frequently claimed that laws forbidding prostitution and the use of marijuana are the contemporary equivalents of Prohibition, and that in each case no action at all would be preferable to the current regulatory schemes.

Over the past 40 years, a variety of modes of regulatory activity have been developed to deal with situations in which markets are alleged to be noncompetitive. Federal control over freight, energy, and airline prices, and government-imposed strictures on safety in the workplace or pollutants out the tailpipe are signal examples. Many of these regulatory efforts have recently come under increasing criticism. It is alleged that they have not accomplished their purposes and in many cases have, on balance, done more harm than good. Thus efforts to promote safety in the workplace, it is charged, have done little to reduce accidents despite their high cost.

Deregulation is currently a lively topic of debate. The targets of censure range from building standards, which ensure, say, that a cast-iron pipe of a certain dimension is used as an exhaust from a bath tub, to the Civil Aeronautics Board, which sets rates and routes for airlines. The more caustic critics suggest that no regulatory intervention at all would be superior to the type of intervention we have at present, or to any other form we are likely to achieve. Many of these critics reinforce their arguments by emphasizing the loss of freedom and private decision making authority when the government steps into the act. This is not the place to dwell on the inadequacies of government in general or its regulatory efforts in particular. It does seem appropriate to warn the reader, however, that the history of interventions to deal with market failure is a history of disappointments. In a variety of areas, programs have accomplished much less than we had hoped, at a cost far greater than we expected. This lesson should be borne in mind as we consider methods for dealing with new problems and new methods for dealing with old ones. In virtually every situation where government intervention has proved counterproductive, it can now be pointed out that the initial effort was misdirected, or that political factors prevented its effective function. Unfortunately, ignorance, biases, and political stresses will always beset the policy formulation process. We should learn to be modest about our abilities to create and operate government programs that will achieve their intended purposes. Moreover, we should recognize that market failure does not mandate government intervention; it just suggests the possibility that such intervention might prove beneficial.

Positive Modes of Government Action

This volume has been directed to the study of situations in which some form of government action is expected to prove beneficial. If action is called for, any of a variety of approaches might be taken. These approaches might be classified along a number of dimensions. We divide them according to the means by which they attempt to improve present performance. The government can (1) attempt to improve the working of the market; (2) require individuals and firms to behave in specified ways; (3) provide incentives that influence the decisions of private individuals and firms; and (4) engage directly in the provision of goods and services.

Government Measures that Attempt to Improve the Working of the Market

Much of our traditional government activity consists of efforts to help the market function more effectively. In many areas, the government provides information to market participants. It grades meat, gathers information on levels of economic activity, accredits institutions, licenses members of various professions, issues information about health and safety standards, and has recently worked out a system to make product warranties more intelligible. All such activities can be viewed as attempts to foster flows of information and thereby improve the functioning of the market. The rationale is that consumers and producers will then have a better understanding of the commodities they are considering for purchase. Our legal system, particularly the specific aspects that revolve around the law of property and contracts, also helps the market function more effectively by making it possible for individuals to engage in exchanges more complex than simple barter.

Antitrust actions represent more aggressive government intervention to promote effective market behavior. The government may seek to prevent buying and selling units from achieving excessive market power. If a single producer or seller becomes the predominant seller in a market, the government may take action to promote competition. Such efforts might be undertaken in the market for gasoline in Concord, New Hampshire, for small generators in the entire United States, or for plasterers in Albuquerque. In the first case, a major oil company might hold the power, in the second a manufacturer, in the third a trade union.

The appropriate weapon for promoting competition varies. In the gasoline situation, the government may outlaw "ruinous competition," efforts by one company to sell gas below cost long enough to drive its smaller competitors out of business and thereby achieve and maintain a monopoly. The government can also scrutinize possible collusive activities among large producers who might have decided to carve up the country, assigning each company a predominant role in some region. To make the small generator market more competitive, the government may require the preeminent manufacturer to license patents on critical components at fair royalty rates so that competitors cannot be locked out of the whole market just because they did not invent a key part. To deal with the plasterers, the government may establish regulations that allow present nonunion members to do a certain amount of work. Such action could take the form of requiring that members of minority groups be allowed to secure apprentice and journeymen positions in the union, or of outlawing labor practices that make it difficult or impossible for nonunion plasterers to compete for work.

Government Measures that Require Individuals and Firms to Behave in Specified Ways

Market-enhancing behavior is not the appropriate tool for all problems. If, for example, a utility has secured market power because of the declining marginal cost nature of the production process, it would hardly be appropriate to undertake action to get two or three substantially less efficient smaller utilities. Thirty years ago there were still areas of the country—Philadelphia was one—where there were two competing telephone systems. However competitive the rates, lots of people could not call each other. When the nature of the production process makes it natural and appropriate to have a single producer, or perhaps two, the government's usual course is to regulate price. The government, in essence, requires the single producer to relinquish its market power and sets a price that strikes a fair balance between the twin objectives of assuring a fair rate of return to the investors and protecting the public from economic exploitation. History has shown that price regulation of this sort is an exceptionally tricky business. Whatever the basis employed to set prices, it is likely to encourage the producer to pursue other than the most efficient means for producing his product. Usually the regulated prices are based on costs. However costs may be defined, inevitably certain classes of costs will not be counted as fully for rate-setting purposes as others. The producer will bias his choices as to inputs or methods of raising capital accordingly. Problems of this sort would arise even if the pricing formulas were set on a highly analytic basis, but they are unlikely to be. In addition, regulatory efforts to set prices are subject to an array of political pressures. The result is much wasteful and expensive activity. Moreover, the prices that are finally set exhibit a certain randomness, depending on the strength of the contending forces in any particular hearing or rate-setting process.

Sometimes the government regulates the quality of a product rather than its price. It can ban from the market products that it considers to be unsafe; food additives are a prime example. It can require compliance with certain quality standards. For example, new cars may be required to meet some minimum mileage capability; individuals who have not been admitted to the bar are prohibited from practicing law even if they make their experience (or lack of it) quite clear. And certain products, such as marijuana and sex, may be barred from sale altogether.

The government also may regulate the way in which goods are produced in order to eliminate unfortunate consequences of the production process. To protect the environment, the government may require that certain types of scrubbers be placed on factory chimneys, or that utilities burn certain classes of fuel. With an eye to the health and safety of workers, the government is now prescribing certain safety features for the capital equipment used in American workplaces. Thus the government may specify that guard rails must be at a certain height, or that forklift trucks must have rollover protection; similarly, workers must not come face to face with open vats of certain chemicals. These stipulations reflect more than mere paternalism, for society as a whole will share in any costs of medical care or disability resulting from inadequate safety. It is a situation that we identified earlier as a financial externality.

In sum, the government has an array of means through which it can dictate what products should be produced in what ways and sold at what prices. It can tell individuals what they can and can't consume. As experience with the 1977 natural gas shortage suggests, it may even try to tell people how warm to keep their homes.

Government Incentives That Influence Decisions of Private Individuals and Firms

Two major classes of adverse consequences result when the government attempts to mandate private behavior: (1) individual freedom of action is restricted, carrying with it an implied threat, although possibly remote, to other liberties; and (2) the government may require behavior that is inefficient or inappropriate. These adverse consequences suggest a tension between government efforts to compensate for the inadequate workings of the market and the desire to allocate society's resources in an efficient manner without infringing on basic liberties. This tension can be reduced or avoided in many important situations if the government employs incentives that attempt to influence individual actions rather than directives that specify them.

The principle behind government incentive mechanisms is readily understood. Certain classes of private actions convey social benefits or impose social costs. Individuals and firms, in their processes of self-interested maximization, do not take account of these social returns. In short, there are externalities. An incentive to correct such a situation takes the form of a payment to an individual if he creates a positive externality or a charge imposed on him if he generates a detrimental externality.

When a person pursues further education, as we observed above, he increases his earning capability and hence his contribution to future tax revenues. His decision to seek education thus yields a positive externality. Yet we would expect that his decision will be based only on the benefits he foresees for himself—and probably on after-tax benefits at that. The excess of social over private gains offers one justification for government scholarship programs and other incentives to undertake further education. Note that an education subsidy does not require an individual to attend school—those who believe they would get little out of it may choose not to—but it makes the option of pursuing further education more attractive.

Conversely, when a plant emits particulates from its smokestack it imposes costs on the citizens of the surrounding community. Yet the plant manager who is seeking to maximize profits will tend to ignore these costs. This is both unfortunate and inefficient. To save the plant $1000 in waste disposal costs, he may send materials up the chimney that result in costs to the community of over $5000. A government-directed incentive scheme might handle this problem by charging the firm for each unit of particulate coming out of its stack. Such charges are usually referred to as effluent charges. If one unit imposes an external cost of $1, the appropriate charge per unit is also $1. (This $1 total cost is computed by assessing the cost imposed on each individual and summing those amounts.) The incentive approach in effect treats an externality as equivalent to another factor of production that must be purchased on the market. A producer can traditionally choose the mix of labor and capital he wishes to employ. Similarly, if the externality is priced, he will have flexibility in determining the least-cost method to reduce it, and indeed the least total cost of producing his ultimate product. The price that the government sets for a unit of the externality, like the price of machines and labor, should be equal to its marginal cost. In this case the marginal cost is the cost that that unit imposes on the rest of society.

The debate between the mandated behavior approach set forth in the previous section and the incentives approach has been a lively one. The vast majority of economists argue strongly for incentives, although some have questioned their practicality. Most economists believe that mandated standards for environmental protection lead to unsatisfactory outcomes.

A regulatory agency cannot know the costs, the technological opportunities, the alternative raw materials, and the kinds of products available for every firm in every industry. Even if it could determine the appropriate reduction standards for each firm, it would have to revise them frequently to accommodate changing costs and markets, new technologies, and economic growth.[4]

In contrast, taxes to provide appropriate incentives are more likely to elicit the desired responses, even when the regulatory agency is far from omniscient. The major arguments against effluent charges relate to their practicality. There is only limited experience to draw on, some of it from related areas such as sewage reduction efforts. The Delaware Estuary Study[5] found that effluent charges would achieve a given water quality for about half the cost of uniform reductions in the emission of pollutants. The potential for the incentive approach in the environmental area, at least, seems enormous. As we remarked earlier, however, the history of regulatory approaches has been a history of disappointments. The only true test of effluent charges will come with their wide application in carefully observed contexts.

The merits of incentives as opposed to mandated behavior carry over to many other areas of policy. For example, present government efforts to promote occupational safety rely almost entirely on a system in which standards are established for physical equipment, heights of railings, guards on machines, and the like. Government inspectors then come around to levy fines if the standards are not met, and to work out procedures for bringing the relevant equipment up to snuff. This system has many disadvantages. Most firms go uninspected; the standards take no account of differences among firms in compliance costs; the emphasis on capital equipment, which is involved in only a small fraction of accidents, means that other factors important to safety are overlooked; potentially important alternative approaches to safety are slighted. In short, this is a rather clumsy form of government intrusion into the workplace. An incentives approach has been proposed as an alternative means to promote occupational safety. Basically, a tax would be imposed when a worker is injured, with the magnitude of the tax depending on the severity of the accident. The major advantages of such a system are the incentives it provides for an employer to pursue all means of promoting worker safety, such as training programs, safety officers, changes in work practices, and so on. We should caution, however, that occupational safety is another area in which only real-world experience can establish whether an approach is truly promising or merely attractive in concept. Conceivably, evidence from the workmen's compensation system, in which an employer's insurance premium is related to his accident experience, could provide suggestive insights.

The incentives approach may also be applicable when consumers'

---

[4] Allen V. Kneese and Charles L. Schultze, *Pollution, Prices, and Public Policy* (Washington, D.C.: The Brookings Institution, 1975), p. 88.
[5] Ackerman et al., *The Uncertain Search for Environmental Quality* (New York: The Free Press, 1974).

behavior generates externalities. Given the current elaborate arrangements, both public and private, whereby most of the costs of one's medical care are shared by other members of society, a person's decision to engage in a health-threatening activity generates negative externalities. Consider Smith, who can smoke or not. If he smokes, there is a .2 chance that he will develop an unfavorable condition. If he does not smoke, that probability falls to .1. It costs society $1000 if he contracts the unfavorable condition. It would then be appropriate for society to charge Smith $[(.2 - .1)($1000)] = 100 for smoking. If Smith's medical costs are to be paid by private insurance, this charge might take the form of a higher insurance premium. If there is national health insurance, we might institute a tax rebate plan to "pay" individuals for not smoking. More simply, we could merely tax cigarettes, as we already do, although calculation of the appropriate externalities might show that the charges should be much higher (or lower) than they are at present.

In sum, incentive approaches merit serious consideration as a means to deal with externalities by influencing the decisions of individuals and firms in favorable directions.

Government Provision of Goods and Services

The mechanisms we have discussed thus far for government action to promote public welfare have all involved efforts to improve the workings of the market. In two classes of issues direct government participation in the market is likely to be the preferred course of action. They involve public goods and income distribution.

Public goods. What is the rationale for collective provision of a good? A salient characteristic of a public good is that its provision is a common objective. That objective can be a park for Greeley, Colorado, the national defense of the United States, or income supplements for the poor. To the extent that the common objective is achieved, everyone who shares the objective benefits—regardless of his efforts to achieve it. Consequently, a person who believes a project will be carried out whether or not he contributes to it may have little incentive to contribute voluntarily. The traditional language that describes this situation refers to the noncontributor as a free rider, or freeloader, recognizing that he tries to get the benefits of a project without paying for them. Although countless organizations—religious, charitable, educational—have long histories of successful reliance on voluntary gifts, most of us would probably agree that the essential business of government cannot and should not depend on voluntary contributions for support. Everyone shares in the benefits of national defense regardless of the sum he pays toward it, but if it were a voluntary charity very few taxpayers would give as much as they now do. Many would choose the role of the free rider—confident that they could not conveniently be excluded from the protection of the armed forces.

On what basis are we to decide whether a certain project should be undertaken collectively? Let's think further about Greeley's proposed park, which would cost $95,000. Suppose that each of Greeley's 20,000 citizens would be willing to contribute as much as $5 for a park. Why doesn't everyone simply give the money? Because the $5 contribution yields no return unless the donor is sure that 18,999 others will also give. Moreover, if the others contribute the required amount, he can enjoy the park even if he gives nothing. Given this situation, few can be counted on to contribute. Yet clearly the park should be constructed; its total value is greater than its cost. The necessary funds can be raised only if all agree to a compact whereby they tax themselves $4.75 each.

Once it is clear that the park should be built, and built collectively, how far should the city go with developing its facilities? We saw in Chapter 9 that the city should continue to spend money on it as long as the additional benefit exceeds the additional cost. And the additional benefit is the sum of the individual marginal benefits of each citizen. In formal terms, development should continue just to the point where

$$MB_1 + MB_2 + \ldots + MB_{20,000} = MC$$

Only at that point is the efficiency condition satisfied.

We saw earlier that the characteristic outputs of governments, those goods and services that affect the common interests of the citizenry, are public goods. They include a vast array of activities, ranging from national defense to bridges and lighthouses, from the maintenance of law and order to the redistribution of income. To achieve efficient levels of output for public goods, collective action is required. In most circumstances, a government is the logical collective unit to ensure that public goods are provided. In a society that stresses the merits of the competitive system of free enterprise, as ours supposedly does, public goods are the justification for a significant range of government activities, for most if not all of the activities through which the government provides goods and services directly.

Income distribution. We mentioned above that the distribution of income produced by the market may be considered unsatisfactory. That is, although it may be reassuring to know that perfectly competitive markets will get us to a point on the utility possibility frontier, we may still prefer other points to the one reached by the free market. Distribution is a foremost policy concern. Through its power to tax, the government directly influences the distribution of income and wealth. Through programs that provide resources to particular groups of citizens, the government affects the distribution of goods and services and hence of effective income. (We observed in Chapter 13, however, that there is no logically deducible procedure for picking one distribution of income over another.) Discussion of the means to accomplish effective and meaningful distribution, moreover, introduces such a tangle of issues that we believe this volume is not the place the delve into specifics. Our decision on this matter is reinforced by the observation that discussion of income distribution policy can easily generate more passion than insight.

Nevertheless, many of the tools laid out in the preceding chapters are well suited to address such questions as: How can we assess the distributional consequences of program X? What mix of programs will provide the equivalent of Y dollars of benefits to group A at least cost to group B? If we take as a constraint the stipulation that no group in society should be hurt by a change in policy, which among a set of alternative policies would yield the highest net benefits? We believe that if more income distribution issues were posed in objective, dispassionate form—and questions such as these are representative—the ultimate consequence would be far greater benefits for the disadvantaged members of society.

Income redistribution as a public good. We have seen that any common objective of a group of individuals can be thought of as a public good. Among such objectives were a park for Greeley, the national defense of the United States, and income supplements for the poor. The ''publics'' in the three cases are the residents of Greeley, the citizens of the United States, and the middle-income residents who provide the income supplement.

Let us formalize the income distribution problem. All middle-income citizens—10,000 of them—live on the East Side of town. On the West Side live 5000 poor people. All East Siders would like to see their poorer townmates made better off, and would pay something to see that objective achieved.[6] Indeed, with the present income distribution, each would give up $1 of his own money to secure benefits of $1000 for the West Side residents. So why doesn't each give the money directly? Quite simply, a single transfer of $1 would yield only $1 in benefits for the West Siders, in other words only 1/1000 of the $1000 that is viewed as necessary to make the transfer worthwhile. Each individual East Sider would contribute nothing voluntarily.

The income distribution in this example is a public good. (More accurately, the redistribution of resources to the West Side is a public good.) Every dollar contributed to the West Side yields one-tenth of a cent (i.e., 1/1000 of $1) in benefits no matter who is the contributor. Thus when Smith contributes $1, he gets the equivalent of one-tenth of a cent in benefits, as do his neighbors Jones and Harris and each of the other 9997 East Siders. Net East Side benefits from the $1 transfer are thus ($.001 × 10,000) − $1 = $9. It would be folly to pass up such an attractive scheme. The way out of the problem is to have the citizens of the East Side contribute collectively. If all agree to tax themselves $200 apiece, they can provide a total of $400 to each West Sider. The net benefit to each resident of the East Side is (.001 × $200 × 10,000) − $200 = $1800.

---

[6] To be sure, they would like it even better if they could be free riders. A particular East Sider's first choice would be to have the rest of his fellow residents contribute to the West Side while he gives nothing. The free rider problem always arises with income distribution problems, as it does with all public goods.

If the benefit relationship remained constant for each dollar transferred, the East Siders would continue to transfer resources until they themselves became the poor. Once the East Siders have made a substantial contribution and are somewhat poorer, however, their egalitarian yearnings may subside. More significantly, the West Siders are now substantially better off. Indeed, suppose that at a contribution level of $200 per East Sider, the East Side benefits per dollar transferred has fallen to one one-hundredth of a cent ($.0001). Even a collective scheme whereby each East Sider contributed an additional dollar, say through tax revenues, would yield $0 in net benefits to the East Siders. Any increase in transfer efforts beyond that point would yield less benefit to the East Siders than the additional costs. As always, the formal condition is

$$MB_1 + MB_2 + \ldots + MB_{10,000} = MC$$

This is just the case when each East Sider is making a contribution of $200. An individual's MB in this example is the benefit he receives from a transfer of one more dollar; the marginal cost is, of course, simply $1. The efficiency condition is thus satisfied.

An Overview of the Government's Role in Achieving Desirable Outcomes

In Chapter 13 we tried to identify goals that society in general and the government in particular should pursue. In this chapter we have outlined the means by which society can proceed. Private decisions by individuals and firms are the allocation mechanisms that are complementary to government actions. These decisions, coordinated through a fully functioning competitive market, will guarantee an efficient outcome. Each individual in society will be at the maximum welfare level that is consistent with the levels achieved by others.

For two broad reasons, government action may be a desirable supplement to market behavior. First, efficiency, the main accomplishment of competitive markets, is only one contributor to social welfare. A concern for equity, for the distribution of goods and services in society, may justify government action to redirect resources from the natural competitive outcome. Second, the market may fail to operate satisfactorily; many goods and services are not provided on competitive markets. Hence an efficient outcome cannot be reached. The government may then find it desirable to intercede to promote efficiency.

Modes of market failure fall under six headings: imperfect information, transactions costs, the nonexistence of markets, market power, externalities, and public goods. How might the government choose to deal with them? One possibility is to do nothing, recognizing that any action may create more problems than it would overcome, and that perhaps private organizations will deal with the issue. In a more interventionist vein, four classes of activities are available to the government. It can take measures that attempt to improve the workings of the market. Government intervention can be subtle, as when the flow of information is improved and private market decisions are thereby facilitated. It can be blunt and overt; citizens may be taxed so that the government can pay for the direct provision of public goods such as police services or money for the poor. In many circumstances the government will not wish to be a direct market participant, but will wish to influence individual actions. Here too a continuum of possibilities is available. The government can order certain behavior, as when it tells a firm how much smoke it can send up its stack or prevents consumers from purchasing unproven or unsafe products by keeping them off the market. Alternatively, the government can influence individual decisions by altering incentives, as when it sets an effluent charge on stack emissions or establishes a system of liability for unsafe products.

Making the appropriate choice among these various modes of intervention requires great skill and careful consideration. The government is often accused of bureaucratic bungling and ineptitude when it attempts to compensate for market failure. Frequently the real difficulty is that an inappropriate mode of intervention has been chosen to deal with the problem at hand. Better management of the particular scheme of intervention would accomplish little; the critical need is a change in the type of intervention. Throughout most of this book we have assumed that the mode of government intervention has already been determined and is not a matter for choice. The reasons were pedagogic: we wanted to develop the essential tools of analysis without continually reopening the discussion of underlying issues. Nonetheless, astute policy makers will not lose sight of the primary questions:

1. Why is the private market not performing satisfactorily in this policy area?
2. What type of government intervention is appropriate?

Public choices will be improved if these underlying questions are kept firmly in mind. The tools of policy analysis presented in earlier chapters should prove helpful in predicting and evaluating the consequences of alternative modes of intervention, and ultimately in choosing among them.

15 Putting Analysis to Work

. . . the will is infinite and the execution confined . . .
the desire is boundless and the act a slave to limit.
                              Troilus and Cressida
                              Act III, Scene ii

The public decision maker has a difficult task. He confronts all the problems of an individual choosing for himself and, because he is acting on behalf of others, many additional problems as well. The environment in which he makes his choices is restricted in a multitude of ways. Resources—whether tax dollars, available space, or talented personnel—are scarce, and their effective allocation may be constrained by political considerations or the limited capabilities of sluggish bureaucracies. Nevertheless, the essence of the public decision problem is that described in the model of choice which was introduced in Chapter 3. There we showed, with the aid of a simple diagram, how effective choices can be made when two essential ingredients can be identified: (1) the alternatives that are available, including a description of the attributes, and (2) the decision maker's preferences among alternative combinations of those attributes. This volume was designed to help analysts arrive at those two critical pieces of information, and to illustrate how they can be combined in practice to make well-informed public choices.

Chapter 1 of this *Primer* set the stage for an analytic approach to public decision making, and outlined a five-step sequence for thinking about policy problems: establishing the context, laying out the alternatives, predicting the consequences, valuing the outcomes, and making a choice. Now let's go back and see how the materials in this volume flesh out that framework.

Establishing the Context

What is the underlying problem that must be dealt with? When contemplating action in any policy area, the first step is to determine whether and why there is a problem at all. In a market-oriented society, the question becomes: Is the market performing satisfactorily in this area, and if not, why not? When you began this book, you perhaps thought of policy problems in rather concrete terms such as cleaning up rivers, protecting consumers from dangerous products or shoddy warranties, or holding down electricity rates. We hope that by now you will see these problems on a more conceptual level, and will perceive them in terms of externalities, or the imperfect flow of information, or market power. It may be helpful to review the range of possible explanations for unsatisfactory market performance outlined in Chapter 14:

1. Information is not shared costlessly among all prospective participants in the market.
2. Transactions costs significantly impede the conduct of beneficial trades.
3. The relevant markets do not exist.
4. Some of the participants in the market exercise market power.
5. Externalities are present, so that the actions of one individual (whether a person or an organization) affect the welfare of another.
6. The commodity involved in the policy choice is a public good.

Under any of these conditions, or if a compelling distributional objective will be served, government intervention may be appropriate. A policy analysis is then merited.

Defining the context of a problem, then, involves moving from the mundane details to a more abstract, conceptual plane. We must diagnose the form of market failure that is encountered. For example, a state environmental commission analyst who is investigating alternative pollution control measures for the Hudson River will undoubtedly find that the essential market failure occurs in the form of externalities. Factories dump industrial wastes, and cities and towns dump untreated sewage into the river, thereby imposing costs on all who would like to enjoy it.

Having identified the nature of the problem, what objectives are we to pursue in confronting it? Too often we lose sight of objectives when we get into the nitty-gritty of a problem. Requiring ourselves to identify the relevant failure of the market is one way to make sure we keep the big picture in mind. Paying careful attention to objectives is another. Consider, for example, the rather commonplace notion that we should "improve" the geographic distribution of physicians. Yet spreading out the doctors is merely a means to an end. The objective, frequently overlooked, is to improve people's health. It is all too easy to imagine a decision maker so concerned with geographic distribution that he blindly pursues some measure of dispersion, while the health of the population becomes a side issue.

Explicit attention to objectives moves us away from platitudes. In the Hudson River problem, we already know the river is dirty because of the externalities; factories and towns have few incentives to restrict their dumping. The next step is to determine what we are trying to accomplish. It may be tempting to say, "We're trying to clean up the river"; certainly it makes for a favorable press. But such a general statement, however well-intentioned, offers little specific guidance; we need to know much more precisely just what we are trying to accomplish. How clean is clean enough? Are we simply trying to create a more attractive environment, or might fishing or swimming be the objective? How much attention should be paid to efforts to keep or attract industry? How critical are the costs imposed on cities and towns? Perhaps these questions cannot be fully answered at this stage of the analysis; much will depend on the tradeoffs that are available and acceptable to society. But the questions must be asked, and subsequent analysis must help to answer them, or we may find years later that we have solved the wrong problem.

Laying Out the Alternatives

With the context of the problem clearly in mind, we can proceed to the second step: *What are the alternative courses of action?* The alternatives for policy choice are often much broader than they first seem. In Chapter 14 we saw that government intervention can take many forms; in any particular situation it is important to determine which type is most appropriate.

Let's stick with the Hudson River a little longer. Practically speaking, the types of pollution control measures that are to be evaluated will probably be narrowly delineated before any analyst arrives on the scene, and he will have to work within those alternatives. Perhaps he is simply to choose one of three possible sites for an aeration plant; perhaps his task is to recommend emissions standards for stationary pollution sources. Still, it would be worth his while to spend an hour or two thinking about all the kinds of interventions that might be undertaken, for his understanding of and approach to the entire problem will be improved if he first thinks about it in a broader context.

Doing nothing at all about the Hudson is one possibility, but the very creation of a commission suggests that positive intervention is desired. Many types of alternatives remain, however, that may perhaps be overlooked if they are not sought out for consideration. In most practical decision contexts, dramatic new approaches may not be feasible for political or historical reasons; still, consider the following possibilities:

1. The government may attempt to improve the working of the market. For the Hudson River, to be sure, this is a tall order. No market for clean water presently exists; "improving the market" would mean establishing one from scratch. Clearly impossible, you say; the river is too big, the sources of pollution too diverse, the population affected has too many different interests. We agree—but we remind you that for a less extensive problem, granting or selling property rights (i.e., arranging matters so that someone owns the water) so that a market can develop may

indeed be a viable alternative.[1] In other situations, where a market already exists, improving the market (by providing information, for instance) may be a relatively easy and surprisingly effective mode of intervention.

2. The government may require people to behave in specified ways. One obvious, if crude, approach is an outright order: STOP DUMPING! Or restrictions may be imposed on the amount of dumping or level of pollution permitted. Directives of this type require that standards be set, performances monitored, penalties established, and regulations enforced. None of these tasks is easy or inexpensive, especially if the number of polluters is large. But to many the approach is esthetically pleasing: it attacks the "right" targets—the polluters are the bad guys and in no uncertain terms. It is quite likely that the Albany analyst would be instructed to concentrate his efforts on interventions of this type. He would then be asked to describe possibilities for action in terms of such specifics as stringency of standards, kinds of pollution, penalties for violations, and monitoring and enforcement procedures.

3. The government can provide incentives that influence the decisions of individuals and organizations. Much of the more technical literature on methods of pollution control deals with various incentive schemes of two general types. In one approach, effluent charges are imposed on polluters; the heavier their discharges, the more they are required to pay and the greater the inducement to install pollution control devices. The second approach is to allow polluters to purchase rights to discharge a certain quantity of pollutants, while all other discharges are prohibited.[2]

In many, many fields incentives schemes are the preeminent means for influencing private decisions. Soil bank payments, investment credits, taxes on alcohol and tobacco, and the proposed escalating taxes on gasoline are all aimed at pushing private choices in a desired direction.

4. The government can engage directly in the provision of goods and services. In this case, the State of New York could go to work and clean up the river itself, removing the noxious substances that others dump. Given the present technology, the prospects for such an approach are not promising. But direct action might be a plausible course of action in another situation, such as cleaning up roadside litter.

Laying out alternatives frequently offers a chance for creative thought as well as hard work. Too often the process is treated as a mechanical exercise; opportunities are lost, and attractive policies are overlooked

---

[1] As a simple example, abutters on a small stream might be granted rights to clean water. They would then have the right to sue an upstream polluter. This arrangement creates the potential for beneficial trades, as abutters could demand compensation for permitting polluters to dump.

[2] The merits and drawbacks of effluent charges and pollution rights are well beyond the scope of this book. In theory, both are far more efficient than the direct approach of setting standards because, if properly administered, they insure that the desired reductions in pollution are undertaken by those who can do them at least cost. Their opponents claim that proper administration is a pipe dream, and that allowing polluters to continue their nefarious practices—for a price—is morally reprehensible.

altogether. On the simplest level, it is important to allow enough time for this review. When starting to consider a policy problem on which you will spend two or three weeks, it is almost certainly worthwhile to take a day or two to explore the available alternatives. The analyst who makes the more traditional allocation of half an hour may miss a great deal; the best option will not always be immediately apparent.

New alternatives may be developed during the analysis; these need not represent major changes in approach. In Chapter 3 we examined a town's choice between tennis courts and softball diamonds. Perhaps a third alternative is possible: tennis courts convertible to hockey rinks or basketball courts in the winter. Sometimes a new alternative involves no more than a change in timing. For example, the town may accept the additional costs of fast-track construction in order to have the courts available for early rather than late summer. Or the new alternative may involve a change in scale; perhaps a 3000-gallon-per-hour aeration plant should be substituted for the planned 5000-gallon plant that gets the water only slightly cleaner.

We make no claims as to which of the alternatives for pollution control—or even which type of intervention—is to be preferred. Indeed, the alternatives have been painted with a very broad brush; a genuine analysis would have to spell them out in much greater detail. Frequently, refinement of alternatives will continue throughout the analysis, as difficulties are identified and more information becomes available.

Can the alternative courses of action be designed so as to take advantage of additional information as it becomes available? A flexible decision process will enable the decision maker to change his course of action as he learns more about the real world in which he must operate.[3] For example, a municipal sewage system often incorporates the town's storm sewers. When rains are heavy, so much additional water floods through the system that the sewage treatment plant can't handle it; raw sewage must then be discharged into the river. Many towns are now trying to correct this condition (with financial assistance from the federal government) by installing separate systems for storm drainage. Alternative plans for pollution control should be designed for easy revision if the separate storm sewers turn out to reduce significantly the pollution caused by a municipal sewage system. Similarly, future technological advances may make it possible to treat discharges of a toxic substance so as to render them harmless at a reasonable cost. Pollution control strategies should not lock decision makers into assumptions based on the existing technology.

Good policy analysis is an iterative process; rarely does it proceed in a straightforward fashion from the definition of the problem to the selection of the preferred action. Rather, it works backward and forward as one's understanding of the problem deepens.

---

[3] Flexibility of this sort is explicitly incorporated in the decision tree, which highlights the feedback aspects of decision processes. Much of Chapter 12 was devoted to the use of information to make decisions in a sequential manner.

Predicting the Consequences

Once the problem is well-defined and the alternative courses of action delineated, the policy analyst must try to predict what will happen. *What are the consequences of each of the alternative actions?* Occasionally, mere reflection will be sufficient to trace the course from actions to outcomes. But in many circumstances unaided intuition may well go astray—or simply run into a blank wall. *What techniques are then relevant for predicting consequences?* The analyst will turn to a model, an abstraction of the real world designed to capture the essential elements of the problem.

In some situations, the model will serve as little more than an intellectual guide. Suppose the director of an outpatient clinic finds that unacceptably long lines of people are regularly waiting for service. She knows that she must work to reduce arrivals, speed up service times, increase the number of servers, or reorganize the way lines are formed and priorities assigned. Just understanding how these elements are likely to interact in a queuing model may be enough to put her on the right track.

The models needed for the pollution control problem—and certainly there will be several—are far more complex. First of all, the analyst must develop a model of how water quality in the Hudson River responds to various types and amounts of discharges and weather conditions. (Realistically, he would probably commission someone with more specialized knowledge to develop it.) Only then can he predict the likely outcomes, in terms of water quality, of alternative methods and degrees of control. A computer simulation is likely to be the most useful type of model in such a situation.

But the impact of various control measures on water quality is only one part of the outcome. The analyst must also try to predict their impact on the individuals and firms affected by them. The economic effects may be substantial, particularly if firms are placed at a serious disadvantage vis-à-vis their out-of-state competitors. Cities and towns may be hard pressed to come up with the necessary funds for sewer improvements. In short, all the effects of proposed policies must be considered, not just the effects desired by the decision maker.

If outcomes are uncertain, what is the estimated likelihood of each? If the consequences of a policy choice are uncertain, and especially if the possible results differ widely from one another, the policy maker may wish to construct a decision tree and estimate the probability of each outcome. Uncertainties are always with us; in the Hudson pollution case, for instance, it will not be possible to predict with complete accuracy either the weather or future developments in pollution control technology, or the vagaries of the political process.

If the pollution control strategy ultimately chosen must be referred to the legislature or another political body, thorough political analysis is in order. A naive study that overlooks political realities might conclude that the best way to reduce discharges into the Hudson is to institute some sort of incentive scheme, even though the legislature has in the past shown a notable lack of enthusiasm for such schemes. The most magnificently conceived plan is useless if the first legislative committee it encounters will vote it down or mangle it beyond recognition. If implementing the pollution controls requires reliance on the state bureaucracy—present or future—this too must be included in the analysis. Too many plausible policy choices have been effectively sabotaged by bureaucrats who feel threatened by changes in policy or increased workloads.

In short, when you build your models, be sure you understand what goes on out there, how the world *really* works. And understanding the real world is not simply a matter of gauging relationships; it's also a matter of getting the facts right. The effective analyst should check out the conventional wisdom and talk to the experts in the field. At the same time, he should look for independent corroboration before relying on those whose past experiences may commit them to particular policies. He should ask questions—tactfully. "How often do the storm sewers overflow?" "How long do the effects last?" "How long would it take to inspect Plant X?" "How often must a plant be inspected to ensure compliance?" Painful though it may be, he should master the empirical details, even though they may seem almost irrelevant to the decision. Not knowing what sulfates are when discussing air pollution, or what common mode failures are when considering nuclear power, or how reimbursement systems work when arguing about new equipment for a hospital, may fatally damage his credibility as an analyst. Above all, it is important to understand the assumptions that are implicit in the models and the definitions that lie behind the data.

Valuing the Outcomes

An individual making a personal decision can define his preferences through introspection. The policy analyst's task is more complicated. Because one of his primary responsibilities is to help the decision maker define his preference function, a substantial part of this book has been devoted to methods for carrying out that task. Chapter 8 considered the preference function itself, while Chapter 9 discussed its application to project evaluation and Chapter 10 took up the question of decisions that have effects over long time periods.

These techniques are not natural laws, nor were they divinely revealed. Rather, they have been derived from a number of basic philosophical principles relating to the fundamental question: What are the ends of public choice? Or, to put the same question in a decision context, what is the standard against which policy choices should be evaluated? The ultimate answer to this question has eluded us, as it has thousands of philosophers, political theorists, economists, and public decision makers. Indeed, however the question is framed, there can be no definitive answer.

We have, however, set forth some working principles in Chapter 13 from which helpful deductions can be drawn.

Valuation is often exceedingly difficult. Sometimes analysts try to avoid it altogether, although it should be clear that rational policy choice is not possible unless the relative merits of alternative options are compared. Because valuation requires considerable sophistication, we have repeatedly returned to the subject in this volume, hoping each time to add a new level of understanding.

How should we measure success in pursuing each objctive? Consider an everyday example of a valuation problem. Massport, the agency that runs Boston's airport, recently investigated an increase in parking rates as a means of limiting airport traffic, which was so heavy as to create a serious externality in the form of congestion. One portion of the analysis conducted for Massport predicted the consequences of alternative price increases on the number of cars coming to the airport. But this alone told them little of what they needed to know: What is the value of a given reduction in congestion? The question is a difficult one to answer. Still, Massport's decision to raise parking rates by $1 or $2, or not at all, should certainly depend on how it values the results of each choice. Otherwise it might as well set its parking fees by the roll of a die.

If the Hudson River analyst is to recommend a rational decision, he must find some way to value the various possible degrees of improvement in water quality. Similarly, if pollution controls impose costs on people (say, by blocking a scenic vista with a treatment plant), those costs also must be valued. We saw in Chapter 9 that in principle the appropriate value is people's willingness to pay to accomplish improvements in water quality on the one hand or to avoid the costs imposed on the other, although estimating that willingness may require considerable ingenuity. Because the impacts of pollution controls will extend over many years, streams of benefits and costs must be discounted.

Some valuation problems, particularly those that involve intangibles, do not lend themselves to quantification. In such a case, analysis can address the issue descriptively. Perhaps a proposed welfare program is perceived as damaging the dignity of the recipients; that fact should be included in the analysis as one output of the program, just as the total dollar cost would be. Identifying the key intangibles is as much a part of the analyst's job as setting forth the hard numbers. Because even honest and well-meaning people can never fully agree, questions of valuation will always be argued. The analyst's job is to increase the probability that debate will be orderly and relevant by making sure that values are assigned openly and explicitly.

Recognizing that an alternative will inevitably be superior with respect to certain objectives and inferior with respect to others, how should different combinations of valued objectives be compared with one another? Assigning values to specific attributes is only a small part of the difficulty in defining preferences. In almost every serious policy choice, painful tradeoffs must be made among valued attributes. Cleaning up the Hudson is no exception. Improvements in water quality will be accomplished only at considerable sacrifice. Manufacturing costs will rise; some plants may have to reduce output; some may even close down altogether. Employment in the region may fall, although some job losses may be offset by jobs in constructing new facilities or providing new pollution control services. New sewers and treatment plants are costly for cities and towns; tax rates and/or borrowings will rise. The state may incur substantial costs in administering the pollution controls. The decision will almost certainly have distributional implications: the benefits of pollution control may be enjoyed by one group of citizens, while the costs are borne largely by another. The public decision maker is elected or appointed to make the tough choices among competing objectives such as these. He will have to decide on behalf of the society how much improvement in water quality its members would choose if they were as knowledgeable about the whole situation as he is.

In Chapter 8 we discussed a variety of techniques for pinning down the decision maker's preferences, ranging from simple pairwise comparisons to a fully formulated objective function. The latter, we saw, is a formal statement of how a change in any attribute (water quality or employment, for example) of the predicted outcome of a policy choice will affect the decision maker's overall evaluation of that outcome. Although most of us, the pollution control analyst included, will rarely—if ever—want to write down an objective function in mathematical terms, its existence is implicit in every decision made. It remains a useful concept that reminds us to look carefully at the tradeoffs that we are willing to make and that are implied by a particular choice.

Making a Choice

When all aspects of the analysis are drawn together, what is the preferred course of action? The last step in policy analysis is a most satisfying one, for the sole objective of that analysis has been to make a better decision. Having struggled hard with defining the problem, specifying the objectives, constructing the necessary models, and valuing the alternative outcomes, the policy maker now pulls everything together to make the preferred choice. The situation may be so straightforward he can simply look at the consequences predicted for each alternative and select the one that is best. At the opposite extreme, it may be so complex that he will have to rely on a computer to keep track of what the options are, how the world will behave in response to the possible choices, and what his preferences are among possible outcomes.

One critical lesson is obvious, yet easily overlooked: the purpose of all this work is to help make a better decision. Yet we all know that countless policy studies have led nowhere. Sometimes the fault lies with public decision makers who don't bother to take advantage of readily accessible information. More often, it is the producers of the analysis who are to blame. Many policy analyses are gathering dust because they are too long or too hard to understand. Remember that the world will never beat a pathway to your door just because you build a better model; analysis is worthless if it can't be communicated to others. The watchword, therefore, is: "Keep it simple." The purpose is to inform the decision maker, not to overwhelm him. Analysis should be presented in such a way that the essential points can be readily grasped and, if necessary, debated.

Too often an analysis is not finished until well after the major decision must be made. If a new energy policy is to be adopted in 1978, there is little point in embarking upon a broad-ranging study of energy availability to be completed in 1979. A less ambitious study that is in hand when policy is debated will be far more valuable. The need for timeliness suggests a tradeoff with thoroughness, as indeed it should. Policy research can rarely aspire to the standards of traditional academic research. Results published in professional journals are supposed to be able to withstand the scrutiny of time, and the continuing probes of fellow investigators. The objective of policy research should be to provide the best analysis possible given the limitations on time, information, and manpower.

The choice among competing policy alternatives is never easy, for the future is always uncertain and the inescapable tradeoffs painful. The methods set forth here cannot eliminate these difficulties, but they can help us manage them. By improving our ability to predict the consequences of alternative policies, and providing a framework for valuing those consequences, the techniques of policy analysis lead us toward better decisions.

Answers to Exercises

Chapter 4

Here are the answers to the five exercises on page 49:

1. $P_1 = (1 + b - d)P_0$

2. $P_1 = (1 - d)P_0 + R$, where R = number of recruits

3. $S_1 = S_0 + 200$

4. $S_1 = (1 + .055)(S_0 + 200)$, or $(1 + .055)S_0 + 200$. The facts are not entirely clear as stated, and sometimes are not in real life.

5. $P_1 = 2P_0$

The generalized answers to the exercises are:

1. $P_n (1 + b - d)P_{n-1}, n \geq 1$

2. $P_n = (1 - d)P_{n-1} + R, n \geq 1$

3. $S_n = S_{n-1} + 200, n \geq 1$

4. $S_n = (1.055)(S_{n-1} + 200)$, or $(1.055)S_{n-1} + 200, n = 1$

   $S_n = 1.055 S_{n-1}, n > 1$

5. $P_n = 2P_{n-1}, n \geq 1$

The solutions are:

1. $P_n (1 + b - d)^n P_0$

2. $P_n = (1 - d)^n P_0 + [(1 - d)^{n-1} + (1 - d)^{n-2} + (1 - d)^{n-3} + \ldots + (1 - d)^2 + (1 - d) + 1]R$. (This expression may easily be simplified; see "A Mathematical Digression," p. 54.)

3. $S_n = S_0 + 200n$

4. $S_n = 1.055^n(S_0 + 200)$, or $1.055^{n-1}(1.055S_0 + 200)$

5. $P_n = 2^n P_0$

The answers to the two exercises on page 66 are:

1. There is a stable equilibrium at 8000 units of public housing.
2. The general difference equation for this situation is

$$P_n = 2P_{n-1} - 100W$$

where P is the staph population at hour n and W is the number of white cells. The equilibrium is given by

$$P_E = 2P_E - 100W$$

$$P_E = 100W$$

It is unstable; if the initial population P_0 is greater than $100W$, it will grow without limit. If less than $100W$, it will be destroyed.

Chapter 9

1.

Monetary Cost	$-\$100,000$
Pollution Cost	$-50,000$
Benefits	$120,000$
Net	$\$-30,000$

The incinerator has a net negative value—don't build it.

2.

	A	B
Monetary Cost	$-\$100,000$	$-\$140,000$
Pollution Cost	$-50,000$	0
Benefits	$200,000$	$200,000$
Net	$\$\ 50,000$	$\$\ 60,000$

Build B if the city can afford it, since it has a higher net benefit.

3. Counting pollution costs as negative benefits, since they are not budgetary expenditures, the projects can be ranked according to their net benefit/cost ratios:

Plant	Total cost	Net benefits	NB/C
3	180	95	.53
1	160	70	.44
6	120	50	.42
4	220	80	.36
5	140	40	.29
2	170	40	.24

The budget constraint is $610,000. Plants 3, 1, and 6 can clearly be built, but there are not enough funds for Plant 4. The next best alternative turns out to be affordable, so you should recommend that Plants 3, 1, 6, and 5 be built. In this case, the indivisibility of Plant 4 forces you to skip it and choose the fifth-ranked project instead. With different numbers, a different set of choices might well be preferred.

Chapter 11

1. *Incinerators and Pollution Control.* First we must ask: What is Burtonville trying to accomplish? In this case, we are told that dumping is far more expensive than burning in any of the incinerators, so savings (S) will be maximized by burning as much trash as possible while complying with environmental regulations.

Next we ask what the control variables are. The city can decide how many tons of trash it will burn in each incinerator; we designate these amounts as X_A, X_B, X_C. Then our objective function must be

Maximize $S = X_A + X_B + X_C$

Next we investigate the constraints. Right away we know that the city can't exceed the capacity of each incinerator:

$X_A \leq 1200$

$X_B \leq 800$

$X_C \leq 1000$

And it must also comply with the environmental regulations:

Sulfur Dioxide $250X_A + 150X_B + 220X_C \leq 400,000$

Particulates $20X_A + 30X_B + 24X_C \leq 50,000$

Finally, we remind ourselves that the incinerators cannot burn negative amounts of trash:

$X_A \geq 0$

$X_B \geq 0$

$X_C \geq 0$

2. *Police Shifts.* First, what is the objective in assigning the necessary policemen? It is to minimize the total number of men (M) used.

Next, what activities can Burtonville control? It can control the number of men on each eight-hour shift. (Note that it does not have full control over the number on a four-hour period.) Consequently we may let X_1 equal the number who work the eight hours from 12 noon to 8 P.M., X_2 the number who work from 4 P.M. to 12 P.M., and so on. Then the objective function is:

Minimize $M = X_1 + X_2 + X_3 + X_4 + X_5 + X_6$

Now for the constraints. The first four-hour period, 12 noon to 4 P.M., will be covered partly by the X_1 men who work from 12 noon to 8 P.M., and partly by the X_6 men who work from 8 A.M. to 4 P.M.; 100 men are needed. Thus we have

$X_1 + X_6 \geq 100$

Similarly,

$X_1 + X_2 \geq 250$

$X_2 + X_3 \geq 400$

$X_3 + X_4 \geq 500$

$X_4 + X_5 \geq 200$

$X_5 + X_6 \geq 150$

334 Answers to Exercises

And of course we must include the nonnegativity constraints:

$$X_i \geq 0, \quad i = 1, 2, \ldots, 6$$

3. *Assignments to Hospitals.* This problem is easier to handle if we first put the technical information in tabular form, as in Table A. We are told that the objective is to minimize total patient travel time, T. The control variables are the number of victims transported from Point A and Point B to each of three hospitals. Designate the victims taken from Point A to Hospital 1 by X_{A1}; the total transport time from A to 1 is then $25X_{A1}$ patient-minutes. The objective function is then

$$\text{Minimize } T = 25X_{A1} + 15X_{A2} + 10X_{A3} + 20X_{B1} + 5X_{B2} + 15X_{B3}$$

The contraints recognize, first, that every victim must be taken to a hospital:

$$X_{A1} + X_{A2} + X_{A3} = 300$$

$$X_{B1} + X_{B2} + X_{B3} = 200$$

Next, no hospital should exceed its capacity:

$$X_{A1} + X_{B1} \leq 250$$

$$X_{A2} + X_{B3} \leq 150$$

$$X_{A3} + X_{B3} \leq 150$$

Finally, again the city cannot transport fewer than 0 victims along any route:

$$X_{ij} \geq 0, \quad i = A, B; \quad j = 1, 2, 3$$

4. *Electricity Generation and Pollution Control.* We have here a problem in constrained minimization. The Municipal Power Company wants to produce its power as cheaply as possible. In other words, the objective is to minimize costs. The control variables are the levels of electrical output produced by the five available processes: present fuel, present fuel with stack filters, low-sulfur fuel, low-sulfur fuel with stack filters, and imported power. We use X_1, X_2, X_3, X_4, and X_5 to designate the levels of these five processes. The costs and pollution emissions for each can be calculated directly; they are given in Table B.

Table A

From point	Estimated casualties	Travel times to hospitals in minutes		
		1	2	3
A	300	25	15	10
B	200	20	5	15
Capacity		250	150	150

Table B

Process	Total cost/mwh	Total pollution emission in lbs
Present fuel	$(3.50)X_1$	$10X_1$
Present fuel with filter	$(3.50 + .80)X_2 = 4.30X_2$	$.1(10X_2) = X_2$
Low-sulfur fuel	$5.00X_3$	$1.2X_3$
Low-sulfur fuel with stack filter	$(5.00 + .80)X_4 = 5.80X_4$	$.1(1.2X_4) = .12X_4$
Imported power	$4.00X_5$	0

We may then write the objective function as:

Minimize $C = 3.50X_1 + 4.30X_2 + 5.00X_3 + 5.80X_4 + 4.00X_5$

Next we turn to the constraints. From the table we can determine total pollution, which must be no more than 2800 lbs/hr.

$10X_1 + X_2 + 1.2X_3 + .12X_4 \leq 2800$

We also know that the city's demand for 2000 mwh/hr must be satisfied:

$X_1 + X_2 + X_3 + X_4 + X_5 \geq 2000$

We note that no more than 200 mwh of power per hour can be imported:

$X_5 \leq 200$

Finally, we must tell the computer that these Xs cannot be negative:

$X_i \geq o, \quad i = 1, \ldots, 5$

As a final postscript for the curious, here are the answers to the four problems:

1. *Incinerators and Pollution*

$X_A = 625$

$X_B = 800$

$X_C = 562.5$

2. *Police Shifts* (This solution is not unique; other combinations that produce the same total of 900 men are possible.)

$X_1 = 250 \qquad X_4 = 100$

$X_2 = 0 \qquad X_5 = 100$

$X_3 = 400 \qquad X_6 = 50$

3. *Assignments to Hospitals*

$X_{A1} = 150 \qquad X_{B1} = 50$

$X_{A2} = 0 \qquad X_{B2} = 150$

$X_{A3} = 150 \qquad X_{B3} = 0$

4. *Electricity Generation and Pollution Control*

$X_1 = 111.1$ $X_4 = 0$

$X_2 = 1688.9$ $X_5 = 200$

$X_3 = 0$

Suggested Readings

Foundations

Feiveson, Harold A.; Sinden, Frank W.; and Socolow, Robert H.; eds. *Boundaries of Analysis*. Cambridge, Mass.: Ballinger Publishing Co., 1976. The companion volume is *When Values Conflict: Essays on Environmental Analysis, Discourse, and Decision,* edited by Laurence Tribe, Corinne S. Schelling, and John Voss.

Scholars in many disciplines take an in-depth look at a paradigmatic problem: Should the Tocks Island dam be built?

Friedman, Milton. *Essays in Positive Economics*. Chicago: University of Chicago Press, 1953.

Chapter 1 presents a controversial but important essay on the need to achieve accuracy of predictions and assumptions when formulating models.

Greenberger, Martin; Crenson, Matthew A.; and Brian L. Crissey. *Models in the Policy Process*. New York: Russell Sage Foundation, 1976.

A useful evaluative survey, with many examples.

Hicks, John R. *Value and Capital: An Inquiry into Some Fundamental Principles of Economic Theory*. 2nd ed.; Oxford: Clarendon Press, 1965.

A cornerstone of modern microeconomics; from it all manner of neoclassical virtues flow, and a few sins as well.

Mansfield, Edwin. *Microeconomics*. New York: W. W. Norton & Co., 1975.

A good intermediate microeconomics text, and a possible follow-on to this volume for those who develop an interest in economics.

Roberts, Marc J. "On the Nature and Condition of Social Science." *Daedalus,* Summer 1974, pp. 47–64.

Simon, Herbert A. "Theories of Decision-Making in Economics and Behavioral Science." *American Economic Review* 49, no. 3 (June 1959): 253–283.

Stigler, George J. *The Theory of Price*. 3rd ed.; New York: Macmillan, 1966.

  A good elementary text.

Zeckhauser, Richard, and Schaefer, Elmer. "Public Policy and Normative Economic Theory." In *The Study of Policy Formation*, edited by Raymond Bauer and Kenneth Gergen. New York: The Free Press, 1968, pp. 27–102.

Nuts and Bolts

Ackerman, Bruce; Rose-Ackerman, Susan; Sawyer, James W. ; and Henderson, Dale W. *The Uncertain Search for Environmental Quality*. New York: The Free Press, 1974.

  A literate review of the application and misapplication of analytic approaches to problems in the Delaware estuary. Politics, law, and engineering are discussed and evaluated.

Ackoff, Russell L., and Sasieni, Maurice W. *Fundamentals of Operations Research*. New York: John Wiley & Sons, 1968.

Baumol, William J. *Economic Theory and Operations Analysis*. 4th ed.; Englewood Cliffs, N.J.: Prentice-Hall, Inc., 1977.

———. "On the Discount Rate for Public Projects." In *Public Expenditures and Public Analysis*, edited by Robert H. Haveman and Julius Margolis. Chicago: Markham, 1970.

Benefit–Cost and Policy Analysis Annual, Aldine Publishing Company (Chicago).
  1971   Arnold C. Harberger et al., eds.
  1972   William A. Niskanen et al., eds.
  1973   Robert H. Haveman et al., eds.
  1974   Richard J. Zeckhauser et al., eds.

  Collections of outstanding and comprehensible pieces of policy analysis.

Bradley, Stephen P.; Hax, Arnoldo C.; and Magnanti, Thomas L. *Applied Mathematical Programming*. Reading, Mass.: Addison-Wesley, 1977.

  Many useful examples highlight this text on linear and more general forms of mathematical programming.

Cole, H. S. D.; Freeman, Christopher; Jahoda, Marie; and Pavitt, K. L. R. *Models of Doom*. New York: Universe Books, 1973.

  A collection of responses to The Limits to Growth.

Dorfman, Robert. "Mathematical or 'Linear' Programming: A Nonmathematical Exposition." *American Economic Review* 43, no. 5, pt. 1 (December 1953): 797–825.

A classic expository piece, to be read as a supplement to Chapter 11.

——. "Operations Research." *American Economic Review* 50, no. 4 (September 1960):575–623.

Drake, Alvin W.; Keeney, Ralph L.; and Morse, Philip M.; eds. *Analysis of Public Systems.* Cambridge, Mass.: M.I.T. Press, 1972.

Contains many useful and accessible illustrations of the use of the procedures presented in the "Nuts and Bolts" chapters of this volume.

Eckstein, Otto. "A Survey of the Theory of Public Expenditure Criteria." In *Public Finances: Needs, Sources, and Utilization,* edited by James M. Buchanan. Princeton, N.J.: Princeton University Press, 1961, pp. 439–494.

Fagin, Allen. "The Policy Implications of Predictive Decision-Making: 'Likelihood' and 'Dangerousness' in Civil Commitment Proceedings." *Public Policy* 24, no. 4 (Fall 1976): 491–528.

Fairley, William B., and Mosteller, Frederick, eds. *Statistics and Public Policy.* Reading, Mass.: Addison-Wesley, 1977.

A useful collection of articles on the role of statistics in public policy formation.

Fisher, Irving. *The Theory of Interest.* New York: Macmillan, 1930.

The classic conceptual work on the valuation of time, renowned yet accessible.

Fuller, Leonard. *Basic Matrix Theory.* Englewood Cliffs, N.J.: Prentice-Hall, Inc., 1962.

Glass, Gene, ed. *Evaluation Studies,* Vol. 1. Beverly Hills, Calif.: Sage Publications, 1976.

A collection of articles on evaluation, with particular attention to social problems.

Goldberg, Samuel. *Introduction to Difference Equations.* New York: John Wiley & Sons, 1961.

Hanke, Steve H., and Walker, Richard A. "Benefit–Cost Analysis Reconsidered: An Evaluation of the Mid-State Project." *Water Resources Research* 10, no. 5: 898–908.

Hansen, W. Lee, and Weisbrod, Burton A. "The Distribution of Costs and Direct Benefits of Public Higher Education: The Case of California." *Journal of Human Resources* 4, no. 2 (Spring 1969):176–191.

Notable for having actually done the calculations.

Haveman, Robert H., and Margolis, Julius, eds. *Public Expenditures and Policy Analysis.* Chicago: Markham Publishing Co., 1970.

A most useful selection from papers originally prepared for the Joint Economic Committee of Congress. It contains excellent chapters on both conceptual and applied issues, including market vs. nonmarket allocation, externalities, uncertainty, distribution, incentives, the discount rate, shadow prices, and program budgeting.

Hinrichs, Harley H., and Taylor, Graeme M. *Systematic Analysis: A Primer on Benefit Cost Analysis and Program Evaluation.* Pacific Palisades, Calif.: Goodyear, 1972.

Hillier, Frederick S., and Lieberman, Gerald J. *Introduction to Operations Research.* 2nd ed.; San Francisco: Holden-Day, 1974.

A good introductory OR text; the next level of difficulty beyond this volume.

Hitch, Charles J., and McKean, Roland N. *The Economics of Defense in the Nuclear Age.* New York: Atheneum, 1965.

The Bible of government analysts when systems analysis was in its ebullient youth. Its wisdom ages well, though it now must be applied to new classes of problems.

Kazmier, Leonard. *Statistical Analysis for Business and Economics.* 2nd ed.; New York: McGraw-Hill, 1973.

A thorough introduction to basic statistics in a programmed learning format.

Keeney, Ralph L. "A Decision Analysis with Multiple Objectives: The Mexico City Airport," *Bell Journal of Economics and Management Science* 4, no. 1 (Spring 1973): 101–117.

———, and Raiffa, Howard. *Decisions with Multiple Objectives.* New York: John Wiley & Sons, 1976.

This book may help move multiattribute utility theory from the mathematician's shelf to the analyst's. Still a bit difficult for the decision maker. Wisdom and examples sprinkled throughout lighten the load.

Kmenta, Jan. *Elements of Econometrics.* New York: Macmillan, 1971.

Krutilla, John V. "Welfare Aspects of Benefit–Cost Analysis." *Journal of Political Economy* 69 (June 1961): 226–335.

Krutilla, John V., and Fisher, Anthony C. *The Economics of Natural Environments: Studies in the Evaluation of Commodity and Amenity Resources.* Baltimore: Johns Hopkins, 1975.

This paperback volume presents a number of fascinating case studies of environmental decisions. They are analyzed with the aid of many of the tools contained in this Primer, *plus a few new ones as well.*

Leibowitz, Martin A. "Queues." *Scientific American,* 219 (August 1968): 96–103.

Light, Richard. "Abused and Neglected Children in America: A Study of Alternative Policies." *Harvard Educational Review* 43, no. 4 (November 1973): 556–598.

An application of Bayes's Theorem to an important policy issue.

Maass, Arthur, et al. *Design of Water-Resources Systems.* Cambridge, Mass.: Harvard University Press, 1962.

The product of a successful multidisciplinary assault on an important class of problems in benefit-cost analysis.

Manne, Alan S. "What Happens When Our Oil and Gas Run Out?" *Harvard Business Review* 53, no. 4 (July–August 1975).

McKean, Roland J. *Efficiency in Government Through Systems Analysis.* New York: John Wiley & Sons, 1958.

A lucid exposition of the basics of systems analysis. This volume concentrates on water problems, which after many years of neglect are regaining attention.

Meadows, Donella H.; Meadows, Dennis L.; Randers, Jørgen; and Behrens, William W., III. *The Limits to Growth.* New York: Universe Books, 1972.

A widely heralded—and just as widely damned—pessimistic prognosis urging us to curb our appetites. A book with enormous influence, its basic analytic technique is no more than difference equations.

Mishan, E. J. *Cost–Benefit Analysis: An Informal Introduction.* 3rd ed.; New York: Praeger, 1976.

Nagel, Stuart, and Neef, Marian. *Legal Policy Analysis.* Lexington, Mass.: Lexington Books, 1977.

Nordhaus, William. "World Dynamics: Measurement without Data." *Economic Journal* 83, no. 332: 1156–1183.

The most cogent theoretical critique of The Limits to Growth.

Raiffa, Howard. *Decision Analysis.* Reading, Mass.: Addison-Wesley, 1968.

If Chapter 12 intrigued you, then you should undertake this effort to broaden your knowledge of decision analysis.

Rogers, Peter. "A Game Theory Approach to the Problems of International River Basins." *Water Resources Research* (August 1969).

An analysis of the Ganges-Brahmaputra river system that includes an easily understood linear programming model of the entire system.

Sartwell, Philip E. "Memoir on the Reed-Frost Epidemic Theory." *American Journal of Epidemiology* 103, no. 2 (February 1976): 138.

Schlaifer, Robert. *Analysis of Decisions Under Uncertainty.* New York: McGraw-Hill, 1969.

> *A highly detailed manual for conducting a decision analysis.*

Singh, Jagjit. *Great Ideas of Operations Research.* New York: Dover Publications, Inc., 1968.

Solow, Robert. "The Economics of Resources or the Resources of Economics." *American Economic Review* 64, no. 2 (May 1974).

> *A delightful and literate essay that explores, among other issues, the relationship of discounting concepts to exhaustible resources.*

United Nations Industrial Development Organization. *Guidelines for Project Evaluation.* New York: United Nations, 1972, Chapter 13, "Intertemporal Choice: The Social Rate of Discount."

Wagner, Harvey M. *Principles of Operations Research.* 2nd ed.; Englewood Cliffs, N.J.: Prentice-Hall, 1975.

> *An advanced and thorough operations research text. Covers difference equations, Markov models, queues, linear programming, and simulations, as well as many other subjects. Must reading for those irresistibly attracted to atrocious puns.*

Ends and Means

Arrow, Kenneth J. *Social Choice and Individual Values.* 2nd ed.; New Haven Conn.: Yale University Press, 1963.

> *The fundamental work in the field; much rougher going than the appendix to Chapter 13.*

Bator, Francis M. "The Anatomy of Market Failure." *Quarterly Journal of Economics* 72, no. 3 (August 1958): 351–379.

———. "The Simple Analytics of Welfare Economics." *American Economic Review* 47, no. 1 (March 1957): 22–49.

> *A meticulous exposition of welfare economics.*

Bergson, Abram. "A Reformulation of Certain Aspects of Welfare Economics." *Quarterly Journal of Economics* 52, no. 2 (February 1938): 310–334.

> *The article that introduced the concept of the social welfare function.*

Brookings Institution (Washington, D.C.), *Setting National Priorities.*
1970   Charles L. Schultze et al., eds.
1971   Charles L. Schultze et al., eds.
1972   Charles L. Schultze et al., eds.
1973   Charles L. Schultze et al., eds.

1974   Edward R. Friedital et al., eds.
1975   Barry M. Blechman et al., eds.
1976   Barry M. Blechman et al., eds.
1977   Henry Owen et al., eds.

A series produced by the Brookings Institution to review and propose policies in a variety of social areas.

Buchanan, James M., and Tullock, Gordon. *The Calculus of Consent.* Ann Arbor, Mich.: University of Michigan Press, 1962.

An early venture in applying economic methods to political processes.

Coase, R. H. "The Problem of Social Cost." *Journal of Law and Economics* 3 (1960): 1–44 (Also in Dorfman and Dorfman *The Economics of the Environment*).

A seminal (and controversial) article on the subject of externalities.

Demsetz, Harold. "Toward a Theory of Property Rights." *American Economic Review, Papers and Proceedings* 57, no. 2 (May 1967): 347–359.

Dorfman, Robert, and Dorfman, Nancy S. *The Economics of the Environment.* 2nd ed.; New York: W. W. Norton & Co., 1977.

A collection of the most useful articles in environmental economics. Externalities, property rights, bargaining, and valuation issues are covered.

Friedman, Milton. *Capitalism and Freedom.* Chicago: University of Chicago Press, 1962.

Chapter II outlines a classical liberal's view of the appropriate role for a government in a free society.

Hardin, Garrett. "The Tragedy of the Commons." *Science* 162, no. 3059 (December 13, 1968): 1243–1248.

A delightful and influential parable that describes problems involving externalities and public goods in terms of an overgrazed common land.

Head, John G. *Public Goods and Public Welfare.* Durham, N.C.: Duke University Press, 1974.

Hirschman, Albert O. *Exit, Voice, and Loyalty: Responses to Decline in Firms, Organizations, and States.* Cambridge, Mass.: Harvard University Press, 1970.

A discussion on the incentives for an organization to provide optimal mixes of services to its members, when preferences may not be known and membership ties may be broken.

Hochman, Harold M., and Peterson, George E. *Redistribution Through Public Choice.* New York: Columbia University Press, 1974.

A predominantly conceptual volume that systematically focuses on distributional issues.

Hochman, Harold M., and Rodgers, James D. "Pareto Optimal Redistribution." *American Economic Review* 59, no. 4 (1969): 542–557.

Poses the income distribution issue as a problem of externalities.

Hotelling, Harold. "The General Welfare in Relation to Problems of Taxation and of Railway and Utility Rates." *Econometrica* 6, no. 3 (1938): 242–269.

An early use of economics to define a regulatory scheme to maximize welfare.

Kahn, Alfred E. *The Economics of Regulation:*
Volume I: *Economic Principles.* New York: John Wiley & Sons, 1970.
Volume II: *Institutional Issues.* New York: John Wiley & Sons, 1971.

Volume I systematically lays out the market failure arguments for alternative modes of regulation, and examines various regulatory mechanisms for meeting those problems.

Kneese, Allen V., and Schultze, Charles L. *Pollution, Prices, and Public Policy.* Washington, D.C.: The Brookings Institution, 1975.

A cogent plea for the use of economic incentives to promote environmental quality.

Musgrave, Richard A., and Musgrave, Peggy B. *Public Finance in Theory and Practice.* 2nd ed.; New York: McGraw-Hill, 1976.

Nordhaus, William D., and Tobin, James. "Is Growth Obsolete?" In *Economic Growth, Fiftieth Anniversary Colloquium., Vol. 5.* New York: National Bureau of Economic Research, 1972, pp. 4–17. (A shorter version appears under the title "Measures of Economic Welfare" in Dorfman and Dorfman, *The Economics of the Environment.)*

Describes how GNP can be refined to take account of gains and losses to society that are not now counted in GNP because they are not bought and sold on markets.

Olson, Mancur L., Jr. *The Logic of Collective Action: Public Goods and the Theory of Groups.* Cambridge, Mass.: Harvard University Press, 1971.

Applies the concept of public goods to explain the inadequate levels of collective activity in a variety of policy arenas.

Rothenberg, Jerome. *The Measurement of Social Welfare.* Englewood Cliffs, N.J.: Prentice-Hall, 1961.

A most understandable book about the purposes of collective decision making. Provides a good review of the literature.

Samuelson, Paul A. "The Pure Theory of Public Expenditure." *Review of Economics and Statistics* 36, no. 4 (November 1954): 387–389. Also "A Diagrammatic Exposition of the Theory of Public Expenditure." *Review of Economics and Statistics* 37, no. 4 (1955): 350–356.

Lays the theoretical foundation for the efficient provision of public goods.

Schelling, Thomas. "On the Ecology of Micromotives." *The Public Interest,* no. 25 (Fall, 1971).

Reward yourself by reading this elegant essay. It explains why uncoordinated private actions may not lead to desirable outcomes, and examines some modes of coordination.

———. "The Life You Save May Be Your Own." In *Problems in Public Expenditure Analysis,* edited by S. B. Chase. Washington, D.C.: The Brookings Institution, 1968.

Sets forth the willingness-to-pay approach to the valuation of life.

Schlesinger, James R. "Systems Analysis and the Political Process." *Journal of Law and Economics* 11 (October 1968): 281–298.

Schultze, Charles L. *The Public Use of Private Interest.* Washington, D.C.: The Brookings Institution, 1977.

A wide-ranging assessment that argues that much existing government action follows the clumsy and inefficient "command and control" approach of direct regulation, and that substantial improvement could be achieved through greater reliance on incentives and decentralized decision making.

Stigler, George J. "The Economics of Information." *Journal of Political Economy* 69, no. 3 (1961): 213–225.

An important early contribution to a field of immediate policy relevance.

Tobin, James. "On Limiting the Domain of Inequality." *Journal of Law and Economics* 13, no. 2 (October 1970): 263–278.

Zeckhauser, Richard. "Optimal Mechanisms for Income Transfer." *American Economic Review* 61, no. 3, pt. 1 (June 1971): 324–334.

Provides a conceptual framework for income transfer systems when improving the welfare of the poor conveys an externality to the rich.

———. "Procedures for Valuing Lives." *Public Policy* 23, no. 4 (Fall 1975): 419–464.

Addresses a wide range of issues pertaining to decisions about risks to lives.

Index